Approaches to Teaching
the Works of Flannery O'Connor

Approaches to Teaching the Works of Flannery O'Connor

Edited by
Robert Donahoo
and
Marshall Bruce Gentry

The Modern Language Association of America
New York   2019

MLA and the MODERN LANGUAGE ASSOCIATION are trademarks
owned by the Modern Language Association of America.
For information about obtaining permission to reprint material from
MLA book publications, send your request by mail (see address below)
or e-mail (permissions@mla.org).

Library of Congress Cataloging-in-Publication Data
Names: Donahoo, Robert, editor. | Gentry, Marshall Bruce, editor.
Title: Approaches to teaching the works of Flannery O'Connor / edited by Robert Donahoo
and Marshall Bruce Gentry.
Description: New York : The Modern Language Association of America, 2019. |
Series: Approaches to teaching world literature ; 158 | Includes
bibliographical references and index.
Identifiers: LCCN 2019011178 (print) | LCCN 2019011998 (ebook) |
ISBN 9781603294072 (EPUB) | ISBN 9781603294089 (Kindle) |
ISBN 9781603294638 (hardcover : alk. paper) |
ISBN 9781603294065 (pbk. : alk. paper)
Subjects: LCSH: O'Connor, Flannery—Study and teaching. | Race in literature. |
Sex role in literature. | Social classes in literature. | Ecocriticism.
Classification: LCC PS3565.C57 (ebook) | LCC PS3565.C57 Z515 2019 (print) |
DDC 813/.54—dc23

Approaches to Teaching World Literature 158
ISSN 1059-1133

Cover illustration of the paperback and electronic editions: Lind Hollingsworth,
The Terrible Thought, mixed media. Collection of Helen Barello. Created for
Southern Discomfort: Art Inspired by Flannery O'Connor, sponsored by
the Flannery O'Connor Childhood Home in Savannah, Georgia.

Published by The Modern Language Association of America
85 Broad Street, suite 500, New York, New York 10004-2434
www.mla.org

CONTENTS

Contexts: Race, History, Film, and Science

O'Connor and Other Authors

Specialized Perspectives

ACKNOWLEDGMENTS

We wish to offer special thanks to the following:

The Department of English at Sam Houston State University, the Department of English at Georgia College and State University, and the College of Humanities and Social Sciences at Sam Houston State University supplied funding and encouragement for our work.

Nancy Davis Bray and the entire staff of Special Collections at the Georgia College Library helped throughout the composition of this volume, especially with many of the details in "Materials."

Rosemary McGee and the entire staff of the Special Collections at Emory University libraries also helped, especially with the handling of Alice Walker's manuscript.

The MFA student assistants at Georgia College who helped with this volume are Leah Kuenzi, Jennifer Watkins, and especially Laura M. Martin, who was instrumental in the preparation of Walker's "Convergence" for publication.

John D. Cox, while he was teaching at Georgia College, provided a great deal of the original inspiration for this project. He continued to work on this collection for years while he employed at the National Endowment for the Humanities, but as his duties with NEH evolved, his continued participation in the project became impossible. We thank John for all his work.

James Hatch and the editorial staff of the Modern Language Association were patient and willing to answer questions and offer guidance in the preparation of the manuscript.

Finally, we thank our wives, Anne Donahoo and Alice Friman, for their support throughout.

Introduction:
Teaching on the Borders

Robert Donahoo

> . . . there is a need to reconceptualize American cultural
> studies as a radically comparative field of studies in which
> a diversity of cultures, languages, practices, and theories
> encounter and interact with one another across the
> borders.
>
> — Betsy Erkkila, "Ethnicity, Literary Theory,
> and the Grounds of Resistance"

> They were frightened by the gray slick road before
> them and they kept repeating in higher and higher
> voices, "Where we goin, Ma? Where we goin?" while
> their mother, her huge body rolled back still against
> the seat and her eyes like blue-painted glass, seemed to
> contemplate for the first time the tremendous frontiers of
> her true country.
>
> — Flannery O'Connor, "The Displaced Person"

At least since Flannery O'Connor's *The Complete Stories* won the National Book Award in 1972—eight years after her death—her fiction has poked its nose into places that seem a long way from the space "between the house and the chicken yard" in rural Georgia that she once described as her general milieu (*Habit* 290–91). In the scholarly world, Ralph Wood grounds her in antiabortion politics in *Flannery O'Connor and the Christ-Haunted South* (240–42), while Patricia Yaeger places her work in a powerful and distinct line of women's writing in *Dirt and Desire* (xiii, 16). Present in most major literary anthologies, O'Connor's work turns up in graduate and undergraduate classes pedagogically focused on a broad range of topics, including twentieth-century American literature and culture, the American South, women's writing, ecocriticism, race studies, the novel, the short story, literature and film, comic literature, and various takes on theology. Apparently, like the trees in "A Good Man Is Hard to Find," the "meanest" of her works—novels, short stories, essays, letters, and even cartoons—sparkle (*Flannery . . . Works* 139).

Not that her work was ever hidden in obscure places. During her lifetime, her novels were published by prestigious houses—*Wise Blood* by Harcourt Brace and *The Violent Bear It Away* by Farrar Straus—and her short stories appeared in prestigious literary journals such as *Kenyon Review* and *Sewanee Review* as well as mass circulation periodicals, including *Mademoiselle* and *Harper's*

Bazaar. Three of her short stories were honored with O. Henry Awards—in 1957, 1963, and 1965. Granville Hicks included her essay "The Fiction Writer and His Country" in his 1957 anthology *The Living Novel: A Symposium*, along with essays by Saul Bellow, Ralph Ellison, and Herbert Gold, the same year CBS broadcast a loosely adapted version of her story "The Life You Save May Be Your Own" as part of the *Schlitz Playhouse of Stars*, in which Gene Kelly played Tom T. Shiftlet (Gooch 288). In 1959, she saw one of her stories, "A Good Man Is Hard to Find," anthologized in Cleanth Brooks and Robert Penn Warren's revised edition of *Understanding Fiction*—a book whose 1943 edition had been a text for her at the University of Iowa's Writers' Workshop (McGurl 534).

Her death at age thirty-nine elicited numerous tributes, but 1972 marks a clear turning point. Along with the National Book Award for *The Complete Stories*, that year saw the birth of a journal devoted to her life and work: *The Flannery O'Connor Bulletin*. Journal articles, essay collections, and monographs have been supplemented by two significant adaptations of her work for film: *The Displaced Person*, a segment of the PBS series The American Short Story (1977), with a screenplay by Horton Foote, and John Huston's *Wise Blood* (1979). In 1988, her work was selected to form one of the first volumes of the Library of America series, and since 2000, eight biographies have appeared, with Brad Gooch's 2009 biography, *Flannery: A Life*, named a National Book Critics Circle Award finalist; a *New York Times* notable book of the year; and a *New York Times* best seller. *A Prayer Journal*, a notebook that O'Connor kept while a graduate student at Iowa, was heavily excerpted in *The New Yorker* in 2013 and experienced strong sales, despite its slim size, when published in hardcover. Most recently, 2014 saw the second National Endowment for the Humanities Summer Institute devoted to O'Connor take place, scholars from around the United States attending. On such evidence, her position in the literary and even popular canon looks secure.

Yet despite her status on readers' bookshelves and in academic criticism, teaching O'Connor has often been problematic. While finishing my graduate studies, I once had a conversation with the scholar Jane Tompkins and asked her about feminist approaches to O'Connor. Her quick response is still audible in my brain: "Why would a feminist be interested in O'Connor?" Similarly, I've long heard the possibly apocryphal story of Eudora Welty's frustration while teaching O'Connor. Supposedly in one class Welty announced her inability to deal with the fiction and asked if there was a Catholic in the room who could explain it, a narrative in line with both Welty's comment that "A Good Man Is Hard to Find" "terrified me so, it was ages before I read any others—and before I understood too well what [O'Connor] was doing" (Welty and Maxwell 181) and what Suzanne Marrs calls Welty's "rejection of religious writing" in general (291).

Both anecdotes point to a persistent imbalance with teaching O'Connor that this volume seeks to remedy: the belief that her work makes sense only when read as belonging in a single category. More specifically, while acknowledging and encouraging teachers to take advantage of O'Connor's spiritual commitments, it rejects the claim that her works' successes and failures are accessible only through theology and her personal religious beliefs. Certainly, O'Connor herself rebelled against narrow categorization. In her essay on the southern grotesque, she lamented being lumped together with certain other southern writers: "Every time I heard about the School of Southern Degeneracy, I felt like Brer Rabbit stuck on the tar-baby" (*Flannery . . . Works* 814). In that same essay, she evoked as guiding lights authors such as Nathaniel Hawthorne (814), Henry James (816), Thomas Mann (817), and William Faulkner (818) and even alluded briefly to Miguel Cervantes (816). In a 1961 letter to John Hawkes, a friend and fellow novelist, she complained, "I am afraid that one of the great disadvantages of being known as a Catholic writer is that no one thinks you can lift the pen without trying to show somebody redeemed" (1146). In a 1962 letter to Cecil Dawkins, she again pushed against enclosure in a religious envelope when she wrote, "I agree that I must be seen as a writer and not just a Catholic writer, and I wish somebody would do it" (*Habit* 464).

Perhaps most radically, she saw the novelists of her day as pushing the boundaries of what novels are:

> The great novels we get in the future are not going to be those that the public thinks it wants, or those that critics demand. They are going to be the kind of novels that interest the novelist. And the novels that interest the novelist are those that have not already been written. . . . The direction of many of us will be toward concentration and the distortion that is necessary to get our vision across; it will be more toward poetry than toward the traditional novel.   (*Flannery . . . Works* 821)

O'Connor had her own interpretations of her fiction, as she made clear in letters (see, e.g., 927, 931, 942) and in her nonfiction (see "On Her Own Work" in this volume). Yet she never insisted that those intentions marked its limits. When Hawkes sent her his infamous essay "Flannery O'Connor's Devil," she responded:

> I like the piece very very much and I hope Andrew [Lytle, editor of the *Sewanee Review*] takes it or if not him somebody else. This is not to say that you have convinced me at all that what you say is perverse is perverse. But you are very fine in pointing out where I disagree with you so I don't feel this does any damage to my views and the quality of the just plain textual insights is so wonderful that of course I hope this will be read.   (1159–60)

This lack of alarm at Hawkes's reading is not mere southern gentility or a singular lapse. Writing in 1959 to her friend Betty Hester, she observed about an earlier comment Hawkes sent her, "I am not sure what he means by 'demonic' as he uses it; frequently he leaves me behind, but I think what he says is just & good" (*Habit* 355). In the face of literary scholarship that has been deemed overwhelmingly dominated by the theological (see Crews 152; Caron, "Bottom Rail" 163–64), O'Connor's letters rejected such categorization: "People are always asking me if I am a Catholic writer and I am afraid that I sometimes say no and sometimes say yes, depending entirely on who the visitor is. Actually, the question seems so remote from what I am doing when I am doing it, that it doesn't bother me at all" (*Flannery . . . Works* 1109–10). Ironically, a particularly well-known O'Connor comment that is sometimes used to support the finding of one true meaning for her work actually points in the opposite direction. When she was contacted by an English professor who wanted her to confirm a reductive Freudian reading of "A Good Man Is Hard to Find," she responded:

> The meaning of a story should go on expanding for the reader the more he thinks about it, but meaning cannot be captured in an interpretation. If teachers are in the habit of approaching a story as if it were a research problem for which any answer is believable so long as it is not obvious, then I think students will never learn to enjoy fiction. Too much interpretation is certainly worse than too little, and where feeling for a story is absent, theory will not supply it.
>
> My tone is not meant to be obnoxious. I am in a state of shock.   (1149)

It is in this spirit of expansion that this volume is based. Rather than suggest one or two preferred or popular methods of teaching O'Connor's work, the essays here demonstrate that her fiction travels well across numerous pedagogical and theoretical borders. It merits space in university classrooms aimed at multiple levels of education, and it is accessible to and makes accessible diverse intellectual disciplines and ideologies.

Indeed, teaching O'Connor requires recognizing the sense of borders that she often brings her characters to. Contemplating "the tremendous frontiers of her true country," Mrs. Shortley of "The Displaced Person" has arrived at a metaphysical border connected to various geographic regions and ethnicities that ironically dot the story, despite its homespun setting in rural Georgia: Poland, "Dutchmen," "Eye-talians," Babylon, Europe, Germans, Africa, and China (*Flannery . . . Works* 286, 292, 301, 310, 319, 323, 324). The priest who brings the Polish Guizacs to the McIntyre farm speaks "in a foreign way" and is seen by Mrs. Shortley as "leading foreigners over in hoards to places that were not theirs, to cause disputes, to uproot niggers, to plant the Whore of Babylon in the midst of the righteous!" (288, 300–01). Ignoring "a map of the universe," Mrs. Shortley dwells on "an inner vision" that reveals "the ten million billion of them pushing their way into new places over here" (291). Despite their differences in class, Mrs. McIntyre shares a similar vision with her farm worker: "She felt," the story states in its final comment on Mrs. McIntyre's subjective existence, "she was in some foreign country where the people bent over the body were natives, and she watched like a stranger" (326).

This pattern and language of borders and frontiers appear in much of O'Connor's work: from the isolated old men in New York longing to return home to the South in the stories that bookend her career, "The Geranium" and "Judgment Day," to Hazel Motes returning from World War II and leaving his rural home for the city of Taulkinham and Francis Tarwater moving backward and forward narratologically through time and geographically between Powderhead and the city. The pattern and language are seen in the journey of Mr. Head and Nelson in "The Artificial Nigger," who find themselves lost in the unknown territory of suburbia; in the travel of the grandmother's family into terror in "A Good Man Is Hard to Find;" and in Mr. Shiftlet's goal of driving to Mobile. They serve as the metaphor for changing times in her late work: the integrated bus of "Everything That Rises Must Converge" and the transformation of the country into sites of recreational retreat in "A View of the Woods."

Because O'Connor herself was so focused on borders and border regions, teachers of her fiction should not resist exploring it beyond their own interpretive safe zones. That her borders are often psychic and metaphysical rather than geological or political hardly undercuts the validity of such an approach. Much of contemporary border studies arises from responses to the British cultural anthropologist Victor Turner and his development of the concept of liminal space as it relates to ritual and myth (93–111; see also Weber 530–32). Moreover, the basic definitions of borders and borderlands by significant border theorists are clearly applicable. Gloria Anzaldúa in her classic work in border studies states, "Borders are set up to define the places that are safe and unsafe, to distinguish *us* from *them*. . . . A borderland is a vague and undetermined place created by the emotional residue of an unnatural boundary" (25). Alejandro Morales echoes this idea and makes some significant additions to it:

> A border maps limits; it keeps people in and out of an area; it marks the ending of a safe zone and the beginning of an unsafe zone. To confront a border and, more so, to cross a border presumes great risk. In general, people fear and are afraid to cross borders. People will not leave their safe zone, will not venture into what they consider an unsafe zone. People cling to the dream of utopia and fail to recognize that they create and live in heterotopia. (23)

Even as O'Connor writes her characters across unnatural boundaries and into "vague and undetermined" places—even as she requires them to leave their safe zones to "venture" into a world defined as a Foucauldian "heterotopia," students can be encouraged to make a similar journey: to look beyond the usual confines of O'Connor criticism and discover what happens when they carry her writing into unexpected and unsafe zones.

These zones will be unsafe because, since the first nonbook review commentary on her work—Paul Engle and Martin Hansford's introduction to the 1955 collection of O. Henry Award winners (9)—critical reception has been dominated by attempts to understand and respond to O'Connor in theological terms. In 1990, Frederick Crews, writing in the *New York Review of Books*, saw discussion of O'Connor split between religiously minded readers who "go most seriously astray . . . in assuming that O'Connor must have chosen the bare ingredients of her artistry . . . with a didactic end already in mind" and secularly oriented critics whom he found equally at fault because they demanded that her fiction "flatter [their] opinions" (162, 161)—often, in the tradition of Hawkes, seeing her work as a radical criticism of religion. Crews called for criticism that "recall[s] that her first loyalty as a writer of fiction was to the cause of vivid, resonant, radically economical art" (167), though exactly how this differs from the demands of the secular critics remains vague.

In 2007, Timothy P. Caron saw the situation in even more dire terms, arguing that O'Connor readers generally fall into one of two camps, "Apostates and True Believers" ("Bottom Rail" 138). Though Caron unquestionably exaggerates the differences to favor his own apostate perspective, he is not wrong in asserting the existence of a "growing consensus" among academic studies of O'Connor that "only a certain type of Catholic reading will generate the correct and proper reading of her work" (142). This consensus makes O'Connor unavailable to all but theological readers and writers, producing the kind of limited response that Betsy Erkkila bemoaned when pointing out that "current paradigms of American literature and studies . . . encourage a separatist and atomized model of literary and cultural studies in which whites do whites, men do men, women do women, blacks do blacks, latinos do latinos, and there is very little dialogue among or cultural encounter beyond these relatively fixed ethnic and gender bounds" (564).

O'Connor is situated at enough borders to forestall such a development. Consider her historical context: writing at the end of World War II and during the first half of the Cold War, she inhabited the moment when the United States was emerging as the dominant power on the world political stage and at the same time completing its transition from a largely rural to a largely urban society. Her career also coincided with the full eruption of the civil rights movements for African Americans and overlapped the South's changing economic scene: the rise of the poor whites Faulkner had chronicled in his Snopes trilogy and the advent of the financial world epitomized by Tom Wolfe's real estate magnate Charlie Crocker in *A Man in Full*. American literature itself was moving beyond the high modernism of T. S. Eliot and Faulkner toward something new—a turn that gained visibility when O'Connor's friend Robert Lowell published *Life Studies* in 1959 (Longenbach 5) and Saul Bellow, her contemporary, published *The Adventures of Augie March* in 1953 (Siegel 625). O'Connor's fiction unquestionably was produced in a historical borderland.

Her fiction borders other territories as well, and the essays in this volume suggest ways to explore many of them, without attempting to limit teachers and students to a single form, text, or even genre. For though her short fiction, collected and published in *"A Good Man Is Hard to Find" and Other Stories*

(1955), carried her into the public and critical eye to a degree her first novel, *Wise Blood*, did not, throughout her life she most often referred to herself as a novelist. She wrote to her editor, Catharine Carver, "I have been asked to talk on The Significance of the Short Story (ugh) at a wholesale gathering of the AAUW in Lansing, Michigan—next April. It will take me from now until next April to find out what the significance of the short story is" (*Habit* 91). Much of her nonfiction she dismissed as moneymaking in support of her work as a novelist (Cash, "Flannery O'Connor" 3–4). Nevertheless, examining the ways her thoughts are manifested and shaped in each genre is key to insights about her achievement.

Many instructors will choose which O'Connor texts to teach according to their availability and the nature of the course. Our goal is to provide a range of approaches that respond to the question Jerome McGann has called "the touchstone of critical and interpretive adequacy": "How much has the subject or problem been opened out by the critic's intervention?" (166). The essays in this volume on teaching O'Connor's fiction are grouped into five categories: the author as teacher, teaching O'Connor and religion, teaching contexts, teaching intertextually, and specialized approaches. In each category, scholars writing out of diverse theoretical positions and commitments attempt to lay out the borders of new ideas, new understandings that await students of O'Connor's writing. We hope that students, crossing these borders, will discover just how tremendous are the frontiers her writing invites them to contemplate.

Part One

MATERIALS

Editions

Our examination of editions of O'Connor's writing begins with her main works of fiction. *Wise Blood*, her first novel and first book publication, appeared in 1952, from Harcourt Brace. A second edition of the novel appeared in 1962, from Farrar, Straus; the only change was the addition of a brief but famous "Author's Note." All stand-alone printings since then have included the note. Her second novel, *The Violent Bear It Away*, appeared in 1960 from Farrar, Straus, and this version of the text is still being reprinted today. Her first short story collection, *"A Good Man Is Hard to Find" and Other Stories*, was published in 1955 by Harcourt Brace, and that edition continues to be reprinted. Her second and last collection of stories, *Everything That Rises Must Converge*, has remained in print since its publication by Farrar, Straus and Giroux in 1965, shortly after her death.

Students also encounter O'Connor's fiction through *The Complete Stories* (1971), edited by Robert Giroux, which arranges her stories chronologically by original publication date and not only includes the nineteen from the two book collections but adds the stories that she submitted for her MFA thesis; portions of her two novels that were published independently and are different from how they appear in the novels; a portion of her unfinished novel, *Why Do the Heathen Rage?*, which was published in *Esquire*; and "The Partridge Festival," a story she never included in a collection. But *Complete Stories* is not complete. Missing are pieces she wrote as an undergraduate at Georgia College, including "Home of the Brave," originally published in *The Corinthian*, a campus literary magazine, and reprinted in a limited edition by Albondocani Press in 1981. Also missing is "The Coat," a story that she submitted for publication while in graduate school at the University of Iowa but that never saw print during her lifetime. It appeared in the journal *Doubletake* in 1995 and is currently available online (www.doubletakemagazine.org/edu/teachersguide/activities/race/oconnor/). Also missing are two versions of the story that began its life as "The Geranium" in her thesis stories and ended as "Judgement Day" in *Everything That Rises*, one of her last pieces of writing. These two middle versions, "An Exile in the East" and "Getting Home," are presented in the variorum edition *Flannery O'Connor: The Growing Craft*, edited by Karl-Heinz Westarp.

Since 1988, the preferred edition of O'Connor's work for purposes of scholarship is the Library of America's *Flannery O'Connor: Collected Works*, edited by Sally Fitzgerald. This one volume contains all O'Connor's published books as well as the six stories in her thesis collection, three unpublished stories ("An Afternoon in the Woods," "The Partridge Festival," her unfinished novel excerpt "Why Do the Heathen Rage?"), eight works labeled "Occasional Prose," and a selection of her correspondence. But, like *Complete Stories*, this volume is not as complete as it appears, omitting "The Coat," "Home of the Brave," "An Exile in the East," and "Getting Home." There is confusion, moreover, involving

"Occasional Prose" and the letters. A reader might assume that the letters in *Collected Works* are those that Fitzgerald edited and collected in her much praised 1979 volume, *The Habit of Being: Letters*. They are not: some of those letters are omitted, and new ones appear; many reprinted from the earlier volume are edited differently, often abbreviated and without the 1979 commentary.

As for the essays in *Flannery O'Connor: Collected Works*, there are significant differences from those published in 1969's *Mystery and Manners: Occasional Prose*, edited by Sally Fitzgerald and Robert Fitzgerald. *Mystery and Manners* consists of fourteen pieces, including essays O'Connor published in her lifetime as well as numerous essays that the editors explain in their introduction were cobbled together from "at least half a hundred typescripts for lectures" and edited "as we feel the author herself would now desire" (vii, viii). In the notes for *Flannery O'Connor: Collected Works*, Fitzgerald states that in this volume she has limited the occasional prose to essays that O'Connor either published or brought to final form (1261–62), but although the pieces here largely are labeled with the same titles as those in *Mystery and Manners*, the texts are not always the same. Which editing is more authoritative is unclear. Nevertheless, *Collected Works* is an invaluable resource for studying O'Connor's fiction in depth, and its worth is increased by Fitzgerald's inclusion of a minibiography in the form of a detailed time line, a discussion about her selection of texts, and notes explaining references possibly unfamiliar to readers.

Instructors interested in using O'Connor's fiction to develop beginning-level research skills can draw on two casebooks for "A Good Man Is Hard to Find." Frederick Asals's casebook in the Women Writers: Texts and Contexts series published by Rutgers University Press in 1993 is the better known. It features a cogent introduction by Asals, the author of a major critical monograph on O'Connor (*Flannery O'Connor*), as well as two O'Connor letters and excerpts from the nonfiction published in *Mystery and Manners*. The ten critical commentaries reflect an array of 1960s–1980s theoretical perspectives. Laura Mandell Zaidman's 1999 casebook for the story in the Harcourt Brace Casebook Series in Literature is designed for courses in which instructors want to limit student research to a dozen sources. The research materials include book and article excerpts as well as selections from O'Connor's letters and essays and Eddie Green's 1917 lyrics to the blues song that shares the story's title. The quality of the scholarly commentaries varies, and, as in Asals's casebook, all are a bit dated: no criticism is more recent than 1984 despite the casebook's 1999 publication date.

Serious study of O'Connor's work requires paying attention to her nonfiction, which has been collected and published since her death. *Mystery and Manners* contains many of her classic critical formulations, but the largely invisible editing raises questions about the manuscript materials used; also there is no clear dating system for the essays compiled from the lecture manuscripts. The book's editors performed a great service in bringing this material to public view, but the shortage of information about the editing process is unfortunate.

Two independent volumes of O'Connor's correspondence have appeared. *The Habit of Being* remains the most comprehensive collection, but readers need to bear in mind that it was compiled while O'Connor's mother, Regina, was alive. Because Regina was worried about offending any of the people mentioned in the letters and also did not want her daughter shown in a negative light, the letters were edited to remove potential embarrassment; deletions were sometimes marked by ellipsis dots, sometimes not. When scholars gained access to the actual manuscripts of O'Connor's letters to Maryat Lee and Elizabeth Hester, the nature of the editing became clearer. For example, in "Where Is the Voice Coming From? Flannery O'Connor on Race," Ralph Wood discusses O'Connor's private use of racist language. Nevertheless, *The Habit of Being* offers a complex view of O'Connor as a writer, a thinker, a committed Catholic, and a friend.

Less known and of less use to instructors is *The Correspondence of Flannery O'Connor and the Brainard Cheneys*, edited by C. Ralph Stephens. Brainard Cheney was a novelist from Georgia who lived in Tennessee with his wife, Frances Neel Cheney, a librarian and teacher at George Peabody College for Teachers in Nashville. He wrote an early appreciative review of *Wise Blood*, and O'Connor shared with the Cheneys a friendship with the novelist Caroline Gordon and her husband, Allen Tate, a poet, critic, and central figure of the southern agrarians, who played a key role in the revival of southern literature in the 1920s. These letters contain friendly gossip and discuss professional matters but seldom show the depth found in *The Habit of Being*. Instructors interested in giving students a close-up look at letter manuscripts should check *Postmarked Milledgeville: A Guide to Flannery O'Connor's Correspondence in Libraries and Archives* (Scott and Nye). This thin volume notes twenty-four archives and university libraries across the United States that own O'Connor letters. The largest number of letters are held by institutions in the traditional South, but Texas, Oklahoma, Missouri, New York, New Jersey, and Massachusetts also have small caches of O'Connor correspondence. Instructors interested in teaching students how to work with such materials and who are close enough to an institution that holds them should take advantage of that opportunity.

A few nontraditional O'Connor volumes deserve mention. *A Prayer Journal*, introduced by W. A. Sessions, a friend of O'Connor, is a journal that she kept between 1946 and 1947 when she was a student in the writing program at Iowa. The book provides both a typescript and a photographic facsimile of the handwritten texts. It not only gives insight into O'Connor's struggles as a young writer but also sheds light on her desire to blend writing into her spiritual life.

Another window into O'Connor's early artistic development comes from her cartoons. These are available in two collections: *The Cartoons of Flannery O'Connor at Georgia College*, introduced by Sarah Gordon, and *Flannery O'Connor: The Cartoons*, edited by Kelly Gerald and with a foreword by the artist Barry Moser. These cartoons make visible the author's sense of humor and thoughts about comedy. An excellent supplement to these collections is Gordon's discussion of connections between O'Connor and James Thurber in her monograph *Flannery O'Connor: The Obedient Imagination*.

From 1956 until her death, O'Connor wrote book reviews, mostly for the Atlanta diocese newspaper, *The Bulletin*. Although many of the books reviewed are Catholic in their focus, as might be expected of a publication from a religious institution, they manage to demonstrate O'Connor's eclectic interests, including fiction by Caroline Gordon and J. F. Powers, Protestant theology by Karl Barth, philosophical history by Eric Voegelin, comparative religion studies by Mircea Eliade, and Zen Buddhism by D. T. Suzuki. These reviews are collected in *"The Presence of Grace" and Other Book Reviews*, compiled by Leo J. Zuber. While not essential reading for undergraduate teaching, these reviews help make the case for the breadth of O'Connor's intellect.

Finally, a word needs to be said about the presence of O'Connor's writings on the Internet. The O'Connor estate for many years worked to protect her fiction from open-access publication, but it has become available nonetheless, and students will likely find it on their own. Available online are the complete text of *Complete Stories*, *"A Good Man Is Hard to Find" and Other Stories*, "A Good Man Is Hard to Find," "Good Country People," "The Life You Save May Be Your Own," "Everything That Rises Must Converge," and "Revelation." Three pieces of occasional prose are also available online—all making use of the versions of these texts found in *Mystery and Manners*: "Some Aspects of the Grotesque in Southern Fiction," "The Nature and Aim of Fiction," and the major portion of "Writing Short Stories." Some of these postings are linked to parties or institutions that do not have permission from the O'Connor estate, so they may suddenly vanish, and the editing that goes into an Internet post is often sloppy. Instructors and students should therefore use these editions with caution.

Also available on the library Web sites for Georgia College and State University and Emory University is the Alice Walker story "Convergence," reprinted as an appendix to this volume.

Reference Works

At the top of any list of reference works for teaching O'Connor are biographies. Though she once declared, "[T]here won't be any biographies of me because . . . lives spent between the house and the chicken yard do not make exciting copy" (*Habit* 290–91), at least eight book-length biographies have appeared in print, and others are in various stages of development. Brad Gooch's *Flannery: A Life of Flannery O'Connor* has dominated critical attention since its appearance. It does not break new ground but is highly readable as well as helpfully indexed and documented. Jean W. Cash's *Flannery O'Connor: A Life* reflects tireless interviewing of O'Connor's contemporaries and excellent archival work, and it offers rich and original insights that other biographers have drawn on. However, the late chapters are organized by a thematic rather than a narrative approach, and because Cash was denied cooperation from the O'Connor estate and the author's living family, some small but inevitable confusions appear involving similar names of relatives. Nevertheless, as the first book-length biography to appear, it merits attention for establishing the basic order and cast of characters in O'Connor's life. Paul Elie's *The Life You Save May Be Your Own: An American Pilgrimage* seeks to study American Catholic culture during the middle of the twentieth century by interweaving biographical studies of O'Connor, Dorothy Day, Thomas Merton, and Walker Percy. His book gives an insightful look at O'Connor's spiritual life against a detailed intellectual history. Somewhat similarly, Patrick Samway's *Flannery O'Connor and Robert Giroux: A Publishing Partnership* provides biographical information as it situates O'Connor in the Catholic intellectual establishment of the United States in the mid–twentieth century, an establishment in which Robert Giroux, her editor, played a key role.

Other O'Connor biographies address specific audiences. Susan Balée's *Flannery O'Connor: Literary Prophet of the South* is part of a series for juvenile readers, Great Achievers: Lives of the Physically Challenged—an emphasis that O'Connor herself might well have disliked given her frustration over a review in *Time* magazine that gave "[a] full medical report" about her lupus (*Habit* 378). Melissa Simpson's *Flannery O'Connor: A Biography*, part of the Greenwood Press's biography series, condenses the basic facts of her life and fiction into undemanding prose that may prove useful to students or even teachers who come to O'Connor with limited knowledge and research time, though it does not offer any fresh insights or much depth. Lorraine V. Murray's *The Abbess of Andalusia: Flannery O'Connor's Spiritual Journey* (2009) focuses on O'Connor's Catholicism, making a case for canonizing her in the Catholic church, and examines her daily life on the farm. Jonathan Rogers's *The Terrible Speed of Mercy: A Spiritual Biography of Flannery O'Connor* gives a credible overview of O'Connor's development as a writer and believer. Its brevity makes it a useful source for lower-level students. Angela Alaimo O'Donnell, who wrote *Flannery O'Connor: Fiction Fired by Faith*, is the first biographer to have access to O'Connor's *Prayer Journal*; she sees the author through the lens of her own theological training, and her highly readable book evaluates O'Connor from a religious perspective.

Three nontraditional biographies offer other insights into O'Connor's life. Sally Fitzgerald's "Chronology," in O' Connor's *Collected Works*, is a highly useful and straightforward presentation of the bare bones of the author's life. Fitzgerald labored for many years on O'Connor's official biography—official in that it was authorized by the O'Connor estate—but died before it could be published, leaving only this readable and accurate time line in print. Bruce

Gentry and Craig Amason's *At Home with Flannery O'Connor: An Oral History* supplies ten interviews with people who knew O'Connor while she lived and worked at Andalusia. Its interesting and quirky observations from those who knew O'Connor offer many insights. *Flannery O'Connor: The Woman, the Thinker, the Visionary* presents some biographical information compiled by a friend and correspondent of O'Connor, Ted R. Spivey.

Students and teachers focused on how O'Connor has inspired other writers should examine some of the collections of creative responses. Rita Mae Reese's *The Book of Hulga* is a poetry collection inspired by the aspects of O'Connor's life that found expression in the character Hulga/Joy Hopewell in "Good Country People." R. T. Smith's *The Red Wolf: A Dream of Flannery O'Connor* is a series of dramatic monologues, generally in O'Connor's voice. Smith also produced a special double issue of the literary magazine *Shenandoah* devoted to fiction, poetry, and essays inspired by O'Connor.

A good bibliography of early publications by and on O'Connor is *Flannery O'Connor and Caroline Gordon: A Reference Guide*, by Robert E. Golden and Mary C. Sullivan. For O'Connor criticism from the early 1970s until just after 2000, R. Neil Scott's massive and well-indexed *Flannery O'Connor: An Annotated Reference Guide to Criticism* is authoritative. It includes sections on movies and videos, dissertations and master's theses, and foreign language criticism. Most O'Connor scholars depend on it, along with searches in the *MLA Bibliography* and other databases. David Farmer's *Flannery O'Connor: A Descriptive Bibliography* is the most scholarly description of O'Connor's publications and includes her books, publications in journals and magazines, translations, film and television adaptations, publications of her drawings, and parodies.

Three volumes collect, reprint, and sometimes summarize the critical reception of O'Connor's fiction. *Flannery O'Connor: The Contemporary Reviews*, edited by Scott and Irwin Streight, contains over four hundred complete reviews as well as citations for the reviews that the editors could not get permission to reprint. It also features a clear introduction discussing the response to each of O'Connor's book publications as well as to her "Introduction to *A Memoir of Mary Ann*," one of her most powerful essays. *The Critical Response to Flannery O'Connor*, by Douglas Robillard, Jr., is broader in time frame but more limited in the number of pieces presented: forty-seven. It provides an overview of responses to O'Connor's fiction in three periods: in her lifetime, from her death in 1964 to the publication of *Collected Works* in 1989, and afterward. Suzanne Morrow Paulson's *Flannery O'Connor: A Study of the Short Fiction* is part of Twayne's Studies in Short Fiction series; it reprints and excerpts twenty-five critical essays in its third section, thus offering a limited and more subjective version of Robillard's project.

An excellent reception history is Daniel Moran's *Creating Flannery O'Connor*. Moran shows how O'Connor's reputation has been shaped and how this shaping has affected readers. Beginning with the early response to *Wise Blood*, he looks at key moments in O'Connor's career and continues his discussion into her online presence today. His book stands as an excellent model for advanced students on the study of authorial reception and reputation. Similarly, Robert C. Evans, in *The Critical Reception of Flannery O'Connor, 1952–2017: "Searchers and Discoverers,"* discusses the full history of O'Connor criticism, organized under the headings of aesthetics, theology, history, region, race, and gender.

The Manuscripts of Flannery O'Connor at Georgia College, by Stephen G. Driggers and Robert J. Dunn, is an irreplaceable source for gaining information about the development of O'Connor's writing. Short of traveling to Georgia College in Milledgeville and using the Flannery O'Connor Collection in person, this is the best way to learn about major revisions in her work and get a sense of how extensive her writing process was. It is also an essential tool for anyone who does plan to study the manuscripts at Georgia College. (There is no similar guide to the O'Connor holdings at Emory University, which also houses a special collection of O'Connor materials.) A useful supplement to Driggers and Dunn is Arthur F. Kinney's *Flannery O'Connor's Library: Resources of Being*, which catalogs the books and some magazines and journals that O'Connor owned at the time of her death and notes the markings and marginal comments she made on them. Kinney's listings are strong evidence of O'Connor's intellectual background, and her markings show what most impressed her in what she read.

A comprehensive source for students looking to begin research on O'Connor is *Critical Companion to Flannery O'Connor: A Literary Reference to Her Life and Work*, by Connie Ann Kirk; it provides "high school and college level students, teachers, library users, and general readers with a current, dependable, and comprehensive introduction to O'Connor's life and work" (xiii). The alphabetically arranged section on her works gives a headnote for each story, novel, or essay: the work's publication history; a synopsis; for the fiction, a commentary as well as a list and description of the major characters; a list of O'Connor letters related to the work; and suggestions for further reading. This section includes *The Habit of Being*, organizing the letters alphabetically by the person O'Connor was writing to, offering a brief look at the correspondent, summarizing the letters for that correspondent in chronological order, and naming any fictional writing by O'Connor that a letter is connected to.

Guide to the Gothic III: An Annotated Bibliography of Criticism, 1994–2003 (Frank), *Encyclopedia of Catholic Literature* (Reichardt), *A Companion to the Literature and Culture of the American South* (Gray and Robinson), and *Short Fiction: A Critical Companion* (Evans et al.), though general reference works, can be of help to O'Connor students. Some focus on a single story (*Short Fiction* deals with "Everything That Rises Must Converge"); others supply an overview of a particular topic. The Gale volume *Southern Women Writers: Flannery O'Connor, Katherine Anne Porter, Eudora Welty* (Wimsatt and Rood), in the *Dictionary of Literary Biography* Documentary Series, contains a significant number of primary documents, including letters, interviews, a generous number of photographs and reproductions of O'Connor's cartoons and manuscripts, and reviews of her books. The sound preface to this volume is worth reading for anyone wishing to see O'Connor in the context of her female peers.

Background Studies

History, religion, and southern culture are the most significant backgrounds that illuminate O'Connor's fiction in the classroom. *Encyclopedia of Southern Culture*, edited by Charles Reagan Wilson and William Ferris, is a treasure trove of information. This one volume published in 1989 has since been turned into a much larger project, *The New Encyclopedia of Southern Culture* (Wilson), which is organized into twenty-four volumes, each focusing on an aspect of southern culture. Most instructors will likely confine themselves to volume 9, which is dedicated to literature, but other volumes (on religion, history, myth, manners, ethnicity, gender, and violence) can be insightful. Robert Coles's *Flannery O'Connor's South* interprets O'Connor's fiction and lays out the background areas most important to it: social structure, religion, and intellectualism. Three recommended pictorial studies, containing both historical and modern photographs of O'Connor's world along with commentary, are Harold Fickett and Douglas R. Gilbert's *Flannery O'Connor: Images of Grace*, Barbara McKenzie's *Flannery O'Connor's Georgia*, and Sarah Gordon's especially beautiful *A Literary Guide to Flannery O'Connor's Georgia*.

Background studies focused on history fall into two categories: those dealing with Cold War America and those dealing with race. In the first category, two books stand out: Jon Lance Bacon's *Flannery O'Connor and Cold War Culture* is a smart thematic look at the ways O'Connor's fiction reflects and influences America in the postwar era. In a similar vein, Thomas Hill Schaub includes a chapter on O'Connor in his *American Fiction in the Cold War*. Good general books on this period are Stephen J. Whitfield's *The Culture of the Cold War* and Jason W. Stevens's *God-Fearing and Free: A Spiritual History of America's Cold War*. *God-Fearing* is particularly relevant to O'Connor's fiction because it links history and religion.

For instructors looking for more specific and briefer historical background studies, Robert Donahoo has written these essays: "On Flannery O'Connor: Recovering the Histories in Flannery O'Connor's Short Fiction," "Recasting the Monuments: O'Connor and Histories of the South," "Beholding the Handmaids: Catholic Womanhood and 'The Comforts of Home,'" "O'Connor and *The Feminine Mystique*: A Southern Slant on Post-war American Women," and "Subject to Limitations: O'Connor's Fiction and the South's Shifting Populations."

Studies of race in the American South have proliferated in the years since the Civil Rights Act, yet race in O'Connor long remained an invisible issue despite its obvious presence in stories such as "The Artificial Nigger," "The Displaced

Person," "Everything That Rises Must Converge," and "Judgment Day." Teachers wishing to examine race as a historical subject might use Taylor Branch's *Parting the Waters: America in the King Years* or Juan Williams's companion volume for the PBS series *Eyes on the Prize: America's Civil Rights Years, 1954–1965*. For an instructor looking for historical pieces to read alongside O'Connor's fiction, excellent sources are *The Eyes on the Prize Civil Rights Reader: Documents, Speeches, and Firsthand Accounts from the Black Freedom Struggle*, edited by Clayborne Carson et al., and *Killers of the Dream*, by Lillian Smith, a fellow southerner and contemporary of O'Connor with an activist stance on civil rights. A narrower but highly suggestive history for understanding O'Connor and race is Jason Sokol's *There Goes My Everything: White Southerners in the Age of Civil Rights, 1945–1975*. Though Sokol makes no mention of O'Connor, his book helps reveal and explore white attitudes about race and sets off numerous echoes with both her fiction and her letters.

There is no monograph on O'Connor and race, but several books have significant discussions, especially Toni Morrison's *Playing in the Dark: Whiteness and the Literary Imagination*. Among the literary scholars who have built on Morrison's insights are John Duvall in *Race and White Identity in Southern Fiction: From Faulkner to Morrison*, Doreen Fowler in *Drawing the Line: The Father Reimagined in Faulkner, Wright, O'Connor, and Morrison*, and Timothy P. Caron in *Struggles over the Word: Race and Religion in O'Connor, Faulkner, Hurston, and Wright*. Ralph C. Wood's "Where Is the Voice Coming From? Flannery O'Connor on Race" opened a floodgate of commentary on the subject. Claire Kahane's "The Artificial Niggers" used race as a whip to chastise O'Connor, but Wood, dealing with unredacted O'Connor letters previously unavailable, offers a more complex discussion.

For background material on religious matters, a teacher might consider Patrick Allitt's *Religion in America since 1945*, whose first three chapters give an overview of the kind of religious sensibility O'Connor encountered as she began her writing career. Will Herberg's *Protestant, Catholic, Jew: An Essay in American Religious Sociology* provides a view of religion from O'Connor's time, capturing well the successes and problems of religion in the postwar era. A briefer version of some of his ideas is also available in his "Religion and Culture in Present-Day America."

Karl Adam, in *The Spirit of Catholicism*, writes about Catholic doctrine as O'Connor knew it: pre–Vatican II. Note that there were two books by Adam in O'Connor's personal library, *The Christ of Faith: The Christology of the Church* and *The Son of God* (Kinney 49–50), and she reviewed his *The Roots of the Reformation* and *The Christ of Faith* (*Presence* 51–52, 54–55). The advantage of *The Spirit of Catholicism* over the books actually connectable to O'Connor is that, for background, it offers a wider discussion of Catholic beliefs.

Those who wish to delve deeper into the religious background would do well to examine the religious thinkers and writers O'Connor declared herself particularly interested in. At the top of the list are the writings of Thomas Aquinas, whose *Summa Theologiae* O'Connor claimed to read "for about twenty minutes every night before I go to bed" (*Habit* 93). Equally important—and not as massive—is Jacques Maritain's *Art and Scholasticism*, which she said was "the book I cut my aesthetic teeth on" (216). Her nonfiction, especially her letters and reviews, point to other texts and thinkers, and in the critical commentary there is vigorous discussion of her contact with a variety of these writers.

Critical Commentaries

Five monographs study O'Connor in more depth. The earliest of these is Asals's *Flannery O'Connor: The Imagination of Extremity*. Without dismissing the religious aspects of O'Connor, his book was groundbreaking when it appeared in 1982, establishing such key ideas for reading her fiction as the importance of doubling, her debts to Edgar Allan Poe, and the sense in which her work offers a "prophetic imagination" (198–233). Four years later, Marshall Bruce Gentry applied the ideas of Mikhail Bakhtin to O'Connor's work in his *Flannery O'Connor's Religion of the Grotesque*. Gentry directed a critical gaze at O'Connor's narrators and the roles they play in her fiction. This push toward a more theoretical examination of the author reached a high point with Jon Lance Bacon's full-throated new historical analysis in *Flannery O'Connor and Cold War Culture*. The return to a focus on O'Connor's religious ideas, combined with an awareness of the developments in literary theory, was evident in Susan Srigley's *Flannery O'Connor's Sacramental Art* and Christina Bieber Lake's *The Incarnational Art of Flannery O'Connor*. Both are remarkably rich studies: Srigley draws on a variety of theological sources to examine the ethics steering O'Connor's fiction, and Lake demonstrates O'Connor's response to thinkers from Emerson to Nietzsche as being grounded in central Christian doctrines.

Monographs that stress O'Connor's theological implications include two by Richard Giannone—*Flannery O'Connor and the Mystery of Love* (1989) and *Flannery O'Connor, Hermit Novelist* (2000). Giannone's more recent O'Connor book has a strong Catholic emphasis, showing her debts to the thought and writings of the Desert Fathers. Also strongly Catholic is George Kilcourse's *Flannery O'Connor's Religious Imagination: A World with Everything Off Balance*. From a Protestant perspective, Wood's *Flannery O'Connor and the Christ-Haunted South* constructs a defense of O'Connor's ideas and Christian beliefs. Each chapter reads as an independent essay and has a clear and strongly held position to argue—especially the chapters on race, southern preaching, and nihilism.

Other studies that are of value but narrower in their approach are Josephine Hendin's *The World of Flannery O'Connor*, Martha Stephens's *The Question of Flannery O'Connor*, and Carol Loeb Shloss's *Flannery O'Connor's Dark Com-*

edies: The Limits of Inference. All three make the case that O'Connor struggled, and sometimes failed, as an artist. Gordon's *Flannery O'Connor: The Obedient Imagination* and Katherine Hemple Prown's *Revising Flannery O'Connor: Southern Literary Culture and the Problem of Female Authorship* perform a clear feminist analysis of the author and show how her manuscripts reveal her process of revising. Teachers who want to explore psychological approaches to O'Connor and her works—as much as O'Connor herself probably would have disapproved—might examine, along with the O'Connor biographies, "Flannery O'Connor's Rage of Vision" by Claire Katz (Kahane), Sherry Lynn Lebeck's examination of mother-child relationships in O'Connor (*Paradox Lost and Paradox Regained*), Cynthia Seel's Jungian analysis (*Ritual Performance in the Fiction of Flannery O'Connor*), and Doreen Fowler's psychoanalytic studies, such as *Drawing the Line*. Even more focused in their angle of approach, Anthony Di Renzo ties O'Connor's theological fiction to medieval traditions of the grotesque in *American Gargoyles*, and Bryan Abel Ragen, in *A Wreck on the Road to Damascus*, one of the first studies to examine closely the automobiles in O'Connor, connects her attention to machinery back to her theological convictions.

Given how little O'Connor wrote, it is not surprising that some of the best critical commentary on her work is found in books that study many authors and in essay collections. Louise Westling's *Sacred Groves and Ravaged Gardens: The Fiction of Eudora Welty, Carson McCullers, and Flannery O'Connor* is a feminist reading criticizing O'Connor's depiction of women. This view has been challenged since it appeared in 1985, but the question remains important. Patricia Yaeger's *Dirt and Desire: Reconstructing Southern Women's Writing, 1930–1990* takes a very different feminist approach to O'Connor among many other southern women writers, linking the author to a variety of tropes that Yaeger sees as defining female writing and identifying her not as critical of women but as belonging to unacknowledged trends in southern women's studies. Farrell O'Gorman's *Peculiar Crossroads: Flannery O'Connor, Walker Percy, and Catholic Vision in Postwar Southern Fiction* argues the centrality of O'Connor to a tradition of Catholic writers in the South before her and to the generation of Catholic writers that followed. John Sykes's *Flannery O'Connor, Walker Percy, and the Aesthetic of Revelation* sets O'Connor in the framework of the Southern Renaissance. While L. Lamar Nisly's *Impossible to Say* also relates O'Connor to Percy, it adds to these connections ones between both Catholic writers and the Jewish writers Bernard Malamud and Cynthia Ozick. Finally, Gary Ciuba's *Desire, Violence, and Divinity in Modern Southern Fiction: Katherine Anne Porter, Flannery O'Connor, Cormac McCarthy, Walker Percy* is less concerned with defining a tradition than in discussing how O'Connor shares particular themes with Porter, McCarthy, and Percy. Ciuba examines her fiction through the theoretical lens of René Girard, whose work in anthropological philosophy sought to theorize the reasons and results of violence. Jessica Hooten Wilson studies O'Connor alongside Dostoevsky (while also applying the ideas of René Girard) in her *Giving the*

Devil His Due: Demonic Authority in the Fiction of Flannery O'Connor and Fyodor Dostoevsky.

Several collections of original essays provide a broad spectrum of approaches to O'Connor's work. The best of these is *New Essays on* Wise Blood. The introductory essay by its editor, Michael Kreyling, argues for the importance of O'Connor's first novel, and the essays that follow, by Jon Lance Bacon; James M. Mellard; Robert H. Brinkmeyer, Jr.; and Patricia Yaeger, display a variety of theoretical approaches and fresh insights. A much longer if uneven collection, with nineteen original essays about O'Connor's first novel, is John J. Han's Wise Blood: *A Re-consideration.* Susan Srigley's *Dark Faith: New Essays on Flannery O'Connor's* The Violent Bear It Away is the only essay collection with O'Connor's second novel as its focus, laying out largely theological interpretations of that book. *The Added Dimension: The Art and Mind of Flannery O'Connor*, edited by Melvin J. Friedman and Lewis A. Lawson, includes essays by such luminaries in the field of American literary studies as Frederick J. Hoffman; Louis D. Rubin, Jr.; C. Hugh Holman; Irving Malin; and Nathan A. Scott, Jr. Their contributions help explain O'Connor's fast elevation into the literary canon. Sura P. Rath and Mary Neff Shaw's *Flannery O'Connor: New Perspectives* contains similar materials from a later generation of scholars, including Gentry, Jeanne Campbell Reesman, Richard Giannone, Gordon, Brinkmeyer, and Yaeger. The essays in *"On the Subject of the Feminist Business": Re-reading Flannery O'Connor*, edited by Teresa Caruso, take seriously gender issues in O'Connor and point to her place in the canon of American women writers. *Inside the Church of Flannery O'Connor*, edited by Joanne Halleran McMullen and Jon Parrish Peede, presents much more of a variety of approaches than its title suggests. *Flannery O'Connor's Radical Reality*, edited by Jan Nordby Gretlund and Karl-Heinz Westarp, is distinguished by its inclusion of several articles by European contributors. *Flannery O'Connor in the Age of Terrorism: Essays on Violence and Grace*, edited by Avis Hewitt and Donahoo, considers O'Connor's fiction in light of changing political realities in the twenty-first century. Finally, Mark Bosco and Brent Little collected essays about the influence of Catholic theology and Catholic literature on O'Connor (with regular attention to her *Prayer Journal*) in their *Revelation and Convergence: Flannery O'Connor and the Catholic Intellectual Tradition.*

Of course, collections that reprint critical essays about O'Connor abound. Harold Bloom has edited at least three; the best of them is his 2009 *Flannery O'Connor*. Robert Reiter's *Flannery O'Connor* is a valuable source for some early responses to O'Connor, including John Hawkes's important essay "Flannery O'Connor's Devil." Volumes that, by including a spectrum of well-known and relatively new critics, merit attention are Robert C. Evans's *Short Fiction of Flannery O'Connor: Critical Insights* and Charles E. May's *Critical Insights: Flannery O'Connor*. In *A Political Companion to Flannery O'Connor*, Henry T. Edmondson III presents a collection of reprinted and new essays to trace the influence of political philosophers on O'Connor and the political implications of her fiction.

Audiovisual Aids

The major film adaptation of an O'Connor work is the feature-length *Wise Blood*, directed by John Huston. The Criterion Collection DVD includes original interviews with Brad Dourif, who plays Hazel Motes; Benedict Fitzgerald, the writer of the film script; and Michael Fitzgerald, a writer-producer. It also includes an archival audio recording of O'Connor reading her short story "A Good Man Is Hard to Find." For many students, hearing O'Connor's voice offers an exciting interpretative moment.

The most important and accessible adaptation of an O'Connor short story is *The Displaced Person*, produced by PBS in the late 1970s and available on DVD. With a screenplay by Horton Foote and a cast including John Houseman, this film was shot in and around Andalusia, O'Connor's farm home in Milledgeville, giving a glimpse into her physical world. Short film versions of her stories are *Good Country People*, *The River*, *A Circle in the Fire*, *The Comforts of Home*, and *The Life You Save*. The last of these is an adaptation made for television during O'Connor's lifetime and featuring Gene Kelly as Mr. Shiftlet; its happy ending, added by Hollywood, generally amuses students and gives them insight into what is often thought of as O'Connor's dark, grotesque vision. All these adaptations can be seen by visitors to the Flannery O'Connor Collection at Georgia College in Milledgeville. Information for buying a video is on the Web site *The Comforts of Home* (www.flanneryoconnor.org/videos.html).

O'Connor herself appears on film twice. One is in a short (and silly) Pathé news item about her success as a young child in teaching a chicken to walk backward, a film that would be easy to skip if it were not for the fact that appearing in it was significant to her. The other is an episode promoting the release of *"A Good Man Is Hard to Find" and Other Stories*, produced for *Galley Proof*, a filmed interview program on New York television. A transcription of this interview is available in *Conversations with Flannery O'Connor*, but currently the only way to see the interview is by visiting the Flannery O'Connor Collection.

Two film documentaries about O'Connor exist. *Uncommon Grace: The Life of Flannery O'Connor*, directed by Bridget Kurt, features many previously unpublished photographs as well as interviews with scholars and friends of O'Connor. It emphasizes her religious thought but is highly informative about many other aspects of her life. In 1974, Nashville Public Television (WDCN-TV) produced *The World of Flannery O'Connor*; because of its proximity in time to her life, it has more interviews with people she knew. However, this documentary appears to be available only in the Flannery O'Connor Collection.

The PBS series Religion and Ethics Weekly produced an episode on O'Connor that focuses almost exclusively on her religious beliefs. It can be found online at www.pbs.org/wnet/religionandethics/2009/11/20/november-20-2009-flannery -oconnor/5043/. This site also has links to extended interviews with Gooch, an O'Connor biographer, and Wood, an O'Connor scholar. Emphasizing O'Connor's importance to Catholicism, Word on Fire Ministries has produced an episode, "Flannery O'Connor," for its series *Catholicism: The Pivotal Players* (vol. 2).

Flannery, a ninety-minute documentary partially funded by the National Endowment for Humanities, will premiere in 2019. Produced and directed by Mark Bosco and Elizabeth Coffman, it includes interviews from O'Connor's friends and family, Sally Fitzgerald, Louise Florencourt, Frances Florencourt, W. A. Sessions, and Robert Giroux; such scholars and writers as Alice Walker, Mary Gordon, Alice McDermott, Hilton Als, and Tobias Wolff; and the actor Tommy Lee Jones.

The Internet offers a number of audio and video materials related to O'Connor. On *YouTube* are amateur films that are based on her work or about her life and career. A friend once commented that, judging from a *YouTube* search, many professors must be encouraging student video responses to O'Connor, and a look at these responses might be helpful to an instructor interested in giving such an assignment. A *YouTube* search will also turn up some audio recordings of O'Connor reading her work and giving one of her lectures as well as videos of scholars lecturing on her—for example, her friend and correspondent Sessions, who before his death in 2016 was working on an authorized biography of her. The Web site for the O'Connor NEH 2014 Summer Institute, Reconsidering Flannery O'Connor, has posted video recordings of seven lectures given during the institute—by Brinkmeyer, Ciuba, Gooch, Fowler, Lake, Virginia Wray, and Nagueyalti Warren (www.gcsu.edu/nehoconnor/institute-lecturers)—as well as creative readings connected to O'Connor by the poets Alice Friman and Martin Lammon. The lectures are directed to other scholars, not to students, but they exemplify some of the academic discussion that O'Connor's work has generated.

Manuscript Collections

Two university libraries offer significant special collections of O'Connor manuscripts and other materials that can serve as a resource for teaching her. The Flannery O'Connor Collection at Georgia College and State University, her undergraduate alma mater, has the largest collection of her manuscripts. Specific information about its holdings as well as other information can be found at lib guides.gcsu.edu/oconnor-collection. Since 2000, Emory University's Stuart A.

Rose Manuscript, Archives, and Rare Book Library has built a strong collection of O'Connor materials that include letters and other objects from the O'Connor estate and from her friends and correspondents. Information about the holdings can be found at pid.emory.edu/ark:/25593/8zqf5.

O'Connor's Childhood Home and Andalusia

O'Connor's first home, in Savannah, and her last home, at the family farm called Andalusia, are open to the public and are continually being renovated and preserved. Both offer valuable programming to visitors, including school groups, and both are compiling and organizing collections of materials that could be of use to scholars. The Web site for her childhood home is www.flanneryocon norhome.org/. The Web site for Andalusia is www.gcsu.edu/andalusia.

Part Two

APPROACHES

Introduction to the Essays

Marshall Bruce Gentry and Robert Donahoo

Why do we teach Flannery O'Connor, and what do we need from a volume about teaching her works? The 149 teachers who answered the online survey for this project reported that it is easy to get started teaching her: as one survey respondent put it, "I would estimate that eighty-five percent of my students find O'Connor's unusual mixture of faith and humor riveting." Teachers said that they used her successfully in classes ranging from freshman English to the graduate seminar. She helped them investigate such topics as "systemic transactions within the family structure," "[t]he South's perception of international affairs," and [h]ow human selves are formed," and many respondents used her works to investigate such topics as race, class, gender, violence, and religion. She is admired and studied for "her modern fictional technique" and even her "presentation of the 'unpresentable.'" She appears on reading lists for courses with titles like Literature and Psychology, Cinematic Modernism, Inquiry into Southern Identities, Generations and Conflicts, and Civil War, Civil Rights.

But with O'Connor, the very topics that intrigue us are the topics that can make a teacher call for help. How does one deal with race in her life and time and in her fiction? Is it all about life in the rural South, about a white underclass living in or near poverty? How does one explain her penchant for the violent climax? Is she antifeminist? And what does one do with the topic of religion? One survey response, in answer to what this volume should address, was, "Not Catholicism!" This is a reasonable response, because so much O'Connor criticism has used a religious approach. Yet many respondents wrote something along the lines of "I struggle with teaching the theological dimension of O'Connor's fiction within a secular context." Another respondent wrote, "[I]s it now time to reconsider O'Connor's fiction in terms of what we now know to be the failure of secularization?" How, and how much, does one address the sacraments, or the Incarnation, or original sin, or the differences between Catholicism and Protestantism? How do we provide "the background [students] need to understand works written when knowledge of the Bible and the classics could be assumed" but no longer can be?

This volume is organized to address the different problems teachers face and the new approaches they would like to try. The first section of articles, "The Author as Teacher," reflects our sense that O'Connor is one of the most powerful interpreters of her work. If teaching her sometimes requires us to leave the safe zone of traditional criticism, teaching within that safe zone has its own challenges. For example, seeing O'Connor as a reader and interpreter of her writing shows students both the value and limitations of her insights. We have included in this volume her comments on her fiction, in the essay titled "On Her Own Work."

O'Connor thought long and often about her craft, and, though her travel was limited by illness, she gave dozens of lectures between the publication of *Wise Blood* in 1952 and her death in 1964 (see Cash, "Flannery O'Connor as Lecturer" 1), honing and repeating ideas about fiction and fiction writing. She used some of this material in the essays she published. After her death, her editors—Sally Fitzgerald and Robert Fitzgerald for *Mystery and Manners* and Sally Fitzgerald for *Flannery O'Connor: Collected Works*—added some of her lectures to her oeuvre. In *Mystery and Manners*, the editors cobbled together essays from various lecture drafts, explaining in the foreword that they "decided to edit the body of the writing as [they felt] the author herself would now desire, having recourse to the same kind of shuffling as she herself so often practiced. [They] cut away most of the repetitions and took interesting arguments in their best available form; where rearrangements and transpositions were necessary and possible, [they] performed them" (viii–ix).

Supplementing O'Connor's essay, Will Brantley offers guidance to using her letters, in which she communicated with a wide range of people: friends, admirers, editors, scholars, and cranks. The publication of the letters, which Richard H. Brodhead has called "the richest volume of correspondence by an American author to have appeared in many years" (451), gives access to O'Connor's "formidable character" (452) as well as to her commentary on her own fiction and life. Brantley helps teachers clarify her views for students and shows how to teach them to engage her in a challenging dialogue.

The section "O'Connor and Religion" addresses what has long been both a mainstay for O'Connor criticism and a stumbling block for teachers: her connection to the Christian faith and how that faith is revealed in her fiction. Her essays plainly show her interest in "the novelist with Christian concerns" (*Flannery . . . Works* 801), and she bluntly states in "The Fiction Writer and His Country":

> I am no disbeliever in spiritual purpose and no vague believer. I see from the standpoint of Christian orthodoxy. This means that for me the meaning of life is centered in our Redemption by Christ and that what I see in the world I see in its relation to that. I don't think that this is a position that can be taken halfway or one that is particularly easy in these times to make transparent in fiction.   (804–05)

Three essays deal with her faith while teaching students with diverse beliefs, an issue that needs close attention. Christina Bieber Lake explores how using basic biblical paradigms such as the story of Jonah provides insight into O'Connor. Lake deepens our understanding of how O'Connor regards her characters as well as her readers. Mark Bosco suggests ways the specifics of O'Connor's Catholic intellectual heritage come into play and offers a demonstration of the value of this Catholic focus centered on "A Temple of the Holy Ghost"—a story that is one of her few that involves a Catholic milieu. In a society that is less and less literate about theological matters, this old safe zone may well seem the most hazardous. Jessica Hooten Wilson demonstrates the value of laying out basic Christian doctrines, like the Incarnation and original sin, to help students see how these open up major thematic concerns in O'Connor's fiction. In an interview about O'Connor and Latino/a fiction, Richard Rodriguez makes this point: "There are very few American writers of her rank in the twentieth century who take religion and religious experience as seriously or as blatantly. . . . It is a scandal that such a crucial aspect of human experience would be ignored or left unspoken in our literature of the last century. Such a cowardice! Such a starvation!" (31).

The "Contexts" section begins by addressing the thorny issue of race. The essays of both Doreen Fowler and John Duvall turn their attention to this concern for O'Connor. Fowler examines, using a psychological approach, how race plays into her understanding and use of the idea of grace. According to Fowler, contact with another color in O'Connor is a way to learn about the divine. Duvall explores the ways her fiction uses and defines whiteness. The result is seeing the extent to which race in O'Connor is a performance, and Duvall's approach uncovers racial significance in stories that seem not to be about race. The following essays address other cultural contexts. Robert Donahoo discusses how the presence of modernism in O'Connor's work expands the themes of her fiction. Jon Lance Bacon argues that World War II is important for an understanding of *Wise Blood*. Doug Davis turns his attention to the role of science and technology in O'Connor's work, how they shape and are responded to by her fiction.

The section "O'Connor and Other Authors" is based on the belief that O'Connor benefits from being moved out of isolation and studied in terms of other authors and that other authors benefit from being compared with and contrasted to her. Her letters and book reviews show that she was an avid reader, despite her frequent claims to have avoided reading for much of her early life. Within two months of corresponding with Betty Hester, O'Connor explained, "I didn't really start to read until I went to Graduate School and then I began to read and write at the same time. When I went to Iowa I had never heard of Faulkner, Kafka, Joyce, much less read them. Then I began to read everything at once" (*Flannery . . . Works* 950–51). Her letters and essays are liberally marked by literary name dropping: from classic American authors such as Poe, Hawthorne, and James to Catholic writers from Dante to Graham Greene. She notes that Vladimir Nabokov's *Lolita* was compared by critics with *Wise Blood* (1175) and describes *The Hard-Boiled Virgin*, by Frances Newman, a largely forgotten writer of the 1920s, as something "I must read" (972) only to later bemoan, "[D]ear Lord, it's all reported; the most undramatic fifty pages I have been exposed to since [Walter Pater's] Marius the Epicurean" (980).

Teaching O'Connor alongside other authors not only allows new views of her to arise but also clarifies literary relationships. Miriam Marty Clark and Virginia Grant suggest the value of searching out strategies and themes shared by O'Connor and James Joyce's *Dubliners*, which helps students understand the nature of literary influence and strengthens their reading skills at various levels. John Sykes looks at the benefits of teaching O'Connor in connection with William Faulkner, whom O'Connor saw as a dominating literary force in her region: the literary equivalent of "the Dixie Limited" whose tracks "[n]obody wants his mule and wagon stalled on" (*Flannery . . . Works* 818). Sykes distinguishes between the southern gothic of Faulkner and O'Connor's vision even while showing how studying their short fiction in tandem offers a master lesson in reading.

Margaret Earley Whitt uses the fiction of Ann Petry, an African American author whose career overlapped with O'Connor's, to examine portrayals of race—a surprisingly fruitful linking of two female writers approaching race from opposite directions. Nagueyalti Warren offers a similar pairing by linking O'Connor and Alice Walker, though her goal is more to show how O'Connor inspired Walker, who responds to "Everything That Rises Must Converge" in "Convergence," one of her earliest pieces. Carole K. Harris and David Wehner write essays about teaching O'Connor in connection to the work of Junot Díaz and Toni Morrison, respectively. Harris encourages linking O'Connor and Díaz to reveal commonalities in their critique of social justice and labor issues. Drawing on Morrison's appreciative commentary about O'Connor's fiction and comparing Morrison's Catholicism with O'Connor's, Wehner clarifies issues of religion and race in both authors. Irwin Streight uses popular music, from Bruce Springsteen to metal bands, as a tool for helping students understand O'Connor's themes and worldview.

The final section, "Specialized Perspectives," describes some highly fruitful teaching approaches that grow out of recent theoretical developments in literary study. Donald Hardy teaches O'Connor by guiding students to analyze her narrative style. Focusing on an often ignored story, "The River," he sees in her style not only a key to understanding her appeal but also to the power of her themes. Christine Flanagan, noting O'Connor's long residence in a rural world, shows how O'Connor's fiction can be taught for its reflection of environmental issues. Where the seemingly unanimous opinion in scholarship as late as the 1990s saw O'Connor as antifeminist, a volume of essays edited by Teresa Caruso suggested that O'Connor's take on gender was more complex, responding to and echoing the changing role of women in 1950s America. In this volume, Julie Goodspeed-Chadwick studies this aspect of her work, elucidating the ways that O'Connor fiction defines and uses and is understood by its place at the border of gender theory and politics. Ben Saxton works with disability and medical studies to teach O'Connor in the context of the physical body. For a writer who famously wrote to a friend, "I have never been anywhere but sick" (*Flannery . . . Works* 997), this approach is particularly apt and opens up teaching O'Connor in nontraditional literary classrooms.

O'Connor provides teachers with texts that can empower students to see the diverse field in which literature resides and to help them, in Betsy Erkkila's words, "to reconceptualize American cultural studies" (589). If we do so, we may find that students can connect to O'Connor in surprising and fruitful ways, since, as Helena María Viramontes reminds us, the author "believed novelists were people who were visionaries" (6). O'Connor's visions do what all good education does: encourage learners to see the limits of their own territory and to peer into the mysterious and beckoning wider world on the other side.

THE AUTHOR AS TEACHER:
O'CONNOR AS SELF-CRITIC

On Her Own Work

Flannery O'Connor

A Reasonable Use of the Unreasonable

Last fall[1] I received a letter from a student who said she would be "graciously appreciative" if I would tell her "just what enlightenment" I expected her to get from each of my stories. I suspect she had a paper to write. I wrote her back to forget about the enlightenment and just try to enjoy them. I knew that was the most unsatisfactory answer I could have given because, of course, she didn't want to enjoy them, she just wanted to figure them out.

In most English classes the short story has become a kind of literary specimen to be dissected. Every time a story of mine appears in a Freshman anthology, I have a vision of it, with its little organs laid open, like a frog in a bottle.

I realize that a certain amount of this what-is-the-significance has to go on, but I think something has gone wrong in the process when, for so many students, the story becomes simply a problem to be solved, something which you evaporate to get Instant Enlightenment.

A story really isn't any good unless it successfully resists paraphrase, unless it hangs on and expands in the mind. Properly, you analyze to enjoy, but it's equally true that to analyze with any discrimination, you have to have enjoyed already, and I think that the best reason to hear a story read is that it should stimulate that primary enjoyment.

I don't have any pretensions to being an Aeschylus or Sophocles and providing you in this story with a cathartic experience out of your mythic background, though this story I'm going to read certainly calls up a good deal of the South's mythic background, and it should elicit from you a degree of pity and terror, even though its way of being serious is a comic one. I do think, though, that like the Greeks you should know what is going to happen in this story so that any element of suspense in it will be transferred from its surface to its interior.

I would be most happy if you had already read it, happier still if you knew it well, but since experience has taught me to keep my expectations along these lines modest, I'll tell you that this is the story of a family of six which, on its way driving to Florida, gets wiped out by an escaped convict who calls himself the Misfit. The family is made up of the Grandmother and her son, Bailey, and his children, John Wesley and June Star and the baby, and there is also the cat and the children's mother. The cat is named Pitty Sing, and the Grandmother is taking him with them, hidden in a basket.

Now I think it behooves me to try to establish with you the basis on which reason operates in this story. Much of my fiction takes its character from a reasonable use of the unreasonable, though the reasonableness of my use of it may not always be apparent. The assumptions that underlie this use of it, however, are those of the central Christian mysteries. These are assumptions to which a large part of the modern audience takes exception. About this I can only say that there are perhaps other ways than my own in which this story could be read, but none other by which it could have been written. Belief, in my own case anyway, is the engine that makes perception operate.

The heroine of this story, the Grandmother, is in the most significant position life offers the Christian. She is facing death. And to all appearances she, like the rest of us, is not too well prepared for it. She would like to see the event postponed. Indefinitely.

I've talked to a number of teachers who use this story in class and who tell their students that the Grandmother is evil, that in fact, she's a witch, even down to the cat. One of these teachers told me that his students, and particularly his Southern students, resisted this interpretation with a certain bemused vigor, and he didn't understand why. I had to tell him that they resisted it because they all had grandmothers or great-aunts just like her at home, and they knew, from personal experience, that the old lady lacked comprehension, but that she had a good heart. The Southerner is usually tolerant of those weaknesses that proceed from innocence, and he knows that a taste for self-preservation can be readily combined with the missionary spirit.

This same teacher was telling his students that morally the Misfit was several cuts above the Grandmother. He had a really sentimental attachment to the Misfit. But then a prophet gone wrong is almost always more interesting than your grandmother, and you have to let people take their pleasures where they find them.

It is true that the old lady is a hypocritical old soul; her wits are no match for the Misfit's, nor is her capacity for grace equal to his; yet I think the unprejudiced reader will feel that the Grandmother has a special kind of triumph in this story which instinctively we do not allow to someone altogether bad.

I often ask myself what makes a story work, and what makes it hold up as a story, and I have decided that it is probably some action, some gesture of a character that is unlike any other in the story, one which indicates where the real heart of the story lies. This would have to be an action or a gesture which was both totally right and totally unexpected; it would have to be one that was both in character and beyond character; it would have to suggest both the world and eternity. The action or gesture I'm talking about would have to be on the anagogical level, that is, the level which has to do with the Divine life and our participation in it. It would be a gesture that transcended any neat allegory that might have been intended or any pat moral categories a reader could make. It would be a gesture which somehow made contact with mystery.

There is a point in this story where such a gesture occurs. The Grandmother is at last alone, facing the Misfit. Her head clears for an instant and she realizes, even in her limited way, that she is responsible for the man before her and joined to him by ties of kinship which have their roots deep in the mystery she has been merely prattling about so far. And at this point, she does the right thing, she makes the right gesture.

I find that students are often puzzled by what she says and does here, but I think myself that if I took out this gesture and what she says with it, I would have no story. What was left would not be worth your attention. Our age not only does not have a very sharp eye for the almost imperceptible intrusions of grace, it no longer has much feeling for the nature of the violences which precede and follow them. The devil's greatest wile, Baudelaire has said, is to convince us that he does not exist.

I suppose the reasons for the use of so much violence in modern fiction will differ with each writer who uses it, but in my own stories I have found that violence is strangely capable of returning my characters to reality and preparing them to accept their moment of grace. Their heads are so hard that almost nothing else will do the work. This idea, that reality is something to which we must be returned at considerable cost, is one which is seldom understood by the casual reader, but it is one which is implicit in the Christian view of the world.

I don't want to equate the Misfit with the devil. I prefer to think that, however unlikely this may seem, the old lady's gesture, like the mustard-seed, will grow to be a great crow-filled tree in the Misfit's heart, and will be enough of a pain to him there to turn him into the prophet he was meant to become. But that's another story.

This story has been called grotesque, but I prefer to call it literal. A good story is literal in the same sense that a child's drawing is literal. When a child draws, he doesn't intend to distort but to set down exactly what he sees, and as his gaze is direct, he sees the lines that create motion. Now the lines of motion that interest the writer are usually invisible. They are lines of spiritual motion. And in this story you should be on the lookout for such things as the action of grace in the Grandmother's soul, and not for the dead bodies.

We hear many complaints about the prevalence of violence in modern fiction, and it is always assumed that this violence is a bad thing and meant to be an end in itself. With the serious writer, violence is never an end in itself. It is the extreme situation that best reveals what we are essentially, and I believe these are times when writers are more interested in what we are essentially than in the tenor of our daily lives. Violence is a force which can be used for good or evil, and among other things taken by it is the kingdom of heaven. But regardless of what can be taken by it, the man in the violent situation reveals those qualities least dispensable in his personality, those qualities which are all he will have to take into eternity with him; and since the characters in this story are all on the verge of eternity, it is appropriate to think of what they take with them. In any case, I hope that if you consider these points in connection with the story, you will come to see it as something more than an account of a family murdered on the way to Florida.

The Mystery of Freedom

Wise Blood has reached the age of ten and is still alive.[2] My critical powers are just sufficient to determine this, and I am gratified to be able to say it. The book was written with zest, and if possible, it should be read that way. It is a comic novel about a Christian *malgré lui*, and as such, very serious, for all comic novels that are any good must be about matters of life and death. *Wise Blood* was written by an author congenitally innocent of theory, but one with certain preoccupations. That belief in Christ is to some a matter of life and death has been a stumbling block for readers who would prefer to think it a matter of no great consequence. For them, Hazel Motes' integrity lies in his trying with such vigor to get rid of the ragged figure who moves from tree to tree in the back of his mind. For the author, his integrity lies in his not being able to. Does one's integrity ever lie in what he is not able to do? I think that usually it does, for free will does not mean one will, but many wills conflicting in one man. Freedom cannot be conceived simply. It is a mystery and one which a novel, even a comic novel, can only be asked to deepen.

In the Devil's Territory

My view of free will follows the traditional Catholic teaching.[3] I don't think any genuine novelist is interested in writing about a world of people who are strictly determined. Even if he writes about characters who are mostly unfree, it is the sudden free action, the open possibility, which he knows is the only thing capable of illuminating the picture and giving it life. So that while predictable, predetermined actions have a comic interest for me, it is the free act, the acceptance of grace particularly, that I always have my eye on as the thing which will make the story work. In the story, "A Good Man Is Hard to Find," it is the

Grandmother's recognition that the Misfit is one of her children; in "The River," it is the child's peculiar desire to find the kingdom of Christ; in "The Artificial Nigger," it is what the "artificial nigger" does to reunite Mr. Head and Nelson. None of these things can be predicted. They represent the working of grace for the characters.

The Catholic novelist believes that you destroy your freedom by sin; the modern reader believes, I think, that you gain it in that way. There is not much possibility of understanding between the two. So I think that the more a writer wishes to make the supernatural apparent, the more real he has to be able to make the natural world, for if the readers don't accept the natural world, they'll certainly not accept anything else.

Tarwater is certainly free and meant to be;[4] if he appears to have a compulsion to be a prophet, I can only insist that in this compulsion there is the mystery of God's will for him, and that it is not a compulsion in the clinical sense. However, this is a complicated subject and requires to be elucidated by someone with more learning than I have. As for Enoch, he is a moron and chiefly a comic character.[5] I don't think it is important whether his compulsion is clinical or not.

In my stories a reader will find that the devil accomplishes a good deal of groundwork that seems to be necessary before grace is effective. Tarwater's final vision could not have been brought off if he hadn't met the man in the lavender and cream-colored car. This is another mystery.

[*The following paragraphs are taken from another context, largely repetitive. They, too, are repetitive but they reinforce a point.*]

To insure our sense of mystery, we need a sense of evil which sees the devil as a real spirit who must be made to name himself, and not simply to name himself as vague evil, but to name himself with his specific personality for every occasion. Literature, like virtue, does not thrive in an atmosphere where the devil is not recognized as existing both in himself and as a dramatic necessity for the writer.

We are now living in an age which doubts both fact and value. It is the life of this age that we wish to see and judge. The novelist can no longer reflect a balance from the world he sees around him; instead, he has to try to create one. It is the way of drama that with one stroke the writer has both to mirror and to judge. When such a writer has a freak for his hero, he is not simply showing us what we are, but what we have been and what we could become. His prophet-freak is an image of himself.

In such a picture, grace, in the theological sense, is not lacking. There is a moment in every great story in which the presence of grace can be felt as it waits to be accepted or rejected, even though the reader may not recognize this moment.

Story-writers are always talking about what makes a story "work." From my own experience in trying to make stories "work," I have discovered that what is needed is an action that is totally unexpected, yet totally believable, and I have found that, for me, this is always an action which indicates that grace has been offered. And frequently it is an action in which the devil has been the unwilling instrument of grace. This is not a piece of knowledge that I consciously put into my stories; it is a discovery that I get out of them.

I have found, in short, from reading my own writing, that my subject in fiction is the action of grace in territory held largely by the devil.

I have also found that what I write is read by an audience which puts little stock either in grace or the devil. You discover your audience at the same time and in the same way that you discover your subject; but it is an added blow.

NOTES

These notes and the bracketed comment on p. 38 are by Sally Fitzgerald and Robert Fitzgerald, from O'Connor, *Mystery and Manners*.

[1] That is, in 1962. These remarks were made by Flannery O'Connor at Hollins College, Virginia, to introduce a reading of her story "A Good Man Is Hard to Find," on 14 October 1963.

[2] This note was written to introduce the second edition of the novel in 1962.

[3] From letters written to Winifred McCarthy, published in *Fresco*, vol. 1, no. 2, University of Detroit, February 1961.

[4] The hero of *The Violent Bear It Away*.

[5] A disciple of Hazel Motes in *Wise Blood*.

O'Connor through Her Letters

Will Brantley

As an undergraduate English major at Georgia State University in Atlanta, I had the good fortune to take courses in the mid-1970s from professors W. A. Sessions and Ted Spivey, both of whom had been friends of Flannery O'Connor, a Georgia author, and each of whom reminisced about her in both lectures and casual conversations. When in 1979 O'Connor's friend Sally Fitzgerald edited *The Habit of Being*, the most encompassing collection of O'Connor's letters to date,[1] I was given the opportunity to hear O'Connor speak in her own voice (or in one of her many voices) to these two influential professors of English language and literature. I could see right away that she intended to shape reader response to her fiction—a body of writing that still challenges us to confront a world that we might prefer to reject as perverse. Critics have mined the letters for insight into O'Connor's creativity, but a near-universal skepticism about the value of authorial intent has kept teachers from using the letters as fully as they might when introducing the fiction—as if that intent has nothing to do with the text that appears on the page. Without claiming too much for the letters, I would like to show how they can be used to encourage students to engage in dialogue with O'Connor, to question her interpretations, and to decide whether or not to take seriously her intent as it is so forcefully stated throughout her correspondence.

When *The Habit of Being* first appeared, Richard Brodhead made an assessment that was shared by many of the book's early reviewers. "*The Habit of Being* is the richest volume of correspondence by an American author to have appeared in many years," he observed, "and one reason for this is simply that letter-writing meant more to Flannery O'Connor than it has to most other authors." The letters, as he accurately describes them, "are sometimes drolly anecdotal, sometimes philosophical, sometimes preachy, sometimes gossipy, but they are always long, and always thoroughly and thoughtfully expressed. They confirm what readers of O'Connor's fiction already know, that she is one of the most gifted users of the American language in our time" (451).

Students, of course, generally begin not with O'Connor's letters but with a frequently anthologized story, such as "A Good Man Is Hard to Find" or "Good Country People," and inevitably they want to know something about the creator of such starkly unusual stories. What they find from the letters is something of a contradiction: a woman who firmly embraced belief in a force beyond herself but who was strikingly independent in her tastes and judgments. Students who read the letters learn that O'Connor was never without humor and could make jokes even about the illness that confined her largely to her mother's farm. They learn that she focused on her fiction for two hours each morning, that "The Artificial Nigger" was her favorite story, and that she gleaned local newspapers for bizarre incidents to use as material. Students witness her passion for theology as well as her impatience with "the vulgarity and rawness of American Catholics" (*Habit* 331). While the letters display her strong opposition to any liberal re-visioning of the Church, students see that on the subject of social change the Georgia writer did not march in lockstep with the segregationists of her era—though she never overtly challenged her region's racial norms, calling herself a "Kennedy conservative" (499) and dismissing segregationists and antisegregationists alike. Through the letters, students discover a writer who was bored by ex post facto accounts of the writing process, disdainful of dream interpreters, contemptuous of education courses, and suspicious of literary theory's intellectualized approaches to the meaning of fiction.

O'Connor produced a sizable body of nonfiction yet did not relish writing essays and giving lectures. "I begin to feel like a displaced person myself, writing papers and not fiction," she complained to Granville Hicks (*Habit* 206). Instead of delivering a speech, she preferred to read aloud one of her stories, noting that the "element of ham" in her sought release (265). Students who have heard her recording of "A Good Man Is Hard to Find" will attest to this element, which is also on display in her letters, documents that she did enjoy writing, so much so that she called mail an "eventful" part of her day (29). O'Connor kept copies of her letters in order to avoid repeating herself and for "other conventional reasons" (*Flannery . . . Works* 928). She knew the letters would resurface and take their place in her larger body of work. "In the future, anybody who writes anything about me is going to have to read everything I have written in order to make legitimate criticism . . ." (*Habit* 442). When she made this statement in 1961, she did not exclude the letters in which she defined herself and clarified her artistic mission.

One of the most frequently cited letters is also one of the most useful for introducing students to O'Connor. After the 1960 publication of *The Violent Bear It Away*, she told fellow writer Andrew Lytle that she had been thinking about "the presentation of love and charity, or better call it grace, as love suggests tenderness, whereas grace can be violent or would have to be to compete with the kind of evil I can make concrete." Focusing on "A Good Man Is Hard to Find," she then made a comment that has grounded many critical appraisals:

> There is a moment of grace in most of the stories, or a moment where it is offered, and is usually rejected. Like when the Grandmother recognizes the Misfit as one of her own children and reaches out to touch him. It's the moment of grace for her anyway—a silly old woman—but it leads him to shoot her. This moment of grace excites the devil to frenzy. (*Habit* 373)

Whether or not O'Connor intended to initiate a critical hunt for this paradigmatic moment in her fiction, her remarks to Lytle, and through him to later readers, may be used to prompt class discussions of this concept and its presence or absence in her work. Is Mrs. May in "Greenleaf" offered a similar moment of grace? O'Connor says the moment is usually rejected, but do any characters—Ruby Turpin in "Revelation," for example—appear to accept the moment that O'Connor describes? Do her remarks to Lytle illuminate or constrict the meaning of her fiction? For those students who reject the notion of grace with all its religious implications—perhaps the very students that O'Connor would most want to engage—instructors might ask what remains for a reader who recoils from O'Connor's worldview and the many violent confrontations that mark her fiction. Does good storytelling in itself suffice?

O'Connor sent a letter to a professor of English who had written her on behalf of himself, two other professors, and roughly ninety students who read and discussed "A Good Man Is Hard to Find" and concluded that the Misfit is not real—that Bailey simply imagines him. Neither the professor nor the students could decide exactly "at which point reality fades into illusion or reverie," so they asked the author if she would provide clarification (*Habit* 436). O'Connor replied that she did not set out to "trick" the reader; nor was she interested in "abnormal psychology." She said the story was stylized and comic rather than realistic in its surface particulars and that Bailey's importance was secondary to that of the Grandmother, who first recognizes the Misfit and whose "superficial beliefs" clash with his "more profoundly felt involvement with Christ's action which set the world off balance for him." O'Connor warned that the "meaning of a story should go on expanding for the reader the more he thinks about it, but meaning cannot be captured in an interpretation." "My tone is not meant to be obnoxious," she closed. "I am in a state of shock" (437). I ask students to consider why anyone would choose to read the second half of this story as a fantasy. Did the English professors and their students wish to avoid the reality of mass murder? I ask my students to debate O'Connor's further warning that too much interpretation of a story is worse than too little and to determine what if any type of interpretation—Marxist, feminist, psychoanalytic—might keep "A Good Man Is Hard to Find" from "expanding" for its readers.

For "A Temple of the Holy Ghost," I turn to the letter in which O'Connor rejected one teacher's notion that the child character in this story is somehow psychologically inverted (*Flannery . . . Works* 925). A few months later she apologized to the letter writer, Beverly Brunson, for her dismissive tone, making it clear that she might disagree with an interpretation but did not wish to lose a thoughtful reader. For students puzzled by the darkness of O'Connor's fiction, the most intriguing part of this letter is her insistence that she did not see life as a tragedy, the extreme violence of her fiction notwithstanding: "I know about violence only from hearsay. I come from very careful people who lock their doors at night and look under all the beds and never find anything" (929). I often ask students to reflect on the discrepancy between her own sheltered life and the violent ends that she imagined for her characters. I also ask them to consider Clara Claiborne Park's suggestion that we take "the letters as primary and the fiction as a gloss upon them, the black repository of all that the letters do not say, of the rebellion and disappointment and anger which the letters show so thoroughly surmounted that we might almost believe they were never felt" (254).

To another teacher, Helen Green, O'Connor noted her distress that some of Green's students had read *Wise Blood* and concluded that she was "a follower of Kafka." O'Connor admitted that she and Kafka provide "a kind of fantasy rooted in the specific," but she said the comparison ends at that point. Her "philosophical notions" derive not from Kafka, nor even from Kierkegaard, but from Saint Thomas Aquinas (*Flannery . . . Works* 897). To Ashley Brown, a student with whom she became good friends, O'Connor added, "I'm no Georgia Kafka. . . . I think I have the Gift of Low Taste that Kafka lacks and that I have been influenced by less fashionable people that nobody mentions—Max Beerbohm and Richard Hughes and maybe, since this is all in the family below the MDixon line, by some of the walled-in monsters of Mr. Poe" (911). Through comparative readings, I invite students to examine the desire to link O'Connor to Kafka. Is there an affinity? I have also witnessed lively debates about what she meant by low taste, and I have urged students to explore some of her self-admitted but lesser-known influences: Beerbohm, the British caricaturist and parodist whose one novel, the satirical *Zuleika Dobson* (1911), ends with the undergraduates at Oxford University all committing suicide; Hughes, the British author of *A High Wind in Jamaica* (1929), a novel that pits a group of pirates against an even more sinister group of unruly children.

Another writer often linked to O'Connor is the American satirist Nathanael West, who shared her penchant for the grotesque. Shortly before she died, she replied to a letter writer who asked her to acknowledge this link. Her response was, "West may have had some influence on me stylistically. I read him when I was in my early twenties and everything was an influence one way or another." Returning to West years later, she was "disappointed" and dismissed his best-known character, Miss Lonelyhearts, as "a sentimental Christ figure." She doubted "if most writers have much idea where their greatest influence came from. For me, I wouldn't say West" (*Flannery . . . Works* 1215–16). A discussion of West and literary influence might easily lead to the far richer discussion of intertextuality—for example, to a comparison of the various Christ figures that populate her fiction with what she perceived as the sentimental figure at the center of *Miss Lonelyhearts.*

Although O'Connor was sometimes suspicious of inquiries from English teachers, she acknowledged that her largest group of readers "will be students" (*Flannery . . . Works* 1162), and she befriended several English professors, including Sessions and Spivey, both of whom had long careers in Atlanta. She offered advice to Sessions about his own stories, but with this warning: "The trouble with being a writer and taking on the activity of critic is that you tend to think everybody else's work should be like your own. You tend to a kind of diffusion which is pretty foreign to my way of writing a story, but after all you have to work out the unity of your way of doing things" (*Habit* 181). O'Connor knew better than to offer a formula or theory, but she did insist, this time to

Spivey, that everything in fiction "has to operate first on the literal level" (299), and she distinguished her sensibility from his: "You said something about my stories dipping into life—as if this were commendable but a trifle unusual; from which I get the notion that you may dip largely into your head. This would be in line with the Protestant temper—approaching the spiritual directly instead of through matter" (304). I have found that her remarks to Spivey not only help students understand the anagogic dimension of her fictional approach but also invite discussion about the defining components of her literary sensibility.

O'Connor cared about both Sessions and Spivey but did not hesitate to disagree with them if she believed that either professor had misunderstood her. To Sessions she made this remark:

> I'm sorry [*The Violent Bear It Away*] didn't come off for you but I think it is no wonder it didn't since you see everything in terms of sex symbols, and in a way that would not enter my head—the lifted bough, the fork of the tree, the corkscrew. . . . Your criticism sounds to me as if you have read too many critical books and are too smart in an artificial, destructive, and very limited way.

She insisted that the "lack of realism would be crucial" if the novel were not in fact a romance in the mode of Nathaniel Hawthorne. Students who feel that they are not quick enough to detect symbols may sense some validation from her trenchant words and from her belief that Freudianism "can be applied to anything at all with equally ridiculous results" (*Habit* 407). On the other hand, students who believe they have been trained to look for symbols everywhere may feel some sympathy for Professor Sessions.

Beyond providing the enjoyment of watching O'Connor mount a self-defense, her letters encourage students to question when something is symbolic or not. She may also make them wonder if she, the creator of Manley Pointer, does not protest too much. Brodhead has noted that "while O'Connor despises the symbol-hunts of academic 'interpritters,' she herself often falls into talking about the religious meaning of her work in a way that recalls the worst academic criticism of the fifties" (455). I agree but stress that O'Connor did not desire to police her fiction. She wanted to be challenged. She asked Spivey—one of her intellectual sparring partners—not to hold back with his critique of *The Violent Bear It Away*: "Thank you for what you have to say about the novel. . . . My feelings are not easily hurt and I am aware of some of the book's limitations, perhaps different ones than you are. Anyway, you have more to bring to it than most & I will listen to you even if I can't agree" (*Habit* 381–82). Spivey, a myth critic with a Unitarian slant, attempted to interest O'Connor in Carl Jung's theories. She demurred: "The kind of 'belief' that Jung offers the modern, sick, unbelieving world is simply belief in the psychic realities that are good for it. This is good medicine and a step in the right direction but it is not religion" (382). She could not reconcile Spivey's embrace of Jung with his rejection of Pierre Teilhard de Chardin, another visionary thinker. She imagined these two philosophers in dialogue with each other, "though one worked with psychic energy and the other dug up bones" (383). She sought the same dialogue from her correspondents and even hoped for it from students if they could move beyond facile readings of her work. I once encouraged a graduate student to explore why O'Connor, an ardent Catholic, and Lillian Smith, a secular humanist and one of O'Connor's southern contemporaries, both embraced the writings of Teilhard de Chardin. Though different in most respects, the two Georgia writers were united in their passion for the theories of this French philosopher and paleontologist. O'Connor's letters to Spivey and to others became central to the success of this student's MA thesis.

The letters provide O'Connor's reflections on many of her contemporaries—reflections that can be cited to help students perceive how she understood her own distinctive vision. Writing to Spivey, O'Connor gave a stringent but self-revealing criticism of the Beats, a group of writers who by the late 1950s had seized the cultural spotlight:

> They call themselves holy but holiness costs and so far as I can see they pay nothing. It's true that grace is the free gift of God but in order to put yourself in the way of being receptive to it you have to practice self-denial. . . . As long as the beat people abandon themselves to all sensual satisfactions, on principle, you can't take them for anything but false mystics. A good look at St. John of the Cross makes them all look sick.
> (*Habit* 336–37)

O'Connor could be harsh in response to other writers—she detested Carson McCullers, a fellow Georgian—but as Jolly Sharp has shown in detail, she was also a supportive mentor and used her correspondence to advance the careers of published authors such as Cecil Dawkins and aspiring authors such as Betty Hester, each of whom solicited her advice. None of O'Connor's correspondents received more attention than Hester, the woman identified only as "A" in *The Habit of Being*. An admirer of O'Connor's work, Hester, whose identity was made known after her death in 1998, initiated a long-term exchange that includes some of O'Connor's most probing letters. Students guided to the Hester correspondence will note that O'Connor valued this Atlanta resident as a sympathetic reader who managed to expand her self-understanding. As Louise Westling noted, Hester "challenged the sexual ambivalence" in O'Connor's early stories and was at least partly responsible for the stronger and more affirmative female characters in the later fiction ("Flannery O'Connor's Revelations" 15). Hester challenged O'Connor on at least three fronts: fictional technique, theology, and gender. Teachers who fear that O'Connor's strong statements of intent preempt more open and radical responses to her work should consider this key admission to Hester: "Perhaps you are able to see things in these stories ['Greenleaf' and 'A Circle in the Fire'] that I can't see because if I did I would be too frightened to write them. I have always insisted that there is a fine grain of stupidity required in the fiction writer" (*Habit* 149). Here O'Connor tacitly sanctions the kind of psychoanalytic questioning that Hester must have provided in her letters.

Through mail O'Connor cultivated the friendship of another strong female presence in her life, the playwright Maryat Lee, a staunch civil rights advocate whose views on race were more conventionally progressive than those of O'Connor. Critics, however, have been split on the value of O'Connor's correspondence with Lee. Fitzgerald says that no other letters are quite as "playful" and that O'Connor "obviously took some mischievous vicarious pleasure in the fluttering of the dovecotes that usually followed the visits of her rebellious and unconventional friend to formal Milledgeville" (*Habit* 193). Melvin Friedman does not agree; for him the letters to Lee seem "forced" and the humor "hollow" or "even incongruous" (9). I have asked students to weigh in on the debate, with attention to letters such as the one in which O'Connor says that she does not care for Negroes of "the philosophizing prophesying pontificating kind, the James Baldwin kind. Very ignorant but never silent. Baldwin can tell us what it feels like to be a Negro in Harlem but he tries to tell us everything else too. . . . If Baldwin were white nobody would stand him a minute" (*Habit* 580). Why might she have thought that no one would listen to Baldwin if he were white? Her remarks to Lee, for all their seeming nearsightedness, help us understand the black characters that she created. I have used these and other comments to Lee to preface what have become crucial questions for contemporary students of O'Connor's work: To what extent were her positions on race and civil rights marked by the dominant cultural forces of her era? To what extent did she manage, in her fiction at least, to challenge these forces?

O'Connor could be brutally direct, but she could also speak through indirection. Quoting Nietzsche's assertion that profundity "loves the mask," Joyce Carol Oates observed that the letters, depending on the recipient, display poses ranging from the "disingenuous hick" and occasional bigot to the self-analyst with a keen ability to assess her own work (195–203). O'Connor, as her correspondence with Sessions, Spivey, Hester, or Lee makes clear, was stimulated by debate, by resisting readers, and by fresh responses to her work. She told John Hawkes, the novelist, with whom she carried on a lively exchange regarding the devil figure in her fiction, that she was "terribly pleased" to hear from him that Lillian Hellman admired her stories: "I had never thought of her even remotely as a person who would read them. It is always a revelation to find out the people who like and dislike them. It is another way of reading the stories" (*Habit* 438).

Citing François Mauriac, O'Connor told Spivey that "God does not care anything about what we write. He uses it" (360). She did not seem willing to wait for God to do all the labor, however. She wanted to shape or at least take part in the critical discourse on her work. Students will see how the letters enabled her to fulfill this aim.

NOTE

[1] C. Ralph Stephens published *The Correspondence of Flannery O'Connor and the Brainard Cheneys* in 1986, and Fitzgerald included twenty-one previously unpublished letters in *Flannery O'Connor: Collected Works* in 1988. See also postmarkedmilledgeville.com, which itemizes letters to and from O'Connor held by collectors and libraries in the United States.

Of Whales and Warthogs: Jonah as Biblical Paradigm for Teaching O'Connor

Christina Bieber Lake

"Blessed are the poor in spirit, for theirs is the kingdom of heaven." According to a recent survey of 1,002 teenagers from a range of public and private schools, nearly two-thirds of these students could not identify biblical quotations from the Sermon on the Mount (Matt. 5.3).[1] The study concluded that although most had a rudimentary knowledge of the Bible, very few had the level of biblical literacy that English professors consider necessary for literary study (Wachlin, *Bible Literacy Report* 25).[2] So we can assume that although most of our students have heard of Jonah and his adventures with a giant fish, few have read the Book of Jonah recently (if at all)—even at a Christian college. Remediating biblical illiteracy is reason enough to assign a reading of the Bible alongside a Flannery O'Connor story, whether one teaches at a faith-based institution or not. The Book of Jonah in particular, terse and full of surprises, can serve as a revelatory paradigm for most of O'Connor's stories.

O'Connor would be the first person to point out that she had no designs to compete with Scripture. What she shares with biblical writers is the conviction that stories point to divine realities, the desire to be taken seriously by readers, and prophetic intensity. So to consider the book of Jonah alongside her stories is not to provide a formula but to open up two of the most important questions that students can address in literary study in general and in O'Connor studies in particular. First, what does her fiction reveal about the relation between the author and her characters, especially as it reflects her views of divine providence and the question of violence? Second, how does that relation go with the deliberately shocking and sometimes off-putting method of the grotesque? For each of these questions, the Book of Jonah provides a revelatory analogue.[3]

Author and Hero

Does O'Connor love her characters? Does her fiction point to or justify divine violence? Is her God a vengeful God?

A persistent issue in O'Connor studies is the nature of the relations among author, implied author, narrator, and characters.[4] Though it is rarely desirable in fiction to equate the author with the implied author or narrator, many critics do it because of O'Connor's comments on her work and because of the remarkably consistent narrative tone across her stories.[5] Through the free indirect discourse that is the hallmark of her writing, the narrator seems to agree with the implied author, the implied author seems to agree with the author, and there has been no compelling reason to think otherwise.

Students should be encouraged to trust their instincts here. O'Connor learned the subtleties of narrative strategies from the Writers' Workshop in Iowa, but the theorist that best describes her use of point of view is probably Mikhail Bakhtin.[6] As Robert Brinkmeyer has illustrated, O'Connor's work is animated by a dialogical tension between her Catholic faith and her characters' Protestant fundamentalism. Bakhtin's early essays, particularly "Author and Hero in Aesthetic Activity" (4–256), reveal how O'Connor might have thought about her relation with her characters theologically. The analogue is not the author as a tyrannical God with power over his or her puppets' fates but the author as a loving other who affirms the creation of particular, free persons as an inherent good (Lake 50–54). In O'Connor's theology, the significance of created persons is central.

Yet O'Connor's satirical and often violent treatment of her characters has generated much disagreement about her love for them. Some argue that her work actually denies her Christian faith, some believe that love is her ultimate motivation, and some find the question itself an obstacle.[7] Jonah's striking similarity to most of O'Connor's characters illustrates why the question should matter to students.

The Book of Jonah begins with a prophet's fleeing from the command of God that he go to the Ninevites and tell them to repent. Jonah boards a ship to escape, accepts blame for the raging sea, is cast overboard by the crew, is swallowed by a great fish in which he lives for three days, finally repents and prays with the acknowledgment that "salvation belongs to the Lord" (Jonah 2.9), is vomited up by the fish, and goes to Ninevah. When the Ninevites repent, Jonah gets angry, seemingly because he wanted God to destroy Ninevah, not save it. The story ends with God's asking him, "And should I not pity Ninevah, that great city, in which there are more than 120,000 persons who do not know their right hand from their left, and also much cattle?" (4.11).

Most of O'Connor's protagonists are runaway or reluctant prophets who try to but cannot get far from God, disobedient or hypocritical believers who do not see themselves clearly, or people who are self-righteous and judgmental of others whom they consider to be below them. Hazel Motes, Frances Tarwater, the Grandmother in "A Good Man Is Hard to Find," Ruby Turpin in "Revelation," Parker in "Parker's Back," and Julian in "Everything That Rises Must Converge" are examples. Although some characters do not necessarily profess faith (for instance, Asbury in "The Enduring Chill" is a self-described atheist), it is often implied that by way of their "wise blood" they know better than to deny God as the ultimate reality. In any case, the fact that the characters are in some kind of spiritual rebellion is the clear focal point of the stories.

Violence befalls these characters. Jonah's shipmates throw him overboard when he admits he is the cause of the storm. O'Connor's Ruby Turpin only gets a book thrown in her face and called a hellish "wart hog" (*Flannery . . . Works* 646), but the Grandmother and her whole family fare much worse in "A Good Man Is Hard to Find." Some stories contain violence that is difficult to stomach: child suicide, rape, goring, and so on.

The severity of the violence, along with the cold and unsentimental way it is described, foregrounds the question of how O'Connor sees her characters and their fates. Is the violence necessary? Does it come from God? René Girard argues that it is not God but human beings who commit acts of violence against human beings. After an original act of violence in a community, people create a culture of violence that is imitated endlessly. Myth is born from the community's desire to justify its scapegoating behavior and hide its complicity with violence. Girard reads the Book of Job as an affirmation of Job's innocence: the community scapegoated the prophet in order to hide their own participation in the cycle of violence.

Bringing Girard's theories to the table in an undergraduate context is not easy, because reading Girard requires an understanding of how his project is both similar to and different from that of such secular structuralist thinkers as Claude Lévi-Strauss. But if the class has at least a few sessions devoted to O'Connor, it is worth presenting, even if only briefly, key ideas from *Violence and the Sacred*.[8] Girard's thesis gives students a more theoretically nuanced way to think about violence as permitted by God but caused by human freedom—a position that allows them greater access to O'Connor's theological vision. Gary Ciuba, for example, sees Tarwater as a character caught in a vicious cycle of imitation of two violence-prone models: Rayber and his great-uncle Mason. Neither breaks the pattern of blaming someone else for the violence and so remain complicit with it. Tarwater continues the pattern by killing Bishop, and and eventually he himself becomes a victim. Ciuba's Girardian reading helps students separate both Tarwater's murderous act of rebellion and his rape from his later acceptance of his calling to preach (*Desire* 152–64). God did not cause or condone his having been raped or his murder of Bishop, nor do we have any reason to believe that O'Connor, the implied author, or the narrator condones them.

Girard's theories do not perfectly fit every biblical story—Jonah, for example, is not an innocent scapegoat randomly selected by a bloodthirsty crowd; aware that he is guilty of running away from God, he offers himself to be thrown overboard. But Girard steers students away from the question of the character's innocence toward something that interested O'Connor more: the response of the victim. Jonah's responsibility, freedom, and complicity with violence are central to the biblical book. His anger because God failed to destroy Ninevah shows his approval of human solutions to evil.[9] Thus the focus of the Book of Jonah, as in the Book of Job, is the distance between human understanding and action and divine understanding and action.

Focusing on character response enables students to ponder the complicated issue of human freedom. What choices does Jonah have? It would seem that here again Girard opens up a way to consider how O'Connor might be developing Jesus's teaching that "whoever is not with me is against me" (Matt. 12.30). Jonah can either be complicit in the violence that is part of the human condition, or he can resist being complicit. This basic struggle is the backbone of most of O'Connor's stories. As Susan Srigley argues, O'Connor's interpretation of the enigmatic verse "the kingdom of heaven suffereth violence, and the violent bear it away" (Matt. 11.12)[10] is in line with that of Aquinas and Augustine, who stressed the need for the violence of a self-sacrificial love in a self-serving world in order to obey God ("Violence" 37). O'Connor's letters emphasize this need for the unnatural violence of love: "I am much more interested in the Nobility of unnaturalness than in the nobility of naturalness. . . . The violent are not natural. . . . [T]his is surely what it means to bear away the kingdom of heaven with violence: the violence is directed inward" (*Flannery . . . Works* 1101, 1171).[11]

Such an insight can permit students to consider that the Grandmother's ultimate choice to transcend her own prejudices (when she is able to see her complicity with human violence) is as costly and heroic as O'Connor believed such a choice had to be. Students might also ask themselves what O'Connor values more than the physical life or comfort of her characters. As promised by Jesus ("the kingdom of heaven suffereth violence"), the Grandmother's choice to reach out to the Misfit causes him to recoil and shoot her three times in the chest. O'Connor preserves not the Grandmother's life but her dignity.

Centering the class conversation around the question of violence done to the characters opens up the possibility of investigating O'Connor's view of the source of ugly human behavior. Asbury, Mr. Head, and Julian all begin to understand that human pride—and chiefly their own—is the primary cause of violence against the African American brother they claim to champion. Mrs. McIntyre, knowing that she allowed the tractor to roll over Mr. Guizac's spine, begins to see herself as more grotesque than any foreigner. Ruby Turpin, having a vision of herself as a hog and of others going ahead of her into heaven, sees a path that she has never known: the choice of a love that accepts the difference of others without ascribing a human hierarchy to that difference.

Author and Audience

Does the grotesque in O'Connor alienate her audience? Does it keep her from communicating her vision?

The author-hero relationship is connected to the relationship between the author and her audience. O'Connor had a high goal: to be an artist who would fulfill God's purpose for her—this is clear in her *Prayer Journal*. To read her letters and essays is to understand how much she valued narrative power: for her, it was a vastly different thing to learn about the concept of obedience than to "[tremble] with Abraham as he held the knife over Isaac" (*Flannery . . . Works* 859). It is therefore important not to lose sight of how students today receive her work, especially at their first exposure (Haddox, *Hard Sayings* 23–36).

Those of us fully entrenched in O'Connor studies can quote from memory the passages in which she explains her spiritual goals. Here are a few of the favorites:

> One of the awful things about writing when you are a Christian is that for you the ultimate reality is the Incarnation, the present reality is the Incarnation, and nobody believes in the Incarnation; that is, nobody in your audience. My audience are the people who think God is dead. At least these are the people I am conscious of writing for.   (*Habit* 92)

> When you can assume that your audience holds the same beliefs you do, you can relax a little and use more normal ways of talking to it; when you have to assume that it does not, then you have to make your vision apparent by shock—to the hard of hearing you shout, and for the almost blind you draw large and startling figures.   (*Flannery . . . Works* 805–06)

> When I write a novel in which the central action is a baptism, I am very well aware that for a majority of my readers, baptism is a meaningless rite, and so in my novel I have to see that this baptism carries enough awe and mystery to jar the reader into some kind of emotional recognition of its significance. To this end I have to bend the whole novel—its language, its structure, its action. I have to make the reader feel, in his bones if nowhere else, that something is going on here that counts. Distortion in this case is an instrument; exaggeration has a purpose, and the whole structure of the story or novel has been made what it is because of belief. This is not the kind of distortion that destroys; it is the kind that reveals, or should reveal.   (*Mystery* 162)

We have all been tempted to rely on these explanations, but the teacher of O'Connor's fiction would do well to resist reading the stories through them. In my experience, it is good to withhold O'Connor's comments from students at first and instead to foreground the question of how convincing they find the stories. Students might be asked, What do you think O'Connor was trying to get you to see? How successful was she in doing that?

Assigning the Book of Jonah is a good way to raise such questions, because O'Connor employs some of the same strategies that it does, especially the grotesque. Geoffrey Galt Harpham explains that the grotesque "consists of the manifest, visible, or unmediated presence of mythic or primitive elements in a nonmythic or modern context" (51). That Jonah's mythic elements (the fish, the ship-threatening storm, the vine-eating worm) function grotesquely for us can help students move beyond their simplistic equation of the grotesque with gross and toward an understanding of it as an artistic strategy for revelation. This view corresponds with Girard's understanding of myth as a distortion of an actual event even as it illuminates it. The power of the grotesque comes from its resistance to rational comprehension.

I lay out three aspects of the grotesque for students: shocking readers to gain their attention, conjoining opposites for the sake of revelation of a mystery (usually one that is hidden in plain view), and functioning in both positive and negative ways.

If students see the grotesque as an artistic strategy to gain attention, they will not worry about the historicity of the Book of Jonah—for example, whether or not Jonah was actually swallowed by a fish and lived to tell the tale. I have taught at Wheaton College long enough to have heard the following joke several times: "The difference between liberals and conservatives is that liberals take Song of Songs literally and Jonah figuratively, and conservatives take Jonah literally and Song of Songs figuratively." Fundamentalists tend to take figurative elements literally, but, as Girard argues, the appearance of mythic elements in biblical or other stories do not necessarily invalidate the possibility of a historical referent (Golsan 151–79). Regardless of their place on the literal-mythical hermeneutical continuum, students can easily see that the monstrous fish is meant to get the attention of Jonah and of the readers, just as the new jesus is meant to get the attention of Hazel Motes and the readers. The grotesque works by simultaneous repulsion and attraction: you don't want to look at a train wreck but can't stop looking. Students realize that O'Connor wants them to pay attention to, and be disturbed by, her various misfits, hermaphrodites, one-legged would-be philosophers, and other grotesqueries.

The grotesque also conjoins dissimilar objects to make a point. Representations of demons on a cathedral are considered grotesque: in a place that is meant to be holy, they remind us that the demonic presence is not far away or, as O'Connor put it, that good and evil are "joined . . . at the spine" (*Mystery* 200). The jolt from the grotesque comes from the surprise of having two unlike objects fused. Ruby Turpin never considered herself on the level of her pigs, yet being called a warthog helps her to see that this metaphor is deserved. That O'Connor makes Bishop, the child with Down syndrome in *The Violent Bear It Away*, the aesthetic center of the novel and aims all the novel's action toward his baptism reveals how we can miss the beauty of creation when seeing it through a rationalist's eyes. I find that this aspect of the grotesque comes most to light for students when

I explain that the Incarnation is the ultimate grotesque. What is more shocking and revelatory of a deep mystery than God becoming a particular man?

The grotesque nature of the Incarnation also serves to illustrate how the grotesque in O'Connor can be positive or negative. The Incarnation is positive: once we get beyond the incongruity, we are drawn to the beauty of God become man. O'Connor employs the grotesque this way with Bishop in *The Violent Bear It Away*. The new jesus of *Wise Blood*, in contrast, is negative, conjoining the idea of a savior with a mummified man in order for Haze and others to understand that this thing cannot save a single soul. He is "all man, without blood to waste" (*Flannery . . . Works* 80). O'Connor insists that the meaning of the new jesus lies in Haze's rejection of it. Marshall Bruce Gentry and other critics believe that O'Connor moved away from the negative grotesque and toward the positive grotesque as she moved through her career (*Flannery O'Connor's Religion*; see also Lake). In this reading, "Parker's Back" is the most supreme example of the new grotesquerie that the Incarnation initiates: that Jesus would make the Church, full as it is of misfits, his body here on earth.

By relying so heavily on this artistic device, O'Connor got the attention of her readers but also annoyed and alienated them. Michael Kowaleski is wise to argue that to give O'Connor's art its due, "we have to resist the temptation to tame or explain away its tempestuous, eruptive power or to dull the sharpness of its humor" (12). To teach O'Connor's fiction well is not to domesticate it.

Neither is the Book of Jonah, or for that matter the entire Bible, domesticatable. Jesus deepens the hermeneutical waters that Jonah is immersed in by saying, "An evil and adulterous generation seeks for a sign, but no sign will be given to it except the sign of the prophet Jonah. For just as Jonah was three days and three nights in the belly of the great fish, so will the Son of Man be three days and three nights in the heart of the earth" (Matt. 12.38–40). Jesus is provoking his listeners to new and uncomfortable depths of inquiry. Both the biblical book and O'Connor's stories provoke readers by what is not given and remains unexplained. Both fail to give us "the rest of the story." The Book of Jonah ends with its protagonist defying God, repeating that it is better for him to die than to live. It also ends, like the Book of Job, with a question from God that puts the protagonists in their place. O'Connor's stories often end without answering the question of what comes next. What will Mrs. Flood do now that Hazel Motes is dead? What is Joy/Hulga thinking up in the loft? How will Ruby Turpin come to terms with the question "how am I a hog and me both" (*Flannery . . . Works* 652)? We are left with only one option: to return to the story itself. And that is the whole point.

NOTES

[1] Except where otherwise attributed, biblical quotations in this essay refer to *The Holy Bible: English Standard Version*.

2 In her summary of the report for the Society of Biblical Literature's Web site, Wachlin included quotations from several of the university professors she surveyed. George Landow from Brown University told her that "the bottom line is . . . far fewer students know the Bible. . . . Our students find themselves cut off from the culture . . . —and don't know it" ("Why").

3 Many thanks to my brother-in-law, David Camera, whose insightful sermon on Jonah sparked my initial approach to this essay.

4 My use of these terms comes from Wayne Booth, who distinguished between the author and the implied author by talking about the latter as a kind of "second self" that exists behind the narrator and may differ significantly from both author and narrator (75).

5 Unlike many modern writers, O'Connor never seems to vary the stance of the implied author toward the narrator or of the narrator toward the characters. I have found Seymour Chatman's *Story and Discourse* to be invaluable in helping students see the importance of her consistency (146–95).

6 I am not arguing for influence, since the works of Bakhtin were not available to O'Connor. The theological aspects of her point of view were an amalgam of approaches she learned from Jacques Maritain, William Lynch, Percy Lubbock, and many others.

7 See, respectively, Giannone, *Flannery O'Connor and the Mystery of Love*; McMullen; Gordon, *Flannery O'Connor: The Obedient Imagination*.

8 I have found Golsan indispensible for this task.

9 It is not given in the text, but it is a good guess that violence is the evil that God says "has come up before me" against the Ninevites (Jonah 1.2).

10 I quote here *The Holy Bible: Douay-Rheims Version*, the translation that provided O'Connor with the title of her second novel.

11 Srigley helpfully concludes that the "violence is against the self, not for selfish purposes or simply self-negation, for but something greater, described in this verse as the Kingdom" ("Violence" 37–38).

Hillbilly Thomist: Understanding O'Connor's Catholic Literary Aesthetics in "A Temple of the Holy Ghost"

Mark Bosco

Everybody who has read *Wise Blood* thinks I'm a
hillbilly nihilist, whereas I would like to create the
impression . . . that I'm a hillbilly Thomist.
— Flannery O'Connor

Throughout her life Flannery O'Connor professed that her Roman Catholic faith was an essential component of her vocation as a writer. Immersed in the currents of Catholic philosophy, theology, and literary aesthetics of her day, she maintained, "I write the way I do because (not though) I am a Catholic. This is a fact and nothing covers it like the bald statement. However, I am a Catholic peculiarly possessed of the modern consciousness, that thing Jung describes as unhistorical, solitary, and guilty" (*Habit* 90). Given such statements, she was much amused when her early critics construed *Wise Blood* as a work of nihilism, as if, through her characters, she were promoting belief in meaninglessness. How, one might ask, could critics suspect her of being a nihilist when in fact she identified herself as a Thomist (81)—someone steeped in the thought of the great medieval scholar and theologian, Thomas Aquinas?

Even though I teach at a Catholic institution, very few—if any—of my students would profess an understanding of Catholicism as an intellectual and artistic lens of American culture, much less know anything about Aquinas. Whether I teach O'Connor for an introductory fiction course or a course for English majors, I always introduce her by assigning one of her short stories (usually "A Good Man Is Hard to Find"), never mentioning her Catholic commitments. After a close reading of the story with students in our first class, I ask them to tell me their reaction, putting words voiced by them on the board—violent, shocking, strange, funny, weird, et cetera. Most of the time, students sense that there is something singular and provocative about the story that they find difficult to articulate. Like many readers, they respond to her work with a sense of admiration and awe but without realizing the significance of that awe as conceived by O'Connor and explicated in her many essays and letters. When I note that her stories are shaped by her deep Catholic faith, there is some initial surprise in the classroom, because students tend to think of sentimental or uplifting narratives as typical of the religious imagination, or of Catholicism as a strict religious code of morals. So the first task is always to discuss Catholicism not primarily as a religious institution but as part of the intellectual and cultural heritage of Western civilization.

In an effort to help students understand O'Connor in the light of her Catholicism and how it is revealed in her work, I first flesh out through lecture and discussion the historical, cultural, and aesthetic assumptions of the twentieth-century Catholic literary revival, of which she was a part, then illustrate the significance of these assumptions in a close reading and discussion of a second story, "A Temple of the Holy Ghost," a particularly clear reflection of O'Connor's Catholic imagination. In this essay I give a summary of Catholic aesthetics as manifested in O'Connor and suggest critical texts helpful in piecing this aesthetic together: first, I contextualize how the intellectual ferment of Catholicism of the time became a larger historical moment in modern American intellectual life during the years when she was writing; second, I argue that Catholicism, like other isms of critical theory, has its own distinctive and fruitful way of engaging the literary arts; and third, I demonstrate how O'Connor's aesthetics and her Catholic understanding of the human condition affect her work. I also include some of the strategies I use in teaching a Catholic literary aesthetic in "A Temple of the Holy Ghost."

A Catholic Moment in American Culture: The Crisis of the Human Person

Although there is a nostalgic sense that the postwar years were a thriving period in American cultural life, the aftermath of World War II was in fact a fraught time for intellectuals and artists struggling to come to terms with what it meant to be human. An enlightenment vision that informed artists' understanding of the world since the eighteenth century crumbled under the rise of totalitarian regimes, two massively destructive world wars, and the horrors of the Jewish and atomic holocausts that engulfed the conscience of the postwar world. Mark Greif contends that after the horrors of the early twentieth century, a generation of writers questioned the purpose of humanity as never before: Was humanity the rational caretaker and spiritual guardian of the planet or its malevolent, reckless tenant? In response to the glaring contradictions between Soviet-enforced communism and an accelerating American individualism, many artists searched for a higher-order account of human purpose. Among these were a group of diverse thinkers and artists who found common cause with a modern update of Thomistic thought, giving Catholicism a surprising place at the cultural table of intellectual debate. Among many thinkers, Aquinas suddenly had renewed currency.[1]

In the 1930s, French Catholic philosophers such as Étienne Gilson and Jacques Maritain advanced a recovery of Aquinas's thought called neo-Thomism, which attempted to take medieval metaphysics and apply it to modern, existential categories. This discourse conceived of the human person as an embodied spirit drawn toward the good, the true, and the beautiful, transcendental properties shared by every living being—even if latent or hidden. Instead of having faith and reason in opposition, as the rationalism of the Enlightenment stressed, Thomistic thought argued that material reality and the spiritual impulse in every person work together to deepen human aspirations. Catholic philosophy and theology became an asset for assessing the existential crises of modernity and a way to rearticulate the transcendental call to human excellence, whether in the political, the personal, the metaphysical, or the artistic dimension of life. O'Connor's southern gothic vision was informed by this Catholic cultural moment.[2] As she notes, "To possess this [sense of crisis] within the Church is to bear a burden, the necessary burden of the conscious Catholic. It's to feel the contemporary situation at the ultimate level" (*Habit* 90).

Part of this Thomistic retrieval focused on art and literature as the cultural fruits of human civilization. Maritain's early work *Art and Scholasticism* used Aristotelian-Thomistic categories of medieval Catholic thought to describe how to judge not only the quality of a work of art but also the quality of the artist. Maritain claimed that good art is not utilitarian or propagandistic; rather, the habit or *habitus* of art is an inner virtue that trains the artist to convey reality in a way that does not separate meaning from experience. The well-made thing—the story carefully crafted to convey what needs to be conveyed—is the primary concern of the writer. The Christian artist, he argued, must develop this *habitus* by striving to create the best work instead of trying to mold art into a dogmatic expression of faith.[3] O'Connor found in Maritain's conception of art a description of herself qua artist. This conception did not romanticize fiction as a form of self-expression or the writer as the primary subject of the work. She wrote to a friend that she had cut her "aesthetic teeth" on *Art and Scholasticism* while studying at Iowa (*Habit* 216), and she often paraphrased Maritain's insights about art in her lectures and readings at colleges and universities around the country.[4]

Catholicism as a Critical Theory of Culture

Literary criticism was also transformed as a result of the postwar American crisis. Called the New Criticism, it was a process of close reading that echoed Maritain's claims about artistic production.[5] At its best, it argued that the form or structure of a text captured human experience in words and gave it significance: the work of art in itself embodied a felt knowledge of life. The New Critics maintained that the craft of fiction writers could be judged in direct relation to how adequately their work communicated this sense of felt experience. In effect, the New Criticism declared that the study of literature could be a valuable means for evaluating and preserving the best of humanistic culture, especially in the light of the dehumanizing ideologies of modernity. Fiction became an arena where the contradictions of modern life could be revealed through an analysis of the formal structures of a work.

The New Criticism paid implicit homage to Catholic conceptions of art that highlighted the ontological truth of a text as a formal expression of reality. A faith tradition that has offered an understanding of the human person in search of transcendence, Catholicism poses its own reasoned and coherent hermeneutic regarding the meaning of life. Paul Giles offers a postmodern analysis of this hermeneutic in his vast study of twentieth-century American Catholic artists.[6] Building on Michel Foucault's interpretation of language as ideological discourse, he observes that Catholicism—like feminism, Marxism, or other forms of critical theory—is one among many discursive strategies available to the maker of cultural texts and notes how the Catholic imaginations of American writers throughout the twentieth century offered different readings of culture. Catholicism, a minority position in America, countered the dominant American narratives, those formed from the Protestant assumptions and biases that dominated the nation's founding. Catholic writers, such as Katherine Anne Porter, Jack Kerouac, Walker Percy, Mary McCarthy, and J. F. Powers, to name but a few in Giles's study, often mapped out alternative visions and fictions about human flourishing, building on the suppositions of their Catholic heritage.

David Tracy has done much to uncover the texture of the Christian imagination from the discipline of Catholic theology. In his groundbreaking *The Analogical Imagination*, he compares two religious languages of faith: analogical and dialectical. Analogical language views reality in terms of ordered relations that express similarity in difference, building on analogy as its reference point and focus; dialectical language views reality as needing radical negations that expose the fundamental illusions in knowledge. Reading the classic texts of Catholic and Protestant theology, Tracy traces the analogical imagination through Catholic Christianity and the dialectical imagination through Protestant Christianity. The Catholic, analogical imagination tends to understand the presence of God as immanent in the world through the analogies of created things, implying that knowledge of God can be discovered in human interaction, in ritual, and in metaphor. The Protestant, dialectical imagination tends to understand God as totally transcendent, absconded from a sinful world, which implies that God can be discovered only by negation and absence, in the complete difference between divine and human. Without absolutizing these tendencies, Tracy offers critiques of Catholic culture in dialogue with a predominantly Protestant cultural heritage.

Tracy's thesis complements the work of William Lynch's *Christ and Apollo*, a book that had a profound effect on O'Connor.[7] Like Thomas Aquinas, Lynch holds that the imagination is an interpretive act of the whole person, not relegated to a separate intellectual act of signification. He critiques the secular constructs of the literary arts of the twentieth century, pointing out exaggerations and distortions that have truncated the religious character of the imagination. In his development of the analogical imagination as a distinctly Catholic construction, he calls it "that habit of perception which sees that different levels of being are also somehow one and can therefore be associated in the same image, in the same and single act of perception" ("Theology" 75). His logic indicates that just as God became incarnate in Jesus, and as Jesus often presented the infinite in finite images, so too the human imagination probes the finite, the limited, as a way of describing the mysteries of the infinite God. The imaginative journey of the life of Christ, and especially the Cross, serves as a model or paradigm of the fullest human life, trusting that the embrace of finite reality will lead to salvation. Lynch maintains that only the drama of Christ captures reality adequately as a narrative of love, loss, and redemption, balancing out an overly optimistic worldview by keeping it firmly grounded in the crucifixion of Jesus. It is a healthier and, for Lynch, more realistic imagination because it considers loss and sacrifice the ultimate inspirations for hope and redemption.

For O'Connor, like Lynch, Tracy, Maritain, and Aquinas, the effect of the Incarnation is not a temporary blessing in history but a constant expansion into the material world of this human-divine revelation—the divine manifest in all creation. In other words, the Incarnation changes everything. One therefore understands O'Connor's lament about the contemporary literary imagination unmoored from Christian thought: "One of the awful things about writing when you are a Christian is that for you the ultimate reality is the Incarnation, the present reality is the Incarnation, and nobody believes in the Incarnation; that is, nobody in your audience. My audience are the people who think God is dead. At least these are the people I am conscious of writing for" (*Habit* 92).

The Basics of an O'Connoresque Catholic Literary Aesthetic

What are some of the basic elements of O'Connor's Catholic literary aesthetic? When teaching O'Connor, I first suggest that what her Catholic faith offered the writer was the technology of the Incarnation. This doctrine, for her, guaranteed that words mattered, that they carried meaning, and that epistemology (what we can know) and ontology (what is real, what exists) are held together in Christ, who contains within himself the finite and infinite, the particular and the universal. As Lynch and Tracy propose, if the Incarnation allows for the possibility of the infinite to be embodied in the finite, then it also allows the finite and particular to reveal the infinite in human experience. O'Connor was committed to this Catholic epistemology of symbolic language, one that affirms that analogies, symbols, and metaphors are not merely conceptual signifiers but also realities that confront the reader in a nonconceptual way. It also affects religious language and ritual, for Catholic epistemology claims that the eucharistic bread at a Catholic liturgy embodies what it signifies: the bread is not, for Catholics, a mere intellectual signification of their savior but their savior under the appearance of bread. That they reverence and adore the Eucharist apart from the liturgical performance suggests that this particular, finite bread has universal meaning and a presence that endures as long as that bread endures.[8]

Second, the doctrine of sacramentalism holds that created things are visible signs that bear within themselves and simultaneously point beyond themselves to an invisible reality. Built on the substance-accident metaphysics of Aristotle and Aquinas, Catholicism explained this most forcefully in the medieval term *transubstantiation* — the divine presence of Christ effected in the bread and wine. *Substance* does not have the modern connotation of physical stuff; rather, it is the underlying reality of a thing. Accidents are the qualities that are contingent reality, such as one's appearance. Thus, in the doctrine of transubstantiation (which became an identity marker for Catholics), the accidents or outward appearances of the bread and wine remain the same even as the substance changes into Christ's own body and blood. In sum, transubstantiation holds out the promise of finite reality's ability to transcend itself. Sacraments therefore incline one to see that the holy lurks in all creation. O'Connor's "Christ-haunted" South (*Mystery* 44) is an apt phrase for the sacramental imagination, because the world is haunted by the sense that the objects, events, and persons of daily life can be revelations of grace. Furthermore, everyone, whether saint or sinner, misfit or freak, can be a conduit of such grace.

Finally, Catholic aesthetics shared with other theories of art in the postwar era a critical discourse on realism that differed profoundly from the nineteenth-century understanding of it. Like the avant-garde theories of surrealism, magical realism, and socialist realism, the Catholic sacramental system shaped what O'Connor adhered to as "Christian realism" (*Habit* 90).[9] All these different ways of viewing realism suggest a paradoxical encounter with reality that extends beyond the visible. So it is with the Catholic literary aesthetic. Indeed, as the critic Ellis Hanson puts it, "Catholicism is itself an elaborate paradox. . . . The Church is at once modern and yet medieval, ascetic and yet sumptuous, spiritual and yet sensual, chaste and yet erotic, homophobic and yet homoerotic, suspicious of aestheticism and yet an elaborate work of art" (7).

A Catholic Transfiguring of the Body in "A Temple of the Holy Ghost"

O'Connor's most explicitly Catholic story, "A Temple of the Holy Ghost," is in many ways a sustained example of the analogical imagination at work. It is one of her few stories that incorporate Catholic characters. She draws out the ramifications of the mystery of the Incarnation as an encounter with bodies: sexual bodies, martyred bodies, sacramental bodies. On the surface a humorous coming-of-age story, the narrative deepens into a moment of revelation in which the body of Christ, as the consecrated bread of Catholic eucharistic adoration, becomes the transcendent reality that, paradoxically, holds together both the apparently secular body of an intersex person and the bodies of young girls as dwelling places of God's spirit, the Holy Ghost.

"A Temple of the Holy Ghost" generates much discussion in the classroom. I encourage a formalist critical approach, examining characters, setting, plot, metaphors, and narrative voice to shed light on how O'Connor's aesthetic is employed. Students consider the main characters, young women formed and educated in a minority Catholic culture set in the Protestant South of the 1950s. I often begin by showing images from the Web depicting American Catholic single-sex high schools, from the 1950s to the present, to accentuate the texture of religious difference that O'Connor is building in the story. We then consider the older cousins, Susan and Joanne, from Mount St. Scholastica Convent School, who call themselves "Temple One and Temple Two." They mockingly laugh at their teacher Sr. Perpetua, who told them what to say in the face of ungentlemanly behavior: "Stop, Sir, I am a temple of the Holy Ghost" (*Flannery . . . Works* 199). We pause to discuss how this trope is analogically rich, for O'Connor creatively puts the comedy of sexual awakening into tension with a deeply Catholic theological theme of the body as temple—humanity made in the image and likeness of God. At this point I ask students to keep a running tab of all the metaphorical words and phrases in the story that O'Connor employs to build a provocative theological insight about the human condition. Students are quick to pick them out, such as the repeated use of the words *sun, temple, tent, circus,* and *freak.*

The quality of Catholic difference is revealed in the humorous linguistic play between Protestant and Catholic hymns. Susan and Joanne are wooed by their arranged dates, Wendell and Cory Wilkins, Pentecostal Protestant boys. In the midst of their flirtation, the reader senses counterimaginations at work: the young men sing their evangelical hymns, "I've Got a Friend in Jesus" and "The Old Rugged Cross," in response to which the young women literally chant the medieval Latin hymn "Tantum Ergo," written by Aquinas. I play recordings of each of the songs and ask students to examine the lyrics. I sometimes divide the class into small groups and ask them to do a quick comparison of the songs. We discuss how the Protestant hymns of personal righteousness and witness to Jesus—classic ingredients of what Tracy calls the "dialectical imagination" of faith—are juxtaposed with the Catholic contemplative analogical hymn of eucharistic adoration, which narrates the mystery of the Eucharist, the host transformed into the presence of Christ for all who have the eyes to see it. We end by focusing on the Wilkins' dismissal of the Latin hymn as "Jew singing" (*Flannery . . . Works* 202), which further conflates the status of Jew and Catholic, both marginalized cultures in the predominantly Protestant South.

I turn the focus of the class to the narrative center of the story, the unnamed twelve-year-old whose imaginative involvement with the mysteries of the Catholic Church structures how she puts together the many dissociated facts accumulated during the story. The grotesque bodies of the freaks displayed in the circus tent advertisements remind the young girl of the pained bodies of the Christian martyrs of the early church. This association causes her to ruminate on a career: she moves from wanting to be a doctor to an engineer to a saint and settles on a romantic reverie of martyrdom as her only option, given her proud, ornery disposition. The story dances around this notion of vocation, of the consequences of being called a temple of the Holy Ghost. O'Connor's analogical layering of symbols connects, through the imagination of a Catholic child, the freak shows of the modern circus to the martyrdoms of the ancient Circus Maximus. The girl's imagination is formed by Catholic hagiography and the popular culture of the postwar period. I show students various images from the Web to dramatize Hollywood's fascination with historical blockbusters on early Christianity: images, posters, and video clips from 1950s Roman gladiator movies and the epic Hollywood films of Christian martyrdom, such as *Quo Vadis*, *The Robe*, and *Ben-Hur*. This material grounds students in the milieu that shaped the young girl's imaginative world.

I direct students' attention to the "hermaphrodite," the intersex body of the freak at the fair. The story turns on the cousins' report to the young girl about the tent of circus freaks. The cousins don't tell her about the intersex person because they think the girl is too young, but she cleverly manipulates them into telling her about the "freak with a particular name" (*Flannery . . . Works* 206). She becomes fascinated by the idea of someone who can be both male and female yet neither male nor female. The circus freak tells the cousins not to laugh, because "God may strike you the same way" (206). This intersex person is entirely marginalized in the world, but the twelve-year-old senses that the person is no grotesque freak of nature but an embodiment of a mystery that she needs to understand. Unable to fathom this mystery, the young girl merges in her dreamlike imagination the circus tent with a tent from a Protestant revival meeting. She has an epiphany as the images converge: the freak becomes a temple of the Holy Ghost, preaching a sermon about the holiness of the body and the ruin that comes from desecrating it. The sermon is underscored by a latent thread of medieval theology—the analogy of being: we are similar to one another because we all share in the divine being of Christ, manifested as the Holy Ghost dwelling within our bodies. Indeed, O'Connor is suggesting that all human bodies are misshapen and broken vessels of the Holy Ghost; it is just a matter of degree in terms of what differentiates us from one another. I show audiovisual clips found on the Web of Protestant tent revivals and the rhetorical flourishes of famous evangelical preachers to demonstrate the analogical complexities of O'Connor's art.

Near the end of the story, during the Catholic ritual of benediction, the young girl arrives at the convent school with her cousins. As she kneels in the school chapel, her "ugly thoughts" halt, and she realizes that she is "in the presence of God" and is prompted to confess her sins, however mindlessly. But her thoughts turn to something unimaginable as she sees the priest raise "the monstrance [a decorative gold vessel] with the Host shining ivory-colored in the center of it" (*Flannery . . . Works* 208). She thinks of the intersex person at the fair saying, "I don't dispute hit. This is the way He wanted me to be" (209). The Eucharist becomes the mysterious place in which two dissimilar realities are held together: the strangeness of the Incarnation of Christ's dual nature as divine and human is found in the strangeness of the intersex body of the circus freak. O'Connor magnifies the analogical tensions by juxtaposing the suffering of the "hermaphrodite" in the circus tent with the suffering of the incarnate Christ on the cross, which is an analogue of the suffering inherent in the human condition. This felt knowledge is brought about not by any conscious, epistemological reflection but by Catholic ritual and belief. It is, I think, O'Connor's most daring analogy, revealing in an original and striking way something about the nature of God and of human life. The story suggests, literally, that God is to be encountered—embodied—in the freak, the stranger, the alienated.

As the child leaves the chapel, a "big nun swooped down on her mischievously and nearly smothered her in the black habit, mashing the side of her face into the crucifix hitched onto her belt" (*Flannery . . . Works* 209). That the child's body is thus physically imprinted with the cross upon her cheek reveals that being a temple of the Holy Ghost means being wrapped up in the suffering and sacrifice of Christ. O'Connor awakens the reader to the risks of taking seriously the words of Christian faith, to the transcendental stakes of the human condition, and to the theological hope that grace is lurking everywhere, especially where we least expect to find it. In the final sentence of the story, the symbolic reach of the girl's imagination is moved to a cosmic horizon: "The sun was a huge red ball like an elevated Host drenched in blood and when it sank out of sight, it left a line in the sky like a red clay road hanging over the trees" (209). We are given a vision of reality that is steeped in the faith and intellectual heritage of Catholicism. The better we understand this vision, the better we understand the artistry of O'Connor.

NOTES

[1] Greif's introductory chapter (3–26) offers a concise summary of the dawning "age of the crisis of man," discussing such diverse thinkers as Hannah Arendt and Jacques Maritain, Karl Jaspers and Leo Strauss, among others, in examining the belief that human nature was under threat. Greif traces how this crisis was treated in the fiction of O'Connor, Saul Bellow, Ralph Ellison and Thomas Pynchon, each testing the universalism of such statements via the discourses of religious faith, race, and technology.

[2] O'Connor's personal library is filled with a wide variety of authors steeped in Thomistic thought of the Catholic intellectual renaissance of twentieth-century Europe: Romano Guardini, Claude Tresmontant, Sigrid Undset, Charles Peguy, Graham Greene, François Mauriac, Baron von Hügel, Pierre Teilhard de Chardin, Henri Daniel-Rops, Paul Claudel, Louis Bouyer, and Henri DeLubac. American writers included Bishop Fulton Sheen, William Lynch, Caroline Gordon, J. F. Powers, Walker Percy, and Thomas Merton.

[3] In his chapter "Christian Art," Maritain advises, "Do not separate your art from your faith. But leave distinct what is distinct. Do not try to blend by force what life unites so well. If you were to make of your aesthetic an article of faith, you would spoil your faith. If you were to make of your devotion a rule of artistic activity, or if you were to turn desire to edify into a method of your art, you would spoil your art" (66).

[4] O'Connor distills the ideas on Aquinas and Maritain in many of her essays, especially "Catholic Novelists and Their Readers" (*Mystery* 169–90).

[5] O'Connor met many proponents of this critical approach while earning her MFA at Iowa. She took classes with Paul Engle, Robert Penn Warren, Robert Lowell, and Allen

Tate and courses on literary criticism, including one taught by Austin Warren, one of the founders of the New Criticism.

[6] When I teach this in a course just for English majors, I have students read Giles's first chapter, "Methodological Introduction: Tracing the Transformation of Religion" (1–31).

[7] The influence of Lynch on O'Connor's occasional prose is ubiquitous but can be found mostly in "The Nature and Aim of Fiction" (*Mystery* 63–86) and "Novelist and Believer" (154–68).

[8] It is often helpful to relay this theoretical point with O'Connor's anecdote in a letter to Betty Hester. O'Connor was taken to a dinner party at the New York apartment of Mary McCarthy, a famous intellectual and ex-Catholic. Near the end of the soiree, the topic of the Eucharist came up. O'Connor relays that McCarthy quipped that "she thought of it as a symbol and implied that it was a pretty good one. I then said, in a very shaky voice, Well, if it's a symbol, to hell with it. That was all the defense I was capable of . . . except that it is the center of existence for me; all the rest of life is expendable" (*Flannery . . . Works* 976–77).

[9] See Schloesser 112–17 for a fuller exposition of this comparison of twentieth-century realisms.

Incarnation and Original Sin:
Teaching O'Connor as a Christian Writer

Jessica Hooten Wilson

Flannery O'Connor's vision can be perplexing to students of every faith—and to those with no faith at all. O'Connor was a Christian writer, but unlike the image that *Christian writer* usually brings to mind, she did not write solely for a Christian audience, and she hesitated to use the label "Christian" for fear that it would mean anyone with a "golden heart" (*Mystery* 192). Because she was a cradle Catholic raised in the Protestant South, her vision of southern religiosity was one both of an outsider and insider. For her, the region was "Christ-haunted" (*Flannery . . . Works* 818), meaning that the ghosts of faith still roamed about but that most churchgoers or self-identified Christians were like her character Mrs. May: they shared "a large respect for religion [but] did not, of course, believe any of it was true" (506). In contrast to Mrs. May and her readers, who "think God is dead" (943), as she put it, she believed in the tenets of the Catholic Church, and these beliefs buttress her stories.

Although O'Connor intended her fiction to express a Catholic vision, her faith does not necessitate a Catholic interpretation of her stories. As Alice Walker, a self-described pagan, says about her, "Her Catholicism did not in any way limit (by defining it) her art" ("Beyond the Peacock" 57).[1] In O'Connor's stories, there are no "religious tracts, nothing haloed softly in celestial light, not even any happy endings," Walker notes (55). O'Connor would never have wanted the mystery of her fiction to be reduced to palliative morals; rather, a Catholic vision meant to O'Connor seeing things as they were and faithfully transmitting that in fiction. In a 1962 interview, she said of her first novel, *Wise Blood*, "The fact that many people can't see anything Christian about my novel doesn't interfere with many of them seeing it as a novel which does not falsify reality" (*Conversations* 87). Her goal was to tell the truth, which makes her narratives often uncomfortable to Catholic, Protestant, and nonreligious readers. Sometimes the ideas undergirding her stories are more than difficult to swallow; they can be a choking hazard for unprepared students. Instead of offering any particular reading of O'Connor's work, this essay suggests ways to teach O'Connor as a Christian writer to religious and nonreligious students by first explaining two key theological ideas behind her aesthetic and then using those ideas to read her use of violence. I then focus on how to teach O'Connor the Catholic to Protestant students.

Seeing Incarnation in Fiction

Although O'Connor's style is often called grotesque, a more apt label would be incarnational or sacramental realism. The term *grotesque* may apply to any picture in which elements, as they appear in reality, are exaggerated by the artist. According to Geoffrey Galt Harpham in *On the Grotesque*, "Most grotesques are marked by such an affinity/antagonism, by the co-presence of the normative, fully formed, 'high' or ideal, and the abnormal, unformed, degenerate, 'low' or material" (11). For O'Connor, the purpose of her grotesque is religious; she depicts reality as grotesque because of her understanding of the Incarnation. In one of her early letters she writes, "One of the awful things about writing when you are a Christian is that for you the ultimate reality is the Incarnation, the present reality is the Incarnation, and nobody believes in the Incarnation; that is nobody in your audience" (*Flannery . . . Works* 943). Her fiction becomes particularly Christian in the way that it relies on the Incarnation for aesthetic principles as well as for the driving action and purpose.

The Incarnation epitomizes the grotesque combination of high and low: God became a human being. As a Catholic, O'Connor believed that Jesus Christ's dual nature as God and man signified the dual nature of every human being as both spiritual and physical, capable of both angelic virtues and beastly vices. The sacraments further the significance of the Incarnation by offering access to spiritual reality through physical means: in the doctrine of transubstantiation, for instance, the Eucharist wafer becomes the body of Christ. In her essay "The Catholic Novelist in the Protestant South," O'Connor explains that the grotesque in literature occurs "when any considerable depth of reality has been penetrated" (*Flannery . . . Works* 860). For her, the "depth of reality" involves the unseen spiritual matters that she believed existed but were not accepted by most of her readers.

Although her fiction is populated by Protestant characters representative of her contemporary southern landscape, with "A Temple of the Holy Ghost," "The Displaced Person," and "The Enduring Chill" being notable exceptions, she defined Christian fiction not as stories with Christian characters but as stories in which the Incarnation of Jesus Christ was central.

To explain the incarnational aesthetic to students, I use the letter in which O'Connor differentiates between symbol and sacrament. To Elizabeth Hester she writes, "I believe the Host is actually the body and blood of Christ, not a symbol. If the story ["Temple of the Holy Ghost"] grows for you, it is because of the mystery of the Eucharist in it" (*Flannery . . . Works* 976 [16 Dec. 1955]). She then relates an anecdote that has become famous for O'Connor aficionados: at a dinner in New York, when Mary McCarthy, a lapsed Catholic novelist, called the Eucharist a nice symbol, O'Connor says she responded, "If it's a symbol, to hell with it." She continues, "[I]t is the center of existence for me; all the rest of life is expendable" (977). The doctrine of the Incarnation and the corresponding sacrament of the Eucharist determine all the artistic choices that she makes. Protestant students may find this anecdote blasphemous, but students of all backgrounds need to understand her point. For O'Connor, there are no mere symbols in her work. In the same way that she believed that the wine becomes the blood of Christ, she means for Enoch Emery to become a gorilla. Like a modern Dante, she wants to embody the spiritual world in physical things—for example, a bull in "Greenleaf" and a tornado in "The Life You Save May Be Your Own" are the retribution of God.

One way to engage hesitant undergraduates to experience the incarnational grotesque in O'Connor's fiction is to encourage them to illustrate her work. For instance, in *Wise Blood* many of the peripheral characters are depicted as animals: the women who sit across from Hazel in the dining car are parrots; the boy working at Slade's car dealership has the thin face of an eagle; the mother in the swimming pool has the teeth of a wolf (*Flannery . . . Works* 7, 38, 48). I ask students to draw scenes from *Wise Blood* and replace the human characters with their animal similes. On the back of the illustrations, they should quote key lines from the scene that correlate with their work. They should discuss what they discovered by creating these portraits. Like Dante's *Inferno*, in which the fourteenth-century poet emphasizes the animal natures of the characters residing in hell to show their dehumanized state, *Wise Blood* embodies this element of Thomistic theology, O'Connor indicating how the beastly nature of people has triumphed over the spiritual.

If the limits of the class do not allow for teaching an entire novel, "The Life You Save May Be Your Own" is a good story to introduce these concepts and practice reading O'Connor's work as incarnational. In education, "I Do, We Do, You Do" is a three-step process that can solidify a new skill in a student. First, model for the student how to read O'Connor's story: begin by reading the first paragraph of the story aloud, possibly showing it on an overhead screen or asking students to follow along in their texts. Analyze the passage for the students, focusing on the concrete particulars that reflect secondary meanings—what, for O'Connor, would be spiritual readings. For instance, the old woman struggling to see is intended to be a physical representation of her spiritual blindness. She shades her eyes from the sun, the source of light. She decides that the approaching Mr. Shiftlet "was a tramp and no one to be afraid of" (*Flannery . . . Works* 172), yet anyone familiar with the story knows that he will kidnap and then abandon her daughter and steal her car in the process. The old woman incarnates poor sight because she judges based on external appearance and not inner character.

Now invite students to find another example of a concrete description in the story that incarnates a hidden reality. They may notice Mr. Shiftlet has half an arm, which may indicate his spiritual brokenness. Ask such questions as, "Why does the breeze seem to push Mr. Shiftlet?" or "Why does the sun balance on the peak of a small mountain?" The purpose is not to elicit right answers but to give students practice in digging for meaning. After the class has tried as a group to read the story this way, either divide the class into groups and pairs, giving each group a different page number or paragraph to read closely, or assign a passage to each person to analyze. This can be an oral or written assignment. Stress that there is not one correct answer to a question.

For a graduate seminar, consider including outside readings from Thomas Aquinas or Jacques Maritain. O'Connor claims in her letters that she read Aquinas for twenty minutes each night (*Flannery . . . Works* 945), and she admits to cutting her "aesthetic teeth" on Maritain's *Art and Scholasticism* (1031). If the course does not have time for much reading, include excerpts from chapter 8 of *Art and Scholasticism* ("Christian Art") or question 76 from Aquinas's *Summa Theologica* on the connection between the body and the soul (available at www .newadvent.org). Consult Marion Montgomery's *Hillbilly Thomist*, Susan Srigley's *Flannery O'Connor's Sacramental Art*, or Christina Bieber Lake's *The Incarnational Art of Flannery O'Connor*.

Original Sin and Violence in O'Connor

For many readers, the violence in O'Connor poses problems, especially because they do not expect so many mutilated corpses in a Christian writer's oeuvre.[2] She chooses not to give tidy moral lessons or feel-good moments but to tell scandalous stories with violent action to prod readers to question their deepest beliefs about reality. For her, human beings have the potential to do evil or good but because of original sin, which she believes is the "bedrock" of all great fiction (*Mystery* 167), choose evil more. *The Catholic Encyclopedia* defines *original sin* as "the hereditary stain with which we are born on account of origin or descent from Adam."[3] O'Connor calls it simply the "flaw in an otherwise admirable character" (*Mystery* 167).

Despite the human inclination to evil and destruction, the biblical Jesus is depicted as sinless. Thus, as the Misfit says in O'Connor's most anthologized short story, "A Good Man Is Hard to Find," "[Jesus] thrown everything off balance" (*Flannery . . . Works* 151). In the Gospel accounts, Jesus not only bears no taint of original sin but also dies as a criminal and resurrects himself, offering his disciples the chance for eternal life. For the Misfit, Jesus has overturned everything by offering an alternative to violence:

> If [Jesus] did what He said, then it's nothing for you to do but throw away everything and follow Him, and if He didn't then it's nothing for you to do but enjoy the few minutes you got left the best you can—by killing somebody or burning down his house or doing some other meanness to him. (152)

As the Misfit sees it, if Jesus was telling the truth, then human beings are eternal and can overcome their sinful nature by following Jesus's example. If he was a liar, there is no reason we should not submit to our lowest desires and maim and destroy. Throughout her fiction, O'Connor presents her readers with this simple choice. Many students, especially those who do not share her faith, may find this either-or troubling: they want room for a middle ground—for human beings to reach a noble ideal without religion, for humanism to be a valid third way, for violence not to be the only alternative to following Jesus. But O'Connor does not negotiate for this option in her fiction, which is why her stories can be so unsettling.[4]

"A Good Man Is Hard to Find" has the highest body count and is probably the most troubling, because that count includes children. The story exemplifies this either-or choice both in the Misfit's words and in the Grandmother's actions. At the first reading, students may find nothing religious or Catholic about it except the words *Jesus* and *pray*. The teacher might ask, "In the story, who's to blame for how rotten the world is?" As students respond, their answers should be put on the board, and they should be asked to support their answers from the text. The Grandmother and Red Sam blame "Europe" (*Flannery . . . Works* 142), while the Misfit blames "Jesus" (151). Students may speculate on how the story's characters would answer. Bailey blames his mother, and Bailey's wife blames Bailey—every character blames someone else. The teacher might follow this question with another: "Is anyone a 'good man' in the story?" The students will probably conclude that no one is good. Walker points out how puzzling it has been to readers "that in [O'Connor's] stories not only does good not triumph, it is not usually present" ("Beyond the Peacock" 55). At this point in the discussion, I have undergraduates spend five minutes reflecting on why a good person should be so hard to find.

Sometimes, when teaching this story, I have compared and contrasted the Misfit with the Grandmother. I solicit questions. What do the characters' names suggest about the characters? How do the names define them? Who do the Misfit and the Grandmother think Jesus is? What do they think about sin? redemption? salvation? The Misfit has a stronger grasp of theology than the Grandmother does: her belief in Jesus is superficial at best, utilitarian at worst. At the conclusion of the story, both appear to have a revelation, encountering a new vision of the way things are. What is that vision for each?

To encourage students to empathize with the story's characters, especially those who seem negative in the text, I assign a character to a pair or group of students. I ask them to rewrite a key scene of the text from that character's perspective. This assignment works well with the ending, where the Misfit and the Grandmother's worldviews are starkly in opposition. Consider dividing the class between the two and allow several students to write from the point of view of either character. Students will see how their creative rendering compels them to choose between various interpretations of the ending.

The Misfit's statement about Jesus provides a strong starting point for discussing other works by O'Connor. In *Wise Blood*, Hazel Motes refuses to follow Jesus—as he explicitly states—and murders Solace Layfield.[5] In *The Violent Bear It Away*, young Tarwater rejects Jesus's calling and kills his cousin Bishop.[6] To heighten the drama of O'Connor's work, students could reenact scenes from it. It lends itself to performance because of the personalities of the characters, their individual voices, and the intense action. Although the stories themselves are unforgettable, performing them can leave a vivid impression in the mind of a student. I once asked a student to play the role of Mrs. Ruby Turpin from

"Revelation": she stood as though above a hog pen, holding tight to her chair as though gripping the railing, and cried out against God, as Mrs. Turpin says in the text, "Who do you think you are?" When another student read the voice of the narrator—"The question . . . returned to her clearly like an answer from beyond"—students held their breath (*Flannery . . . Works* 653). Then one of them broke the silence, saying, "I have goosebumps."

Teaching the Catholic Writer to Protestant Students

I have primarily taught Protestant students in my tenure as a professor at both major universities and small colleges with strong religious ties. I've found that my Protestant students approach O'Connor in a way that is different from that of my students who are not religious. As readers they are familiar with safe best sellers from the Christian aisle at the bookstore, so anything too strange—or too violent—prompts them to resist.[7] Wary of atheistic writing in general, they desire the assurance that O'Connor's work stems from a devout faith. If they trust the author, they may suspend their outrage and engage in discussions about her stories.

In a course dedicated to O'Connor, I have my students read Jonathan Rogers's biography *The Terrible Speed of Mercy*, which, unlike Brad Gooch's biography, focuses on the author's religious life. In a broad course in which O'Connor is one author among several, her letters in *The Habit of Being* reflect her theological commitments in briefer form. A handful of them provide enough insight into her mind, especially those in which she defends the faith to Betty Hester ("A") or T. R. Spivey and especially the May 1962 letter to Alfred Corn after he lost his faith (*Flannery . . . Works* 1163). Her *Prayer Journal*, edited by W. A. Sessions, reveals the young woman when she was enrolled at the Iowa Writers' Workshop in 1946, before she had published any of her work. She shows her struggle with authentic faith and her desire to create art that reveals God to an unbelieving culture. Once students approve of her personal story, I turn the tables on them—I write on the board O'Connor's claim: "If you're studying literature, the intentions of the writer have to be found in the work itself and not in his life" (*Mystery* 126).[8]

The Christian aspect of O'Connor's work that will most attract Protestant readers is her use of the Bible. Her stories are laced with biblical references, and two scholars have written monographs on her dependence on the Bible, calling her stories "a kind of *rewriting* of Scripture" that speaks to contemporary readers (Michaels 9).[9] Near the end of her life, O'Connor recommended to others that the best way of examining her stories is through their connection to Scripture (Letter). In addition to attending church daily (in which she would have heard from the liturgy the Bible in its entirety over the course of three years), she was an avid Bible reader, as she admits in her letters: "As for me, I don't read anything but the newspaper and the Bible. Everybody else did that it would be a better world" (*Flannery . . . Works* 1206). Considering how much she read (see the long list of titles that compose her library in Arthur Kinney's annotated resource or those works she reviewed in the edited collections of her reviews, *The Presence of Grace*), this statement is hyperbolic. However, it emphasizes the importance that she places on the Bible. For deeper reading in graduate courses, students should note that she used a Catholic Bible, the Douay-Rheims edition, so some of her references will not be found in Protestant students' NIVs (New International Versions) and ESVs (English Standard Versions).

In discussing so-called American Catholic novelists, Walker Percy brings up Flannery O'Connor but then jokes, "although she's a Georgia fundamentalist" (47 [interview by Charles Bunting]). Percy's humor is accurate, because O'Connor, despite her Roman Catholic worldview, not only depicts fundamentalists but also adheres, in many cases better than they do, to their orthodoxy. In *Flannery O'Connor and the Christ-Haunted South*, Ralph Wood explores her connections to fundamentalism and shows how Protestants should engage her fiction; this book is a good introduction for teachers at Protestant universities who venture to teach O'Connor.

In a presentation to English teachers, O'Connor acknowledged her lack of experience as a teacher and felt humble before the group, but she spoke as a novelist about how she believed stories ought to be taught: "In the standing dispute between the novelist and the public, the teacher of English is a sort of middle-man, and I have occasionally come to think about what really happens when a piece of fiction is set before students. I suppose this is a terrifying experience of the teacher." Students, she supposes, all approach novels "according to [their] particular interest" (*Mystery* 122). Yet the teacher should redirect the student to see the world as the characters do, as the novelist does, instead of on the student's terms, and to register these new ways of seeing. O'Connor invites students first and foremost to consider how a "story is made and what makes it work as a story" and to contemplate the "mystery in the whole work" rather than track down "an expressible moral or statement about life" (129). When teaching O'Connor as a Christian writer, then, the goal should be not to teach answers but to inspire questions, to discover the vision and enjoy the story.

NOTES

[1] Walker's essay "Beyond the Peacock: The Reconstruction of Flannery O'Connor" is a good introduction to the value of teaching O'Connor as a religious writer from a non-Christian perspective.

[2] Thomas Haddox addresses the problem well in *Hard Sayings*: "My avowedly secular students, upon hearing of O'Connor's religious orthodoxy, are puzzled and sometimes intrigued by what they perceive as the exoticism of her position. . . . My Christian students, on the other hand . . . are usually shocked" (25). He gives examples of perplexing vio-

lence and explains, "Unfortunately, only the body is in the text; whatever grace and lines of spiritual motion there may be exist only in O'Connor's intentions, in the responses of readers to them, and in the coductions that readers might formulate in ongoing conversations about them" (25). According to Haddox, O'Connor's violence makes her text a battleground for various worldviews.

³ Read Thomas Aquinas's question 82 from *Summa Theologica* on the essence of original sin.

⁴ Over the years my students have been uncomfortable with this inflexibility: follow Jesus or commit violence. Some scholars, such as Joanne Halleran McMullen, echo their discomfort. McMullen writes, "For those schooled in a more humanistic view of Christianity, [O'Connor's] vision becomes impenetrable" (70).

⁵ At the beginning of *Wise Blood*, Hazel Motes accosts two women on a train, "Do you think I believe in Jesus?" Although the women are uninterested in his answer, he continues, "Well I wouldn't even if He existed. Even if He was on this train" (*Flannery . . . Works* 68).

⁶ Tarwater has been instructed by his Uncle Mason to become a prophet for Jesus and to fulfill this calling by baptizing Bishop. Although Tarwater baptizes his cousin, he denies that this was following Jesus. As he tries to explain to the driver who has offered him a ride, "It was an accident. I didn't mean to. . . . The words just come out of themselves but it don't mean nothing. You can't be born again" (*Flannery . . . Works* 458). To prove that he is not following Jesus, Tarwater drowns Bishop as he baptizes him.

⁷ Some Protestant students fear confronting other belief systems because they do not want to lose their faith. Lawanda Smith discusses this problem: "Most of my students either cling tenaciously to propositions of an unexamined Christian theological tradition . . . or knowing no other theological options, they reject their inherited theology, seeing it as inadequate" (95).

⁸ Harold Bloom contests, "O'Connor was ardent in proclaiming Original Sin and the Fall, but I trust the tales and not their teller" (*Flannery O'Connor* [1999] 9). Is he right to suggest that the tales suggest a different interpretation of the stories from the Catholic vision that O'Connor intended? I press students to examine her text.

⁹ Jordan Cofer also calls O'Connor's stories "biblical rewriting" (16).

Race and Grace
in O'Connor's Fiction

Doreen Fowler

> In Southern Literature, the Negro, without losing his
> individuality, is a figure for our darker selves, our
> shadow side.
> > —Flannery O'Connor

> . . . there is nothing that screams out the tragedy of the
> South like what my uncle calls "nigger statuary."
> > —Flannery O'Connor

> Whatever you did not do for one of the least of these, you
> did not do for me.
> > —Matt. 25.45

For Flannery O'Connor, "contact with mystery" is "what makes a story work"
(*Mystery* 111), and students certainly find her fiction mysterious—particularly her representations of race. For example, her seemingly casual use of the
N-word troubles students, and they find offensive her use of the racial slur in
the title "The Artificial Nigger," a story that she called her "favorite" (*Habit* 101).
Students are even more mystified when I tell them that O'Connor defended the
title, saying, "I don't think the story should be called anything but 'The Artificial
Nigger.'"[1] But what students find most mysterious in her fiction is the relation
between white racism and the action of grace. Why, they ask me, are racially

charged confrontations between white and black characters often the occasion for a moment of grace? In "The Artificial Nigger," why does the mysterious lawn jockey, a white-created caricature of an African American, have a healing effect on the quarreling grandfather and grandson, Mr. Head and Nelson? In "Everything That Rises Must Converge," why does the violent collision of a black lady and Julian's mother call forth the action of grace for Julian?[2]

The mystery of the relation between race and grace in O'Connor's work attracted the attention of a leading authority on race in America, Toni Morrison. In *Playing in the Dark*, Morrison issues a call to scholars to interpret the way "a black presence" is used in the works of white authors: "The contemplation of this black presence is central to any understanding of our national literature and should not be permitted to hover at the margins of the literary imagination" (5). She points to O'Connor as an author whose figurative uses of race have been overlooked by scholars; commenting on this critical neglect, she posits that there is a "connection between God's grace and Africanist 'othering'" in O'Connor that scholars have not seen (14).

Any study of racial figurations in O'Connor's works has to consider the story that seems to epitomize racial mystery, "The Artificial Nigger," and a class discussion of it needs to address first the author's use of the racial slur in her title. The title of course refers to Mr. Head and Nelson's demeaning term for the grotesque yard statue of a black boy that appears at the story's conclusion. The instructor should call students' attention to O'Connor's deliberate, repeated pairing of "artificial" with "nigger," which suggests that the inferiority signified by the racial slur is artificial—that is, it is a fiction constructed by what Morrison calls the "dominant cultural body" (10) to define a white identity as normative and superior in a binary opposition.[3] In other words, both the title of this story and the racist lawn jockey to which it refers are racist representations that expose white constructions of raced identities. At this early stage of the discussion, students may not yet divine O'Connor's antiracist purpose, but, as the class interprets subsequent passages, it should become evident.

The story tells of a poor white grandfather, Mr. Head, and his ten-year-old grandson, Nelson, who live alone together in the country. The story takes on a journey motif as the grandfather and grandson leave their outpost to take a trip to the big city, Atlanta. Mr. Head's purpose in making this journey is to teach his grandson to respect him, and race figures importantly in the story because Mr. Head believes that in Atlanta he will be able to impress Nelson with his racial superiority. In Mr. Head's words, Atlanta will "be full of niggers," and Nelson has never seen an African American before, because, as Mr. Head tells him proudly, "There hasn't been a nigger in this county since we run that one out twelve years ago and that was before you were born" (*Flannery . . . Works* 212). He means to use the boy's lack of experience with people of color to show him that "you ain't as smart as you think you are" (211). The ensuing events in Atlanta conform to a frequently repeated pattern in O'Connor's fiction: both Mr. Head and Nelson discover that they are not as smart as they thought they were; more than that, they discover that they are not even who they thought they were.

The instructor should focus students' attention on the interactions between the grandfather and grandson and African Americans in Atlanta, including the well-dressed African American man who passes them on the train, the "large colored woman" whom Nelson asks for directions (222), and of course the story's central icon, "the plaster figure of a Negro," which seems to embody "the mystery of existence" (229, 230). It is important for students to note that each of these experiences is a moment of contact with people of color that subverts the idea of natural white superiority. *Contact* is a key word in O'Connor's lexicon. She uses it frequently to talk about the mystery of grace. Grace is a moment of "contact" with the divine life (*Mystery* 111). In "The Artificial Nigger," the old man and the boy make contact with people whom they have always defined as other, and that contact works to close the gap between them and the divine other.

The first time Nelson sees an African American, he does not find any racial difference. When a well-dressed, bejeweled "coffee-colored man" proceeds down the train aisle, Mr. Head asks his grandson, "What was that?" Looking "as if he were tired of having his intelligence insulted," Nelson answers, "A man." When his grandfather repeats the question insistently, Nelson, "beginning to feel that he had better be cautious," answers, "A fat man," and then, with increasing "foreboding," "An old man." When Mr. Head triumphantly says, "That was a nigger," and proclaims Nelson "ignorant," Nelson feels "a fierce raw fresh hate" for the man (*Flannery . . . Works* 215, 216). The instructor should ask the class to discuss the boy's inability to identify a person as racially different. Students will understand that this inability of the child to see race difference shows that racial difference is not natural but taught and that the untutored child's ignorance drives home the meaning implicit in the title: the racial inferiority signified by "nigger" is an artificial, white attribution. The other important racial meaning to be gleaned from the incident has to do with the origin of race hatred. I ask my class, Why does Nelson hate the man who walked down the aisle? As they debate the answer, students come to see that Nelson hates the African American because he feels ignorant and blames the man for that ignorance—in other words, racial hatred arises because the hater needs to project onto another his feeling of inferiority.

The interaction between Nelson and the woman of color whom he asks for directions can help students see the connection between race and grace. When Mr. Head and Nelson become hopelessly lost in a black section of Atlanta, the older man is unwilling to ask a black person for help and tells his grandson to ask the way back to the train station. Nelson approaches an African American woman and is mysteriously overcome with a desire for contact with her: "He suddenly wanted her to reach down and pick him up and draw him against her and then he wanted to feel her breath on his face. He wanted to look down and down into her eyes while she held him tighter and tighter. He had never had such a feeling before. He felt as if he were reeling down through a pitch-black tunnel" (223). To interpret this powerful desire, students should recall that Nelson's mother died when he was a year old. According to Jacques Lacan, in the first months of life an infant has yet to develop a sense of a separate self and experiences existence as continuous with the mother. Read in this context, Nelson seems to desire to return to this early mother-child attachment, which is represented in the text by his feeling that he is "reeling down through a pitch-black tunnel," an image suggestive of a return to the womb.[4]

In an important gloss on the mysterious interaction between Nelson and the woman of color, O'Connor suggests that the boy's need to return to an early mother-child closeness is a pathway to grace: "I meant for her in an almost physical way to suggest the mystery of existence to him. . . . I felt that such a black mountain of maternity would give him the required shock to start those black forms moving up from his unconscious" (*Habit* 78). Given that, for O'Connor, the mystery of existence is always the mystery of our participation in the divine life, we can read her statement to mean that the ten-year-old boy's desire to return to an early boundaryless condition creates an openness to others that makes him open to the divine other. This openness to the racial other is also suggested by her reference to "black forms moving up from [Nelson's] unconscious." Throughout their trip to Atlanta, he is "half conscious of . . . black forms moving up from some dark part of him into the light" (*Flannery . . . Works* 225). According to psychoanalytic theory, a black form rising up from the unconscious mind is the uncanny double or alter ego—that is, the other self, the return of something just like the self that we have estranged. Throughout the story, Mr. Head and Nelson, to distinguish themselves as superior whites, have estranged people of color and buried in their unconscious minds a recognition that these people are just like them.[5] During the Atlanta trip, however, their social contact with African Americans has triggered a breakdown of psychological barriers, and the repressed is returning in the form of the double, the "black forms" rising up from the unconscious.[6]

Denial of relatedness figures again in a scene in which Nelson, fearful that he has been abandoned by his grandfather, frantically runs into a woman and knocks her down. When Mr. Head catches up to Nelson, the old man is surrounded by a crowd of women "massed in their fury like a solid wall to block his escape." Feeling threatened, he says, "This is not my boy. . . . I never seen him before," and the women "drop back . . . repulsed by a man who would deny his own image and likeness" (226). Mr. Head denies his own "image and likeness" in the same way that he denies African Americans. I ask students if the words "his own image and likeness" sound familiar. The biblical quote is well known, and students quickly recognize that O'Connor is alluding to the Genesis account of man as created in God's "own image" (*The Holy Bible: New International Version*, Gen. 1.27). This biblical allusion links those whom Mr. Head denies—Nelson and African Americans—to God. This link should lead students to see the connection between God's grace and the denial of others. When Mr. Head distances himself from those who are "his own image and likeness," Nelson and the people he racializes, he distances himself from those who are exactly like him and share a likeness with God.

Mr. Head is returned to Nelson and to God through the mediation of the racist lawn jockey. When he has lost all hope, "the plaster figure of a Negro" appears "like a cry out of the gathering dusk," and the old man and the boy gaze at the yard statue full of wonder as at "the mystery of existence" (*Flannery . . . Works* 229, 230). This allusion to the "mystery of existence" is our first clue that the yard ornament will be the occasion for the action of God's grace. To help students understand the relation between the breakdown of racial repression and the advent of grace, the instructor needs to explain that in the segregated South in the 1950s and 1960s it was common practice for white southerners to decorate their homes and gardens with sculptures of black people, which had features that exaggerated racial difference. Images of these lawn jockeys might be shown, and students might be asked why whites would want to feature in their homes and yards these demeaning representations of African Americans. In Morrison's terms, these white-constructed images embody racial "othering" (*Playing* 14). In her study of white representations of race, Susan Gubar goes further and points to the lawn statue in "The Artificial Nigger" as an example of a "blackface performance" that "justified and replicated white violence against the black body" (85).

But O'Connor's text suggests that, despite white people's efforts to construct stark racial polarities by denying likeness, that likeness is undeniable. The plaster figure of the African American, despite its strangeness, bears an uncanny resemblance to both Mr. Head and Nelson.[7] Students pick up on a number of similarities among the grandfather, the grandson, and the racist lawn jockey. The statue is described as "about Nelson's size"; its "wild look of misery" (*Flannery . . . Works* 229) reflects the "ravaged and abandoned" (228) expression on Mr. Head's face; it is "pitched forward at an unsteady angle" (229) that mirrors the stance of the old man and the boy, who lean with "their necks forward" (230); all three seem to be of indeterminate age—"the artificial Negro," we are told, could be "young or old" (229), and grandfather and grandson are described as looking like "brothers not too far apart in age" (212); finally, the racist artifact is a mysterious black form, and Nelson has been feeling "black forms moving up from some dark part of him into the light" (225).

This last similarity between the lawn statue and a psychological process in Nelson suggests that, like the "black forms" rising up from Nelson's unconscious mind, the statue is a representation of the uncanny double, the disguised return of what has been denied. The appearance of the double always signals a breakdown of denial (or repression) and a recognition of similarities between the self and others. In this case the racial repression by which we wall off a white self is breaking down, and O'Connor suggests that this dissolution of racial othering triggers a moment of grace for Mr. Head and Nelson. They stand mesmerized by the dark form "as if they were faced with some great mystery, some monument to another's victory that brought them together in their common defeat.

They could both feel it dissolving their differences like an action of mercy" (230). The "action of mercy" is O'Connor's term for God's grace, and its action "dissolv[es] differences."

When asked about redemptive grace in her fiction, O'Connor said that the "mystery" of "our participation in" what she called "the Divine Life" (*Mystery* 111) has its "roots" in "ties of kinship" (112). In "The Artificial Nigger," white people manufacture a stark racial polarity by refusing to acknowledge kinship with African Americans, and this denial separates them from God. But this story also illustrates the psychoanalytic tenet that "repressed, it reappears" (Lacan 297). In Atlanta, social contact with African Americans precipitates a breakdown of psychological and social barriers, which enables a moment of grace. It is important to note that this dissolution of artificial lines drawn to make some people other entails a loss of ego-protecting boundaries and leaves us in a terrifying boundaryless state.[8] This dissolution of self-identifying boundaries, I would argue, is the "considerable cost" that O'Connor said accompanies a moment of grace (*Mystery* 112). For her, grace is always a moment of "contact" and an "intrusion" (111, 112); in story after story, her characters experience grace when they are stunned, shattered, pierced, lost, and helpless. At the end of "The Artificial Nigger," Mr. Head again feels "the action of mercy touch him," and this "touch[ing]" is a conflagration, a dissolution of a secure self-identity: he "burned with shame," and "the action of mercy covered his pride like a flame and consumed it." But in the same instant that he felt the dissolving "action of mercy touch him," he also felt "ready . . . to enter Paradise" (*Flannery . . . Works* 230–31).

NOTES

[1] This quote appears in O'Connor's letter to John Crowe Ransom, dated 12 Jan. 1955 (Fitzgerald, Letter).

[2] Three essays are essential reading for teaching O'Connor's racial themes: "Beyond the Peacock: The Reconstruction of Flannery O'Connor," by Alice Walker; "Where Is the Voice Coming From? Flannery O'Connor on Race," by Ralph C. Wood; and "A Teachers' Forum: O'Connor and the Issue of Race," by Laura Zaidman, Margaret Whitt, and Jane Vogel.

[3] This reading aligns with contemporary theories of race. Omi and Winant, for example, explain that racial designations "are an unstable 'decentered' complex of social meanings constantly being transformed by political struggle" (68).

[4] Perreault argues that O'Connor attributes "body" to the African American woman in the story and in so doing "subverts her own deeply held belief in the necessity of unifying body and spirit for true spiritual integrity" (389–90).

[5] O'Connor was familiar with Freud: "As to Sigmund, I am against him tooth and toenail but I am crafty: never deny, seldom confirm, always distinguish. Within his limitations I am ready to admit certain uses for him" (*Habit* 110). She also writes of *The Violent Bear It Away* that "a Freudian could read this novel and explain it all on the basis of Freud" (343). In other words, she was aware that her fiction was amenable to a Freudian interpretation but insisted on distinguishing herself from Freud.

[6] In his essay "Repression," Freud makes the point that "repression itself . . . produces substitute formations and symptoms, . . . indications of a return of the repressed" (*Standard Edition* 14: 154). Lacan, who revises Freud in terms of language theory, states this idea simply: "Repressed, it reappears" (297). Repressed material often returns in the form of the uncanny double. In "The Uncanny," Freud writes that the uncanny "is in reality nothing new or alien, but something which is familiar and old-established in the mind and which has become alienated from it only through the process of repression" (17: 241). He goes on to theorize that uncanny strangeness occurs in a moment of recognition, when the veil slips and this alien is recognized as one's own (217–56).

[7] A number of critics have noted this resemblance. Kahane observes that the "complicated network of psychological involvement and mutual dependency between black and white . . . is one of the more ignored themes of [O'Connor's] fiction" ("Artificial Niggers" 187). Brinkmeyer maintains that the racist image reveals to the grandfather and grandson that "they share with blacks and with all people a common identity as a fallen people" (80). MacKethan finds correspondences between Mr. Head, Nelson, and the plaster figure of the African American (31). Nesbitt suggests that the grandfather and grandson "perhaps have come to recognize their own essential and shared 'blackness'" (168).

[8] In an early, astute psychoanalytic reading of O'Connor's fiction, Kahane notes that a fear of loss of ego boundaries drives racial repression: "Thus it would seem that one important reason for the Southerner's insistence on racial distinctions . . . is that these barriers block the fear of an ego-annihilating fusion with blackness. In short, non-integration prevents disintegration" (191).

O'Connor and Whiteness Studies

John N. Duvall

Teaching Flannery O'Connor in the twenty-first century can make for some unsettling classroom moments. Some of her most interesting stories are also the most troubling for contemporary readers because of their depictions of African Americans and of the unreflecting racism many white characters exhibit, even if it is ironically depicted. But students can be shown that O'Connor's fiction does productively contribute to contemporary thinking about race if we shift our attention from the black characters to the white ones. Although O'Connor insisted that her Catholic faith provided the best context for understanding her fiction, bringing a critical whiteness studies approach to the classroom helps students see that southern whiteness is a socially constructed metaphysics of privilege that has as much to do with class as it does with race. This essay discusses how a senior-level course on the literature of the American South can use short critical readings on white appropriations of blackness by Toni Morrison, Susan Gubar, and E. Patrick Johnson to underscore the ways in which O'Connor's fiction racializes whiteness by showing the anxiety of white characters about their racial status. Such an approach helps move class discussion of race beyond representations of black characters and toward a recognition of the imbricated relation of race and class in the twentieth-century South. Students ultimately come to see the extent to which O'Connor's narratives make whiteness visible as a race and how whiteness is intimately tied to performance.

Before coming to O'Connor, the class has read Mark Twain's *Pudd'nhead Wilson* and William Faulkner's *Go Down, Moses*. In the ending of Twain's farcical and satirical treatment of miscegenation and the nature-nurture question, students first encounter the thematic that extends through our discussion of Faulkner and O'Connor: characters who are racially white but culturally black. Once Pudd'nhead Wilson exposes Roxy's act of having switched her light-skinned son, Chambers, with her master's son, Tom, Chambers, now recognized as black, is sold down river. Restored to his privileged white status, the true Tom simply cannot play his part: "His gait, his attitudes, his gestures, his bearing, his laugh—all were vulgar and uncouth; his manners were the manners of a slave. . . . The poor fellow could not endure the terrors of the white man's parlor, and felt at home and at peace nowhere but in the kitchen" (121).

If Twain's novel ends at the point where a racially white man cannot play his proper role, such awkward performance is precisely what Faulkner's tragic exploration of miscegenation makes central. At this point, I break up the reading of the various narratives that compose *Go Down, Moses* with the material from Morrison, Gubar, and Johnson. Morrison's now iconic study, *Playing in the Dark: Whiteness and the Literary Imagination*, which claims that whiteness knows itself only in relation to the imagined otherness of blackness or the "constituted Africanism" of white writers (44), becomes an excellent jumping-off point for students to consider what is at stake in white appropriations of blackness. Gubar's term "racechange" is also salient. For Gubar, racechange represents a broad range of possible crossings of racial boundaries, including whites posing as blacks (as in blackface minstrelsy) or light-skinned blacks passing as whites. In the twentieth century, racechange becomes a "crucial trope of high and low, elite and popular culture, one that allowed artists from widely divergent ideological backgrounds to meditate on racial privilege and privation as well as on the disequilibrium of race" (5). Despite the ostensible neutrality of this claim, Gubar ultimately finds that every white impersonation of blackness undermines "black subjectivity in a way that will inevitably rebound against the ethical integrity of whites" (36).

Before approaching Faulkner's Isaac McCaslin stories, I give students Johnson's introduction to *Appropriating Blackness*; it provides an excellent counterpoint to Morrison and Gubar, because it does not in advance see every white artistic use of blackness as an aesthetic or ethical failure. Using a performance studies approach to the issue of the appropriation of blackness, Johnson argues that blackness is not an essence but rather always an enactment, no matter what the race of the performer. He is fully aware of the dangers of stereotypes and fetishization that can accompany white appropriations of blackness, evident for example in the language of white rappers. He is, however, willing to imagine, in ways Morrison and Gubar are not, that "cross-cultural appropriation of blackness" need not result simply in "colonization and subjugation" and at times may actually "provide fertile ground on which to formulate new epistemologies of self and Other" (6).

In a more significant way than Twain's narrative, Faulkner's story of Isaac McCaslin helps set the stage for reading the whiteface minstrelsy that one finds in O'Connor. In *Go Down, Moses*, Ike's life follows the trajectory of the pliant African American male. He is referred to as "boy" in his youth but never acquires the honorific "Mister," the minimal marker of white southern masculinity. In other words, he is never called Mr. Isaac, the required form of address that African Americans would use when speaking to him. His failure to become a mister results from his decision to refuse his inheritance: when he repudiates his patrimony—his property, the McCaslin plantation—because of his grandfather's incestuous miscegenation, he simultaneously repudiates his proper white identity, even if he recognizes his racial reassignment no more than the rest of the white community. Ike's refusal to accept his legal and cultural legacy creates a profound social misrecognition. If Ike were black, his degraded status among the next generation of white hunters would be conventional in southern culture. But that Uncle Ike gets no respect is precisely the point, signaled by the fact that he is addressed as a polite southerner would address an elderly African American man. Uncle Ike is racially white but culturally black. Effectively, he is a whiteface minstrel, a character who performs blackness in whiteface.

If Faulkner uses a whiteface minstrelsy to trouble white southern masculinity and to point to the social and psychological costs to white southerners who fail to acknowledge their black kin, O'Connor intertwines the white performance of blackness with her theological concerns. For her, the narrative arcs of her fiction lead to painful and sometimes fatal instances of grace. A unit on her fiction, however, can lead students to see that these moments of grace are also very often moments of race. To show students the link between race and grace, I have assigned Claire Kahane's essay "The Artificial Niggers," because it sets up precisely what a whiteness studies perspective can add to a discussion of O'Connor and race. Kahane is useful because she sees how the Negro becomes a trope in O'Connor and takes up every story I want students to read, but Kahane limits the discussion of race to O'Connor's failure to imagine the interiority of African Americans. At the same time, she sounds an important warning against universalizing black victimhood. In other words, she presents O'Connor on race before we began to think about the social construction of whiteness. But what happens when we approach O'Connor with the frame suggesting that whiteness serves not as the unmarked universal against which one can measure African American difference but rather as an unstable social construct that is always performative?

Her story "Revelation" directly depicts the performance of whiteness. For white southerners in her fictional world, whiteness is not a given but must be properly performed on a daily basis. To fail to do so is to risk falling into the abject status of "white trash." Mrs. Turpin is one of O'Connor's characters who maps social distinctions of race and class. Apparently confident in her whiteness, she spends her time in a doctor's waiting room categorizing people as either white or "white trash" by such clues as the kind of shoes they wear. Tellingly, at one point she thinks about the choice she would make if Jesus were to make her decide whether to "either be a nigger or white trash"; she decides she would rather be "a neat clean respectable Negro woman, herself but black" (*Flannery . . . Works* 636). While Mrs. Turpin is careful to correctly perform her whiteness, her obsession with identifying herself as white actually marks an anxiety about her racialized position in particular and the contingency of whiteness more broadly. Being Caucasian is a necessary (but finally insufficient) condition of southern whiteness. Through Mrs. Turpin O'Connor shows that reducing southern racial politics to skin color overlooks the crucial elements of class and breeding in the construction of southern whiteness.

The term "white trash" is a designation that her characters are comfortable using in many of her stories. Like Mrs. Turpin, these rural characters reveal a deep anxiety about their whiteness and use the poor white to confirm their racial identities, so that the otherness of class becomes completely imbricated with the otherness of race. In "The Displaced Person," although Mrs. Shortley and her husband are hired labor, she is certain that she is white and not "white trash." After all, she has conversations with her employer, Mrs. McIntyre, about previous employees, all of whom are identified as "white trash." Mrs. Shortley is equally certain that the Guizacs, the Polish Catholic family of war refugees that Mrs. McIntyre has sponsored, do not belong on the farm, even though Guizac immediately proves himself to be a much better worker than Chancey Short-ley. However, after learning that she and her husband (rather than the black hired help or the Guizacs) have been let go, Mrs. Shortley suffers a fatal stroke and dies. In her death throes, her face turns "an almost volcanic red" (303); quite literally, at the moment of her loss of whiteness, she becomes a col-ored person. That the Shortley family leaves without a word only confirms for Mrs. McIntyre that they are indeed "white trash."

A short paper that can be assigned before students read "The Displaced Person" asks them to bring their reading of Morrison to bear on O'Connor's fiction:

> In your response, draw on Toni Morrison's argument that white writers use the racial other to confirm white identity. Do poor whites and the insulting designation "white trash" function in O'Connor's fiction in ways similar to or different from the ways black characters and the racial epi-thet "nigger" function? To what extent is the poor white another other?

As originally published in 1954, "The Displaced Person" ends with Mrs. Short-ley's death. In expanding the story for inclusion in "*A Good Man Is Hard to Find*" *and Other Stories*, O'Connor extends the displacement of whiteness to Mrs. Mc-Intyre, who quite literally loses her place. Although appreciating Guizac's work, she is horrified to discover that Guizac is trying to arrange the marriage of his niece with Sulk, one of her black workers, so that the niece can escape the displaced person camp in Europe. For Mrs. McIntyre, Guizac's inability to un-derstand the southern prohibition against miscegenation makes him a monster, someone who is not fully white, and she identifies him as just another in the series of "white trash" workers she has always had to deal with. Deciding that she must get rid of the Pole, she rehires Chancey Shortley, who along with Sulk plots Guizac's murder.

Mrs. McIntyre, dressed in black, sees the murder (staged as a tractor accident) unfold but fails to save Guizac by calling out to him. In that moment, "[s]he had felt her eyes and Mr. Shortley's eyes and the Negro's eyes come together in one look that froze them in collusion forever" (*Flannery . . . Works* 325–26) as she hears the tractor wheel break Guizac's backbone. In this shared gaze, the three become displaced people. Chancey and Sulk leave the farm, but Mrs. McIntyre has lost the moral certainty of her white privilege that allowed her previously to designate those who fell short of the mark of southern whiteness. She loses her farm, her sight, and her voice, all figures of the very whiteness that, like Mrs. Shortley in the story's first half, Mrs. McIntyre has now lost.

"The Comforts of Home" is one of O'Connor's uncanny stories that plays along the color line in the total absence of racially black characters. All the char-acters are white: thirty-five-year-old Thomas (still living at home), his mother, and the wayward teenage girl whom Thomas's mother attempts to save by bringing the girl into their home. The plot turns on his horribly failed plan to remove the girl from his home, and until the very end of the story he serves as the angle of vision.

By this point in the semester, students are usually able to pick up on a number of details that point to the whiteface performance of the girl whom Thomas loathes. On the story's second page, the performative element of her character is marked by a particular piece of physical description: her "face was like a comedienne's in a musical comedy—a pointed chin, wide apple cheeks and feline empty eyes" (*Flannery . . . Works* 573). As a genre, musical comedy derives from vaudeville and minstrelsy. In the minstrelsy of the girl known as Star Drake but whose real name is Sarah Ham, everything about the way she is delineated, except for her apple-cheeked whiteness, suggests cultural blackness: she is quick to laughter; she's often drunk; she is promiscuous; she is, in Thomas's judgment, "a congenital liar" (578); and when she wakes ". . . in the morning, her voice throbbed out in a blues song that would rise and waver, then plunge low with insinuations of passion about to be satisfied" (585). When I say "cultural blackness," I mean neither black culture nor the actual behavior of African Americans but rather refer to the racialist assumptions or cultural stereotypes of blackness common from before the Civil War through the civil rights movement.

Racially white, Sarah has no claim to southern whiteness because, as Thomas asserts, she is "[b]orn without the moral faculty" (575). If Star/Sarah were racially black, she would be the stereotyped embodiment of the Negro. The girl's name is another clue to her enactment of cultural blackness. Just as her racial whiteness masks cultural blackness, her assumed name serves as a screen that deflects attention from the implication of her given name: Sarah suffers from the curse of Ham, that often used antebellum southern justification for the enslavement of African Americans.

"The Comforts of Home" ultimately undoes the presumption of whiteness by showing that Thomas's confidence that he was born with a moral faculty (and so can identify those who lack one) is simply untenable. The mother's ultimate justification for bringing Sarah into their home is a maternal concern for Thomas. Whenever he presses her regarding her charity toward Sarah, the mother responds, "[S]uppose it were you?" (574). In the logic of the narrative, if Sarah, as a congenital liar, embodies cultural blackness, that is precisely what Thomas is moving toward; he undergoes a process of becoming culturally black, and by the story's end, that process is completed.

The internalized voice of the father becomes increasingly insistent in Thomas's mind. After Sarah fakes a suicide attempt, the mother urges Thomas to lock up his father's handgun, which he keeps in his desk. To the mother's concern that Sarah might truly do away with herself, Thomas responds in a racially coded way when he says, "Don't you know that her kind never kill themselves?" (587). This assertion resonates with the racist belief that happy-go-lucky Negroes don't commit suicide because they lack the psychological depth ever to fully feel the human emotion of despair that would lead to suicide. But when the gun disappears, Thomas finally gives in to his father's voice and goes to see Sheriff Farebrother, whom he invites to come to the house that evening to search Sarah's room. Returning to his study, Thomas discovers just a few minutes before Farebrother is to arrive that Sarah has replaced the pistol in his desk. Heeding his father's instructions again, he places the gun in Sarah's purse, but the girl catches him doing so.

Thomas's mother claims that her son could not have put his pistol in Sarah's purse, because "Thomas is a gentleman." She believes that honesty is his essential nature. Racial ideology says that blacks are congenital liars, so Thomas, because he is white, wouldn't act in a devious fashion. The girl tells the mother to come look in the purse, but Thomas says, "I found it in her bag! . . . The dirty criminal slut stole my gun" (593). In the climactic moment, his lying undercuts his mother's claim and his own belief in his honesty, which is the ground of his whiteness.

When he fires the gun to kill Sarah but accidentally kills his mother, Thomas is stripped both of his control of the story's point of view and, like Mrs. McIntyre, of his whiteness. He ceases being a moralizing subject and becomes a stereotyped object. Whiteness depends on the ability to define and name the difference of the other. Sheriff Farebrother becomes our angle of vision in the last two paragraphs, and in the sheriff's eyes Thomas is now merely a placeholder in a narrative that could be the lyrics of one of the blues songs that Sarah sings each morning: "Over the body, the killer and the slut were about to collapse into each other's arms. The sheriff knew a nasty bit when he saw it" (594). Thomas is demoted from white southern gentleman to amoral Caucasian with a blackened interiority.

O'Connor told John Hawkes that in "The Comforts of Home" "nobody is 'redeemed'" but goes on to say that "if there is any question of symbolic redemption, it would be through the old lady who brings Thomas face to face with his own evil" (*Habit* 434). We might recast this slightly to say that what the mother brings Thomas face to face with is the contingency of his whiteness. In becoming an abject other to the white community, he now opens himself to the possibility of salvation. It is a recurring theme in O'Connor's fiction that the matter of grace is always intimately tied to the matter of race, even when African American characters are absent. Like Faulkner, O'Connor helps make whiteness visible as a race precisely through a minstrelsy of whiteness.

From O'Connor, one can move on to other southern women authors, such as Harper Lee, Carson McCullers, and Dorothy Allison. In Lee's *To Kill a Mockingbird*, for example, Dolphus Raymond adds to the sense of the performativity of race. Raymond is from a prominent southern family but has lost his claim to full southern whiteness because he consorts with blacks and lives with a black woman with whom he has fathered mixed-race children. He is presumed to be an alcoholic because he is always seen drinking publicly from a bottle in a brown paper bag. Raymond, however, reveals to Dill and Scout that his alcoholism is pure performance, since his bottle contains only soda. As he explains, his presumed alcoholism deflects the prejudice of the community, giving people a convenient narrative to explain his degeneracy.

In McCullers's *The Member of the Wedding*, one can emphasize the extent to which Frankie codes her adolescent gender anxiety in racial terms, such as her identification with the African American Honey Brown (as well as with black criminality more generally) and her decision, after the humiliation of not being included in the honeymoon, to ride home in the back of the bus "with the colored people" (135). In *Bastard Out of Carolina*, Allison so thoroughly blurs the boundary between "white trash" and "nigger" that the class difference of the Boatwright family cannot be thought of apart from race. Allison's sexually abused protagonist, Bone, who is figuratively associated with blackness, also underscores the problematic status of the bastard in southern culture. With her father's identity stamped as unknown, this official document can in no way assure the community of her racial whiteness.

The ultimate value of the critical whiteness approach is that it allows students to distinguish between white characters who consciously appropriate blackness (such as Lee's Dolphus Raymond and McCullers's Frankie) and those who are appropriated by blackness (such as Faulkner's Ike McCaslin and O'Connor's Mrs. Shortley and Thomas). In the latter group, O'Connor's fiction centrally contributes to an understanding of whiteness as an unstable racial identity.

Teaching O'Connor in Context:
Modernism as Historical Artifact

Robert Donahoo

Teaching Flannery O'Connor generally begins with the desire to establish a context for her work that enables insight into its value and values. Harold Bloom stakes out his admittedly minority view on this point when he offers O'Connor as one of a hundred examples of genius, concluding:

> Her admirers praise Flannery O'Connor as a Roman Catholic moralist, an estimate I find odd. I celebrate her genius as another authentic prophet of the American Religion, at once the source of our individuality in literature and in life, and the origin also of our endemic violence, which [Nathanael] West parodied, as O'Connor did also, but with a certain ambivalence.
> (*Genius* 579)[1]

Whatever Bloom means by his terms here, his goal—one I ask my students to emulate—is plain: to both connect O'Connor to and disconnect her from certain literary traditions and artists.

That O'Connor herself shared an interest in context and connection is evident in the title story of her first professional collection. "The Grandmother didn't want to go to Florida," the opening sentence of "A Good Man Is Hard to Find" declares. "She wanted to visit some of her connections in east Tennessee and she was seizing at every chance to change Bailey's mind" (*Flannery . . . Works* 137). She fails, of course, and the family heads off for a disconnected vacation in the disconnected (disconnected from the traditional South) state of Florida. At the key moment when the story begins its transition from satiric comedy to something more deadly, the cat Pitty Sing, disconnected from the context of Gilbert and Sullivan's *Mikado*, leaps onto Bailey's shoulder, causing him to lose control of the car and disconnect it from the road. This "ACCIDENT!" is explained by the Grandmother's sudden realization that the house she has detoured the family to see "was not in Georgia but in Tennessee" (144, 145); she had remembered it in the wrong context. Before long, even the Grandmother's language struggles with context: "Finally she found herself saying, 'Jesus. Jesus,' meaning, Jesus will help you, but the way she was saying it, it sounded as if she might be cursing" (151).

The Misfit too struggles with context and connection, blaming his actions on an inability to connect his empirical knowledge to the claim that Jesus raised the dead: "It ain't right I wasn't there because if I had of been there I would of known. Listen lady, . . . if I had of been there I would of known and I wouldn't be like I am now." Only in death does the Grandmother reconnect and find her proper context—when she reaches out and mistakes the Misfit for "one of my own children" and when the Misfit orders, "Take her off and thow her where you thown the others." Now a bullet-ridden corpse, she is where she belongs: with her bullet-ridden family. The Misfit's last words form a final disconnect. Having previously explained his philosophy that "it's nothing for you to do but enjoy the few minutes you got left the best way you can—by killing somebody or burning down his house or doing some other meanness to him. No pleasure but meanness," in the context of pumping three bullets into the Grandmother, he now declares, "It's no real pleasure in life" (152, 153).

For students who have studied O'Connor largely as a product of her theological commitments and beliefs, such a reading—presented in a lecture or developed by students themselves when they are asked to follow the language and images of connection in the story—will likely appear odd or unreflective of authorial intent, but in fact it can open the door to having them examine contextualization, particularly O'Connor's frequent concern about context expressed in her nonfiction. When they read her essay "The Fiction Writer and His Country," which grew out of her earliest lectures, they discover that she bemoans the idea of writers from the South being deemed part of a mythical "Southern school," which "conjures up an image of Gothic monstrosities and the idea of a preoccupation with everything deformed and grotesque," adding, "Most of us are considered, I believe, to be unhappy combinations of Poe and Erskine Caldwell" (*Flannery . . . Works* 802). Students will note her own definition of her context, when she directly declares, "I see from the standpoint of Christian orthodoxy. This means that for me the meaning of life is centered in our Redemption by Christ and that what I see in the world I see in its relation to that" (804–05). Less theologically adamant, her lecture "Some Aspects of the Grotesque in Southern Fiction" seconds her concern about context, whether it be the context of readers demanding realism—"I am always having it pointed out to me that life in Georgia is not at all the way I picture it"—or "the modern romance tradition" or the Faulknerian influence: "Nobody wants his mule and wagon stalled on the same track the Dixie Limited is roaring down" (814, 818).

She addresses having to write within the context of tired readers who want their hearts lifted:

> I used to think it should be possible to write for some supposed elite . . . , but I have since found that though you may publish your stories in *Botteghe Oscure*, if they are any good at all, you are eventually going to get a letter from some old lady in California, or some inmate of the Federal Penitentiary, or the state insane asylum or the local poorhouse, telling you where you have failed to meet his needs.   (820)

Moreover, by her reference to writers from Dante to Hawthorne to Henry James and Wyndham Lewis (820, 818, 816, 819, 804), she implies her way into a literary context that sends its own signals to her readers. Students can be asked to examine her letters to see how they reflect her continuing attempt to construct her sense of context—especially the letter sent to fellow novelist and friend John Hawkes, who famously saw her as an unconscious member of the devil's party. Far from being offended, she responded to him, "You haven't convinced me" (1156), and in yet another letter to Hawkes she shows her willingness to leave her context in question: "People are always asking me if I am a Catholic writer and I am afraid that I sometimes say no and sometimes say yes, depending entirely on who the visitor is. Actually, the question seems so remote from what I am doing when I am doing it, that it doesn't bother me at all" (1109–10).

The diversity of O'Connor's attempts to contextualize her writing is something upper-level students can see mirrored in the critical discussion of her work. A reviewer of her first novel, *Wise Blood*, announced that "it reads as if Kafka had been set to writing the continuity for L'il Abner" ("Southern Dissonance" 20). Reviewing the same novel, Isaac Rosenfeld linked her to Faulkner and Carson McCullers (22), while Joe Lee Davis suggested that O'Connor was grafting Evelyn Waugh onto Erskine Caldwell while reading Raymond Chandler (24). Later southern scholars continued to struggle with her place in the southern literary tradition. In the mid-1970s, Walter Sullivan judged her work as damaged by spanning two contextual worlds, claiming, "After [1955] there were no more strictly southern stories" (61). For Sullivan, "the deterioration of myth and community" pushed her work outside the southern context to a more comic and Christian one (63). Lewis Simpson in his 1980 *The Brazen Face of History* argues for disconnecting O'Connor from the mainstream of southern modernism: "Flannery O'Connor suppresses the motive of the southern literary imagination known to Faulkner, Eudora Welty, and Warren: a tension between memory and history" (247). A decade later, both Thomas Hill Schaub and Jon Lance Bacon strove to examine O'Connor in the context of the Cold War, and in 2004 Teresa Caruso, building on such works as Louise Westling's *Sacred Groves and Ravaged Gardens*, edited a volume designed to view O'Connor through the context of feminism. Theological critics have honed or narrowed their context for understanding O'Connor—see, for example, the monographs by Susan Srigley (*Flannery O'Connor's Sacramental Art*) and by Ralph Wood (*Flannery O'Connor*).

Just what context best serves for understanding the fiction of O'Connor? What connections should students, like the Grandmother, be exercising all their wits to make? I would answer that all connections should be made. Any context will serve students, provided it does not distort or ignore the texts themselves. Our usual teaching agenda tries to prove that O'Connor belongs only to one context, one set of connections, but I would argue that students at all levels should come into contact with as many aspects of O'Connor's fiction as possible and that the nature of context itself should be examined. In this essay, I suggest taking advantage of O'Connor's relation to literary modernism.

Modernism is a hotly debated term, so instructors may have their own definitions of or approaches to it. Daniel Joseph Singal has written a relatively succinct, highly readable, and useful consideration of it in an article that focuses on modernism "as a full-fledged historical culture much like Victorianism or the

Enlightenment" and names "one of the foremost tendencies of Modernism" to be "the desire to heighten, savor and share all varieties of experience" ("Towards a Definition" 8, 11). His article has material useful for arguing that O'Connor's fiction should not be labeled modernist—something recent O'Connor scholars such as Farrell O'Gorman take almost for granted (6–9). But if, following Singal, modernism is considered a period, it becomes possible to lead students to see it also as a historical subject for O'Connor's fiction: one can see how broad and familiar generalizations about modernism are then embodied and treated by O'Connor.

Two common generalizations are Virginia Woolf's famous "in or about December, 1910, human character changed" ("Mr. Bennett" 320) and Willa Cather's equally broad "[t]he world broke in two in 1922 or thereabouts" (Prefatory Note). Both statements are seemingly simple declarations about modernism and frequently make an appearance in courses where modernism is discussed. But when read closely, both offer images of modernism that describe situations and conditions visible in O'Connor's fiction, and exploring them can both ignite a discussion of modernism and create an entrance into her fiction that places her work in relation to the literature that precedes and follows it.

After introducing the idea of context by encouraging a reading of the images and the language of connection in "A Good Man Is Hard to Find," instructors can lead students back to that story in the company of Woolf. If students are unfamiliar with Woolf, point out that this is the kind of startling move that O'Connor would surely have approved of—startling, since "A Good Man" consists more of stereotypes than of the kind of psychologically rich characterizations generally associated with the author of *Mrs. Dalloway*, characterizations that "record the atoms as they fall upon the mind in the order in which they fall" and see life as "a luminous halo, a semi-transparent envelope surrounding us from the beginning of consciousness to the end" (Woolf, "Modern Fiction" 107, 106). In contrast, O'Connor's sanctimonious Grandmother, psychotic killers, bratty children, and vacuous parents are drawn with broad and exaggerated lines.[2] But if O'Connor eschews the kind of delicate character development practiced by Woolf, she makes the crux of the story the Grandmother's confrontation with a changed human nature: the historical reality found in Woolf's generalization about the modernist era. The story provides students an opportunity to discuss how the idea of a changed human nature functions thematically in O'Connor's tale: to what extent are her characters aware of this change, and how does this awareness provide a way to evaluate them either with or without making use of traditional theological judgments? Discussion and lecture will likely lead students to find that in the Grandmother a simplistic and stable sense of the basic goodness of human beings is at work—an essentially Romantic view in opposition to that of modernism.

In the story's opening paragraph, the Grandmother is sure of the Misfit's character, telling Bailey, "I wouldn't take my children in any direction with a criminal like that aloose in it" (*Flannery . . . Works* 137). Yet, if such a statement suggests that she does not hold a rosy view of humanity, her failure to push her protest beyond words and her joining the family trip implies that her protestations are merely ploys to redirect the family trip northward, toward Tennessee rather than Florida. Once on the road, her soft chastisement of her grand-children reinforces this view: she sees their departure from the way children behaved "[i]n my time" as a lapse, not a true change of character; they can be steered back to the path of normalcy. When they see an African American child standing near the road, the Grandmother names him a "cute little pickaninny" and explains, "Little niggers in the country don't have things like we do" (139). She does not demonize African Americans but uses slurs that freeze any sense of character change. Even though she laments to Red Sammy that "[p]eople are certainly not nice like they used to be," her pronouncement that Red Sammy is "a good man" contradicts that claim (141, 142). If Red Sammy is as nice as people ever were, human character has not changed. Her assumption of good explains her efforts to attract the attention of the Misfit's "hearse-like automo-bile" when she spots it after their accident: surely these good people will help a family in distress (145). Even after the Misfit sends Bailey and John Wesley off to the woods to be murdered, the Grandmother insists, "I just know you're a good man" (148). She consistently fails to know and accept Woolf's claim about life in the modern age, that it has changed. But readers are shown the reality as O'Connor relentlessly records "the atoms [and bodies] as they fall" with all their "disconnected and incoherent . . . appearance" (Woolf, "Modern Fiction" 107).

After the instructor has demonstrated through discussion and lecture the ap-plication of Woolf's ideas to the grandmother, students can be directed to try a similar move with the Misfit through a short writing assignment or an essay on an exam. They should be able to discover that the story unfailingly stresses the Misfit's "disconnected and incoherent appearance" as well, though it follows a reverse trajectory from that given the grandmother. Although the grandmother has quite accurately labeled him as evil in the opening paragraph, he materializes in the tale more as a good Samaritan who stops to assist the car-wrecked family and addresses them with constant politeness even as the murdered bodies of an infant, children, and parents pile up in the woods to contradict his appearance. The Misfit is not a good man, and neither the Grandmother's insistence nor his mannerly speech will make him so. As a gentleman caller, a link to Tennessee Williams, whose work O'Connor disliked (*Flannery . . . Works* 974), he is worse than a disappointment; he is death. Whereas the Grandmother, in the context of Woolf's phrase defining modernity as a change of human character, is imagined as someone coming in contact with that change, Woolf's view also enables the Misfit to be read as a manifestation of the embodiment of that change.

Just how erratic this embodiment is becomes manifest in the meeting of these two individuals. O'Connor herself tries to direct the reader's view of it when she writes in a lecture:

> The Grandmother is at last alone, facing the Misfit. Her head clears for
> an instant and she realizes, even in her limited way, that she is responsible

for the man before her and joined to him by ties of kinship which have their roots deep in the mystery she has been merely prattling about so far. And at this point, she does the right thing, she makes the right gesture.
(*Mystery* 111–12)

She goes on to refer to this gesture as the story's "action of grace in the Grand-mother's soul" (113), so it is not surprising that critical opinion has tended to see the Grandmother's "instant" of clearheadedness, her murmur "Why you're one of my babies. You're one of my own children" (*Flannery . . . Works* 152), as denoting a salvational epiphany (see J. May 63; Giannone, *Flannery O'Connor and the Mystery* 52; Cofer 55–63). Yet reading in the context of Woolf's view of a character's change opens an additional dimension for students and makes the scene an entrance into the modern. This entrance has consequences; as Woolf also wrote, "And when human relations change there is at the same time a change in religion, conduct, politics, and literature" ("Mr. Bennett" 321). In this light, Woolf's sense of modernism does not contradict O'Connor's read-ing of her story but opens additional possibilities. Because Woolf refuses to characterize modernist change as inherently positive, stressing only its multiple impacts, the passage critics and O'Connor see as carrying the story's theological content can be read theologically or in purely secular terms: the instant of clear-headedness can be seen as a crystallization of the Grandmother's insistence on seeing human character as good, a confirming of her premodern sense of char-acter as unchanging—an attitude that is as dead as the Grandmother herself will be soon after she utters this line. Woolf's ideas allow the passage to remain a moment of judgment while expanding what the judgment can be.

In focusing on the term *change*, I have stressed a small part of Woolf's phrasing, but advanced students examining in more detail its source, the essay "Mr. Bennett and Mrs. Brown," will discover that such a stress is warranted. Woolf writes near the end of that essay:

> Your [the reader's] part is to insist that writers shall come down off their plinths and pedestals, and describe beautifully if possible, truthfully at any rate, our Mrs. Brown. You should insist that she is an old lady of unlimited capacity and infinite variety; capable of appearing in any place; wearing any dress; saying anything and doing heaven knows what. But the things she says and the things she does and her eyes and her nose and her speech and her silence have an overwhelming fascination, for she is, of course, the spirit we live by, life itself.
>
> But do not expect just at present a complete and satisfactory present-ment of her. Tolerate the spasmodic, the obscure, the fragmentary, the failure.   (336–37)

Whether or not O'Connor thought of herself as modernist—whether or not she belongs to that group—seeing the story in the context of Woolfian modernism creates insights into its two main characters while emphasizing the story's chiasmic structure, which begins with the Grandmother—a static, Romantic protagonist—and then supplants her with the Misfit, a dynamic and complex character well described by Woolf's modifiers: "spasmodic," "obscure," "fragmentary," "failure." The Misfit's about-face in the story's final sentence makes sense now. Having previously proclaimed, "No pleasure but meanness" (*Flannery . . . Works* 152), he lurches to a different position, whose tone is far less declamatory, far more provisional.

This vacillation is in sync with the pessimism of World War I literature and culture that William Barrett sees defined by "a rage to destroy, as if the culture itself were bent on working toward conclusions that destroy its own premises" (23). O'Connor, however, created a disconnect when she explained her reading of the Misfit's last line in remarks that Sally and Robert Fitzgerald shaped into the essay "On Her Own Work":

> I don't want to equate the Misfit with the devil. I prefer to think that, however unlikely this may seem, the old lady's gesture, like the mustard-seed, will grow to be a great crow-filled tree in the Misfit's heart, and will be enough of a pain to him there to turn him into the prophet he was meant to become.   (*Mystery* 112–13)

In a letter to Hawkes, she echoes this view: "The Misfit is touched by the Grace that comes through the old lady" (*Habit* 389). Students need not accept her interpretation as gospel truth, but these statements underscore the point that modernism is present in her work. "A Good Man" dramatizes the move to modernism not by recording the personal psychological workings of the characters but by observing the disruptive arrival of its change enacted on a very small stage. In this way, O'Connor is able, in Frederick Crews's words, to "[cast] a cold eye on the whole modern world, whose recent cataclysms are just what it deserves . . . for having taken up with the Enlightenment's fatal substitution of reason for revelation" (157).

Advanced students can be encouraged to go beyond Woolf and deal with Cather's comment on modernism, that "[t]he world broke in two in 1922 or thereabouts." This comment is relevant to O'Connor's fiction in a way that Woolf's statements are not, in its image of breaking. Students should almost immediately notice the difference in the two authors' selection of dates for the advent of modernism and observe that Cather offers no explanation for her choice of 1922. Either through lecture or assignment, students can speculate whether Cather had in mind the publication of *The Waste Land* or *Ulysses*.[3] However, the geographic location of Woolf and Cather may explain the difference in their date for the birth of modernism: America—especially outside the centers of culture—was delayed in getting the news. An instructor may wish to link this delay to such historical facts as Robert Frost's inability to launch successfully his poetic project before he left North America for England in 1912,[4] as well as Eliot's rise in poetic circles only after he was living in England. Such thinking should be seen as in line with Singal's sense of modernism as an era, one that need not show up around the globe at the same moment but rather dawns slowly in various locales.

Students should explore the historical context of modernism in the South, a region that research suggests was particularly slow to modernize. David Minter writes:

> During the late nineteenth and early twentieth centuries, when for the nation at large being an "almost chosen people" seemed clearly to mean being chosen for wealth and power, the South made small gains and yet fell farther behind. By 1929 it was in large part a land of hominy grits and hookworms, sharecroppers and subsistence farmers, moonshine whiskey and feuding clans, cultural backwardness and a strict and often brutal system of racial segregation. When, infrequently, the larger nation paused to think about the subject, it regarded the South as an embarrassment. (205)

Focusing on Georgia during a time nearer to O'Connor's settings and dates of composition, Numan V. Bartley asserts that, despite such surface signs of modernization as increased urbanization and "turbulent change," "significant currents of continuity" remained. In particular, he notes that because "the family and the church survived the transition from farm to city with many basic values intact," "the achievement of the civil rights movement's integrationist goals was necessarily limited." He quotes Charles P. Roland on this last point: "The vast majority of the members of the two races lived as far apart in the 1970s as they had in the 1940s. Possibly they lived further apart" (375).

If students do additional historical research or put together a time line for literary modernism in the South, they will discover such facts as that the Fugitives out of Vanderbilt University burst forth in 1922, and the group lasted only three years as a coherent body. Of that group, Allen Tate did not publish his best-known example of southern modernism, "Ode to the Confederate Dead," until 1928. William Faulkner's *The Sound and the Fury* did not appear until 1929, the same year that saw Thomas Wolfe's *Look Homeward, Angel*, with much of the central writing of the Southern Renaissance—the southern stronghold of modernist writing—appearing in the 1930s and 1940s.

This late arrival of modernism is present in O'Connor's stories, especially in "A View of the Woods." If students, either individually or in groups, are asked to survey some of the scholarship on the story, they will find that scholars have generally focused on the doubling device in it (e.g., Asals, *Flannery O'Connor: The Imagination* 69–70, 99–102) or on its religious images and ideas (e.g., Giannone, *Flannery O'Connor and the Mystery* 175–81; Desmond 70–73). Nevertheless, the basic details of the story support reading it in the context of modernism. Its conflict arises from Mark Fortune's self-assigned mission to wrench his rustic world into the modern age, opening on a scene in which an unnamed "machine" "systematically ate a square red hole in what had once been a cow pasture" (*Flannery . . . Works* 525). For Mr. Fortune, the land's owner, this is "Progress" and "improvement" as well as revenge on people like his son-in-law, who "would let a cow pasture or a mule lot or a row of beans interfere with progress" (527, 528). But progress here is ironized: it's the construction of a "fishing club" (525) on lake lots for the escape of southern urbanites and a gas station to fuel that escape (533)—in other words, a fleeing of the urban and industrial for a temporary retreat into rusticity.

Race relations, a useful measuring rod for social progress in the South, remain oddly static in "A View of the Woods." Mr. Fortune answers complaints by his beloved granddaughter, Mary Fortune Pitts, with words that indicate a clear separation of the races: "And I'm a Poland china pig and black is white!" (531) and "And black is white . . . and night is day!" (531, 533). Tilman's store "was divided into two sections, Colored and White, each with its private nickelodeon" (535). The only African American character to appear is a "Negro boy, drinking a purple drink . . . sitting on the ground with his back against the sweating ice cooler" (536)—a stereotyped image of idleness juxtaposed to the hardworking machine. First published in the fall of 1957, this story is set decades later than Cather's 1922, but read in conjunction with Cather, it supports a view of modernism as existing over a range of time and place—an insight that will allow students to be creative in their literary analysis and expand their understanding of modernism.

Cather's image of the effect of modernism, a world broken in two, is also useful for helping students explore the complex images of the closing paragraphs of O'Connor's story. When his ten-year-old granddaughter physically assaults the seventy-nine-year-old Mr. Fortune, they end up on the ground, "her face exactly on top of his." That they visually form a split globe is emphasized when Fortune "managed to roll over and reverse their positions." In their struggle, Mr. Fortune and his granddaughter form a two-part world, only to have the text add a horrific image of brokenness: "With his hand still tight around her neck, he lifted her head and brought it down once hard against the rock that happened to be under it. Then he brought it down twice more" (*Flannery . . . Works* 545).

In his anger and insistence on the modern, Mr. Fortune has not only broken apart the unified planet he and his granddaughter formed at the story's start but also the globe of his granddaughter's head, murdering her in a logical climax to their growing separation over the issue of selling the part of his farm that the Pittses think of as theirs. The story's conclusion reinforces the idea of a splitting earth:

> . . . the old man felt as if he were being pulled . . . through the woods, felt as if he were running as fast as he could with the ugly pines toward the lake. He perceived that there would be a little opening there, a little place where he could escape and leave the woods behind him. He could see it in the distance already, a little opening where the white sky was reflected

in the water. It grew as he ran toward it until suddenly the whole lake opened up before him, riding majestically in little corrugated folds toward his feet. He realized suddenly that he could not swim and that he had not bought the boat. On both sides of him he saw that the gaunt trees had thickened into mysterious dark files that were marching across the water and away into the distance. He looked around desperately for someone to help him but the place was deserted except for one huge yellow monster which sat to the side, as stationary as he was, gorging itself on clay. (546)

In these surrealistic dream images, students should be able to hear an echo of Cather's world breaking. The break is seen from the inside, with Mr. Fortune running out of the woods into the sunshine of the lake where he will surely drown, attended only by a creature-machine whose function is to break the earth. If from the typical theological perspective this can be seen as a baptismal trope of death as part of the birth into a new life, it can also be read as a record of Mr. Fortune's sense of being born into a true modernism—that is, of being broken in two. That O'Connor narrates this break as a series of sensations existing only in Mr. Fortune's mind implies her focus is on how it felt to enter modernism. She supplies a register of the emotional toll caused by modernism's arrival in her region.

Read without Cather's image of modernism, the story could also stand as a conservative defense of agrarianism. But using Cather's image suggests something further. Mr. Fortune and his eventual nemesis, Mary Fortune, are united in the story's opening pages in their celebration of the machine's devouring of the land. When they diverge, it is not over the loss of a rural, agricultural environment to urban development but over the loss of the family's "lawn" (532)—a term more associated with urban than rural life. The story's true agronomist, Mr. Pitts, is a sadistic figure, "a man of a nasty temper and of ugly unreasonable resentments" who beats his daughter with a belt in response to his anger and frustration with Mr. Fortune (529). The story may paint Tilman, the man to whom Mr. Fortune sells the lawn, as a snakelike and therefore satanic figure (542), yet this Lucifer is relatively passive. If O'Connor intended her story to be part of what Mark McGurl labels her "project of unconventionally intense conventionality, conventionality radicalized and thus recoded as reactionary critique" (531), she makes a mess of it.

Cather's idea of modernism creates a context in which we see the story as breaking all conventions, even those associated with literary modernism. It suggests that O'Connor's fiction is engaging modernism without strenuous concern for adhering to any particular literary method. Is such an engagement intentional? The case for intentionality is hard to make.[5]

Nevertheless, as teachers who want our students not only to gain a better knowledge of literary authors but also to think creatively about literary periodization, literature's place in social movements, and the conversation that literary works create with each other, using modernism to open up O'Connor's texts and add to the ways they can be understood is fruitful. Jeff Wallace in his introductory study of modernism offers a pedagogical "gambit": *"modernism is the moment at which art stops making sense"* (3). If instructors find this gambit attractive, let them use it to show students how writers like O'Connor, writing in the wake of modernism's solidifying stature in the canon, brought the work of modernism into their writing even when they resisted modernist ideology and techniques. Some classes may even elect to explore how these writers' engagements with modernism contributed to their success in entering the canon, how using the context of modernism created the literature that followed it.

NOTES

[1] Christina Bieber Lake makes a strong anti-Bloom argument (2–3, 39–40).

[2] In her essay "The Fiction Writer and His Country," O'Connor writes about the need "to make your vision apparent by shock—to the hard of hearing you shout, and for the almost blind you draw large and startling figures" (*Flannery . . . Works* 805–06). She constructed this dictum in late 1956 for an arts festival lecture at Wesleyan College in Macon (Manuscripts [folder 238a 7])—well after the writing of "A Good Man."

[3] Michael North has discussed the importance of 1922 to modernism in great detail in his *Reading 1922*, including a discussion of Cather's sense of distance and her "stern antimodernism" (173). Yet Cather's published letters make no reference to James Joyce, *Ulysses*, or *The Waste Land*. The only reference to Eliot is in a 1937 letter to Zoltan Engel, who asked her if she was interested in a medallion of Rudyard Kipling. Cather answered, "I am led to believe that just at present most colleges would be more interested in a portrait medallion of Mr. T. S. Eliot!" (*Selected Letters* 527). Her biographers have made few connections to Joyce and Eliot. James Woodress, in his discussion of her novel *One of Ours*, notes it appeared the same year as *The Waste Land* but asserts, "There is no influence of one work on the other" (329). He also mentions that a reviewer of *Not under Forty* tied Cather to Eliot in a way negative to Cather (474). For a thematic discussion of Eliot and Cather, see Newstrom; Jabbur.

[4] John Evangelist Walsh offers one of the best discussions of Frost's reasons for leaving the United States for a two-year sojourn in England. He explains that Frost's motivations were complicated and not completely clear (29–33), but it is obvious that Frost saw the move as necessary to advance his poetic project.

[5] Kinney reports that O'Connor had three books by Woolf in her personal library (15, 165), including a copy of *Mrs. Dalloway* that O'Connor signed and a copy of *Hours in a Library*, a work that deals, in part, with one of O'Connor's favorite subjects: the average reader. But O'Connor's limited and largely negative comments about Woolf in her letters fail to suggest a significant connection between the two writers (see *Habit* 98, 109, 451). Both her essays and collected letters show no sign of Cather, although Cather wrote one of the best-known novels on Catholicism: *Death Comes for the Archbishop*. At the same time, O'Connor reviewed a number of books discussing the self-defined modern. These reviews are found in *The Presence of Grace*. The seven book titles there dealing with the modern are *The Metamorphic Tradition in Modern Poetry*, by Sister Bernetta Quinn (31–32); *Christian Asceticism and Modern Man*, edited by Louis Bouyer (71–72); *The Modernity of St. Augustine*, by Jean Guitton (90–91); *Modern Catholic Thinkers*, edited

by A. Robert Caponigri (103–04); *Evidence of Satan in the Modern World*, by Leon Christiani (139–40); *Seeds of Hope in the Modern World*, by Barry Ulanov (157–59); and *The Modern God*, by Gustave Weigel (162–63). I make no claims for the idea of the modern or modernism in any of these works, but O'Connor's reviews of them do suggest her interest in the concept.

Restoring Connections:
An Interdisciplinary Perspective on *Wise Blood*

Jon Lance Bacon

As she herself was acutely aware, Flannery O'Connor is not the easiest author for students to understand. In 1961, she famously—and rather curtly—reprimanded a group of English professors and undergraduates for their "fantastic" misinterpretation of "A Good Man Is Hard to Find" (*Habit* 437). The problem derives in part from her literary strategy: her decision to "shout" at her readers, making her vision "apparent by shock" (*Flannery . . . Works* 805–06). This strategy produced fiction that is intense and unforgettable, but also, for many students, more than a little disorienting.

Of all her works, perhaps the most jarring is *Wise Blood*. The 1952 novel features a superabundance of shocking actions, from murder to self-mutilation, performed by its protagonist, Hazel Motes. At first glance, these actions seem rooted exclusively in his religious obsessions: an odd, unprecedented mixture of evangelical Protestantism and medieval Catholicism. Even to students who identify themselves as Christian, Hazel can be a puzzling character, with bewildering motivations. To students from other religious traditions, or those with no religious leanings, he can seem completely opaque.

In *Wise Blood*, O'Connor intentionally violates "a novelistic orthodoxy" by ignoring the "connections which we would expect in the customary kind of realism" (*Flannery . . . Works* 814, 815). The instructor who plans to teach her novel needs to restore these connections, giving students a way into the text that recognizes its social and cultural context. This approach does not mean discounting the religious aspects of the work; the instructor, instead, should ground them in historical terms that students can readily appreciate. Before we address the issues of belief and unbelief that obsess Hazel, I ask students to consider the literal situation in which he finds himself at the beginning of the narrative. He is first and foremost a soldier returning from war—specifically, World War II. This fact can serve as the basis for an interdisciplinary discussion, incorporating other cultural representations of veterans in the years immediately following the war, the years in which O'Connor was writing her novel.[1] Apprised of the parallels between these representations and the character of Hazel, students should find his actions more comprehensible.

To prepare students for such a discussion, I have them read a set of excerpts from *The Veteran Comes Back* (1944) by Willard Waller, a prominent sociologist at Columbia University. With the end of the war in sight, Waller predicted the consequences of massive demobilization, describing the millions of new veterans as "Our Gravest Social Problem" (6). His description may sound curious, coming at a time when veterans would soon be celebrated nationwide for their victory over the Axis powers. Waller was not alone, however, in his views regarding ex-servicemen. There was considerable anxiety over their ability to make a successful transition from combat to civilian life. In 1945, David A. Gerber observes, Americans had "a sharply divided consciousness that both honored the veteran and feared his potential to disrupt society" (70). According to social workers and other experts, the veteran was vulnerable to a wide range of problems, including anger, alcoholism, and mental instability (72–76). Most disturbingly, the experts warned, he could be prone to violent behavior, even homicide. The reason for this was obvious to Waller: "The soldier must kill, must make a study of the art of killing, and overcome all his inbred repugnance to the taking of life. Perhaps he comes to enjoy killing." If the "mental shocks" of warfare could lead to crime, so could the veteran's alienation from the "controls" of civilian life (124). "The veteran is dangerous to society," Waller wrote, "not only because he is embittered but because . . . he lacks a stake in the social order" (186). The question, clearly, was whether the veteran would find his place in that order—whether he could reconnect with the life he had left behind.

The definitive response to the question—the response with the greatest cultural currency, that is—came from Hollywood. Before the war had even ended, studios began developing films about returning servicemen. The most acclaimed, and certainly the most famous, is *The Best Years of Our Lives*, which won the Academy Award for Best Picture of 1946. For purposes of class discussion, though, I have the students watch a similar film, *Till the End of Time*, released the same year.[2] Both films follow a trio of World War II veterans as they struggle to reconnect with their families and communities, but *Till the End of Time* has clearer parallels with *Wise Blood*. Its main protagonist, an ex-Marine named Cliff Harper (Guy Madison), has much in common with Hazel—in terms of action as well as characterization.

To initiate class discussion, I ask students to consider a key scene in the novel and the film: the moment of homecoming. In each case, the veteran's return home is disappointing, to say the least. Hazel finds no one waiting for him, all his relatives having died. His childhood home is empty, an abandoned "shell" that offers neither comfort nor security; he sleeps on the floor in the kitchen, where a board falls from the roof and cuts him (*Flannery . . . Works* 13). Cliff likewise returns to an empty house. Though his parents are away only temporarily, he describes his homecoming as "kind of spooky." Later on, when Cliff and his parents are reunited, he still feels emotionally separated from them. His mother refuses to discuss the most pivotal events in his life, namely, his combat experiences. The first time he mentions the war, Mrs. Harper (Ruth Nelson) cuts him off: "Don't talk about it, Cliff. I know you don't want to talk about it."

The parallel between the homecomings in *Wise Blood* and *Till the End of Time* leads naturally to the subject of alienation, the feeling of social isolation that afflicts both Hazel and Cliff. The disappointment experienced by Hazel, for instance, extends beyond his family home; Eastrod, his hometown, is empty as well. During his four years in the army, all his neighbors died or moved elsewhere. As a result, he finds himself adrift, with "no place to go" (15). Having lost his family and his community, he doesn't really care where he ends up. "You might as well go one place as another," he says (6). Cliff is equally adrift, noting that "I feel out of things." He describes himself as "edgy" and "lonesome," lost in postwar society: "A lot of things don't make sense." Without any plans for the future, he goes from one unfulfilling job to another. "It's me that's wrong," he laments. "I guess I just don't fit anyplace yet." Quite literally, the film presents Cliff as a misfit: on the day he comes home, he changes out of his uniform and discovers that his old civilian clothes are too small for him.

At some point during the discussion of alienation, students are bound to mention another important parallel between *Wise Blood* and *Till the End of Time*. In both works, veterans are not just emotionally isolated but also physically disabled. Hazel was wounded in combat, in his chest, and he feels as if the shrapnel were "still in there, rusted, and poisoning him" (12). The wound has left him with a permanent disability: "He got money from the government every month for something the war had done to his insides" (120). Cliff is physically unharmed—or "lucky," as he calls himself—but his two close friends from the Marine Corps have serious disabilities. Bill Tabeshaw (Robert Mitchum) suffered a severe head wound, necessitating a silver plate that causes constant pain. "My head—it's busting wide open," Bill tells Cliff. "Always this pressure—it's like clamps on my skull." Perry Kincheloe (Bill Williams) is a double amputee, and, like Bill, he suffers extreme physical pain, complaining that his artificial legs "murder" him. Compounding his pain is an overwhelming sense of despair: "You've no idea what a feeling I get, letting my mother look at me like this. I get sick in my stomach when she has to help me in the chair—when she has to lift me back in the bed. I'm twenty-one, and I'm dead." Students will undoubtedly pick up on Waller's assertion that the disabled veteran is "more emotionally intense and unstable than other veterans" (161). He is, as Waller puts it bluntly, "the bitterest veteran" (159).

Not surprisingly, such bitterness culminates in violence in both the film and the novel. Cliff, Bill, and Perry get into a bar fight with other ex-servicemen—the members of a racist veterans organization—while Hazel commits acts of escalating brutality. At first the violence in *Wise Blood* seems harmless, even comical: Hazel hits Enoch with a stack of religious tracts. The next time he hits Enoch, however, he uses a rock. Finally, he uses his car to kill Solace Layfield. He commits the murder coldly, methodically, like a trained killer—which, of course, he is. Warfare has changed him in the very way described by Waller. Before the war, Hazel shows no sign of being violent toward others. In fact, he considers harming himself, shooting himself in the foot, to avoid combat. After the war, killing comes easily to him. With a face "like a gun no one knows is loaded" (37), he seems to personify deadly violence.

Students are likely to note that warfare has also affected Hazel's relationships with women. Before his time in combat, he never went to a brothel; as he tells his fellow recruits during training, he wouldn't go "for a million dollars and a feather bed to lie on" (12). After he returns from the war, he frequents the home of a prostitute, Mrs. Leora Watts. His meaningless encounters with her will surely remind students of Waller's observation regarding the veteran's sexual proclivities: still hearing "the fevered pulse of war" and believing that he lives on "borrowed time," the veteran seeks out "furtive amourettes with quick and easy women" (128).

By the same token, Hazel's interaction with Sabbath Lily Hawks affords the opportunity to discuss a widespread concern about gender relations in postwar America. During the war, American women made significant gains in economic independence and sexual freedom—a worrisome development for many social commentators. As *Wise Blood* conveys the fear of dangerous veterans, so it reflects this anxiety about newly liberated women. Sabbath Lily personifies the troubling idea that the war had weakened the morals of American girls, making them sexually precocious. Though identified consistently as a "child," Sabbath is anything but the "innocent" youth that Hazel believes her to be (62). She is, at fifteen, one of the postwar teenagers Waller describes as "a disorganized generation," a group with "an unusual percentage" of female "sexual delinquents" (84). Aggressive and amoral, Sabbath tries repeatedly to seduce the clueless Hazel. She is certain of her sexual appeal, which she explains in a letter to Mary Brittle, the advice columnist: "I have this personality that makes boys follow me" (67). In actuality, Sabbath follows Hazel everywhere, forcing him "to protect himself" from her advances (82). When she sneaks into his room, wearing a nightgown, he drives her away with a chair. Later, she waits for Hazel in his bed, and she tells him she likes being bad, "just pure filthy right down to the guts" (95).

Students should have no trouble spotting similarities between Sabbath Lily Hawks and Helen Ingersoll (Jean Porter), a college freshman who lives next door to Cliff and his parents. Like Sabbath, Helen embodies an unsettling combination of childishness and sexual precocity. The first time we see her, she seems too young to be attending college: she wears her hair as a little girl would, in a pair of long braids tied with ribbons, and she keeps referring, in her high-pitched voice, to what "Daddy says." Despite her childish appearance, Helen flirts aggressively with Cliff, making a series of suggestive remarks. When he asks whether she has ideas of her own, apart from Daddy, she eyes Cliff up and down and says, "Oh, for a returning Marine, I've got some super ideas." To make sure he doesn't miss her point, she arches her eyebrow on the last word. In later scenes, she pursues Cliff as ardently as Sabbath pursues Hazel. She sends her boyfriend on an errand, for instance, so she can get Cliff alone; as they sit together on a garden swing, she scoots closer and assures him, "I'm not so young." In reality, the actress playing Helen was several years older than the character, adding to the sense of precociousness.[3]

Male anxiety about female sexuality extends even to the character with whom Cliff falls in love, a war widow named Pat Ruscomb (Dorothy McGuire). When he sees a tipsy Pat return from a date and kiss another man, Cliff gets angry and calls her a "tramp." The filmmakers, to their credit, side with Pat here. After storming off, Cliff comes back to apologize. Eventually, he overcomes his doubts about Pat's moral fiber, deciding he wants to spend the rest of his life with her. His decision, I would stress, represents a major step toward social reconnection. For Cliff, Pat plays the role assigned to women by Waller and other experts on the "problem" of the veteran: the supportive mate who helps him readjust to civilian life. As Gerber notes, these experts, mostly male, advised women "to devote themselves to the domestication of the returning men" (74). To quote Waller, Pat helps Cliff "find his bearings again" (288). At the end of the film, he says he is finally "all right," adding that "I'm going to *stay* all right." The closing shot has Cliff and Pat embracing, the background music swelling as they kiss. They will be together, as the title of the film suggests, "till the end of time."

At this point, class discussion of the film and the novel could turn from similarities to differences. Obviously, Hazel does not get a romantic Hollywood ending with Sabbath Lily. The sexual delinquent, ill-equipped for the role of helpmate, ends up in a house of detention (121). Whereas Cliff finds "a good job" that enables him to settle down with Pat, Hazel remains unemployed, deprived of any stabilizing social influence. Unlike Cliff, he fails to secure a place in postwar society. Beset with the "demoniacal restlessness" that Waller attributes to returning veterans (127–28), Hazel is more attached to his car than to the people of Taulkinham. Toward the end of the novel, he decides "to move immediately to some other city," where he can "make a new start with nothing on his mind" (*Flannery . . . Works* 105).

Talking through the differences between *Wise Blood* and *Till the End of Time*, we soon arrive at the most significant contrast: Hazel's alienation has a religious dimension that is wholly absent from Cliff's. To describe his sense of displacement, Hazel uses biblical terms. "In yourself right now is all the place you've got," he tells his listeners on the street. "If there was any Fall, look there, if there was any Redemption, look there, and if you expect any Judgment, look there, because they all three will have to be in your time and your body . . ." (93). The biblical language harks back to his childhood, when his grandfather traveled three counties preaching Christian fundamentalism and Hazel planned to become a preacher himself. Wartime service put an end to his plan, turning him into an atheist: "He had all the time he could want to study his soul in and assure himself that it was not there." In this respect, he follows the lead of his fellow soldiers, who "told him he didn't have any soul" (12).

Students should be informed that O'Connor started writing *Wise Blood* in 1946, at a state university teeming with recently demobilized soldiers.[4] According to one of her biographers, the veterans she met in the Iowa Writers' Workshop "had absolutely no interest in the religious faith that was so dear to O'Connor" (M. Simpson 10). This observation is quite relevant to an interdisciplinary discussion of *Wise Blood*, in that Waller makes a similar statement regarding World War II veterans, describing them as "overwhelmingly indifferent to religion" (69).

In his own attitude toward religion, Hazel goes well beyond indifference, attacking belief at every turn. As fiercely as he promotes his atheism, however, he retains the religious forms of his past. When he throws away his army uniform, stuffing it in the trash, he replaces it with a suit and hat appropriate for a fundamentalist preacher. Even when he seems to be "going forward after something," he is really moving backward: his failure to connect with postwar society pushes him toward the faith of his childhood (*Flannery . . . Works* 120–21). To demonstrate this point, I bring up the manner in which he punishes himself at the end of the novel. Specifically, I ask students where he gets the idea to put stones in his shoes. Attentive readers will recall that he did the same thing in Eastrod, in his youth, as a way to "satisfy" God (36).

Ultimately, the "longing for home" that Hazel feels as a displaced veteran is a longing for the faith that once united his family and community. He may think his "misery" has "nothing to do with Jesus" (13), but O'Connor suggests otherwise. By making his emotional struggle explicitly religious, she reframes the cultural depiction of the returning soldier. The instructor teaching *Wise Blood* would do well to start with this depiction. Students will feel freer to participate in a classroom discussion that doesn't foreground theological concepts like the Fall, redemption, and judgment. Regardless of their religious views, they will be more invested in the novel and, as a result, less inclined to dismiss it as some kind of literary freak. Having identified the connections between *Wise Blood* and contemporaneous works, they will come to see Hazel's story as part of a larger cultural conversation—one to which O'Connor makes an extraordinary contribution.

NOTES

[1] For a different perspective on Hazel's identity as a veteran, see a recent essay by Stacey Peebles, who argues that *Wise Blood* dramatizes the psychological impact of military service. Instead of focusing on the period after World War II, she offers a more general analysis, linking the novel with war narratives from the 1890s to the 1990s.

[2] Students interested in watching *The Best Years of Our Lives* would benefit from reading Gerber, whose take on the character of Homer Parrish (Harold Russell) is astute and enlightening. For additional viewing, I recommend *The Men* (1950), which deals with the same issues as the two earlier films. What's more, it features the screen debut of Marlon Brando, who plays a paraplegic veteran.

[3] A year before she played Helen Ingersoll, Jean Porter appeared in a lightweight comedy, *Twice Blessed*, that also voices fears about juvenile delinquency in the aftermath of war. "Our children are running wild," says one of the characters in *Twice Blessed*, an expert on child psychology. "Reports from welfare authorities are alarming. Shall we permit our sons and daughters to frequent jukebox rendezvous and public dance halls?"

[4] The G. I. Bill of Rights, passed in 1944, gave millions of American veterans the chance to attend college after the war. The bill provided various forms of financial assistance to address the readjustment issues delineated by Waller and other social commentators.

Teaching O'Connor with Science and Technology Studies

Doug Davis

When I teach Flannery O'Connor, the following question inevitably arises: Why are her stories so violent and grotesque? More often than not, my literature students are surprised to learn that one answer lies in the history of science and technology. In this essay I discuss how I teach my students a critical vocabulary drawn from the field of science and technology studies (STS) that empowers them to be close critical readers and astute historicists of O'Connor's fiction.

STS is a diverse interdisciplinary field of study whose practitioners use the analytic tools of the humanities (such as literary criticism and critical theory, discursive and rhetorical analysis, and cultural studies) and of the human sciences (especially history, sociology, and anthropology) to situate science in culture and produce new understandings of both scientific development and technological practice. STS scholars variously study the relation of scientific knowledge to technological and social systems; the roles of language, representation, and ideology in the sciences; the ways that science and technology form the modern subject; the culture of laboratory communities; and the politics of scientific knowledge and technology. STS scholars accordingly offer new, revised histories of science and technology as encultured, socially situated practices. They also propose new methods of socially, politically, and environmentally self-conscious technoscientific research and development. In the model lesson plans that follow, I show how concepts drawn from STS enable students to analyze O'Connor's fiction as representing the technocultural forces transforming life in her era.

Because many literature students come to O'Connor knowing one thing—that she is a religious writer—I like to begin by assigning an essay that allows me to connect the author's views on religion with her views on technology, "Some Aspects of the Grotesque in Southern Fiction." In this essay, she laments how readers in our era of scientific realism have blinkered vision because they have been trained "since the 18th century" to ignore the mystery of spirituality. Americans in particular believe that "the ills and mysteries of life will eventually fall before the scientific advances of man" (*Flannery . . . Works* 815). She explains that the violence and grotesques in her stories are her way of "forc[ing]" her modern characters to "meet evil and grace and . . . act on a trust beyond themselves" (816). Her tormented modern characters thus demonstrate the limits of technocultural optimism and ask readers to put their faith in spirituality as much as in science and technology. For O'Connor, to be a writer of faith in the modern era requires always grappling with the relations of science, technology, and spirituality.

Once students understand O'Connor's project, they are ready to explore the literary techniques she uses to enact it. Returning to "Aspects," I direct them to her repeated description of herself as a "realist of distances" who explores the spiritual mysteries that reside behind the concrete details of daily life (817, 819). While her ultimate subject may be spirituality, O'Connor believes that modern characters—and modern readers—must connect with the mysteries of the spirit precisely by connecting with the real, everyday technocultural situations and things that shape their lives. I ask my students to consider the following passage from another O'Connor essay, "The Nature and Aim of Fiction," which contains one of her few public comments on her era's most violent and grotesque technology:

> The longer you look at one object, the more of the world you see in it; and it's well to remember that the serious fiction writer always writes about the whole world, no matter how limited his particular scene. For him, the bomb that was dropped on Hiroshima affects life on the Oconee River, and there's not anything he can do about it.   (*Mystery* 77)

My class discussions reveal that students know little about the atomic bomb, from its science to the psychology of it. Wrapped in national security, the bomb for most people is as mysterious as the soul. Its radiological effects are unseen. Its economic costs are incalculable. Its psychic toll is immeasurable. Its science is arcane. The bomb is as much a part of the mystery of everyday life as the other things that O'Connor writes about, such as illness, pride, cruelty, and murder.

Once students understand that modern technologies are as mysterious and compelling to O'Connor as religion, they are ready to begin learning a critical terminology drawn from science and technology studies that will help them read her fiction as a record of what her region and the rest of the world were becoming. I introduce my students to STS by assigning them the first two chapters of Bruno Latour's *We Have Never Been Modern*, "Crisis" and "Constitution," in which Latour develops his critique of modernity. I pair these two chapters with O'Connor's "The Nature and Aim of Fiction," which contains her critique of modernity. I use the two chapters from Latour to teach students both STS's new critical vocabulary, such as *hybrids* and *networks*, and also Latour's concept of "the modern constitution," the modern, disciplinary habit of mind that treats nature, society, and divinity as wholly separate worlds (13).

Before beginning my class discussion of Latour, I ask the literature students what they think nature and culture are and to provide examples of both. Chances are they will think like Latour's moderns and come up with binary lists, citing such things as books and beliefs as examples of culture and rocks and scientific theories as examples of nature. After coming up with these lists, we discuss what all those things have in common. Aren't books the products of science and engineering? Where does literary culture end and book technology begin? And aren't rocks described in not only geology textbooks but also in "A Good Man Is Hard to Find" (*Flannery . . . Works* 138)? Where does the literary rock end and the natural rock begin?

Questions such as these are not easy to answer, students find. They may refer to the different disciplines of the sciences and humanities that focus exclusively on rocks or books, assuming that the divisions of the academy reflect real divisions in nature. Once students start responding as disciplinary thinkers, I introduce them to Latour's interdisciplinary concept of the modern constitution. Latour argues that the sciences and technology connect people to natural forces and things in new ways through a process he calls translation. Every artifact, device, and expert technique is part of vast networks of nature and culture stemming from the constant interaction of human beings and nonhuman beings. The true state of our modern world, Latour concludes, is hybridity. But through a cultural process he calls purification, our modern understandings of nature and culture are predicated on discourses in both the sciences and the humanities that ignore the networks and hybrids that make up the modern world, treating science and culture, along with the human, the nonhuman, and the divine as entirely separate things. Modernity thus speedily creates more and more of what Latour calls "monsters"—unaccountable hybrid assemblages of natural processes and social institutions, such as the ozone hole over the Antarctic—precisely because moderns do not take the time to problematize the interrelation of the social order and the natural order (42–43).

Drawing special attention to section 2.9 of *We Have Never Been Modern*, "The Crossed-Out God," I discuss with students the provocative resonances between Latour's analysis of the modern constitution and O'Connor's critique of "the modern spirit" (*Mystery* 68), which treats the world as if "grace and nature have been separated" (82). How closely, I ask my students, can we align Latour's and O'Connor's critiques of modernity? I direct them in particular to O'Connor's observation in "The Nature and Aim of Fiction" that modern culture is scientistically obsessed with "problems, not . . . people," resulting in a compartmentalized modern literature that ignores both everyday details and the presence of the supernatural: "all those concrete details of life that make actual the mystery of our position on earth" (68).

I ask students to apply Latour's insights about the networked, hybrid nature of modern society to O'Connor's violent and grotesque stories by focusing on the technological and hybrid imagery O'Connor uses to describe the modernizing South. As Patricia Yeager reminds us in her study of southern women's writing, *Dirt and Desire*, O'Connor's violent and grotesque imagery represents in a coded way her region's changing social and political circumstances (25–32). If Latour is correct that modernity is an unchecked, unaccountable process of creating monstrous, society-transforming networks of hybrids, then O'Connor's grotesque and violent characters and situations can be read as representing the increasing, sometimes violent hybridization of the American South in her day. I ask students to keep track of all the technologically augmented and mechanically adroit characters they encounter in her stories. I also ask them to record all the fusions—literal and figurative, helpful and fatal—between animals, machines, and people they find in those stories. The result can be long lists of mechanics, farmers, and philosophers who are variously run over by tractors, gored by bulls, and conned out of everything from their cars to their artificial limbs. O'Connor's fiction, students learn through this exercise, is full of hybrids. I then ask my students to read her many hybrids through the terms of Latour's analysis, exploring how many of them can be described as specifically modern people or modern problems. The hybrid monsters of modernity that Latour identifies find their grotesque expression in many of the characters and situations with which O'Connor fills her pages. The procession of grotesquely and often violently fused, penetrated, wounded, and augmented bodies in her stories represents what she — much like Latour — believes to be the condition of modernity.

Having introduced my students to the critical language of STS and shown them how Latour's concept of the hybrid can illuminate O'Connor's violent and grotesque literary craft, I turn to a series of lessons that foreground the role of science and technology in her stories. In the model lesson plans that follow, I show how students use STS to analyze O'Connor's grotesque characters and violent situations as representing her era's new technological subjects and global networks.

To demonstrate how O'Connor writes about the social context of the great technocultural feats she witnessed in her day, I assign two works of social history, Mary Barbara Tate's "Flannery O'Connor at Home in Milledgeville" and selections from James C. Cobb's *Away Down South*. I also assign the "Chart of the Development of O'Connor's Fiction" from Stephen Driggers and Robert Dunn's *The Manuscripts of Flannery O'Connor at Georgia College*, which shows students when O'Connor was working on each of her stories (xx). I ask my students to read two of her stories, "A View of the Woods" and "The Lame Shall Enter First," and before we discuss the stories, I bring them to a computer lab.

With Driggers and Dunn's chart in hand, I have my students research the history of Georgia's dams and the American space program. For the history of the dams, I direct them to the *Georgia Aerial Photographs* database of the Digital Library of Georgia (dbs.galib.uga.edu/gaph/html/). Here students can witness the creation of the entirely new Lake Sinclair in Baldwin County, which was O'Connor's inspiration for "A View of the Woods." I have students compare the photomosaics of Baldwin County from 1951, the year of O'Connor's return to Milledgeville, with those from 1956 and 1960 to see the geographic effects of the new dam built by the Georgia Power Company on the Oconee River. Watching these waters rise is a fine visual demonstration for students of the connection between engineering, electrification, regional culture, and O'Connor's literature.

For the history of the space program, I have students do a general Web search and write down all the connections they find between it and "The Lame Shall Enter First." I give a virtual star to the first student who recognizes that the protagonist of O'Connor's story has a name very similar to that of America's first man in space, Alan Shepard. Is this a coincidence? I direct my students back to Driggers and Dunn's time line and also to Driggers and Dunn's record of the changes O'Connor made to her manuscript between 1961 and 1962 (121). O'Connor, students learn through this brief foray into archival and historical research, changed the name of her protagonist from Dr. Radclaw to Sheppard only after the flight of Shepard's *Freedom 7*. We return to our regular classroom to discuss the significance of these respective geographic and editorial changes.

Having explored O'Connor's technological settings, we consider all the technologies and artifacts that play a significant role in her plots. These include cars, guns, tractors, a bus, a pig parlor, several milking parlors, a racist statue, a couple of staircases, an infamous artificial leg, and a tattoo. I stress to my students that none of these things are independent, self-contained. Instead, they both communicate meaning beyond their commercial value and connect to networks of production and sociality that weave throughout the nation and the world.

When discussing O'Connor's things, from cars to the atomic bomb, I introduce my students to the concepts of big science and technological systems developed by historians of science to describe the massive scope of American science and industry. I assign the first chapter of Thomas P. Hughes's *American Genesis*, "The Technological Torrent," in which Hughes argues that the defining activity of Americans over the past hundred and fifty years has been massive "technological-system-building" for commerce and war (2–4). After reading this chapter, students recognize how O'Connor's characters become modern by networking themselves with technological systems that become part of their everyday lives.

Everyday networks and systems abound in O'Connor's fiction, from the telephone network to the city bus network to sewer networks to the network of the nation's roads. I illustrate the prevalence of such networks by assigning "The Life You Save May Be Your Own" and *The Violent Bear It Away*. When I teach the novel, I ask students to first discuss all the networks they use every day, from the sewer system to *Facebook*. I then ask them to note the networks young Tarwater encounters as he leaves his "not simply off the dirt road but off the wagon track and footpath" farm (*Flannery . . . Works* 336) in the novel's first chapter.

I also explore the character Meeks with my students, because Meeks is Tarwater's guide to modern America. Why does he sell copper flues, of all things? I tell my students to take out their smartphones, get on the campus Wi-Fi network, and google the terms *flue* and *copper*. The images and advertisements for pipes and tubes designed to convey hot gases that the first search reveals illustrates the little networks that any house with a stove or gas possesses; the second search reveals an element that is the backbone of our modern electronic society. I show students how Tarwater becomes a modern subject when he becomes a part of modernity's material networks, first of paved roads and then of the copper wires of the telephone network.

I close-read the novel's second chapter with students to discover just how Tarwater's transformation occurs. I direct students to pay close attention to both Meeks's advice and O'Connor's imagery. Students notice that the first book Meeks directs Tarwater to is the telephone book, in which people become numbers (*Flannery . . . Works* 364), and that Meeks refers to the boy's future as a "line" (367). In Tarwater's recollections, O'Connor uses the more organic network imagery of "veins" and "bloodstreams" (368–69). We consider how these organic networks differ from the ones Tarwater is currently encountering with Meeks. Finally, I close-read the chapter's closing scene, Tarwater's first encounter with a telephone (382–84). How has Meeks made Tarwater modern? Students recognize that this modernization occurs when he takes Tarwater for a drive, plugs him into a telephone, and tells him "to learn to work every machine he [sees]" (383). I ask my students if learning to work every machine is really useful advice about how to be successful in today's society.

While I teach O'Connor's novel as a tale of becoming modern, I teach her "The Life You Save May Be Your Own" as a commentary on America's automotive technoculture. To provide a critical and historical context for this story, I assign two works: the chapter on Fordism from David Harvey's *The Condition of Postmodernity* and Bruno Latour's essay "Give Me a Laboratory and I Will Raise the World." Harvey's chapter shows students how the regime of automotive production developed by Henry Ford came to define the twentieth century's "rationalized, modernist, and populist democratic society" (126). Latour's essay shows students how anybody who uses a machine such as a car becomes part of a technocultural network. Each new technology is really the successful completion of an experiment first conducted in a laboratory, Latour argues; technology becomes a part of society by remaking society and people in the image of the laboratory and its workers. Latour and Harvey help students describe the kind of man Tom T. Shiftlet is: a Fordist man who naturally sees the old Ford in the Craters' garage as a more integral part of his modern life than the farm girl he just married.

Beyond recording instances of O'Connor's technological characters and plots, I direct students to keep track of the similes and metaphors O'Connor routinely uses to describe people as animals and elements of the natural world. The purpose is to show how her prose operates as a hybridizing force in her fiction, registering in figurative language the networks that STS scholars describe as composing the modern world. In the classroom we draw together five texts: letters O'Connor wrote to Maryat Lee and Betty Hester, Edgar Allan Poe's story "The Man That Was Used Up," O'Connor's story "The Displaced Person," and Donna Haraway's essay "A Cyborg Manifesto." I begin with the 11 February 1958 letter in which O'Connor tells Lee, "I owe my existence and cheerful countenance to the pituitary glands of thousands of pigs butchered daily in Chicago, Illinois at the Armour packing plant" (*Habit* 266), and her 28 August 1955 letter to Hester, in which she describes her childhood fascination with a Poe story "about a fine figure of a man who in his room removed wooden arms, wooden legs, hair piece, artificial teeth, voice box, etc., etc." "[T]his is an influence," she tells Hester, "I would rather not think about" (98). We then read the Poe story to which she refers. I discuss with my students what the influence of this story and O'Connor's experience as a medical subject might be on her fiction, using these two letters and story to illustrate her personal experience with human-animal and human-machine networks.

We then read "The Displaced Person" along with "A Cyborg Manifesto." Before reading Haraway, who is an STS scholar, I ask my students to locate all the similes and metaphors that O'Connor uses to describe her characters. Students soon recognize that the things in her prose are never just what they are, especially human beings. Her characters are described variously as animals, machines, rocks, mountains, ice, fossils, and light. After my students have located O'Connor's figurative hybrids, I introduce them to Haraway's concept of the cyborg, a hybrid subject bred from the Cold War's militarized networks of transnational capitalism who has the ability to create wildly different futures ranging from dystopias of total alienation and "the final appropriation of . . . bodies in a[n] orgy of war" to postracial utopias built on global labor politics and "lived social and bodily realities in which people are not afraid of their joint kinship with animals and machines" (154). I discuss with my students how O'Connor's displaced person, Mr. Guizac, possesses the cyborg's world-altering powers; when her traditional southern characters confront him, they are confronting one of Haraway's cyborg futures. I ask my students to find evidence of these two futures in O'Connor's story, directing them to passages such as Mrs. Shortley's vision of the orgy of war (*Flannery . . . Works* 287), her warning to Astor and Sulk about the future (297), and the mechanical Mr. Guizac's race-blind global reasoning (314). I find that students can easily devote an entire class period to analyzing this story as an exploration of what Haraway calls cyborg politics.

Teaching O'Connor with STS empowers students to be close, critical, and historicist readers of her fiction. The field's terminology reveals subjects in her fiction that the author herself did not have the vocabulary to describe in her interpretive essays. Most important, though, teaching O'Connor with STS shows students how her mid-century stories are about their world and their times too. Our students live on global networks, social and otherwise; they negotiate technological systems every day; they learn new technical skills and experience new, hybrid ways of life each time a new app or device becomes a part of their lives. Taught through STS, students learn that the world they live in now is the same world that O'Connor saw her region turning into over a half century ago.

Eternal "Greenleaf":
O'Connor's Environmental Imagination

Christine Flanagan

> Do you know Joyce's story "The Dead"? See how he
> makes the snow work in that story. Chekhov makes
> everything work—the air, the light, the cold, the dirt.
> —Flannery O'Connor

Give literature students this deceptively simple task: Catalog the items of nature in Flannery O'Connor's "Greenleaf." Ecocriticism, the application of ecological principles and environmental ethics to the study of literature, promises a uniquely rewarding exploration of her work. Landscape and nature, for O'Connor, first serve to anchor setting and to expand character description. Beyond this, her deliberate use of nature influences, then transcends her characters' powerful desires. Her oeuvre easily lends itself to ecocriticism; but of her most anthologized stories, "Greenleaf" in particular offers an ecocritical analysis that is accessible to and satisfying for students. Saw-toothed tree line or silver moonlight, beast or human, sun or sky or elements of weather—all these images allow O'Connor to grapple with the social implications of race, class, and gender; they free her to investigate the liminal space between concrete matter and divine mystery.

Ever evolving, ecocriticism "remains the preferred term for environmental literary studies," writes Lawrence Buell, ecocriticism's most prolific scholar (*Future* 138). From the perspective of creative writing pedagogy, Janet Burroway defines setting as "the layers of history and social forces around characters as evidenced in their buildings, their inventions, their appliances, their transportation, their agriculture, their efforts to control and tame nature" (166). Likewise, ecocritical place, says Buell, is "bounded and marked as humanly meaningful through personal attachment, social relations, and physiographic distinctiveness" (*Future* 145). Generally, ecocritics distinguish first-wave ecocriticism as that which focuses on nonfiction nature writing, such as first-person narratives or natural history texts (think Thoreau, Emerson, Crèvecoeur). Second-wave ecocriticism examines both literature and other artistic genres; discussion progresses from wild nature to human constructions, even farmhouses and urban landscapes (L. Johnson 8). Ecocriticism's most accessible questions include the following: "How is nature represented in this sonnet? What role does the physical setting play in the plot of this novel?" (Glotfelty xxviii–xix). Ecofeminist critiques—the examination of the twin domination of women and nature—offer unexplored avenues in relation to O'Connor's work, which might "not read as if it were written as a feminist polemic, or . . . particularly gender emphatic" (Murphy 29). A final avenue of interest to O'Connor scholars might be ecotheology and, in particular, the 2015 publication of *Laudato Si'*, Pope Francis's environmental encyclical, which warns, "If we approach nature and the environment without this openness to awe and wonder, if we no longer speak the language of fraternity and beauty in our relationship with the world, our attitude will be that of masters, consumers, ruthless exploiters" (par. 11).

Ecocritical scholarship of O'Connor has grown steadily since ecocriticism's entrance into the academy, circa 1990.[1] Sarah Petrides proposes that O'Connor's landscape reveals "social preconceptions and desires; it reflects history and influences the future" (9). Louise Westling sees images of nature populating O'Connor's fiction: "The land, the trees, the sky, and the relentless eye of the sun are so powerfully charged in her fiction that they become some of its most powerful characters," she writes (*Sacred Groves* 6). Mark Graybill reenvisions O'Connor as a peer to deep ecologists, comparing elements of her work and life to Rachel Carson's. Any of these texts—from Buell to Westling and Pope Francis—are excellent secondary sources for reading O'Connor through the lens of ecocriticism.

In undergraduate courses, I often present O'Connor alongside other nonfiction nature writers. I first ask students to compile a literary field notebook: While reading O'Connor, what images of nature do you encounter? How might we classify these images of nature? My science majors recall Linnaean taxonomy (the eighteenth-century system that delineates kingdom, class, order, etc.). Even Carl Linneaus admits that his taxonomy is "no more than a crude stab at divining nature's pattern" (Warne). Nonetheless, he believes that understanding nature is a spiritual enterprise, a way to "read the Divine Order of God's Creation" (see "Carl Linnaeus"; Engel-Ledeboer and Engel). Two centuries later, O'Connor proposes that the "moral basis" of writing is "the accurate naming of the things of God" in order "to render the highest possible justice to the visible universe" (*Flannery . . . Works* 978, 981). Describing nature—the seemingly simple choices she makes related to setting and characterization—becomes a moral imperative for her, one that intimately connects the craft of writing with her Catholic faith.

Teaching "Greenleaf"

Students are startled and puzzled by O'Connor's "Greenleaf." An ecocritical examination, however, provides an intriguing new experience of this story. We might begin with how each character is connected to the natural world. What hierarchy is established as the story progresses? "Greenleaf" is concerned with the ownership of nature and the questions that surround it. Mrs. May owns a farm, having inherited the land from her husband. Her job is difficult because she is at war with the elements of nature: the weather and the dirt and even the help, Mr. Greenleaf. When a scrub bull crosses onto her property, she wants the bull removed. "Whose bull is he?" (*Flannery . . . Works* 511, 504), she asks Mr. Greenleaf. The bull also trespasses as she sleeps, penetrating her dreams. She hears

> a steady rhythmic chewing as if someone were eating one wall of the house. She was aware that whatever it was had been eating as long as she had had the place and had eaten everything from the beginning of her fence line up to the house and now was eating the house and calmly with the same steady rhythm would continue through the house.   (501)

This bull doesn't seem frightening; he is "squirrel colored, with jutting hips and long light horns," and he ambles down the road, slightly regal (512–13). Why is he a threat? Literally, he is "scrub," a contagion to her purebred herd. He also interrupts the pastoral vision of farmland that "calm[s] her," with cows "grazing on two pale green pastures." O'Connor's extended description undermines a serene landscape, however. Mrs. May's pastures are surrounded by "a black wall of trees with a sharp sawtooth edge that held off the indifferent sky" (511). She is steadied not by beauty but by the landscape's clear and stable definition. Frederick Asals notes that Mrs. May is "doubly enclosed, sealed up sterilely behind the protecting fence of the hedge and the 'black wall of trees' bounding her property" ("Mythic Dimensions" 322).

The bull, it seems, alerts Mrs. May to the danger that the boundaries all around her are unstable. Mr. Greenleaf leaves the gate ajar; that's how the scrub bull enters. For three days, the bull inhabits her property. Mr. Greenleaf insists that he "put him in the bull pen but he torn out of there" (*Flannery . . . Works* 502, 503). The ineffective farmhand observes, but cannot—does not want to?—stop the bull. Mr. Greenleaf is as casually resigned to nature's ways as he is to his wife's prayer healing in the woods. Mrs. Greenleaf howls in the woods, "a huge human mound, her legs and arms spread out as if she were trying to wrap them around the earth." Mrs. May, who is "returning through a wooded path that separated two pastures" (note the boundary line), finds Mrs. Greenleaf "sprawled obscenely" (507) in filth. We learn that Mrs. Greenleaf "cut[s] all the morbid stories out of the newspaper—the accounts of women who had been raped and criminals who had escaped and children who had been burned. . . . She took these to the woods and dug a hole and buried them and then she fell on the ground . . ." (505). Her religious devotion has no church and knows no rational boundaries. Mrs. May, who calls herself a "good Christian woman with a large respect for religion," believes that "Jesus" is a word suited for "inside the church," though she doesn't "believe any of it [is] true" (506). Whenever she encounters nature, we see that her desire for clear and defined boundaries is undermined by both nonhuman and human nature. She can't separate the profane from the sacred any more than she can remove the scrub bull from her purebred herd.

The pasture's open gates in "Greenleaf" also seem to signal a shifting social hierarchy in the human world. O. T. and E. T. (also landowners) are the twin sons of the "scrub human" Greenleafs. Because Mrs. May can't tell the twins apart—both are "long-legged and raw-boned and red-skinned" (507)—she relies on her folksy, irrational beliefs: you can "always tell the class of people by the class of dog," and the Greenleaf dogs are "part hound, part spitz" (513). It shouldn't be a surprise, then, that the scrub bull belongs to O. T. and E. T. She crosses onto their property, a farm two miles down the road, to confront their neglect. There, she tours a new landscape: the post–World War II South. She realizes uneasily that O. T. and E. T. have transcended their "lower" class through military service. Their army uniforms disguise everything except their rank. Now, they are "some kind of sergeants" who have pensions and are able to purchase land. They marry French wives, and "they hadn't married French trash either." They attend the university's agricultural college and build a new "brick duplex bungalow" on their farm (508). Mrs. May notices that an absence of nature ("a treeless hill") surrounds their "warehouse with windows," which she considers "the kind of house that everybody built now" (513). O'Connor quietly links the flattened, government-subsidized architecture with the impending cultural transformation of the 1950s. When the Greenleafs' hired help enters the scene, the African American "boy" pauses "at a respectable distance" from Mrs. May. He is "dressed in the cast-off army clothes of the Greenleaf twins" (515) and seems equally poised to march across the dissolving boundaries of race and class. Throughout her visit to the Greenleaf farm, Mrs. May never articulates the spiritual or economic costs of a changing world. She only recognizes, in horror, that one day O. T. and E. T.'s children will be "society" (508). Before leaving the farm, she delivers her message: she will shoot the bull if O. T. and E. T. don't retrieve it.

The rise of O. T. and E. T. has one notable component: they embrace and can afford the luxury of technology to help them manage nature. Mrs. May observes that their house is air-conditioned (513); their farm utilizes modern equipment, like "a forage harvester and a rotary hay baler." The milking parlor is mechanized, and "[t]he milk runs in pipes from the machines to the milk house" (514). Inside the Greenleaf barn, she feels breathless. She sees that "[t]he spotless white concrete room was filled with sunlight that came from a row of windows head-high along both walls. The metal stanchions gleamed ferociously and she had to squint" (515). Whether she finds the barn "evocative of a church" (Graybill 9) or is simply astonished by the evolution of agribusiness, she is disturbed enough to imagine the sun is "like a silver bullet ready to drop into her brain" (*Flannery . . . Works* 515).

O'Connor's imagery, often stark and vivid, is difficult for students to digest. The same year O'Connor wrote "Greenleaf," Leo Marx (one of ecocriticism's forefathers) published an essay on nature and technology in Nathaniel Hawthorne's writing. Hawthorne's imagery, Marx said, was "designed to get at circumstances which gave rise to conflicting emotions, and which exceeded, in their complexity, the capacities of understanding" ("Machine" 31). A decade later, Marx remains convinced that American literature was "singularly useful . . . in getting at the more elusive, intangible effects of change—its impact on the moral and aesthetic, emotional and sensory, aspects of experience" (*Machine* 370). I like to offer students excerpts of Marx's writing alongside a more recent consideration of O'Connor's work (not expressly ecocriticism) that comes through Doreen Fowler, a feminist scholar who interrogates cultural and literary assumptions about race and gender. Any cultural or biological construction (black vs. white, male vs. female) relies on definitional boundaries. For Fowler, the boundary between dual and opposing items (high/low, outside/inside) is not a solid line of demarcation. A boundary is

> the middle, a mysterious, dangerous, two-in-one place that differentiates between the one and the other precisely because it is both the one and the other. It is not exclusion but doubleness that forms a boundary; and when we draw a boundary, we always occupy a threatening, liminal, in-between space; and we always experience a cross-identification with the other. (141)

Fowler's proposition seems to illuminate the "more elusive, intangible effects" of human and natural boundaries in "Greenleaf." One example is that before leaving O. T. and E. T.'s farm, Mrs. May searches for a stable, defined hierarchy. She asks their African American farmhand, "Which is boss, Mr. O. T. or Mr. E. T.?" Neither, he says: "They like one man in two skins" and "they never quarls" (*Flannery . . . Works* 516). We can see Mrs. May's peril: her world of distinctions is dissolving or—even worse—is false.

That evening, Mrs. May's sons "quarls" until they violently upend her dinner table. Unlike the Greenleaf twins, her sons are utterly different: they "never had the same reaction to anything" (504). Wesley is a "thin and nervous and bald" intellectual who had rheumatic fever as a child and now doesn't like nice girls; Scofield is an insurance salesman with a "broad pleasant smiling face" who "never had a day's sickness," and the nice girls don't like him (504, 509). My students, still sorting through their images of nature and now armed with Fowler's concept of boundary, argue with me. Wesley and Scofield are also twins, they say, and are equally disengaged with nature. "Neither of them cared what happened on the place"; neither values his inheritance of land. Mr. Greenleaf tells Mrs. May that "her boys don't know hay from silage" (504, 507). Both disrespect their mother. Oddly, Wesley and Scofield's disconnection from nature reflects a shrinking circle of existence: they are unmarried and "impotent" (Westling, *Sacred Groves* 158). Wesley "talked about Paris and Rome but he never went even to Atlanta" (*Flannery . . . Works* 509). Like their mother, they will not expand their horizons.

Students who struggle with the ending of "Greenleaf" typically echo Louise Westling's observation that "[we] should still be troubled by the lack of interior development in Mrs. May's character to prepare her for the spiritual revelation she is supposed to experience in the final scene" (*Sacred Groves* 166). As the story concludes, Mrs. May closes the open gate to secure the pasture's boundary. She is "encircled by woods" (*Flannery . . . Works* 521). The bull approaches, bounding "at a slow gallop, a gay almost rocking gait as if he were overjoyed to find her again." But the image suddenly changes: he transforms into a "violent black streak." His horn pierces her, and her view of nature changes: "the tree line was a dark wound in a world that was nothing but sky—and she had the look of a person whose sight has been suddenly restored but who finds the light unbearable" (523).

What are we to make of this ending? Compare it with the ending of "A Good Man Is Hard to Find," where the Grandmother realizes that the Misfit is like a son. The Grandmother's realization leads her to reach out and touch him. He recoils and shoots her. In contrast, Mrs. May stands "in a freezing unbelief," utterly passive, as the bull approaches her, horns lowered (523). She has done nothing to precipitate the attack; she experiences no epiphany. Or does she?

Grace, writes Fowler, "is an experience at the border of the self, the borderline place that is dual, where self and other or human and divine make 'contact'" (73). O'Connor insisted that the subject of her fiction is the "action of grace in territory largely held by the devil" (*Mystery* 118). Most readers take this insight as an opportunity to discuss grace instead of territories. In O'Connor's terrain, my students see elements of a natural world that resist claims of ownership but still hint at hierarchy. Images of ladders, for example, repeat in "Greenleaf," from the opening image of the bull outside Mrs. May's window, when "bars of light slid across him" (*Flannery . . . Works* 501), to the image of Mr. Greenleaf at Mrs. May's back door near the end of the story: "[T]he sun was moving down slowly as if it were descending a ladder. Mr. Greenleaf squatted down on the step, his back to her, the top of his hat on a level with her feet" (518). It is Mrs. May's ownership of nature that places her above Mr. Greenleaf, a hired hand, on the hierarchical ladder.

As Mr. Greenleaf stands below Mrs. May, an essential moment occurs: she tells him that he will have to shoot the bull that belongs to O. T. and E. T. He delays. She insists, asserting her authority. Her firm stand is accompanied by a realization: "Do you know the real reason they didn't come for that bull? . . . They didn't come because I'm a woman. You can get away with anything when you're dealing with a woman" (518–19). There is fiction, writes Patrick D. Murphy, an ecocritic, that perhaps unintentionally "weaves themes of nature, gender, and culture into a single fabric that the reader feels compelled to appreciate by not only looking at it, but also by feeling its texture and reflecting on its frayed ends" (29). Carol Shloss, when exploring the territory of skin in O'Connor's fiction, proposes that "far from being a shallow integument, [the skin] serves always as a signifying system with a complex relationship to that which is presumed to lie beneath it and outside of it" ("S/kin" 70). Mrs. May's skin is her female identity, the landscape that the bull will pierce. He is animal;

she is human—as different as two creatures can be, until they meet: he wears a "hedge wreath"; she wears "green rubber curlers" (*Flannery . . . Works* 501).

She inhabits a woman's body but a male experience. She is the embodiment of a false definition, a dissolving boundary. She is a woman whose husband has died and whose sons have no interest in taking ownership of the farm. She did not choose to be the head of the household, family provider, landowner, or business manager. When Mr. Greenleaf reaches her, the bull's horn is "curved around her side," and she is "bent over whispering some last discovery into the animal's ear" (524).

Who owns nature? *To own* is not simply "to possess." It means also to admit or acknowledge, to yield or acquiesce, to become aware. "To assent to the rhythms of nature or to the Christian vision," writes Asals, "is to accept also the forces of time, suffering and death" ("Mythic Dimensions" 323). The absurdity of finding life in death, finding meaning in suffering, says Asals, "can be justified by only the greatest absurdity, by the death of a God from which sprang the fertility of true Life" (325). This is O'Connor's final vision, her last whispered discovery.

Paradox—Christian and secular—inhabited every realm of O'Connor's life. Many critics have observed that she "needed to escape from the Southern ideal of the lady if she ever wanted to succeed as a writer" (Westling, *Sacred Groves* 173). She shared this conflict with her literary mentor, Caroline Gordon, an award-winning author of nine novels, three story collections, and two nonfiction books on the craft of fiction, who described her own ambivalence as a writer: "While I am a woman I am also a freak. The work I do is not suitable for a woman" (qtd. in Boyle 44). More than any other influence, Gordon taught O'Connor that images of nature were essential elements of art. She complimented a draft of *Wise Blood* ("You are like Kafka in providing a firm Naturalistic ground-work for your symbolism") but suggested more details of landscape: "You have to imitate the Almighty and create a whole world—or an illusion of a whole word, if the simplest tale is to have any verisimilitude (qtd. in S. Fitzgerald, "Master Class" 832). Before O'Connor published "A Good Man Is Hard to Find," Gordon instructed her to expand her "composition of scene" when the Grandmother's family is shot offstage, in the woods: "Remember that the Lord made the world before He made Adam and Eve. Events take place in time and space. . . . I'd show the grandmother's reactions to what is happening, or what she barely suspects may happen by the way the world—these trees, this road—looks to her" (O'Connor and Gordon 59). To revise "The Artificial Nigger," Gordon insisted, "You ought to set this scene more carefully . . . for it is the 'forest' out of which your action will emerge" (109).

At every turn, O'Connor embraced Gordon's suggestions. From gaunt pine trunks and corrugated red earth to pale blue skies fringed with treetops, images of nature become the constellation that is the trademark O'Connor landscape, what she called her "country," which, she said, "suggests everything from the actual countryside that the novelist describes, on, to, and through the peculiar characteristics of his region and his nation, and on, through, and under all of these to his true country, which the writer with Christian concerns will consider to be what is eternal and absolute" (*Flannery . . . Works* 801).

Sixty years after the publication of "Greenleaf," Pope Francis said, "Human life is grounded in three fundamental and closely intertwined relationships: with God, with our neighbour and with the earth itself" (par. 66). Buell argues:

> Athough the creative and critical arts may seem remote from the arenas of scientific investigation and public policy, clearly they are exercising, however unconsciously, an influence upon the emerging culture of environmental concern, just as they have played a part in shaping as well as merely expressing every other aspect of human culture.
>
> (*Environmental Imagination* 3)

O'Connor's fiction remains relevant—timeless—because we still struggle to navigate the shifting hierarchies and false boundaries of our own time. We seek to understand other human beings, who we imagine are so different from us. Finally, we seek to preserve a connection to the disappearing landscapes and societies we cherish so dearly.

NOTE

[1] Even before 1990, scholarly articles investigated O'Connor's landscape and her treatment of nature (see Chow; Cleary). Additional resources I recommend are Buell, *Environmental Imagination*; Fowler; Glotfelty and Fromm; and the Web site for the Association for Literature and the Environment (www.asle.org). The association's mission is to explore "the meanings of the natural environment and the complexities of human relationships with each other, and with the more-than-human world, and to deepening the impact of these explorations both within and beyond the classroom." Their Web site is a hub of scholarship, references and resources, and archives, including information on the association's scholarly journal *ISLE* (*Interdisciplinary Studies in Literature and the Environment*).

O'Connor in the Company of *Dubliners*

Miriam Marty Clark and Virginia Grant

It will not come as news to those who have taught Flannery O'Connor's fiction that most students are far more interested in interpretive questions than in questions of narrative technique; whatever liberties they may take with theme and symbol, the mysteries of narration itself remain more or less intact. But *Wise Blood*, O'Connor's first book, begun while she was a student at the Iowa Writers' Workshop, offers an unusually good opportunity to think with students about her method of telling, both as an element of her developing craft and as an expression of her distinctive way of seeing and being in the world. At the end of the essay we suggest assignments both for literature students, whose attention might be turned from unresolvable questions about meaning to more productive ones about how O'Connor's stories work, and for creative writing students concerned with honing their own craft of narration.

Mark McGurl, who calls O'Connor "the first major figure to emerge from an MFA program" (529), argues that what she encountered at the workshop was not one but several powerfully influential institutions: the "institution proper," the workshop itself, its situation, its faculty, and its pedagogical practices; the "circulating aesthetic institution created by New Critical textbook-anthologies"; and the "institution as 'established practices'" and as established writers like Henry James and James Joyce (533).[1] In this essay we focus on O'Connor's extended encounter with Joyce's *Dubliners* during her time in Iowa. Reasoning from notes in her copy of the book and successive drafts of *Wise Blood*, we show the importance of the encounter—and the institution constituted by those established writers who had the endorsement of workshop faculty members and

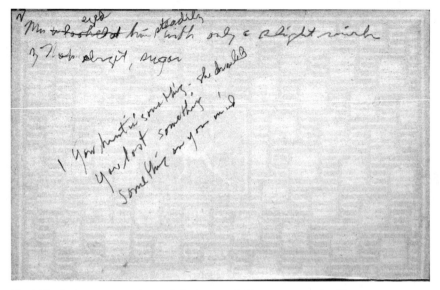

Fig. 1. Handwritten notes on the inside back cover of O'Connor's copy of *Dubliners*.

the New Critics—to the development of her craft, not only for *Wise Blood* but for the stories that followed (fig. 1).

Brad Gooch, O'Connor's biographer, has traced her interest in Joyce to her undergraduate days at Georgia State College for Women, noting that "A Little Cloud" is marked with a star in her copy of a required short story anthology and that at least one short essay she wrote mimics the style of "Araby" (102). By O'Connor's account, less precise than Gooch's on this point, her first experience of *Dubliners* took place while she was a student at Iowa. There, she later wrote to a friend, she "began to read everything at once," including "Faulkner, Kafka, and Joyce," "all the Catholic novelists," "all the nuts," "the best Southern writers," "the Russians," and Joseph Conrad, whom she admired greatly (*Habit* 98). *Dubliners* was one of two books she chose to focus on in a seminar on literary criticism taught by the well-known critic Austin Warren in the fall of 1946 (Gooch 133), and she returned to it in the months that followed as she worked on *Wise Blood*.

O'Connor's Modern Library copy of *Dubliners*, now housed with the rest of her library at Georgia College, is only lightly annotated—a few passages underlined in pencil. But the inside back cover of the book offers much more tantalizing evidence of Joyce's importance to her development as a fiction writer. In numbered lines scrawled diagonally and then sideways down the page is a passage of dialogue:

> 2 Mrs [something scribbled out] eyed him steadily with only a slight wink
> 3 That's alright, sugar
> 1 You huntin' something—she drawled

You lost something
Something on your mind

In the final version of *Wise Blood*, published a few years later, this passage is fleshed out but otherwise virtually unchanged:

"You huntin' something?" she drawled.
    If she had not had him so firmly by the arm, he might have leaped out the window. Involuntarily his lips formed the words, "Yes, mam," but no sound came through them.
    "Something on your mind?" Mrs. Watts asked, pulling his rigid figure a little closer. . . .
    Mrs. Watts eyed him steadily with only a slight smirk. Then she put her other hand under his face and tickled it in a motherly way. "That's okay, son," she said. "Momma don't mind if you ain't a preacher."
                                                        (*Flannery . . . Works* 18)

For a brief but critical moment, then, sometime in 1947 or 1948, *Dubliners* became a field of composition for O'Connor. Exactly what happened between Joyce's stories and her developing novel is unknowable; it may well have been a mystery to O'Connor herself. As she wrote and revised her book, she was attuned to many voices—teachers, friends, other writers, agents, publishers—and intent all the while on honing her mature style. Gooch's biography offers a detailed and convincing account of her labors over *Wise Blood*, including her reading and the formative conversations she had with others. Paul Elie also writes about this crucial period, noting that during the fall of 1947, after a summer in Milledgeville, O'Connor settled into an Iowa City boardinghouse and "got to work in earnest."

There, independent of relatives and teachers for the first time, she was transformed into a novelist. She was twenty-two years old, pretty, funny, healthy, ambitious. Her work, so far skillful but unremarkable, suddenly became original both in style and in what she was trying to accomplish; her desire to be a writer turned into an urgent sense of calling.
    There is no telling just how it happened.   (151)

Still, the connection with Joyce, represented in a few scribbled lines, strikes us as unusually important, an invitation and a provocation to readers of her fiction.
    Among the things O'Connor took from Joyce was a narrative technique. Like many other twentieth-century fiction writers, including Joyce, she relies on third-person heterodiegetic narrators—that is, narrators who are not themselves involved in the action of the story. In modern and contemporary fiction,

such narrators are very rarely omniscient, the kind Jean Puillon has described as "voices behind" the action of the story who "tell more than any and all of the characters know" (qtd. in Prince 442). More typically they have access to the interior experiences—the perceptions, thoughts, and feelings—of one or more characters in the story, which is to say they narrate from within the story without being actors in it. Their narratives are focalized through a character or characters.

Focalization in third-person narratives allows readers to get inside fictional minds, to see and feel as the characters do. But the fact that the story is told in third person creates the expectation that the interior perspective it offers will be complicated, enlarged, even corrected by an external perspective, often provided by a focalizing narrator who, though not omniscient in the old sense of the term, is able both to see as and to look at the story's characters. Ernest Hemingway's Nick Adams stories offer good examples of this kind of narration. Less commonly, the external view takes choral form, focalizing a community's perceptions of a character and the character's situation. Willa Cather's "Paul's Case" is a remarkable example of this kind of choral response, a community's perspective on Paul's circumstances and his increasingly desperate actions.

Without this kind of external view, a third-person narrative can seem flat, lacking both in vividness and in insight. It is not hard to see the absence of external perspective on a focalized character as the central problem in "The Train," the short story O'Connor wrote as a graduate student at Iowa that later became the basis for *Wise Blood*. Hazel Wickers, the story's protagonist, has a mind nearly as rich and strange as Hazel Motes's, but "The Train" is focalized exclusively through him. We see things as he sees them but never get a look at him; the story offers no external account of his appearance or mannerisms. His encounter with another passenger on the train, which O'Connor later develops into the crucial opening scene of *Wise Blood*, is represented in the story only by his thoughts and perceptions and the words they exchange.

> "Are you going home?" Mrs. Hosen asked him. Her name was Mrs. Wallace Ben Hosen; she had been a Miss Hitchcock before she married.
>
> "Oh!" Haze said, startled—"I get off at, I get off at Taulkinham."
>
> Mrs. Hosen knew some people in Evansville who had a cousin in Taulkinham—a Mr. Henrys, she thought. Being from Taulkinham Haze might know him. Had he ever heard the. . . .
>
> "Taulkinham ain't where I'm from," Haze muttered. "I don't know nothin' about Taulkinham." He didn't look at Mrs. Hosen. He knew what she was going to ask next and he felt it coming and it came, "Well, where do you live?"
>
> He wanted to get away from her. "It was there," he mumbled, squirming in the seat. Then he said, "I don't rightly know, I was there but . . . this is just the third time I been at Taulkinham," he said quickly—her face had

crawled out and was staring at him — "I ain't been since I went when I was
six. I don't know nothin' about it. Once I seen a circus there but not. . . ."
He heard a clanking at the end of the car and looked to see where it was
coming from. The porter was pulling the walls of the sections farther out.
"I got to see the porter a minute," he said and escaped down the aisle.

(Flannery . . . Works 755)

In the later and more technically sophisticated version of this scene, O'Connor
shifts the focalization, for one crucial moment, from Haze's head to that of
Mrs. Wally Bee Hitchcock, the woman he meets on the train. This "fat woman
with pink collars and cuffs and pear-shaped legs that slanted off the train seat
and didn't reach the floor" offers readers a vivid description of Hazel Motes's
appearance and his mannerisms:

> "I guess you're going home," she said, turning back to him again. He
> didn't look, to her, much over twenty, but he had a stiff black broad-
> brimmed hat on his lap, a hat that an elderly country preacher would
> wear. His suit was a glaring blue and the price tag was still stapled on the
> sleeve of it.
>
> He didn't answer her or move his eyes from whatever he was looking
> at. The sack at his feet was an army duffel bag and she decided that he
> had been in the army and had been released and that now he was going
> home. She wanted to get close enough to see what the suit had cost him
> but she found herself squinting instead at his eyes, trying almost to look
> into them. They were the color of pecan shells and set in deep sockets.
> The outline of a skull under his skin was plain and insistent.   (3)

The technique O'Connor uses here — a sharp pivot from one character's perspective to another's — is distinctive, different from the more commonly used
fictional strategy that sets a character's limited perspective against the narrator's
more authoritative, more comprehensive knowledge, or against the fixed and
steady ideas of a community. She uses the technique again a few pages later, at
the end of chapter 2, in the scene that takes shape around the lines she'd first
jotted in *Dubliners*. There the focal point shifts abruptly from Hazel Motes to
Leora Watts, the prostitute he visits as soon as he arrives in Taulkinham. Smirk-
ing and coaxing, she notes Haze's "rigid figure" and the nervous, restless way he
touches things around her room (18). When he reappears the next day, we once
again see him through her eyes, staring back, his black "Jesus-seeing hat" sitting
squarely on his head (33).

It is a technique readers of Joyce's *Dubliners* will find familiar. In "The Dead,"
a story that clearly appealed to O'Connor as a model for fictional character
development, Joyce uses it twice, each time pivoting from Gabriel Conroy's

keen and self-regarding internal perspective to an equally keen, if less chari-
table, external perspective. The first time the focalization pivots, it is to Lily, his
aunts' housemaid. As the story begins, Lily greets Gabriel and his wife, Gretta,
who have arrived a little late for a party hosted by his elderly aunts. Soon the
aunts—Kate and Julia—and Gretta turn to go upstairs. Since only Lily remains, the perspective we are offered must be hers. At first, Gabriel is described
in more or less neutral terms, an anxiously awaited, late-arriving guest at the
Misses Morkan's annual dance. But after an exchange of what he has clearly
intended to be pleasantries, Lily's perspective darkens, and the description of
Gabriel reveals physical and temperamental qualities readers could not see if
the story were told only from his point of view. These qualities will prove critical
to the story's unfolding. "O, then, said Gabriel gaily," after learning that Lily has
finished school, "I suppose we'll be going to your wedding one of these fine days
with your young man, eh?"

> The girl glanced back at him over her shoulder and said with great
> bitterness:
> —The men that is now is only all palaver and what they can get out
> of you.
> Gabriel coloured as if he felt he had made a mistake and without look-
> ing at her, kicked off his galoshes and flicked actively with his muffler at
> his patent-leather shoes.
> He was a stout tallish young man. The high colour of his cheeks pushed
> upwards even to his forehead where it scattered itself in a few formless
> patches of pale red; and on his hairless face there scintillated restlessly the
> polished lenses and the bright gilt rims of the glasses which screened his
> delicate and restless eyes.   (178)

The second and more important pivot shifts the focalization of the story for
a crucial moment from Gabriel to Miss Ivors, a "frank-mannered, talkative
young lady" with whom he has been paired for one of the evening's dances.
"I have a crow to pluck with you," she tells him as the dance begins (187).
In the exchange that ensues, she offers a courteous but insistent challenge
to his political leanings, questioning his decision to write book reviews for a
West Briton newspaper rather than an Irish one and his practice of traveling to France and Belgium each summer rather than venturing west, more
deeply into Ireland. As their conversation advances, the story offers an external
view—not the author's or the narrator's but Miss Ivors's—of Gabriel, who col-
ors, knits his brow, blinks his eyes, murmurs lamely, and appears perplexed and
inattentive (188–89).

The image that emerges is strikingly different from the urbane, charis-
matic image he has hoped to present as well as from the self-image he actually

holds—his belief in himself as a person of good character, goodwill, some intellectual standing, and some well-concealed uneasiness in social situations. Eventually the focal point pivots back to him. For this return pivot, Joyce begins with terms that could describe either feeling (internal perspective) or appearance (external); in other words, they could represent either Miss Ivors's perceptions or Gabriel's. At the end of the scene there comes a moment of mutual regard: he feels her hand on his; she looks at him; he looks at her looking at him "from under her brows" (190). Only then does the perspective again become clearly, exclusively Gabriel's. "Gabriel tried to cover his agitation," Joyce writes, "by taking part in the dance with great energy. He avoided her eyes for he had seen a sour expression on her face. But when they met in the long chain he was surprised to feel his hand firmly pressed. She looked at him from under her brows for a moment quizzically until he smiled" (190). At this point Gabriel's engagement with Miss Ivors appears considerably more sophisticated and complex than any pivot involving Hazel Motes. In the gradual return of focalization to Gabriel, Joyce's story creates an interval that gives his protagonist time to internalize and process Miss Ivors's perspective—a moment of wincing realization, then a correction or refinement in his thinking, and finally a deepening or enlargement of his understanding.

The pivots in *Wise Blood*, by contrast, are abrupt, unsparing, and fiercer than anything anywhere in Joyce. If Joyce's characters deepen and expand, O'Connor's shrink and twist at the pivot point. Shifts in focalization are a way of painting or seeing characters, the main thing O'Connor thought a writer might learn from "The Dead." Both writers recognize the comic potential of focal pivots, particularly where the elevated self-regard of one character is met by the withering assessment of another. But the difference between O'Connor's use of the technique and Joyce's is significant and illuminating. Gabriel is a sympathetic figure whose feelings the story invites us to share and whose sensibilities, we are made to understand, are noble ones, if still in need of chastening. He is, in his touching, imperfect way, the story's hero. Hazel Motes refuses sympathy and, in his strangeness, repels identification. Even as we see the world through his eyes, we know that he is no figure of the artist as Gabriel Conroy was; we know that we are not like him in any way. Each of his encounters in the novel becomes a confrontation; each confrontation is a violent twist to the rigid, already damaged figure he bore into the story.

The focal pivot soon evolves in O'Connor's fiction into a dyadic form of storytelling in which perspective pivots back and forth between two characters: Mrs. Pritchard and Mrs. Cope in "A Circle in the Fire," Mrs. Freeman and Mrs. Hopewell in "Good Country People," Mrs. McIntyre and Mrs. Shortley in "The Displaced Person," and virtually every significant parent-child pair in O'Connor's stories. Here perspectives are not enlarged or modulated by a heterodiegetic narrator, someone who brings a wider or more balanced or less distorted view of the world. What we see, we see through the narrow, shortsighted, blindspotted vision of the characters themselves. What we know, we know through their fraught and savage relationships to each other, their cunning refracted as foolishness, their self-assured goodness as hard-edged hubris. It is both a fallen world and a comic one that opens between characters; no narrative voices intervene to correct distortions and misapprehensions or to offer a fuller sense, a deeper analysis, a gentler reckoning, or a wider set of possibilities.

The focal pivot, which shifts external perspective from narrator to characters, makes this kind of narrative restraint or standing back possible. Not long after O'Connor received copies of *"A Good Man Is Hard to Find" and Other Stories*, where many of her most dyadic stories appear, she wrote to Robbie Macauley, "I read [the stories] over and over and laugh and laugh, then get embarrassed when I remember I was the one who wrote them" (*Habit* 81). A reader might likewise read the stories and laugh without much thought of their tellers. This unobstructed, if darkly comic, view of human nature and human relations is one of the pleasures the stories offer.

Suggestions for Teachers

This approach to *Wise Blood* creates an opportunity for students to consider how we come to understand and form our images of fictional characters. Teachers might ask students to create knowledge maps of the text or portions of it, indicating where readers get the information. Is it based on knowledge or a perspective provided by a third-person narrator? based on the thoughts, actions, or statements of the story's protagonist? or based on things another character says or thinks about the protagonist? Comparing knowledge maps for stories by different writers can help students see key differences in narrative technique and gain a sense of how it shapes our experience of a story.

In many of the short stories O'Connor wrote after *Wise Blood*, she uses pairs of characters, figures whose competing interests, conflicting beliefs, and comically withering perspectives on each other are central: Mrs. Freeman and Mrs. Hopewell in "Good Country People," Mrs. Cope and Mrs. Pritchard in "A Circle in the Fire," Asbury and his mother in "The Enduring Chill," Julian and his mother in "Everything That Rises Must Converge." Even the Grandmother and the Misfit in "A Good Man Is Hard to Find" emerge as a dynamic pair at the end of that story. It is possible to see O'Connor's use of pairs as a logical extension of what she learned from Joyce's *Dubliners*. Students might be asked to consider her use of pairs in one of these stories, to identify moments when the perspective shifts from one character to the other, and to reflect on how these shifts shape our understanding of the story.

In creative writing courses, students might be asked to rewrite a passage from their own work or someone else's, introducing a focal pivot—a sharp swing from one character's perspective to the other's—into an encounter between two characters. What happens when the detached perspective of the third-person narrator is replaced by the perspective of another character?

NOTE

[1] McGurl cites Jeffrey Williams on the range of meanings of *institution*.

Teaching O'Connor
in Conversation with William Faulkner

John D. Sykes, Jr.

By the time Flannery O'Connor began seriously to prepare herself for a writing career, William Faulkner cast a long shadow. In 1945, when she enrolled in the Iowa Writers' Workshop, his best-remembered novels had already been published, and Malcolm Cowley was editing *The Portable Faulkner* for the Viking Portable Library series (*Novels* 1094 ["Chronology"]), a volume that would secure Faulkner's reputation with a wide segment of the American reading public. The Nobel Prize in Literature would follow five years later, well before O'Connor published her first significant work, *Wise Blood*, in 1952. Although in letters written in the 1950s she said she had not read Faulkner before she got to Iowa (*Flannery . . . Works* 950), it is certain that her graduate school instructors made sure she paid attention to him. After Iowa, Caroline Gordon, an established writer whose judgment O'Connor trusted, included Faulkner among her models in her detailed comments on O'Connor's drafts. Although O'Connor only occasionally mentions Faulkner in her letters and addresses, the reason is not difficult to surmise. It is plainly implied in her frequently quoted remark in "Some Aspects of the Grotesque in Southern Fiction": "The presence alone of Faulkner in our midst makes a great difference in what the [southern] writer can and cannot permit himself to do. Nobody wants his mule and wagon stalled on the same track the Dixie Limited is roaring down" (818). She did her best to avoid comparison with Faulkner, but she was very much aware of him. Her relative silence speaks loudly. Despite her wishes, at the remove of more than fifty years, teachers should feel a right if not an obligation to lead students to make comparisons between the two.

In this essay I lay out suggestions for three extended comparisons that might be incorporated into undergraduate courses. The first would work effectively in a freshman- or sophomore-level introduction to literature course that includes short stories. Faulkner's "A Rose for Emily" and O'Connor's "Good Country People" are often anthologized—both are in Nina Baym's *The Norton Anthology of American Literature*, for instance—and the pair makes for a revealing contrast. The second suggestion would find a more natural place in a junior-level fiction, theory, or period course in which special attention is paid to stylistics. Here, the focus is on two monuments steeped in the racial history of the South: the Confederate monument invoked at the end of Faulkner's *The Sound and the Fury* and the lawn ornament in O'Connor's "The Artificial Nigger." Finally and more broadly, for a senior-level novel course or a course in twentieth-century southern literature, I outline an approach to *Wise Blood* by way of Faulkner's *Light in August*.

"Good Country People" and "A Rose for Emily"

Students coming to O'Connor for the first time through this story are likely to be struck by the double revelation at the story's climax: Manley Pointer's bizarre fetish and Joy-Hulga's humiliation. I recommend discussing the story with only a brief introduction, allowing students to gravitate toward what they find compelling. Almost inevitably, conversation will turn to Pointer's collection of body parts and Hulga's abandonment in the hayloft. From these points of engagement an instructor may proceed along two lines of inquiry, both of which are enhanced by reading the story alongside "A Rose for Emily." The first is stylistic and the second thematic. Contemporary student readers will likely place Pointer's unusual sexual tastes in the context of such recent books and films as *The Silence of the Lambs* or *Fifty Shades of Grey*. Or they may have registered the news, reported by *The Guardian* on 26 June 2014, that the convicted pedophile DJ Jimmy Savile stole a glass eye from a corpse and had it made into a necklace (Halliday).

Faulkner's story can show students that O'Connor is working from a tradition that goes back in American literature at least to Poe but that also had a specific name and place in 1955—"southern gothic." With little prompting, students will find gothic elements in "A Rose for Emily"—the refusal to see death as an absolute border, the fascination of forbidden love, the importance of ritual, the violation of taboo—all of which coalesce in that long-locked bedroom opened to the reader at the end of the story. Students can be led to see these elements in altered form in O'Connor's story. No lovers die in "Good Country People," but Hulga is preoccupied with "nothing," and her seducer finishes her off metaphorically by telling her, "I been believing in nothing ever since I was born" (*Flannery . . . Works* 283). Hulga's turn away from Joy (and from joy) and toward nihilism began with a brush with death in the hunting accident that cost her her leg and gained momentum when her father departed. In this way, Hulga is a kind of anti-Emily, or attempts to be, and the events in the story expose her failure and leave her with a longing not so different from Emily's mad desire. Hulga, like Emily, or indeed like the narrator of Poe's "Ligeia" (*Complete Stories* 97–107), is drawn to a lover she should not have. The boundaries in both cases are social. The man Emily is attracted to is a Yankee and a commoner who cannot pass muster with her stern father and reputation-conscious aunts. Hulga lives in a South where such strictures have loosened but not fallen away. Her mother's condescending praise of "good country people" shows her class awareness (271). Although Hulga has freer rein in her mother's house than Emily could claim in her father's, the restraints are real enough that Hulga can take perverse delight in pursuing a man she knows her mother considers beneath her. Of course her pursuit of the bible salesman is also forbidden in the sense that she intends to make him violate his own code, which she assumes to be a puritanical biblicism.

Fantasy ritual orders the love nest in both stories. Emily has carefully laid out the bridegroom emblems of her would-be wedding night: the precisely placed suit and shoes, the tie and collar, the monogrammed silver toilet articles, and the desiccated corpse in its rotted nightshirt. Manley, for his part, insists that Hulga follow a prescribed pattern in their lovemaking, one that most memorably includes the removal of her prosthetic leg and the careful display of Manley's obscene playing cards and box of condoms, "in an even-spaced row, like one presenting offerings at the shrine of a goddess" (282). Both love affairs violate taboos: Emily refuses to bury the dead and indeed suffers from a form of necrophilia; the bible salesman practices a similar violation of the body, stealing artificial body parts meant to rectify deformities and deficiencies.

Pointing out ways in which O'Connor is making use of a genre that Faulkner explored some twenty-five years earlier (in 1930) can lead to further stylistic comparisons. Two fruitful directions to pursue are the roles of the respective narrators and the related issue of irony. On the topic of the narrator, I would suggest beginning with "A Rose for Emily," whose narrator is easy to identify and whose relationship to Miss Emily is straightforward. The narrator is a spokesman for the town, and his attitude is one of curiosity and detached interest. Students may want to explore the implications of having Emily Grierson's story told from the point of view of the town; the narrator uses plural first-person pronouns. This corporate point of view is at odds with the norm for modern literature and perhaps echoes the use of choruses in ancient Greek drama. It also highlights the power of the community in shaping and constraining personal desire. The notion that a town has a right not only to enforce laws having to do with assessing and collecting taxes but also to enforce mores establishing standards of decency and propriety may itself be a subject of classroom debate. It will also provide a segue to O'Connor's story.

In "Good Country People," the unidentified narrator shows that Hulga resents her mother's slavish adherence to convention, an adherence suggested by Mrs. Hopewell's reverence for "good country people." Mrs. Freeman has a disproportionate influence on Mrs. Hopewell's opinions precisely because she forcefully if illogically expresses the views of the common people; the bible salesman also worms his way into Mrs. Hopewell's good graces by casting himself in the conventional role. But O'Connor's narrator is not an enforcer of conventional values. The chief indication of the narrator's distance is her use of irony. Students can be asked to find examples of irony directed toward Mrs. Hopewell, Joy, and Mrs. Freeman in the first six paragraphs of the story. An example for Mrs. Hopewell is, "Mrs. Hopewell had no bad qualities of her own but she was able to use other people's in such a constructive way that she never felt the lack" (*Flannery . . . Works* 264). An example for Joy is, "[T]he large hulking Joy, whose constant outrage had obliterated every expression from her face, would stare just a little to the side of her, her eyes icy blue, with the look of someone who has achieved blindness by an act of will and means to keep it" (264–65). Most comically ironic is Mrs. Freeman's reply to Mrs. Hopewell's truism that everybody is different: "Yes, most people is" (265). Although the first section of the story is observed from the limited point of view of Mrs. Hopewell, the use of third person and the irony indicate that this narrator is removed from the action and does not share the characters' judgments. This removal can lead to a discussion of the relation between narrator and author in the two stories.

Clearly, Faulkner is not the narrator of "A Rose for Emily." Is O'Connor the narrator of "Good Country People"? What difference does the difference between narrator and author make? In Faulkner's story, setting the main character over against the narrator reinforces Miss Emily's rebellion against communally enforced mores. O'Connor's irony seems directed not only at small-minded conventionalism but also at smug rebellion. Her narrator seems to be pushing the reader to make judgments that require a wisdom none of the characters has achieved, although Joy-Hulga may be on her way to it. Although one may find ironies in Faulkner's story—the contradiction between Miss Emily's standing as a lady and the horrid smell emanating from her house, for example—the Jefferson world as a whole is not ironized in the way that the Hopewell farm comes to be. In this way students can be alerted to techniques writers use to imply what they do not state. The instructor might also ask which author places a greater demand on readers to come to their own conclusions.

From these considerations of technique, the instructor can delve more deeply into thematic issues, and two that stand out are gender and theology. Again, "A Rose for Emily" may serve as the point of departure. The most vivid image of Emily in the story is the tableau of the Grierson family imagined by the town: "Miss Emily a slender figure in white in the background, her father a spraddled silhouette in the foreground, his back to her and clutching a horsewhip, the two of them framed by the back-flung door." The "back-flung door" expresses the notion that "[n]one of the young men were quite good enough for Miss Emily" (1000). Grierson keeps Emily as closely as Capulet keeps Juliet, and the story sounds the same theme as Shakespeare's play: individual desire in conflict with patriarchal duty. Students can be encouraged to work out the progression of this conflict: Emily has no suitors before she turns thirty. She goes on her first date the summer after her father dies. The man she goes out with is the kind her father would never have approved of, "a Northerner, a day laborer" (1001). The ladies of the town take action on behalf of decorum, asking the male minister to intervene. He in turn has his wife write Miss Emily's distant relations, who send two cousins to restore order. But eventually they depart, and Miss Emily's beau returns one final time, never to be seen thereafter. The conclusion toward which we are led, finalized by the single gray hair on the pillow next to Homer Baron's corpse, is that Emily finally found a way to have the man she loved without having to submit to him. Poisoning her lover was an act of revenge and a private declaration of independence.

Hulga's fate makes an interesting contrast against the backdrop of what might be called the pathological feminist protest of Miss Emily. Hulga's rebellion against convention is rooted in protest against standards of femininity that she does not accept, at least in part because she cannot measure up to them. Emily's formative years were spent in the shadow of a domineering father; the young Joy's father is himself a shadowy figure long ago divorced by Mrs. Hopewell. Where was he during the hunting accident that claimed the ten-year-old girl's leg? Did he fire the gun? The absence of the father is the most powerful unacknowledged factor in Joy-Hulga's psychology. If Miss Emily's frustration eventuates in a hidden act of revenge, Hulga's resentment is turned against itself when she falls victim to the man she planned to victimize. Students might well want to discuss whether her comeuppance carries an antifeminist message. Her desire to live according to her own lights and her entirely understandable irritation at the inane insinuations of Mrs. Freeman and the trite practicality of her mother seem completely justified. Is her humiliation at the hands of Manley Pointer a vindication of the sexist status quo? Instructors might pose the ironies raised by pairing a male author in 1930 creating a female character who poisons and preserves her lover for forty-three years against a female author in 1955 whose intellectual female protagonist is seduced out of her prosthetic leg by a simple bible salesman and left helpless in a hayloft.

The gender issue in O'Connor's story cannot be adequately addressed without recourse to the theological debate initiated by Hulga. Here is the area of starkest contrast between O'Connor and Faulkner, and it can be highlighted by assigning "Some Aspects of the Grotesque in Southern Fiction." O'Connor has a theological agenda for incorporating elements of southern gothic in her fiction that Faulkner did not share, and it is evident in "Good Country People." Hulga's plan to seduce the bible salesman is not intended by Hulga only as a demonstration of her power as an independent woman; it is also and primarily meant to teach a religious lesson. She intends to corrupt the naive hayseed in order to show him that sin is an illusion and thus turn him into an atheist. Thus her struggle to free herself from her mother's control and from the straitjacket of gender norms in a patriarchal society is mixed with the wish to deny the God that the shallow people around her uncritically believe in. Spiritual warfare of the sort that she wages against Manley is entirely missing from "A Rose for Emily," and it is an example of what sets O'Connor apart from earlier southern writers and indeed from most of her contemporaries. Her theological concerns also help explain the stylistic differences noted above. She cannot afford an external narrator who pieces together evidence in order to make inferences about the central character; she needs to get inside Hulga's mind to show the psychomachy taking place there.

All these considerations should come into play in discussing the thematic climax of the story: Hulga's humiliation. Students should tackle the question, What has Hulga learned? Manley has certainly revealed her presumption, proving to her that "you ain't so smart" (*Flannery . . . Works* 283). But the larger question is whether her conviction that love is an illusion and God does not exist has been refuted. If the answer is yes, does the defeat of her rationalist nihilism also cancel out her criticism of patriarchal gender norms? Have Mrs. Hopewell and Mrs. Freeman been vindicated?

"The Artificial Nigger" and The Sound and the Fury

A junior-level class on modernist fiction or twentieth-century southern fiction could benefit from a study of symbol in two well-known scenes from O'Connor's and Faulkner's work. Students will of course be familiar with the term *symbol*, but they may not be aware that the concept has a history that brought it to prominence at the end of the nineteenth century. Assigning the entries *symbol* and *symbolism* in a reference work such as *The Bedford Glossary of Critical and Literary Terms* (Murfin and Ray) will give quick and helpful context. The form of modernism embraced by Faulkner places a premium on the role of symbol, as the instructor can explain in a fifteen-minute lecture. I have a brief discussion of the topic in my essay "How the Symbol Means," which compares Faulkner and O'Connor and also cites other helpful sources in making the following case.

An important element of high modernism's aesthetic grew from the conviction that art had the power to bring a coherence to experience that it otherwise lacked and that indeed art was a more complete form of knowledge than the sciences or religion or philosophy could provide. Symbol has an essential epistemological function in literary art. It provides what Malcolm Bradbury and James McFarlane describe as "the hard objective centre of energy, which is distilled from multiplicity, and impersonally and linguistically integrates it" (50). Although Faulkner was not inclined to theory, he absorbed much of his aesthetic from writers he admired and emulated, such as Joyce. Students will be interested to hear that he said Joyce had been "electrocuted by the divine fire" (*Faulkner* 280) and that he tracked down Joyce in Paris in 1925 but was too shy to approach him (Blotner 159). A short lecture can set the stage, but students can best be led to the theory by the same route Faulkner took: close attention to technique in the fiction.

O'Connor inherited a modernist notion of the symbol, both directly through instruction and indirectly through imitating models. But, as students can be encouraged to see for themselves, she bent symbol in a different direction. For a pure modernist such as Faulkner, the effectiveness of symbol derives from the work of art that gives rise to it. Its cognitive function is realized through a collaborative effort between the reader and the linguistic universe the artist has created. For the scholastically influenced O'Connor, symbol has an added dimension: it may function by analogy to the Christian sacraments, becoming a means by which transcendent truth is conveyed to the reader. Faulkner's symbols act as lures, inviting us to tease out their meaning; O'Connor's important symbols are typically confrontational, demanding that we submit to them. The difference emerges vividly when we compare two monuments prominent in their fiction.

Students can be alerted to the symbolic freightedness of "The Artificial Nigger" and the conclusion of *The Sound and the Fury* by brief readings on the Confederate monument phenomenon in the South, which continues to this day.

These memorials were the most visible sign of Lost Cause religion and could be found from the prominent street, Monument Avenue, dedicated to them in Richmond, the former Confederate capital, to the courthouse square of nearly every county seat in the region. The Oxford, Mississippi, that Faulkner knew had two such monuments, one on the courthouse square and one on the University of Mississippi campus. His grandmother, a former president of the local chapter of the United Daughters of the Confederacy, was a driving force behind the erection of the courthouse statue (Blotner 21–22). After the Stars and Bars, the battle flag of the Army of Northern Virginia that became the Confederate flag in popular parlance, the monuments were the preeminent symbol of the Old South. It is for this reason that the racist killings at Emanuel African Methodist Episcopal Church in Charleston, South Carolina, in 2015 triggered a wave of reaction against the monuments, leading to the dismantling or relocation of dozens of them.

Students may be less aware of a second statuary phenomenon widespread in the South of O'Connor's youth: the lawn jockey. Although not unique to the region, these ornaments had a strong resonance in the South because of its history of slavery. Originally designed as hitching posts, the statues were intended to suggest welcome, and white jockeys were portrayed as well as black ones. But the features of the "Jocko" style of African American jockey, with its large lips, white eyes, and slouching posture, fall clearly in the category of racist stereotypes perpetuated in minstrel shows.[1] Add the nineteenth-century associations of pre-automobile American travel, and it is difficult not to see the black lawn jockeys as reminders of slavery. Certainly, O'Connor implies the connection in "The Artificial Nigger." The lawn jockey thus serves as an arresting, parodic counterpoint to the Confederate monument. The monument represents the official, heroic version of the South's struggle in the Civil War; the jockey can be seen as an expression of popular white myths justifying slavery—the African American caricatured in it is grinning and servile, an eternal child in need of white parents. Images of both types of statues are easy to find on the Internet and make striking classroom illustrations.

Comparisons between the two works of fiction will be most effective if students have read the entire Faulkner novel, but it is not necessary for them to do so. A workable shortcut is to assign the novel's final seven pages, beginning with page 314 of the Vintage International corrected text edition. It will be necessary to supply some background on the decline of the Compsons' fortunes, Benjy's love for Caddy, and Dilsey's heroic efforts to hold black and white families together, but the scene between Benjy and Luster stands well on its own. Students are as likely to be surprised by Benjy's outburst at going the wrong way around the square as is Luster. One explanation given by critics that students may well echo is that Benjy is objecting in his inarticulate way to the violation of one of his personal rituals. It is a small jump from this explanation to a larger point concerning the breakdown of order in the social world the Compsons inhabit: history has left them behind, and the old values have not sustained them.

Benjy's cry is the sound and fury signifying nothing, an idiot's protest against change he is powerless to prevent. But it is possible to go deeper into Faulkner's technique by asking students to figure out what Benjy is actually looking at when he howls. A careful reading of the final paragraphs shows that his accustomed route has him facing away from the square. An effective teaching strategy is to ask students to map the route of the surrey. The final sentence of the novel tells us that "his eyes were empty and blue and serene again as cornice and façade flowed smoothly from left to right, post and tree, window and doorway and signboard each in its ordered place" (321). The scenery moves from left to right because, instead of staring straight ahead at the back of the driver's head, Benjy always turns to the right, and when he is driven counterclockwise around the square, his attention is directed to the surrounding buildings. Reversing the usual circuit thus brings him face to face with the Confederate soldier.

Once one makes this connection, it takes on great significance: the statue, which memorializes a dead past of glorified defeat, also represents the failure of the Compsons to accommodate themselves to a changing world. The passage implicitly identifies Ben with the figure on the pedestal. In the Compson family, Benjamin has been a living symbol of failure, disappointment, and even shame. His mother originally called him Maury, after her brother, but on discovering his mental disability, she renamed him using the name the biblical Rachel gave the last of Jacob's children before dying from childbirth. The Hebrew means "son of sorrow," and, as the final Compson child, he seems to signify the demise of the family line. When Faulkner uses imagery and action to identify Ben with the statue, he lifts the Compson tragedy into the context of southern history, making the family an example of a larger cultural failure. His method is subtle and indirect. In addition to the detective work required to work out what Benjy is seeing when he begins to howl, the reader is required to recall the description of Luster and Benjy's arrival: "They approached the square, where the Confederate soldier gazed with empty eyes beneath his marble hand in wind and weather" (319). The imagery here is strikingly similar to that used to describe Benjy in the sentence quoted above. The soldier's eyes are empty; Benjy's are empty and serene. The soldier looks from beneath a marble hand; Benjy sees cornice and facade. Both men are monuments, signifiers, the one a kind of blackly comic parody of the other.

If, as I have suggested, Faulkner intends for the Confederate monument to be the central symbol in the final scene of his favorite novel, his handling of it stands as an excellent example of modernist indirection and deferral. Having read *The Sound and the Fury* half a dozen times, I still needed Daniel Singal's treatment of the passage to open my eyes to the fact that Benjy is facing the statue for the first time when he begins to howl (*William Faulkner* 141–43). After the brief mention when the buggy approaches, the statue drops out of sight, so to speak; we can find it again only by following Benjy's gaze. Likewise, the meaning of the symbol, and of Benjy's outburst, is withheld from us. The scene is vividly rendered; we know what happened. We can even be confident, given all clues concerning Benjy's love of ritual, that the literal cause of his bellowing is unwanted deviation from familiar routine. But the metaphorical meaning that we long for, and that Faulkner has whetted our appetite for from the beginning by giving his novel its allusive title, is held back. We are not content to have the tale told by the idiot signify nothing, yet our conclusions about what it does mean are constantly delayed by the incompleteness of the evidence and the refusal of the author to give us the answer.

O'Connor's technique in "The Artificial Nigger" is the opposite of Faulkner's. To prepare students to see the difference, an instructor can assign a couple of O'Connor's essays. Unlike Faulkner, O'Connor traveled the speaker's circuit and left behind brief but revealing declarations on her writing principles. "The Fiction Writer and His Country" announces a didactic purpose Faulkner did not share. This essay contains the often quoted line "to the hard of hearing you shout, and for the almost blind you draw large and startling pictures" (*Flannery . . . Works* 806). Another excellent theoretical statement of her intentions as a writer is to be found in "The Nature and Aim of Fiction," which is not included in the *Collected Works* volume but may be found in *Mystery and Manners*. A second essay in *Mystery and Manners*, "Writing Short Stories," specifically mentions symbols (98–100). The best illustration, however, is to be found in the story itself.

O'Connor calls attention to her monument through the title, which alerts us to the importance of the story's central symbol before we read the first word. When the two principal characters encounter the statue at the story's climax, they do so directly, exclaiming in turn, "An artificial nigger!" This double proclamation is part of a pattern in which the grandson is made out to be the image of his grandfather, and both resemble the statue, which is "about Nelson's size." When the two stand before the plaster figure "with their necks forward at almost the same angle," they strike the pose of the jockey, which is "pitched forward at an unsteady angle" (*Flannery . . . Works* 229, 230). This identification through imagery is similar to the more subtle parallel Faulkner leads us to see between Ben and the Confederate soldier. However, the narrator's commentary that follows injects a new note. We are told, "They stood gazing at the artificial Negro as if they were faced with some great monument to another's victory that brought them together in their common defeat." The word *monument* here takes us back to *The Sound and the Fury* and the link with the most common type of civic memorial in the South; moreover, the sentence as a whole posits a conclusive judgment about the epiphany that the two have simultaneously received. Despite the "as if," we have little doubt that O'Connor intends this moment to be one of grace. In the story's penultimate paragraph, we are told that on his safe arrival home, Mr. Head "felt the action of mercy touch him again" (230). Further, he now recognizes that "no sin was too monstrous for him to claim as his own, and since God loved in proportion as He forgave, he felt ready at that instant to enter Paradise" (231). There is no deferral of meaning here: O'Connor is drawing in large and startling figures, confronting us with what she would call the analogical meaning of the fictional event, just as the characters are confronted by the unexpected statue. She does omit one connection that is implied without being stated, that the lawn jockey is, in this story, a Christ figure. Students may well wish to discuss both why she thinks this to be an appropriate connection and why she does not make it directly.

Wise Blood *and* Light in August

A course in twentieth-century southern fiction or one on religious themes in modern literature might well feature O'Connor's first novel and Faulkner's most sustained novelistic treatment of religion in the South. The theme of this section of the course could be O'Connor's phrase, "the Christ-haunted South," and it would focus on two fanatical, violent, peripatetic characters whose journeys are fraught with religious meaning. Faulkner's Joe Christmas is the victim of a racist theology who becomes an ironic Christ figure. Hazel Motes of *Wise Blood* dies a victim's death after losing a long, vociferous battle against God.

The heart of *Light in August* is the story of a child born out of wedlock to a white teenage girl and a swarthy circus hand of unknown origin. The child's grandfather is convinced that the long-gone father is black and that the baby is therefore cursed. Doc Hines, as the grandfather is called, thus condemns the boy on theological grounds: he is not only a bastard and therefore the product of sin but also a son of Ham, the race that God has cursed. Hines follows the child to the orphanage in which he was placed, apparently believing it to be his mission to see that the curse is revealed and the sin punished. Hines believes both that the child's course is ordained and that he, Hines, must participate in executing the design. This is but one example of a pernicious form of Calvinism that circumscribes Christmas's life and that he partially internalizes. Three sets of Calvinists do, in fact, shape his destiny: the grandfather, his adoptive parents, and the abolitionist's daughter with whom he has a fatal love affair.

Two sorts of background reading are helpful for coming to terms with this aspect of the novel. The first is brief reading in the history and theology of Calvinism, which can be supplied through reference works and reliable Web sites. William Shurr's book *Rappaccini's Children* is devoted to the Calvinist influence on American literature, and his introduction (esp. 6–8) is helpful and succinct. Shurr summarizes the so-called five points of Calvinism. The emphasis should be on the forms Calvinism took in the United States; students need to know that although it is most often associated with New England and figures such as Jonathan Edwards, it was also a force in the South. A fifteen-minute lecture comparing the religious views of the fiery abolitionist John Brown to those of the Confederate hero Stonewall Jackson could show that Calvinist belief in preordination was equally strong on both sides of the slavery issue. A handy summary of major theological convictions can be found in the Westminster Shorter Catechism, which McEachern, Christmas's adoptive father, tries to force him to memorize. Also helpful is reading specifically on race. Students can be pointed to articles on "the curse of Ham" and on the "one drop rule" of racial classification. *The New World Encyclopedia* has an article on the first topic ("Curse"). For the second, sociologist F. James Davis has a short article on the pbs.org Web site in connection with the *Frontline* story "Jefferson's Blood."

These sources provide the context to make sense of Joe Christmas's self-hatred. He is at once a rebel who refuses to submit to unjust authority and a wounded soul who believes in the curse that has been pronounced on him. He fights against a fate he knows he cannot escape, and the uncertainty of his parentage only exacerbates his anxiety. He becomes a kind of anti-Christ, murdering the lover who prays over him and preaching racial hatred from the pulpit of a black church he has violently seized. His death is an ironic martyrdom; after a final fruitless escape, he allows himself to be shot by a Nazi-like vigilante whose racist bloodlust sickens his own comrades. I use the term *martyrdom* advisedly here; Christmas is more accurately a scapegoat. The cause for which he is martyred is that of the racial classification scheme on which southern society is built. His death is a sacrifice to the ideology that against his will he internalized and ultimately submitted to. Students might benefit from knowing that in 1908 a black man named Nelse Patton was lynched on the square in Faulkner's Oxford, the crowd acting after a judge and several ministers failed to dissuade them (Blotner 31–33). The literature on the horrible lynching phenomenon in the South of Faulkner's youth is extensive.

This line of thought can in turn lead to a discussion of the puzzling aftermath of Christmas's death, in which the town is restored to peace, the sound of its Sunday church services seeming to signal that from the point of view of the white citizens, the social order has been vindicated and God is pleased. Gail Hightower, the disgraced Presbyterian minister who is helpless to prevent what amounts to a lynching, muses resignedly and ineffectually in his dark house. The possibly biracial Joe Christmas, whose name and age clearly recall Jesus Christ, becomes in the novel an entirely ironic religious figure, the sacrificial victim for a God who has ordained the racial divide as an eternal reminder of human sin.

O'Connor's Hazel Motes is a blackly comic character and therefore quite different from Christmas. An exercise that provides relief from the grim tragedy of Christmas is to ask students to bring in favorite comic lines from *Wise Blood* — perhaps one passage of narration describing Motes and one in which he or another character speaks a humorously framed truth about him. Motes has an innocence lacking in the dangerous, world-weary Christmas, yet he is equally determined in his efforts to escape the religion of his youth. Having left east Tennessee for the army, he and his naive faith are belittled by his more cosmopolitan buddies, and he returns determined to disabuse others of their Christianity. He adopts the methods of his grandfather, who "carried Jesus in his head like a stinger" (*Flannery . . . Works* 9–10). Motes, however, preaches the Church without Christ, an anti-Gospel that needs no savior. Comically mistaken for a conventional preacher wherever he goes, he is a driven man, scrupulous in his blasphemy and conscientious in his licentiousness. Motes and Christmas make for an interesting study in compulsive behavior. Both are pre-occupied with purity and see sex as a kind of evil, which they turn to in order to defy the moralism they resent. Both act for reasons they don't understand and cannot articulate. Both struggle against forces operating on their psyches that they cannot control. The big difference between them is that Joe fights against notions society has inflicted on him through upbringing and social mores, whereas Haze's struggle is ultimately with God.

This difference, which is likely to be the subject of classroom debate, can be posed by juxtaposing two actions occupying similar points in the narrative arc of the respective novels. Christmas, for reasons not readily apparent, escapes from jail and then allows himself to be cornered and killed. Motes, having lost the automobile that represented to him his complete autonomy, blinds himself with quicklime. Christmas's death is described twice, both times from the point of view of witnesses. The first account, that of the lawyer Gavin Stevens, describes his final actions in racial terms as the result of a battle between his black blood and his white blood: Christmas grew tired of the struggle and wanted simply to die. Stevens surmises that he "crouched behind that table and defied the black blood for the last time, as he had been defying it for thirty years. He crouched behind the overturned table and let them shoot him to death, with that loaded and unfired pistol in his hand" (449). The second description, narrated in the third person from the point of view of the posse, emphasizes the vicious resolve of Percy Grimm and the passive suffering of Christmas after Grimm has shot and mutilated him: "He just lay there, with his eyes open and empty of everything save consciousness, and with something, a shadow, about his mouth. For a long moment he looked up at them with peaceful and unfathomable and unbearable eyes" (464–65).

Motes puts out his own eyes, following through on a resolution he undertakes as soon as the deputy pushes his car over the embankment. Like Christmas, he is guilty of murder, but it is not remorse over this misdeed that prompts his action. We are never told the reason, which entirely eludes Mrs. Flood, his landlady. But we can make inferences based on his laconic remarks to Mrs. Flood after the fact. In contrast to Christmas, Motes's suffering is active and intentional; he seems to be seeking something rather than escaping through his pain. When he extends his mortifications of the flesh to wearing glass in his shoes and wrapping his chest in barbed wire, he says he is doing so "[t]o pay" (*Flannery . . . Works* 125). "I'm not clean," he says on another occasion (127). He is performing acts of penance aimed at a reconciliation beyond the law and indeed beyond the visible world. "If there's no bottom in your eyes, they hold more," he asserts (126). His earlier rejection of the very notion of sin has turned into recognition of himself as a sinner; his flight from God has turned into a pilgrimage.

Read in the way I am suggesting, Motes's death is not a tragedy, as Christmas's surely is. The vision given the landlady who holds his dead hand is hopeful:

> She shut her eyes and saw the pin point of light but so far away that she could not hold it steady in her mind. She felt as if she were blocked at the entrance of something. She sat staring with her eyes shut, into his eyes, and felt as if she had finally got to the beginning of something she couldn't begin, and she saw him moving farther and farther away, farther and farther into the darkness until he was the pin point of light.   (131)

If Motes has become the pinpoint of light, the haze lifted from his eyes, his story has become a kind of divine comedy. Faulkner's portrayal of Christmas is a brilliant example of modernist psychological realism; O'Connor's Motes partakes of the romance tradition practiced in American literature by Hawthorne. Where Christianity in general is concerned, Faulkner is in his novel primarily exposing the corruption of a culture religion that props up a racist society. O'Connor is determined to replace a superficial and therefore false conventional Christianity with the real thing.

Students should take away from this comparison a better understanding of two approaches to the role of religion in fiction and an insight into the history of race and religion in the American South in the first half of the twentieth century. For Faulkner, religion is one dimension of culture that art may explore and expose. For O'Connor, religion, or more accurately the action of God in the world, is the prime subject; everything else is secondary. In short, she's a bit like Hazel Motes. Having been introduced to this comparison, students may wish to explore in a research project the biographical and personal differences between Faulkner and O'Connor. I have attempted to frame their different conceptions of the artist in "Portraits of the Artist: O'Connor's 'The Enduring Chill' and Faulkner's 'Elmer.'" The topic of the intertwining of race and religion in the South is also a fruitful one for research presentations and papers. Faulkner's description of how Calvinism reinforces racism can be juxtaposed with O'Connor's determination to put issues of divine-human interaction above social issues in such works as "The Artificial Nigger" and "Everything That Rises Must Converge." Students who pursue the issue of race in connection with these authors should have no trouble generating a lengthy bibliography. Detailed comparisons of the two writers are rare, however, and thus the opportunity for plagiarism is diminished and the scope for original thinking is wide.

NOTE

[1] Although legend attributes the name Jocko to a twelve-year-old African American boy who died heroically while serving under George Washington during the Revolutionary War, most historians find the story highly unlikely. More plausible is the explanation that the name comes from the jockey's costume in which the figure is dressed, which is consistent with the use of the statues as decorative hitching posts. See Pilgrim.

The Physical and Psychological Violence of Race Relations in Ann Petry and O'Connor

Margaret Earley Whitt

Over a century ago, W. E. B. Du Bois began his *The Souls of Black Folk* with this now famous line: "The problem of the twentieth century is the problem of the color-line" (9). More than a half century later, when Flannery O'Connor and Ann Petry wrote their respective short stories that emphasize issues of race, the "problem of the color-line" was in the air they breathed, and it remains so as we find ourselves in the first decades of the twenty-first century. T. C. Tanner, white, is the protagonist of O'Connor's "Judgment Day," and Charles Woodruff, black, is the protagonist of Petry's "The Witness": both characters find themselves in New York because circumstances in Georgia and in Virginia, respectively, have dictated that staying home is no longer a viable option. While O'Connor's violence is physical and racial—a white man at the hands of a black man—Petry's violence is psychological and racial: a black man at the hands of white teens. Both from the South, Tanner and Woodruff carry with them preconceived notions about the other race as they move to the North. In both stories, violence is also religiously and historically haunted. In the end, both men, one dead and one living, return to their homes in the South. In a course that privileges the study of race in O'Connor, "Judgment Day" paired with "The Witness," deepens the discussion from both sides of that color line.

Ann Petry, like her father before her, trained as a pharmacist and worked in the family drugstore in Old Saybrook, Connecticut, her home for most of her life. Her first novel, *The Street* (1946), distinguished her as one of the "most successful follower[s] of the 'Richard Wright School of urban protest'" ("Ann Petry").[1] But Petry bristled at the idea of having her writing categorized, believing that the universal human condition of struggle was inherently more interesting than the particular struggles of race. In the 1940s, she also published short stories, in mostly black journals, and in the same year that O'Connor published her first story, "The Geranium" (1946), Petry's "Like a Winding Sheet" was named to the *Best American Short Stories* volume. Although her short stories were published over several decades (1940s–1971), her only collection appeared in 1971; she was the first African American woman to have a collection of her stories published (Lubin 8). "The Witness" was first published in the February 1971 issue of *Redbook Magazine* and is among the thirteen stories included in *"Miss Muriel" and Other Stories*. In 1995, Gloria Naylor selected "The Witness" for inclusion in her volume *Children of the Night: The Best Short Stories by Black Writers, 1967 to the Present*. Petry's stories appear often in literary anthologies, and contrasting them with Zora Neale Hurston's stories shows the difference between the school of protest writing (Petry) and the school of celebratory writing (Hurston). O'Connor finished "Judgment Day" the summer she died, in

1964, but it was first published in her 1965 collection *Everything That Rises Must Converge.*[2]

"Judgment Day" is often paired with "The Geranium," because the comparison helps us observe the growth of the writer over the years. The northern African American writer and a southern white writer both understood the perils of race and demonstrated their awareness by making a consciousness about race control their characters' actions. Because both Petry and O'Connor are deliberate in their assignment of character to race, I show in this essay how pairing them offers a fresh view of their themes and a better perspective on the nature of the violence they depict: plot points in both stories turn on race, location is shaped by thoughts on race, and race cannot be separated from the violence that results. Indeed, violence happens because of attitudes about race.

Class discussion could begin by having students unpack the titles of these stories. Judgment Day will come, according to the New Testament, at the end of the world, when Jesus returns and judges the good and bad deeds people have done to one another. Sarah Gordon suggests that this title gives "fresh meaning" to familiar phrases; the reader will be well served by rethinking even "the most ordinary use of language" (*Flannery O'Connor: The Obedient Imagination* 134). In O'Connor's story, on the literal level, the title is a joke that Tanner concocts about his return to his Georgia home in Corinth and to his lifelong friend Coleman. *Witness*, used as a noun in Petry's title, is one who watches and can give evidence in a court of law. Woodruff is kidnapped by delinquent youths who want him to be their "pro-tec-shun" (222) as they gang-rape a girl they have pushed into their rattletrap car.[3] But Woodruff, straitjacketed into his expensive new winter coat and blinded by a wool cap pulled over his eyes, does not see, and his word against that of the teens—that "he hadn't touched the girl"—would only suggest that he was a participant in the crime because others would assume that where there is "smoke there must be fire" (229).

Though the titles suggest on the literal level that "judgment day" is a joke between two men—Tanner, who is white, and Coleman, who is black (coal man)—and "the witness" is ironically a man who cannot see the story's pivotal action, they resonate far more deeply. "Judgment day" affects Tanner's daughter, the changing laws of the South, and Tanner's relationship with the next-door neighbor in New York, who is an actor, not a preacher. "Witness" extends to the whole of white Wheeling (in New York, not West Virginia) and the changing laws that may or may not affect the town's thinking. It is interesting that each title comments on the contents of the other story, because a judgment day has arrived for Woodruff, in which he serves as judge and jury on himself, and Tanner becomes a witness, like Woodruff, who cannot see beyond what his region has taught him about the other race.

The settings, another class discussion topic, can open the similarity of both men's responses to the North and the South. The two stories emphasize the cold, indifferent, violent, biased worlds that Woodruff and Tanner find when they arrive in the North. Wheeling, the fictional setting of "The Witness," appears in three other Petry stories;[4] in each case, the whiteness of the setting is emphasized. "Witness" opens in a more-suffocating-than-beautiful snow that has been falling for twenty-four hours (211). The cold and the white are literal here, but when Woodruff is introduced, we meet a competent teacher in an "all-white community" who was hired by a "little frozen Northern town" that needed to integrate and was looking for a black teacher. Woodruff spent his entire adult working life at Virginia College for Negroes. He retired with plans to write a first-year English grammar, but when his wife died, everything seemed "inconsequential" (213), so he answered an advertisement for a position to teach academic-oriented high school seniors in the North. It was, he thought, an easy way out from his loss, memories, and pain. But he took the South (the protected enclave of a black school) with him to the North, where nothing was as good as what he left behind. Even the stale dryer smell of clothes not properly rinsed offended his nose, as he longed for the smell of "new-mown hay and flower gardens and—Addie" (222).

In "Judgment Day," when Tanner arrives in New York, he takes only a one-time fifteen-minute sightseeing tour to learn that this is "no place for a sane man" (*Flannery . . . Works* 686). From the window looking out on a brick wall in an alley "full of New York air, the kind fit for cats and garbage," he knows he is in "no kind of place" (676). He writes these words in his note to Coleman, which he pins inside his pocket, and he repeats his summing up of the "pigeon-hutch of a building" with its foreigners and their strange ways of behaving: It is "no kind of place" (686). In Corinth, Georgia, Tanner had only a shack and Coleman, who treated him "like he was white" for the past thirty years (684). The shack offered "air around it. . . . [And] he could put his feet on the ground" (686). In the South, Tanner understood both his environment and its worldview. A man could breathe the clear air of the South, because the superiority of white over black there was unquestioned. As Bruce Gentry points out, when Tanner goes north to the "land of miscegenation," he needs to worry about his becoming "tanner" ("O'Connor" 197) and thinks that becoming a "nigger's white nigger" might have been more tolerable than life in the North (*Flannery . . . Works* 685). The South is indeed his kind of place. The unknown in New York represents uncertainty and violence, as it does for Woodruff.

Both Tanner and Woodruff are aware of civil rights activities and changes in laws, but both also know that the mind-set of people can lag far behind what a new law dictates. Both use generalizations to put all black people or white people into stereotypical categories. Having students list stereotypes before reading the stories may help illuminate the characters for them when they do read. Though Woodruff is an educated professional black man, he doubts that his New York acquaintances—Shipley, the preacher with whom he participates in a class held for seven white teen delinquents, and his fellow teachers and students, who all have given him high marks for what he knows and how he conducts himself—will take his word over the word of the seven delinquents. Tanner is a working white country man, who used to manage a half dozen black workers at a sawmill, owned a piece of land until he lost it, and then with Coleman built a shack on someone else's land and lived contentedly. The buyer of the land on which he squatted was a "brown" doctor, "only part black" (680), who assumed that Tanner and Coleman ran a still somewhere, so he reasoned in his stereotypical way: Wouldn't Tanner want to run that still for him? With his back against his own set of beliefs, Tanner confirms that though he is aware that the laws have changed, the "governmint ain't got around yet to forcing the white folks to work for the colored" (684). Tanner and Woodruff both regret their choice to go north; for both, the violence that meets them there adds a new layer of complication that did not exist for either in their comfortable southern locales.

To represent her professional black man, Petry uses the "nigger" epithet only once and puts the word in Woodruff's mouth to refer to himself. He does this knowing that those white people around him, deep down, must see him that way. The white delinquents call him "ho-daddy," with no affection attached (222). O'Connor uses "nigger" more than twenty times—mostly by Tanner in reference to Coleman, his closest friend, where affection is present. Tanner's daughter uses the word once to show that her mother taught her not to dally with the race, suggesting, ironically, a tribute to her sophistication. A classroom discussion of the use of such words, with particular attention paid to context, could deepen students' understanding of how language by itself can be a kind of violence.

Tanner has no wife—though he has three sons and a daughter—but, typical of so many of O'Connor's stories, a single parent is the norm. Yet Coleman is a mate in many ways. The two live together in the shack they built. Coleman sleeps at the "foot of Tanner's bed" (679), he cooks, cuts Tanner's firewood, and empties his slop. At the beginning of their relationship, Tanner whittles a pair of eyeglasses, which he gives to Coleman so that Coleman might see better. The glasses take on a mystical, surreal quality; they bring to mind the biblical story of Paul, also a tanner,[5] in his letter to the people of Corinth, also the Georgia town from which Tanner hails, that perhaps he has seen through these glasses darkly but will one day see God face to face (1 Cor. 13.12). Coleman wears the glasses and sees a white man, who expects to be treated as such. The glasses appear to be the means through which Tanner and Coleman understand their relationship.

Glasses play an important role with Woodruff and his wife, Addie, as well. When the youths break his glasses, he has to pull out an old pair on his return home. It was Addie who insisted that he stop wearing them, for although he thought they gave him the air of a "careful scholarly man," she believed they would make it easy for his students to "caricature him," suggesting also that the steel-rimmed frames made his eyes look "as though they were trapped behind those little glasses" (228). Addie appears to be the boss of Woodruff. In both stories, those who wear glasses, Coleman and Woodruff, are directed and led by those who know better, Tanner and Addie. In these stories, glasses do not improve vision. Students could be asked what more Addie and Tanner tell us about Woodruff and Coleman.

Keith Clark posits that while "no tangible evidence suggests that Petry read the most gothic of southern women writers, Flannery O'Connor, 'The Witness' nonetheless demonstrates Petry's similar tropologizing of space" (138). After Tanner has used his southern knowledge to try to make friends with the new black couple next door—the knowledge that all black men are flattered when they are called "Preacher," all want to go fishing, and all miss their southern homes—he decides this neighbor's home must be south Alabama. But this man is an actor, his home is New York City, and he has no interest in taking "crap . . . off no wool-hat, red-neck, son-of-a-bitch peckerwood old bastard" (*Flannery . . . Works* 690). The man's female partner tries to get around Tanner in the hall, "as if she were skirting an open garbage can" (689).

When Tanner repeats the name "Preacher," the actor retorts, "I'm not a preacher! I'm not a Christian. I don't believe in that crap. There ain't no Jesus and there ain't no God." When Tanner claims that he isn't white and the actor isn't black, the New York City man becomes violent, and Tanner is "slammed," "yanked," "grabbed," "shoved," and finally "knocked" through the open door of the apartment, where he falls "reeling" and "crack[s]" his head. From the blow, he has a stroke (690). When his daughter leaves for the store, he tries to make his way down four flights of stairs, wanting to return to Corinth and Coleman, only to pitch forward and fall again. When his daughter returns, she finds her father "head and arms thrust between the spokes of the banister" and his "hat . . . pulled down over his face and head" (695). With the hat over his face, Tanner becomes the same kind of witness that Woodruff is: he does not see, and he cannot change.

After the Sunday night class, Woodruff, returning to his car, sees the delinquents forcing a young girl into their car. Though he speaks to them with a voice of authority, he also hears himself do so as "a black man speaking with a white man's voice" (221). The youths attack him: they shatter his glasses; take his cap, keys, and wallet; reverse his coat so that it becomes a straitjacket; and push him into their car, with a black wool cap pulled over his eyes and nose. He cannot see, has difficulty breathing, and cannot be heard over the noise of the car. When they finally arrive at their destination—a maintenance shed at a cemetery—Woodruff is taken inside and made to stand facing the wall with the coat and cap still restricting his movement and vision. He cannot see Nellie being gang-raped but hears the sounds, manages to see shadows on the wall. The violence toward him is more psychological than physical. When the boys are done with Nellie, they twist Woodruff around, take off his coat and cap, and offer him his turn. He does not move, but they force his hand to touch her thigh and breasts. Then they laugh at him and leave him there, taking Nellie, "half-naked, head hanging down limply," to their car (227).

Woodruff plans to call the police on his return home but realizes that he cannot. He must get out of Wheeling and return to the only place where he understands life. All the luxury items he bought in his new life in the North, including his beloved coat, are now associated with the crime. He can and does leave, but he will be haunted forever by the memory of what took place in the cemetery.

What died for Woodruff that night was his "whiteness," which he sought through his dress (he was called a "prince" by the slick New York City salesman who sold him the expensive cashmere coat [212]) and through his delight that the seven youths were white but he, along with Dr. Shipley, the Congregational minister, was in a position of authority over them, which "niggerized" the youths (Clark 144). When Tanner comes to his own end, literally pilloried into the banister, his blackness dies with him. He never saw himself as black and would no doubt take umbrage at the suggestion, but his best friend is black. He prefers Coleman's company to that of his own daughter.

Not a moment in either story is separated from race. If Woodruff were white, would he call the police? Would he leave town? For that matter, would he have been taken by the teens to serve as "witness"? If Tanner were black, would his daughter have suggested that he come to New York? Would he have objected to working for the new part-black owner of the land in Corinth? Without race, would there have been violence? Would there even have been a story?

Physical violence ends Tanner's life. But he gets what he wanted most, to return to Corinth, where his faith in race was certain and comfortable. Psychological violence ends Woodruff's life in the North; he will return to his Virginia home and a death-in-life existence.

To date, no anthology carries both "Judgment Day" and "The Witness." There are a number of anthologies of best stories by black writers, but none of best stories by white writers. A quick look through any anthology of short stories will indicate that most are by white writers, though progress toward diversity has been made over the last several decades. O'Connor is considered by all to be a major canonical writer, but the status of Petry depends entirely on who is asked that question. O'Connor and Petry, who never met and who most likely never read each other's work, might well have found in each other an empathetic companion.

NOTES

[1] In his seminal "Blueprint for Negro Writing," Wright set forth a paradigm that would emphasize the inequality of the races in this country. "Protest writing" became the easy name for the writers who would follow his "blueprint," and some scholars began also to identify these African American writers as belonging to the literary left.

[2] The content of "The Geranium" occupied O'Connor for the rest of her life. The story became "An Exile in the East" in the mid-1950s, then "Getting Home," and, finally, "Judgment Day" in 1964. For an overview of the story's various drafts, culminating in how the first published version in *Everything That Rises Must Converge* is different from the final wording in the Library of America edition, see Westarp, "'Judgement Day.'"

[3] All quotations from and references to this story are taken from *"Miss Muriel" and Other Stories*.

[4] The Wheeling stories are "Miss Muriel," "The New Mirror," and "Has Anybody Seen Miss Dora Dean?"

[5] "According to a tradition recorded by Jerome, both Paul's parents came from Gischala in Galilee. His father was of the tribe of Benjamin. It is evident that the family had a leather factory or weaving mill, where they manufactured the famous 'cilicium' textiles. This was made of the hair of goats bred on the Cilician plateau. Soldiers and sailors favoured this warm clothing. Working rough goat hair was an awkward business and often made one's hands bleed. The church fathers called Paul a tanner or tentmaker" ("Paul's Childhood").

Teaching O'Connor's "Everything That Rises Must Converge" and Alice Walker's "Convergence" in the Twenty-First-Century South

Nagueyalti Warren

For years, Sally Wolff and I discussed team teaching a class in southern literature for undergraduate students at Emory University. However, as associate deans in the college, we could not find the time. Her research on William Faulkner and mine on Alice Walker provided for interesting conversations, and finally, in 2008, after both of us had returned to full-time faculty positions, we proposed Reading Southern Literature in Black and White as an undergraduate seminar cross-listed in English and African American Studies. We chose to teach Margaret Walker and Eudora Welty, William Faulkner and Richard Wright, and Flannery O'Connor and Alice Walker. The course went well, and we plan eventually to publish a book with the same title as our course. Teaching O'Connor and Walker together led to my renewed interest in O'Connor's works. She and Walker, both Georgia writers, have both parallel and converging lives.

In 2009, Emory University Libraries acquired Walker's papers, and I discovered her unpublished story "Convergence." Teaching O'Connor and Walker together enables a bifocal view that illuminates a particular era in southern life and history. Even before discovering the story, I had spent time discussing the southern geography that helped form and inspire the fiction of both writers. O'Connor and Walker once lived within a few miles of each other in middle Georgia, just off Route 441, yet were separated by age, race, and class. Biographical information may not be essential to teaching O'Connor or Walker, but it is important for fully understanding their work. In the twenty-first-century classroom, where some students, both black and white, assume they are living in a postracial society, O'Connor's work read next to Walker's is eye-opening. The classroom atmosphere has changed significantly since 2008, when my colleague and I team-taught the course. We did not have the advantage of reading Walker's "Convergence" then, but as I taught the works after the shooting deaths of Trayvon Martin, Michael Brown, and Tamir Rice and in the wake of Black Lives Matter demonstrations, students were asking what had changed since the 1950s and 1960s described in the stories. The effect of these twenty-first-century killings has been similar to the response of many Americans to the Emmett Till murder that took place in 1955. The history and context that inform both stories are a catalyst for discussing the deep concerns that students have about justice in the United States.

In 1961 O'Connor wrote in a letter to Brainard Cheney that "Everything that Rises Must Converge" was her reflection on the race situation (*Correspondence*

134). Before writing this story, it seems she was intent on ignoring the race situation so apparent in the South. The integration of the University of Georgia, the Freedom Rides with the bus burning in Anniston, Alabama, the murder of Herbert Lee for registering black voters, the Savannah boycott, sit-ins, pray-ins—this was 1961 in the South.

My seminars are small, consisting of no more than fifteen students. Limiting the number of students tends to increase the participation of those who would remain silent in larger classes. Issues about race and racism often are part of our discussions. The question posited by many African American students is whether O'Connor was a racist. I cannot answer definitively if she was or was not, but by reading about her life, they can decide for themselves. I also introduce an alternative question: it may not matter if she was racist; the real issue might be whether or not her work is. In a letter dated 3 May 1964, O'Connor writes, "You know I am an integrationist by principle and a segregationist by taste anyway. I don't *like* negroes. They all give me a pain and the more of them I see, the less I like them. Particularly the new kind" (qtd. in Michaels 180). This letter is not included in *The Habit of Being*, which is part of the suggested reading for students; it is in the Flannery O'Connor Collection at Georgia College and State University. I only recently became aware of this O'Connor statement but will share it with my students along with her better-known statement about James Baldwin.[1]

Not surprisingly, O'Connor's influence on southern African American writers has received little attention, because there is not much, but her influence on the work of at least one African American writer is clear. There are two essays in which Walker affirms her connection with O'Connor. The first, "Saving the Life That Is Your Own: The Importance of Models in the Artist's Life," clearly acknowledges O'Connor as a model (*In Search* 8). In the second, "Beyond the Peacock: The Reconstruction of Flannery O'Connor," she reveals that in 1952 she had lived down the Eatonton-to-Milledgeville road from O'Connor. As a college student at Sarah Lawrence, she encountered O'Connor's writings and "read her books endlessly, scarcely conscious of the difference between [O'Connor's] racial and economic background and my own" (42). Thus O'Connor and Walker converge on several grounds. Caught in the paradoxical milieu of the American South—Georgia pines, red clay earth, smoldering heat, front porches and folk vernacular, shrouded in religion and violence—both writers convey the uniqueness of the twentieth-century South. In the landscape of New York, Walker found herself at home with O'Connor. Parallel lines led both writers to New York, but whereas O'Connor returned to the South and remained there for the rest of her short life, Walker returned to work in the civil rights movement but then left to make her home in California. Both writers suffered from physical disabilities: O'Connor suffered and died from lupus; Walker is blind in her right eye because of a shooting incident when she was eight years old. These similarities and differences enable students to understand better the works of both writers. It encourages them to imagine living without hope of recovery from an illness, as O'Connor did, or seeing the world with only one eye, as Walker has done. To ignore the racist, sexist, religious, and provincial small towns in which both writers grew up is to miss or misread significant aspects of their works.

Richard Giannone writes that Pierre Teilhard de Chardin, whose writings inspired the title of O'Connor's story "Everything That Rises Must Converge," provided O'Connor with the "phrase 'passive diminishments' to describe the inescapable afflictions that could be spiritualized into creative forces" (*Flannery O'Connor and the Mystery* 24). Her disease was a passive diminishment. For Walker, racism and partial blindness are diminishments that she also has used to fuel her creative productions. Whereas O'Connor believed that her sickness led her to the need to meet God, Walker believes that racism, sexism, and all the other isms must lead to activism. One might say that O'Connor's focus is on the hereafter and Walker's is on the here and now.

Another troublesome issue for students is connected to the first: O'Connor's use of the word "nigger." In teaching the story "The Artificial Nigger," my colleague attempted to explain the spiritual significance of the story. Her explanation reminded me of the lecture I had received as an undergraduate regarding the merits of Joseph Conrad's *Heart of Darkness*. Chinua Achebe's and Ngũgĩ wa Thiong'o's responses to Conrad's work years later finally articulated how I had felt about the work as a student. O'Connor identifies "The Artificial Nigger" as her favorite story. She says, "What I had in mind . . . was the redemptive quality of the Negro's suffering for us all" (*Flannery . . . Works* 931). Some students understood redemptive suffering as merely rendering black people as scapegoats.

Toni Morrison's *Playing in the Dark* is helpful in discussing the inarticulate black presence in O'Connor. Morrison points out that critics (and readers) often "see no connection between God's grace and Africanist 'othering' in Flannery O'Connor" (14). According to Morrison, race is a metaphor, "a way of referring to and disguising forces, events, classes, and expressions of social decay and economic division far more threatening to the body politic than biological 'race' ever was" (63). Interestingly, it is O'Connor's dispassionate and piercing description of white characters that inspired Walker:

> It was for her description of Southern white women that I appreciated her work at first, because when she set her pen to them not a whiff of magnolia hovered in the air . . . and . . . I could say, yes, these white folks without the magnolia (who are indifferent to the tree's existence), and these black folk without melons and superior racial patience, these are like Southerners that I know.   (*In Search* 52)

Perhaps most important of all is O'Connor's spirituality—not her religion, not the Catholicism, but the acknowledgment of mystery. Walker recognizes this in O'Connor when she says that if the work is about anything, "then it is 'about' prophets and prophecy, 'about' revelation, and 'about' the impact of supernatural grace on human beings who don't have a chance of spiritual growth without it" (53). Ironically, Walker as a pagan and O'Connor as a devout Catholic have more in common than one might expect. Their point of convergence is mystery, but their place of departure is the unknown that the Catholic Church and organized religion seek to answer and one that Walker is content to accept.

One way to approach the teaching of O'Connor and Walker is to have students read Walker's statement about stories. She says southern "black writers and white writers seem to . . . be writing one immense story—the same story, for the most part—with different parts of this immense story coming from a multitude of different perspectives" (5). Thus O'Connor's "Everything That Rises Must Converge" is "only half a story" (51). Walker wrote but never had published the other half. In a manuscript titled "Convergence," she writes back to O'Connor, saying, in the subtitle for her story, "The Duped Shall Enter Last: But They Shall Enter" (Walker Archive box 72, folder 8). Just as "Convergence" speaks to "Everything That Rises Must Converge," Walker's subtitle is a double-voice parody of O'Connor's "The Lame Shall Enter First." I ask students to compare the parallels between "Everything That Rises" and "Convergence" and discuss the complete meaning that emerges from both writers.

Students discuss O'Connor's influence on Walker through the idea of there being just one story. I ask students to think about how stories grow out of other stories and to pay attention to the intertextuality of the two stories. For African American writers, acknowledging literary precursors was not always acceptable. Henry Louis Gates, Jr., has observed how uncomfortable it may be for African American writers to revise the works of others, which may explain why Walker never had her story published. Gates wrote, "Revision is a curious and perhaps even ironic matter to pursue in the black tradition, if only for the odd role that originality has assumed in black letters" (113). Historically African American writers were thought to not have the ability to write, or even to think, for that matter. Those writers who did not conform to the prevalent belief regarding the inability of African American people to be original were called imitators. As a result, originality came to mean more to African American writers than it did to those who criticized them. Any number of writers are known to borrow freely from others and some without acknowledgment.

The parallels between the two stories are striking, beginning with the names of the central characters. In Walker's story, Adrianne is the counterpart to Julian. Both have classical names, and both have mothers who appear trapped in the pre–Civil War and pre–civil rights era. Both Julian and Adrianne attempt to change their mothers' minds, and both also hold the aging women in contempt.

O'Connor completed "Everything That Rises Must Converge" at the time of the integration of the University of Georgia and the landmark 1961 Freedom Rides to desegregate interstate bus and train stations throughout the South. In 1960, the *Boynton v. Virginia* court case ruled segregated buses unconstitutional. Regarding the massive social and political movements swirling around her, O'Connor refers to them, when she acknowledges them at all, as "topical" issues (*Habit* 436). One might expect a deeper analysis coming from one whose piercing vision aims at prophecy. Nevertheless, there is no clear statement in "Everything That Rises" that racism is sinful. In *Passing by the Dragon*, J. Ramsey Michaels suggests that O'Connor sees "racism as a corporate sin, the sin of a particular culture and a particular time, not the sin of an individual . . . like Mr. Head in 'The Artificial Nigger'" (178).

O'Connor's story centers on a white woman who cannot adjust to the changes that social movements have brought to the South and on her college-educated son who tries to make her aware of the new world around her. Walker, in a conversation with her mother about this O'Connor's story, says, "O'Connor thought that the South, as it became more 'progressive,' would become just like the North. Culturally bland, physically ravished, and, where the people are concerned, well, you wouldn't be able to tell one racial group from another" (*In Search* 50). Therefore, an expensive, outlandish, purple-and-green hat that Julian's mother purchases symbolizes a certain uniqueness. The mother says, "[Y]ou only live once and paying a little more for it, I at least won't meet myself coming and going" (*Flannery . . . Works* 486). But this is precisely what happens. On the integrated bus that she refuses to ride alone, forcing her son to accompany her to the YWCA weight-reducing class every Wednesday evening, she is confronted by an overweight (as is the mother) black woman sporting the identical hat. Morrison's definition of "metaphysical condensation" helps explain this "black double" in the story. According to Morrison, metaphysical condensation allows writers "to transform social and historical differences into universal differences. Collapsing persons into animals prevents human contact and exchange; equating speech with grunts or other animal sounds closes off the possibility of communication" (*Playing* 68). When the black woman enters the bus and sits next to Julian, the narrator says that she "muttered something unintelligible to herself. He was conscious of a kind of bristling next to him, muted growling like that of an angry cat." O'Connor has Julian tell his mother that the black woman is her "black double" (*Flannery . . . Works* 499) while simultaneously reducing the black woman to an animal by referring to her as the "Negress," by analogy to *tigress* or *lioness*. The other reference to the black woman as animal or simian occurs when Julian's mother looks at the black woman "as if the woman were a monkey that had stolen her hat" (496).

The mother attempts to ignore the black woman sitting on the bus in front of her. Walker observes that the white woman "chooses to treat the incident of the identical hats as a case of monkey-see, monkey-do. She assumes she is not the monkey, of course" (*In Search* 50). Because the white woman is so out of touch with the times, she begins to flirt with the black woman's "cute" little son, oblivious to the black woman's anger, and when they get off the bus, she offers the boy "a bright new penny" (*Flannery . . . Works* 498). Insulted by the condescension of the white woman, the black woman smacks her with a large red pocketbook. Julian tried to warn his mother about her attitudes and behavior—she views black people as "inferior" (497)—but she refuses to listen. She believes that his "radical ideas" are due to his lack of experience. Julian claims to be "free of prejudice and unafraid to face facts" (491–92). Reeling from the blow, his mother completely loses her grip on her sanity. Julian is contrite, but it is too late to make amends to his mother. Her demise ushers him into a world of "guilt and sorrow" in classic O'Connor style (500).

Walker's mother, to whom the O'Connor story is told, feels sympathy for the disoriented old white woman, exclaiming, "poor thing," a response that Walker identifies as "a total identification [with this horrid woman] that is *so* Southern and *so* black" (*In Search* 51). The so-black sympathy is where Walker picks up the thread for her own story. When her mother asks her why she makes trips back to the South, Walker tells her that she is searching for wholeness. She claims that the truth of any situation "only comes when all the sides of the story are put together, and all their different meanings make one new one. Each writer writes the missing part of the other writer's story. And the whole story is what I'm after" (49). In writing the missing part of the O'Connor story, Walker creates a story that is whole. She completed it 28 June 1966 and dedicated it "to the memory of Flannery O'Connor." It is an early work, preceding the publication of her first collection of poems, and Walker was only twenty-two years old.

"Convergence" tells of an African American mother similar in age and size to Julian's mother. Her daughter, like Julian, is educated and politically aware. Adrianne, however, because she is African American, is more sophisticated than her white counterpart. Whereas Julian has an inflated sense of himself, believing that a "Negro professor or lawyer" would happily spend an evening with him (*Flannery . . . Works* 494), Adrianne is clearheaded in her understanding of her relationship to whites. Adrianne and Mrs. Katie Taylor are juxtaposed not only to Julian and his mother but also, in "The Lame Shall Enter First," to Norton; to his father, Sheppard; and to Rufus Johnson. Mrs. Taylor not only mirrors Julian's mother but also reflects aspects of Norton's father. To her daughter's chagrin, she acquiesces to whites and does not demand respect or her civil rights. Her passivity causes her daughter to shout, "Won't you ever understand that the white man doesn't give a damn about you!" (1). Adrianne is as exasperated as is Julian when he demands that his mother look around and see where she is.

The blindness that affects both mothers affects Sheppard, but for different reasons. He attempts to save Johnson, a juvenile delinquent, from a life of crime and fanatical religious beliefs but, blind to the needs of his own son, ends up losing both Johnson (to crime) and Norton (to suicide). His stance toward the incorrigible Johnson is not unlike Mrs. Taylor's toward white racism: both are in denial. Mrs. Taylor tells her daughter that black people should know their place and stay in it. Walker introduces another reference to O'Connor when the mother says that "all 'new generation' people were 'mix-placed' and 'mis-placed' persons" (4), clearly referring to O'Connor's story "The Displaced Person." Mrs. Taylor is against school integration and believes that white people are naturally smarter than black people—except for her daughter.

Julian's mother refuses to emerge from the past because she and her family were part of the southern aristocracy. Mrs. Taylor's refusal stems from her fear, not unfounded, of white violence. Her brother, militant and angry like her daughter, was lynched and burned to death by white townspeople. Despite their blackness, the Taylors are coming up in the world, as the aristocrat in O'Connor's story has come down. That the Taylors "scraped and saved to send [their daughter] . . . to school" (1) and that they own an ancient blue-and-white Packard, polished and still beautiful, even though it does not run well, is important, considering that Julian and his mother take public transportation.

Unlike Julian's mother, who makes excuses for her son's attitude regarding integration and disdain for her, Mrs. Taylor is forthright with her daughter. In response to Adrianne's anger over the fact that her mother is sewing up "that filthy white man's drawers," Mrs. Taylor says, "They ain't done nothing to me. Ain't done nothing to you neither." For sending her to school, she says she gets "nothing but disrespect and abuse from you who ain't even dry behind the ears yet" (1). Just when Andy (her mother's name for her) thinks that there is no hope for her mother and her retrograde attitude, they run into a demonstration taking place in the center of the small town. Andy is taking her mother to work at Mrs. Kelly's home. Black students are picketing the town's drugstore where they may purchase a coke but cannot sit at the counter to drink it. The town's whites are reacting as they actually did to the black push for civil rights — violently, gathering into a mob attempting to intimidate the protestors. In the middle of the gathering mob, Mrs. Taylor sees the son of the white people for whom she works. He should be in school, and she thinks it her duty to see that he goes. Adrianne is appalled at her mother's misreading of the situation.

Mrs. Taylor forces her daughter to stop the car and let her out. Against her better judgment, Adrianne pulls the old car to the curb, all the while warning her mother about the danger of the white mob. Mrs. Taylor ignores Andy just as Julian's mother ignores Julian when she insists on giving the little boy, Carver, a shiny penny — which Gilbert Muller identifies as tokenism. Andy's mother pushes her way through the white mob in order to save the thirteen-year-old Tommy Kelly. Muller writes, "When characters resist the need to revaluate their own preconceptions, the world frequently disintegrates before their eyes" (69). The attack on Julian's mother sends her sprawling on the sidewalk and into the mythic past. Her request for Caroline to come to get her (420) represents the juvenile and narcissistic aspect of antebellum southern culture that depended so completely on the people whom it oppressed.

Mrs. Taylor's world also disintegrates, but unlike Julian's mother, she becomes politicized by Tommy's mean-spirited and disrespectful behavior. Hers is a moment of radical revisioning and transformation. Tommy, confronted by her, is not sure how to respond. His inner voice says that this elderly black woman is his friend, but groupthink, mob rule, and peer pressure override his conscience, and he punches her and calls her a "nigger." Mrs. Taylor believed that there was safety in knowing and staying in one's place. Her daughter tried to convince her that the "don't rock the boat" attitude doesn't work, because the boat can sink when one sits still. Andy's words to her mother could have been said by Julian to his mother: "Don't you realize you don't know these people, have never known these people, and if you keep going on this way, *will* never know these people?" (8). Mrs. Taylor is shocked to discover that her goodwill, Christian precepts, and keeping her place fail to protect her. When Tommy hits her, she is disoriented; but instead of retreating into the past, as Julian's mother does, she is moved by her anger to a radically different position: the mother joins the protestors.

O'Connor's story leads to regret by the son, who recognizes racism in his mother but is blind to his own bigotry. Giannone writes, "What seems racist is nothing more than a desire for dignity displaced onto conventional antebellum nostalgia" (*Flannery O'Connor and the Mystery* 163). Most of my students have responded to this statement with their own: "What seems racist is racist." Giannone fails to recognize the racism in the mother's desire but correctly identifies Julian's inability to respect his mother. Unlike Julian, Andy clearly loves her mother and understands her mother's sacrifices. Mrs. Taylor, like Julian's mother, acts according to her beliefs, and her inherent inferiority is one of them. The transformative moment for both mothers is a physical assault.

Critics trace O'Connor's story to the influence of Teilhard de Chardin and the idea of the omega point or Christ consciousness, where unity prevails. Albert Camus's essay *The Rebel* and its idea of metaphysical rebellion likely influenced Walker, a recent college graduate who wrote her thesis on Camus. Unity for Walker's characters is with the mystical self. The daughter, already well integrated with her political, historical, and spiritual persona, is a paradigm for her mother, who finally realizes that wisdom comes "Out of the mouths of babes" (10).

Because Christianity enables O'Connor to view race as a topical issue instead of as a spiritual dilemma, she can use black characters as catalysts for the development of her white characters. Katherine Hemple Prown writes, "Black 'suffering' and the racist response it inspires does not in itself become a theme in ["The Artificial Nigger"] but functions instead as a means of uniting the pair and propelling them on the journey that will ultimately culminate in redemption" (72). This observation holds true for Julian and his mother. Walker refuses the platitude of redemptive suffering embedded in the symbol of the cross and challenges the idea of redemptive black suffering in her novel *Possessing the Secret of Joy*. From the *African Saga*, by Mirella Ricciardi, Walker quotes, "Black people are natural, they possess the secret of joy, which is why they can survive the suffering and humiliation inflicted upon them" (in the unpaged preface to *Possessing*). Her characters are not catalysts for white redemption or even for their epiphanies. She is aware, as is Morrison, that white writers often use black people as shadow figures, signifiers, and what Jonathan Rogers classifies as "black doppelganger(s)" (146). "Everything That Rises Must Converge" is O'Connor's contemplation on the issue of race, even though critics point out that the story fails to engage race, focusing instead on the relationship of mother and son. There is no convergence between blacks and whites and no real coming together of the son with his mother until it is too late. Walker's story, on the other hand, does achieve, with the mother's conversion into a self-actualizing adult, a convergence between the mother and daughter.

Teaching O'Connor and Walker in the twenty-first-century South is an opportunity to engage students in a conversation about race, current events, and the past. Most of the students I teach are not from the South. The largest number come from the Northeast, the next largest from the Midwest and West. My students often are repelled by both Julian and his mother, as Walker was. But one purpose of the humanities is to cultivate human understanding. The sympathy that Walker's mother felt for the old white woman represents a difficult pedagogical challenge today. Liberal education at its best, according to Paulo Freire, results in acts of cognition, not in the transmittal of information. Stories have the power to enable us to recognize our own foibles. Walker has written of this cognition as a "revelation, when the individual comes face to face with her own limitations and comprehends 'the true frontiers of her own inner country'" (*In Search* 56). For some people, this cognition comes after they contemplate O'Connor's story and realize, as Walker's mother must have done, that racism, prejudice, bigotry, snobbery, and spiritual blindness are human failings that diminish us and make us prone to hatred. Convergence is possible only if we empathize with others, because empathy eliminates the idea of the other. As Walker wrote, "We are the Ones!" (*We Are the Ones* 3).

Both writers embrace the idea of unity but articulate it in different ways. Unity in O'Connor's Christian nomenclature is being one in Christ or what Teilhard identified as the omega point. Walker's vision includes a oneness with the earth and all that is in it, including other animals, rocks, trees, flowers—a oneness with all nature. I try to make clear to students that the important concept to grasp in both writers is that in unity there is no other and that the othering of people and things is a root cause of prejudice, racism, and discrimination. I am only partially successful. The twenty-first-century South is still the Bible Belt. Some students from southern states and some black students from traditional Christian backgrounds find it difficult to embrace Walker's oneness, and the black students find themselves disliking O'Connor's unity because they cannot get beyond the fact that she was a racist. But I am gratified that a few students are intrigued enough to want to continue their study of both authors.

NOTE

[1] In a statement about Baldwin found in a letter to Maryat Lee dated 21 May 1964—the letter is in a collection at Georgia College and State University, Milledgeville—O'Connor said that Baldwin was "very ignorant" and made other disparaging remarks about him and Martin Luther King, Jr.

Language, Class, and Social Power: Teaching O'Connor and Junot Díaz at City Tech

Carole K. Harris

When I taught Flannery O'Connor at Yale University; Bennington College; the University of California, Irvine; and Saint Ann's School, a private school in Brooklyn Heights that is a short walk from the City University of New York (CUNY) college, where I teach now, students gave her a lukewarm reception. By contrast, at City Tech,[1] students erupt into laughter or become very angry when reading her stories aloud. Why is that?

An accidental encounter in the classroom between O'Connor and the Dominican American writer Junot Díaz gave me an unexpected chance to reflect on this question and expand my approaches to teaching O'Connor. In the spring of 2012, Díaz was the guest speaker at City Tech's Literary Arts Festival. I used the occasion to add his *Drown* (2008) to my Introduction to Fiction syllabus, which included story collections by other authors who witness the poetry and politics of place: James Joyce's *Dubliners*, Edwidge Danticat's *Krik? Krak!*, Donald Ray Pollock's *Knockemstiff*,[2] and O'Connor's *Complete Stories*. The stories in any one of these volumes paint a portrait of an entire people, exposing their dirty laundry, their silences and taboos, to themselves. As the semester got under way, students expressed an interest in reading all of *Drown*, and the course became an intensive workshop on O'Connor and Díaz. Both authors probe the sticky, discomfiting issues of race and class in their respective cultures at moments of seismic change—for O'Connor, the end of segregation in the American South; for Díaz, the explosion of immigration from the Dominican Republic to the United States. They thus offer a critique from within a community—a "moral history," in Joyce's words—to wake their people up.[3]

Díaz and O'Connor write against a sentimental, mythologizing narrative unique to their culture. In *Drown*, Díaz questions the "Dominican Dream," which celebrates the success of some Dominicans who move to the United States and then return home with the "accoutrements of an upper-class lifestyle" (Pessar xii). However, measuring themselves against this cultural expectation to achieve success, poor Dominicans who emigrate to the United States in search of a better life, especially in the recent decades of economic struggle, and then return to the Dominican Republic feel compelled to exaggerate their achievements abroad and deny their struggles. The returning emigrants' idealized stories about life in America inspire subsequent waves of Dominicans to emigrate and, unprepared, face economic hardships in the United States. By his own account Díaz wrote *Drown* as an antidote to this glorified vision of emigration perpetuated by the Dominicans themselves.[4] O'Connor challenges the myth of the Old South's glorious past of heroes and landed gentry depicted in such works as *Gone with the Wind*.[5] This myth denies or whitewashes the oppressive history of slavery and its aftermath, which forced generations of black southerners, first as slaves and later as free blacks, to migrate north in search of freedom and economic opportunity. Each author's home culture, the Dominican Republic or the American South, thus has its own history involving a diaspora in which large numbers of people sought a better life in the big urban centers of the United States, such as New York and Chicago. Furthermore, Díaz and O'Connor break down foundational codes of their respective cultures: Díaz, Dominican machismo; O'Connor, the southern code of manners.[6]

That City Tech students are drawn to Díaz's stories is not surprising: many grew up in or have family ties to the Caribbean. But their equally passionate response to O'Connor's work is unexpected. Although few City Tech students are from the American South, their response to O'Connor might have something to do with the imagined Global South as represented by their immigrant, working-class backgrounds.[7] Often the first in their families to go to college, many City Tech students work long hours in bakeries, pizzerias, fast food restaurants, and newspaper stands, work as janitors, health care aides, retail and office workers, to pay their own way. Many are bilingual and come to English as a second language: with thirty-two percent of its students identifying as Hispanic, City Tech is a federally designated Hispanic serving institution. According to the *College Fact Sheet*, eighty-three percent of the student body is of color — that is, black, Hispanic, or Asian (www.citytech.cuny.edu/about-us/facts.aspx). In my ten years teaching there, I've heard many black male students report having been stopped and frisked by the police. City Tech students, who know we don't live in a postracial world, are trained in everyday encounters to read between the lines of those speaking in positions of authority, to detect how race, class, gender — and command of English — tip the balance of power against them. My students, appreciating that O'Connor never sugarcoats power struggles between black and white, boss and hired help, parent and child, write spot-on papers about her that have been published and won awards.

Scholars tend to pigeonhole O'Connor as a Catholic writer, a regional writer, or a writer of the southern grotesque. They often explain the conflict in her stories in religious or aesthetic terms. City Tech students, by contrast, who howl with laughter when reading aloud dialogues between O'Connor's self-satisfied landowners and their sassy farmhands, understand the conflict and humor in her stories in terms of social justice and labor issues. Living as refugees, as immigrants, or as low-wage workers, these students are leading the way to a paradigm shift in O'Connor studies.

The Ritual of Work, the Politics of Work

"As immigrants we were exposed to the ritual of work," Díaz explains to his fellow Dominican Silvio Torres-Saillant in a 1996 interview. "All you see all your life is your parents working" ("Fiction" 895).[8] In "Negocios," the final story of *Drown*, Díaz poignantly portrays the hardships of Ramón, a first-generation immigrant father like his own, who is absent from most of the collection, as Ramón arrives to find work in America. His leaving his family in the Dominican Republic in search of work haunts the entire volume.[9]

We are not surprised that the immigrant work ethic is a theme in Díaz's writing, but O'Connor also vividly portrays that ethic in her story "The Displaced Person," through Mr. Guizac, a Polish immigrant come to work on a southern farm, bringing his wife and two children with him. Because he works harder than any of the Americans, black or white, the landowning Mrs. McIntyre describes him as her "salvation" (*Flannery . . . Works* 294). On the first day of discussing this story, the hand of Olga Dziakiewicz, a usually quiet Polish student, shot up; she said she identified with Mr. Guizac because of his work ethic.[10]

Many City Tech students bring their understanding of their parents' sacrifice for them to their analyses of Díaz's and O'Connor's immigrant characters. Lordia Cenatus wrote about her father, who emigrated to the United States from Haiti, in her final paper on immigrant fathers in "The Displaced Person" and "Negocios." "Like Ramón, my father was once a displaced person," she said, using O'Connor's term to explain her father's predicament. "He left his country of Haiti only being able to speak Haitian Creole and French. He knew no word of English, but he got himself an apartment with another fellow Haitian in Brooklyn, New York." Cenatus spoke with admiration about her father for his overcoming hardship to provide for his family. Despite Ramón's sometimes unsavory actions, Cenatus discussed his life in America with respect and empathy. In earlier papers, she had struggled with basic sentence structure and organization, but in this paper she was clear and forceful with a strong sense of purpose: by making visible her father's struggles, she found her voice.

City Tech students, especially those who struggle with ESL issues, are quick to see that the immigrant fathers in both stories lose social status in America because they don't speak English well. About Mr. Guizac, Seng Yeal Kang, a Korean student, wrote:

> If the war had not occurred, he might be middle class in his home country. However, his social status on Mrs. McIntyre's farm is much below that of Mrs. Shortley or the black workers because he does not know English or the culture of the U. S. . . . . If Mr. Guizac were a citizen of the United States, Mrs. McIntyre could not have taken advantage of him as just another displaced person.

About Ramón's first low-wage job in the United States, Kang continued, "Most immigrants who cannot speak English start with this kind of job and are classified as low-level in society."

In addition to Mr. Guizac and his family, O'Connor gives us a large cast of American characters from the American South who have a similarly disciplined work ethic and feel displaced. Her repertoire of hardworking female landowners — Mrs. Hopewell, Mrs. Greenleaf, Mrs. McIntyre, and Mrs. Turpin, to name a few — are modeled in part after her own mother, Regina Cline O'Connor. When Flannery's father died and Flannery was fifteen, her mother inherited and managed a small dairy farm (originally named Sorrel Farm but renamed Andalusia by Flannery), an unusual role for a woman in 1950s small-town America. Flannery left home to attend the MFA program at Iowa but was forced to move back to Andalusia in 1951 after a devastating diagnosis of lupus. In her letters, the adult O'Connor entertained white friends such as Maryat Lee by writing down the conversations she overheard between her mother and her mother's farmhands, both black and white. However hilarious to O'Connor and her correspondents, these conversations were also negotiations about power. She reshaped this material to compose dialogues between landowners and hired help in her farm stories: "Good Country People," "The Displaced Person," "A Circle in the Fire," "Greenleaf," and "Revelation" — all good to include in a syllabus with Díaz.

From the perspective of Regina O'Connor, her workers became "a regular part of the family," a phrase that revealed her unexamined privilege as a white landowner — the workers themselves would probably never have used such a phrase to describe their position.[11]

Many O'Connor scholars have examined how her mother affected her psychologically, but fewer have paid attention to how her mother's work ethic, as a managing boss, affected her (for admirable research here, see Cash, *Flannery O'Connor*; Gooch). My students, by writing about workplace politics in stories like "The Displaced Person" and "Revelation," thus shake up the usual ways scholars read O'Connor, both in her fiction and in her life. Consider that O'Connor wrote nearly all the stories for her two collections after she returned home to live with her mother on the farm. There she was a keen observer of the politics of everyday conversation between workers and boss. Listening to her mother on the job must have developed her voice as a writer. City Tech students, vulnerable workers themselves — in retail, construction, and home health care, for instance — are alert to workplace politics, pick up on this voice, identify with it, and use their insights to reconsider the site of conflict in her stories in terms of social justice and labor conflicts.

Family Politics and the "Terrifying Work Ethic" of Immigrant Parents

Díaz understands the inadequacy many children of immigrants feel around issues of work. "I think immigrants have a terrifying work ethic," he explains. "What is most insane is the feeling that you can never be adequate to your parents" ("Fiction" 895). This feeling gives us a new way to think about O'Connor both as a daughter and as a writer.

Flannery's mother was not an immigrant, but her forebears came from Ireland, so Regina's work ethic may have had cultural roots.[12] Furthermore, as a widowed woman in the South, Regina had to prove herself as landowner and manager of a farm. Flannery was a sharp observer of the power dynamics involved as her mother handled herself with the townspeople and other farmers, often male and white, as well as with the hired hands. For example, Flannery often accompanied her mother to auctions where Regina bid on cattle. Because Flannery modeled so many of her fictional mothers on her own, Díaz's insights about the inadequacy children of immigrants feel give us a new way to understand her often negative portrayal of resentful adult children still living at home. Hulga ("Good Country People"), Julian ("Everything That Rises Must Converge"), and Asbury ("The Enduring Chill") witness their mother's "terrifying work ethic" and feel unable to duplicate it in their own lives: Hulga lives at home because she failed to find a job as a professor, Julian lives at home because he failed to make it as a writer, and Asbury has struggled unsuccessfully to make it as a writer in New York. In the eyes of these characters, the labor of their mothers, who made sacrifices so they could go to college, highlights their own failures to find meaningful work.

Students in my classes, who often live at home with their parents to save money, frequently do not like O'Connor's adult children, but they understand the predicament and write with a combination of compassion and criticism about the enmeshed relationships these characters maintain with their parents. City Tech students feel pressure from their parents to go to college, get a degree, find a well-paying job, and be successful, but the parents, who in many cases did not go to college themselves, don't always know how to be a support to their children in their studies. Often there is resentment on both sides.

Talking "Inside" the Community

> Unless the novelist has gone utterly out of his mind, his aim is still communication and communication suggests talking inside a community.
>
> *(Flannery . . . Works* 844)

> I don't explain cultural things, with italics or with exclamation or with side bars or asides. . . . I had so many negative models, so many Latinos and black writers who are writing to white audiences, who are not writing to their own people. If you are not writing to your own people, I'm disturbed because of what that says about your relationship to the community you are in one way or another indebted to. You are only there to loot them of ideas, and words, and images, so that you can coon them to the dominant group.   (Díaz, "Fiction" 900)

Díaz and O'Connor share a common goal of talking "inside" their community in order to engage in a critical dialogue with their audience, whom they see, or should see, as their own people. According to O'Connor, who was forced by ill-ness to return to her native Milledgeville, an author's true audience lies at home, and only by living as a member of that community does she stay connected—concretely, not abstractly—to the people, language, and daily rituals that are the writer's material and life source.

Díaz knows the importance of talking inside a community but qualifies his audience as the diasporic community, which he defines variously as the Do-minican diasporic, the Spanish-speaking diasporic, or even the African diasporic community.[13] He was born in the Dominican Republic to Dominican parents and moved to New Jersey at age seven. As a Dominican American living in the diaspora, his notion of home, audience, and community is complex and mul-tiple. Díaz consistently uses the plural when talking about his audience or his people. For example, in the interview with Torres-Saillant, he responds to a question about his literary role models:

> Torres-Saillant: I suppose that once you're able to be critical of your own people, you gain possession of a model that you may equally apply to others.

> Díaz: Yes, definitely, but I'm just a lot more passionate about having a critical dialogue with my communities. Exposing white racism and white arrogance is important, but, if I don't criticize myself and my peoples, how are we going to get better?   ("Fiction" 901)

We see O'Connor cast her critical gaze on exactly the "white racism" and "white arrogance" of the southern whites she grew up with, people who were seeing the world as they knew it coming to an end. She feels indebted to them, so in her life she follows the proper southern code of manners, but in her sto-ries, she is, as Díaz would put it, having a critical dialogue with her communi-ties. Hilton Als writes about O'Connor's project with regard to using her family and townspeople as material: "O'Connor's most profound gift was her ability to describe impartially the bourgeoisie she was born into, to depict with humor and without judgment her rapidly crumbling social order" (White Girls 119). Als's observation about her position in the bourgeoisie can be supplemented by her own claim, borrowed from Thomas Mann and expressed in her essay "Some Aspects of the Grotesque in Southern Fiction," that the grotesque is "the true anti-bourgeois style" (Flannery . . . Works 817).

One of the ways Díaz and O'Connor actively talk inside their respective cul-tures is by experimenting with different kinds of dialects and languages. Díaz, who writes primarily in English, sprinkles Dominican slang into his stories, in-cluding curse words and sexual terms, without translating them or setting them off in italics. O'Connor showcases her ear for dialect through her characters' dialogues, including both the pleasant language of her middle- and upper-middle-class characters and the ungrammatical speech of "poor white trash."

Students hear the humor and vitality of this language by reading the stories out loud.

Reading Díaz's stories out loud had an unexpected outcome in my classroom: Spanish-speaking students, who felt their culture was being acknowledged with dignity, stepped forward and became discussion leaders. Reading *Drown* gave them permission to write about their own immigrant families, to talk inside their community and criticize it from within.

Community and Critique in the Classroom

Díaz's use of Spanish without any translation sets into motion a classroom situation in which those who understand Spanish shine and feel solidarity with one another: they are part of an insider group that understands his references. Students who do not know Spanish may feel excluded, but their curiosity often leads them to ask a Spanish speaker to explain. In the spring of 2012, when I first taught the course, the Spanish-speaking students in my class educated their peers (and me) on Spanish slang and curse words. Many of these students, who had remained quiet during our discussions of O'Connor, now came out of the woodwork with great authority. One student who grew up in the Dominican Republic voluntarily wrote up a dictionary of sixty-three Spanish words that appear in *Drown*; class members broke out in laughter when he instructed us matter-of-factly on vulgar words for sex or body parts.

The students quickly picked up on all the unspoken cues in "Fiesta, 1980" of Papi's affair with the Puerto Rican woman—when he comes home from work, for example, he races to the shower—and chimed in with stories from their own families. A number of Spanish-speaking students from other countries (Columbia, Ecuador, and Peru) also regularly offered their observations about the pressures on young men in their cultures to have sex early and about the entitlement men feel later to have multiple affairs. To Díaz's description of the father's returning home from work (in the opening scene of "Fiesta 1980") and staring in a threatening way at his sons, the students responded, as if in chorus, "My father is just like that." In other words, silent, aloof, authoritarian, dispensing punishment without explanation.

My students, who are in effect doing the work of cultural criticism, agree with the scholars on Díaz. For example, the scholar Katherine Miranda tells Díaz, "I see your work as deeply critical of Dominican machismo, and the ways that it can perpetuate forms of both domestic and institutionalized violence" (Díaz, "Junot Díaz" [Miranda] 35). My student Sandra Oteng wrote in her final paper:

> At the same time that this story of marital infidelity seems to arrive at a quiet ending, it is also told from a man's—macho's—point of view. In many cultures, such as Hispanic cultures, men's sexual adventures are tolerated, whereas women who engage in the same behavior are looked

upon very harshly. We notice, for instance, that Yunior and Rafa go over to the Puerto Rican woman's house for dinner . . . without questioning whether such behavior might be hurtful or disrespectful to their mother.

Oteng continues:

> Nor does the story investigate Mami's feelings. We don't ever see her weeping or screaming or throwing her husband's clothes out the window. In this way the story itself "circumnavigates" the core moral issue affecting this family. This is a story about adultery, a sin heavily proscribed in many cultures and in some even demanding the death of its participants. But that is not where this story goes. Papi's adultery is "nothing out of the ordinary."

Many students in that class from Spanish-speaking cultures and other immigrant backgrounds identified deeply with the harsh aspects of family life portrayed in *Drown* (especially in "Fiesta, 1980"), a life based on evasion, euphemism, and circumlocution. They also readily saw parallels with the family life pictured in O'Connor's "The Artificial Nigger" as well as in her other stories of childhood: "The River," "A Circle in the Fire," and "A Temple of the Holy Ghost," for example. Their identification with her fictional families was especially strong after they had read Díaz and were looking back a second time at her stories. Students discovered that the foundational codes in both cultures — machismo and the southern code of manners — structured relationships at home and at work in similar ways.

Reading "The Artificial Nigger" Out Loud

O'Connor dramatizes the taboos of race and class in the lives of her southern characters. She shines a light on the everyday, chilling relationships of power in the workplace and at home. If my students don't get this about her right away, they hear the punch in her stories when they are read out loud. Once I noticed this, reading them out loud became my key approach. One student reported she didn't understand "Good Country People" at all until she went home and read it out loud with a friend, taking turns reading the dialogue. Taking my cue from this student, I now plan my lessons accordingly. When teaching O'Connor's "Revelation," for example, I organize class discussion around student performances of key scenes rich in dialogue: Mrs. Turpin chatting with the white pleasant lady in the doctor's waiting room or seeking consolation from her black female hired help. In small groups, students choose roles and prepare their scenes, which they then perform for the big group. These performances give everyone a chance to air their questions, including basic ones about the narrator, farm vocabulary, or cultural references. The funniest moments occur when male students take on the voice of the "white-trash" mother or the black female help or when black students impersonate Mrs. Turpin.

For "The Artificial Nigger," which is rarely included in literature anthologies, I use cross-race or cross-gender casting to motivate my students to see O'Connor in a new light.[14] Typically I have students rehearse a dialogue that takes place early in the story between Mr. Head, a white grandfather and father surrogate, and his ten-year-old grandson, Nelson, who resists his authority. Mr. Head takes Nelson on a day trip to Atlanta to "show him all it is to show." On the train ride there, when a black male passenger, described by the narrator as "a huge coffee-colored man" (*Flannery . . . Works* 215), followed by two young black women walk past them down their aisle, Mr. Head seizes on his first opportunity to quiz Nelson:

> "What was that?" he asked.
> "A man," the boy said and gave him an indignant look as if he were tired of having his intelligence insulted.
> "What kind of a man?" Mr. Head persisted, his voice expressionless.
> "A fat man," Nelson said. He was beginning to feel that he had better be cautious.
> "You don't know what kind?" Mr. Head said in a final tone.
> "An old man," the boy said and had a sudden foreboding that he was not going to enjoy the day.
> "That was a nigger," Mr. Head said and sat back.   (216)

The postperformance discussion varies according to who plays the role of Mr. Head. In one performance, George Williams, who is African American, shared afterward how it felt to play the role of a white racist grandfather; he hammed up his performance by delivering Mr. Head's lines in a loud, sarcastic voice, which made the other students laugh. During this student's caricatured performance, Mr. Head looked more foolish than powerful, but when the laughter died down, students had a serious conversation about the use of the N-word: how its meaning and effect change depending on who is using it and who is hearing it. At City Tech, classes are so diverse that no one ethnic or racial group predominates, which relieves everybody from bearing the burden of being perceived as representative of a given group.[15] Out of this variety emerges passionate and often surprising debate.

After performing parts of "Revelation" and "Everything That Rises Must Converge," this same group of students erupted into a spontaneous, student-led firing out of questions that culminated with one student's exclaiming the question that had been brewing for weeks: "Is Flannery O'Connor a racist?" This question changes register when posed by an African American student surrounded by other students of color rather than by a white scholar surrounded by other white scholars at an academic conference. The questioner at first defended O'Connor by saying that in her stories she was merely witnessing or recording her culture, which was racist, without taking a stand, but he concluded that her remaining neutral was a moral failing. A fellow student, also African American, chimed in: she considered O'Connor to be a racist, but her stories were nevertheless interesting to her because the student had always wondered what white people discussed together when no black person was around. Reading O'Connor made her feel as if she were eavesdropping on a white conversation.

Williams later wanted to write a paper either on James Baldwin's "Sonny's Blues," a story he loved and whose characters he deeply identified with, or on "The Artificial Nigger."[16] He chose O'Connor's story because, in his words, "I hated Mr. Head so much, hated what he was doing to Nelson." Williams, who felt empathy with Nelson, talked about writing his essay as if it were an intervention on Nelson's behalf. About the scene in the train, he wrote:

> This is Nelson's first experience actually trying to distinguish a difference between Blacks and Whites, and the language that Mr. Head uses in teaching Nelson this lesson is very important. "What is that?" Mr. Head asks Nelson when he points out a Black stranger. The way Mr. Head phrases the question gives Nelson the message that the Black man is an object rather than a person. This language is deliberate and intended to teach Nelson to objectify Negroes.[17]

Williams's experience in class of taking on the voice of Mr. Head pushed his written analysis forward by helping him understand his initial, emotionally raw response. His cross-race performance and the discussion it provoked helped other students, many of whom had never written an essay about literature, to write with insight. Reading O'Connor dramatically out loud, especially in combination with cross-race, cross-gender, or cross-nation casting, created an atmosphere of trust and solidarity among students, which facilitated classroom discussion of sensitive or explosive topics.

Teaching Tips

The techniques I've discovered through teaching O'Connor alongside Díaz, which take advantage of City Tech students' expertise, including their ability to code-switch in the classroom, based on their immigrant, working-class backgrounds, can be adapted for other student populations and institutional cultures.

The shared laughter and sheer fun of acting out the parts of O'Connor's characters who are obnoxious create solidarity and trust among the students and may inspire shy or reluctant students to step out of their comfort zones and participate in difficult discussions on race and class. Students who have never written a paper about literature before express their ideas more fluently on the page after having rehearsed them thoroughly with fellow students in a discussion group.

For a paper, I give students the choice of topics based on themes common to Díaz and O'Connor—for example, workplace politics, family politics, gender politics, language politics. Students then choose their own story pairs to analyze, one from each writer—for example, "A Temple of the Holy Ghost" and "Ysrael," "The Artificial Nigger" and "Fiesta, 1980," "Revelation" and "Drown." I include a creative writing option. For example, students can write a story about a family conflict, perhaps having to do with immigration, with the requirement that they use flashbacks and introduce Spanish words or another home language, as modeled by Díaz in his story "Fiesta, 1980." This option gives students permission to write as insiders about their family, with the result that students put into practice Díaz's goal of having a "critical dialogue" with one's own people—in Joyce's words, holding up a mirror and exposing their taboos (*Letters* 64). As writers, students learn to see their family in a larger cultural context.

I use contests and publication opportunities as incentives to motivate my students, including those in developmental classes, to showcase their writing to a larger audience. In this way, they see themselves as part of a community of writers. For example, every spring, to prepare students for the CUNY-wide Making Work Visible contest, I ask them to write about the kinds of work they do outside school—in retail, fast food, and home health care. The mission of the contest, as articulated on the Web site, was "to expand student engagement with the underappreciated history of work and workers in this country, and to re-vitalize the study of labor history at CUNY" (www.laborarts.org/exhibits/contest2016, click on "Rules for 2016–2017 Contest"). In the process of writing about the work they do, they discover its value and bring this understanding of work to their reading of Díaz and O'Connor, and to literature and writing in general.

From Displacement to Diaspora

Reading O'Connor and Díaz in dialogue complicates and gives a more accurate picture of O'Connor's notion of one "true country" (*Flannery . . . Works* 801). This term of O'Connor's has had a powerful afterlife because many scholars have used her religious idea to deflect political readings of her stories that take into account language, class, race, and social justice (for compelling critiques of this practice, see Caron, "Bottom Rail"; Végsö). Given the South's legacy of slavery, segregation, and racism, O'Connor's notion of community is closer to Díaz's: it is not one but multiple; it is not coherent but contested.

Díaz is painfully aware of the complications inherent in calling oneself Dominican, and he uses his mother as an example. She lived in New Jersey for over thirty years but still saw herself as Dominican. "What do you do with someone like that," he asks with fascination and exasperation, "who's literally, physically living in a place thirty years non-stop and yet that place is more insubstantial than memories from her first thirty years?" ("Junot Díaz" [Miranda] 24). This mind-set reverberates in O'Connor's depiction of the southern white gracious ladies that people her stories, ladies who are clearly modeled after her mother. In "Everything That Rises Must Converge," for example, the plantation home-stead from the childhood of Julian's mother is more real to her than the shabby apartment complex she currently inhabits in postintegration Atlanta. She, too, is living in diaspora.

O'Connor has been labeled in various ways — as a regional writer, a Catholic writer, a master of the southern grotesque. Critics take their cue from her own eloquent writing about her work; editors make their selections of her stories for their anthologies accordingly, with the result that high school teachers and college professors present her a certain way. We direct our students to look for the self-satisfied character who encounters a shock, which results in a moment of grace. It sounds like a formula. Our way of thinking about O'Connor has be-come a cliché.

Reading O'Connor and Díaz together with my students at City Tech has chal-lenged me to reconsider O'Connor, metaphorically at least, as a diasporic writer. Her true country is as complex and multiple as Díaz's, and her consciousness of race and class is as split and as conflicted as his. My students, who as outsiders grapple with the American dream with a similarly double consciousness, take notice of her own struggle with the tricky, sometimes deadly, crises of workplace and family politics. They are leading the way for a paradigm shift in O'Connor studies.

We need to listen to them.

NOTES

[1] New York City College of Technology — City Tech, as it is affectionately known — is one of twenty-four campuses that compose CUNY, the largest public urban university in the United States. Located in downtown Brooklyn in a commercial district known as Metrotech, City Tech enrolls over 17,000 full- and part-time students.

[2] In *Knockemstiff*, named after a town in Ohio, Pollock explores interrelated charac-ters whose lives have been devastated by a methamphetamine epidemic. He has been called an heir to O'Connor's hardscrabble worldview.

[3] Díaz calls the Dominican Republic in 2009 an "exploded society" with "multiple existences" ("Junot Díaz" [Miranda] 23). The same terms could describe the Ameri-can South in the aftermath of the 1954 Supreme Court decision *Brown v. Board of Education*. About O'Connor's writing, the cultural critic Hilton Als writes, "O'Connor was not a polemicist, but her work is implicitly political given the environment she drew from — the South during its second failed Reconstruction, otherwise known as Inte-gration" (*White Girls* 118). On Díaz's notion of "the historical moment" and its great potential for writers, see "Junot Díaz" (Miranda) 24. Joyce viewed *Dubliners* as provid-ing a "moral history" for the Irish people as well as a "looking-glass" in which they could

see themselves reflected (*Letters* 62–63, 64). On Díaz and Joyce, see Díaz, "Junot Díaz" (Danticat) 92.

[4] On the damaging effects of the "fiction of success" on Dominicans, see Pessar 15–17. On Díaz's challenging the myth of the Dominican dream, see Moreno.

[5] About this tradition, Als writes, "It's remarkable to consider that O'Connor started writing less than a hundred years after Harriet Beecher Stowe published *Uncle Tom's Cabin*, and just a decade after Margaret Mitchell's *Gone with the Wind*, two books whose imagined black worlds had more to do with the authors' patronizing sentimentality than with the complicated intertwining of black and white, rich and poor, mundane and sublime that characterized real Southern life—and O'Connor's portrait of it" (*White Girls* 113).

[6] On Díaz's critique of Dominican masculinity, see Frydman; Riofrio; and Díaz's interview with Miranda. Miranda states, "I see [Díaz's] work as deeply critical of Dominican machismo, and the ways that it can perpetuate forms of both domestic and institutionalized violence" (Díaz, "Junot Díaz" [Miranda] 35). Matthew Day eloquently demonstrates that O'Connor is critical of the "foul underbelly" of the southern code of manners, as epitomized by the southern "gracious" lady (141).

[7] When speaking about the countries of the Caribbean, social scientists often use the term *Global South*, a catchall neologism that has come to replace *Third World*. The American South has traditionally been defined in binary opposition to the American North, but in recent scholarship it has also been productively imagined as part of the colonized or Global South. Both the Dominican Republic and the American South share a common colonial past, marked by racism and stark class divisions between plantation owners and workers. On imagining the American South as part of the Global South, see Buffington; Cobb and Stueck; Dirlik; Donaldson; Jansson; McKee and Trefzer; Peacock et al.; Ring; and Smith and Cohn. On the concept of internal orientalism in the United States, see Jansson; on the concept of southern orientalism, see Yaeger, "Southern Orientalism."

[8] As a professor of humanities at Syracuse University, Torres-Saillant served as Díaz's early mentor. He went on to found the Dominican Studies Institute at City College, CUNY, which he directed until 2000. See the article he wrote with Ramona Hernández, "Dominicans: Community, Culture, and Collective Identity."

[9] In "Ysrael," the first story of the collection, Ramón's sons, Rafa and Yunior, ages twelve and nine, share a similarity with Ysrael, the boy whose face was eaten by a pig: their fathers live and work in the United States and send money home. On the trauma of absent fathers in *Drown*, see M. Miller; Riofrio.

[10] This student also identified with Mr. Guizac's poor command of English: "I felt that his language barrier was an obstacle I faced myself when I first came to the States. As much as I understood everything people were saying, I had no confidence in myself and felt very insecure. I couldn't express my thoughts out loud for quite some time even though I'd been taking private English lessons since kindergarten. For the first two years I felt like a stranger and that is the reason I kept myself apart from others." For a teaching-friendly analysis of how Guizac as immigrant and outsider disrupts the farm's binary power structure based on race, see Harris, "Politics"; Taylor.

[11] The phrase "regular part of the family" comes from Barack Obama's memoir *Dreams from My Father: A Story of Race and Inheritance* and captures the paternalistic attitude many white families displayed toward their black help under segregation. Obama remembers a shocking conversation he had with Frank, an elderly black friend of his white grandfather, Stanley Dunham (1918–92), who would have roughly been a contemporary

of O'Connor. Stanley and Frank grew up near each other in Wichita, Kansas, in the days of segregation. As a young couple Stanley and his wife, Madelyn, hired a young black girl to look after Obama's mother; in a tone of sarcasm Frank reported to the teenaged Obama how Stanley viewed her role: "Told me how she became a regular part of the family. That's how he remembers it, you understand—this girl coming in to look after somebody else's children, her mother coming in to do somebody else's laundry. A regular part of the family" (90).

12 On cultural connections between O'Connor and Joyce, see G. Robinson. On cultural ties between Ireland and the American South, see Quinlan.

13 Díaz says, "I was writing for, in a larger context, African diasporic and in the most narrow context, a Dominican diasporic. So I just assume that, you know, there is going to be a lot of things that people are going to understand. I mean, I just assume that this is my audience, if I am writing to them, I didn't necessarily need to translate things . . ." ("Junot Díaz" [Torres and Vásquez] 29).

14 In 2004, the New York choreographer Bill T. Jones, in collaboration with Toni Morrison, created a dance piece out of "The Artificial Nigger," entitled *Reading, Mercy, and the Artificial Nigger*. Jones insisted on cross-gender and cross-race casting, so that by the end of the piece, every dancer in his ethnically and racially diverse troupe had performed the role of either Mr. Head or Nelson. See Jones's interview with Roberts.

15 As a graduate student at Yale, I remember feeling nervous teaching Morrison's *Beloved* for the first time. I was a white teacher, and all my students were white, with the exception of one. When a question came up regarding the black experience, I would catch myself, to my great shame, looking to her for a response.

16 On teaching O'Connor and Baldwin together in a literature class, see Als, *White Girls* 130–31; Harris, "James Baldwin" and "On Flying Mules." Roland Végső, in a close reading of "The Artificial Nigger," demonstrates that the question of race in this and other of O'Connor's stories ("The Enduring Chill" and "Everything That Rises Must Converge") "is not only a division that takes place along lines of skin color; it also produces violent divisions within white American culture as well" (69). Influenced by the approach of Jon Lance Bacon, whom he acknowledges, Végső analyzes O'Connor's texts in the cultural context of her time.

17 Williams's essay was published in *City Tech Writer*, the journal on our campus for outstanding student writing from all disciplines.

Teaching O'Connor and Toni Morrison from a Nonsecular Space

David Z. Wehner

> This is a here-and-now world, that's what I mean when I say "secular"; and the religious side of it, even the moral side of it—well, there's a lot up for grabs.
> —William Carlos Williams

> Our age is very far from settling into a comfortable unbelief.
> —Charles Taylor

In 1996, the first year of my master's in literature at the University of Colorado, Boulder, the English department's powers that be handed me the syllabus I would use for Introduction to Literature. As a neophyte college instructor, I breathed a sigh of relief when they told me what to teach. A selection of Flannery O'Connor's short stories and Toni Morrison's *Beloved* made up part of that syllabus, and, since then, these two authors have returned frequently in my scholarship and teaching, appearing in my courses Multicultural Literature, American Women Writers, and one I currently teach called Literature, Faith, and Secularization. This last course examines the interplay among religion, secularization, and literature from the mid–nineteenth century to the present, and it mostly focuses on O'Connor and Morrison as two writers responding to the secularization of their day, O'Connor defending her religious tradition against its critics and Morrison questioning religion in order to make it more inclusive.

Of the three terms in the course's title—literature, faith, and secularization—the students most take for granted yet understand least the term *secularization*, so on the opening day I hand them their first reading: the *Oxford English Dictionary*'s three-page definition of the word *secular* in all its manifestations. I begin our second class by discussing the definition, hoping to impress on them that *secular* exists as both an old and a new word. *Secular* dates to the thirteenth century and denotes a monk who did not live in the monastery but lived outside the church, "in the world." We still have this understanding of *secular*, but since the thirteenth century what it means to live outside the church and in the world has changed. Having been jailed for blasphemy for his atheist views, George Jacob Holyoke coined the word *secularism* in 1851 to denote a morality system based on this world rather than a future one. Eighteen years later, Thomas Huxley introduced the word *agnostic*, so the nineteenth century birthed a new vocabulary to describe a position outside the church and in the world.

Early in the course, I lay out the framework for students for three waves of secularization theory, which closely follow the three waves of feminist theory. In the first wave, late-nineteenth-century writers like Karl Marx, Charles Darwin, Friedrich Nietzsche, and Sigmund Freud forged philosophies that "had no place for God," and in the 1950s and 1960s, a second wave of writers — Peter Berger, Harvey Cox, C. Wright Mills, J. Hillis Miller, and Michel Foucault — extended this secularization thesis (Armstrong, *History* 346). Miller begins *The Disappearance of God* (1963) with "Post-medieval literature records, among other things, the gradual withdrawal of God from the world" (1), while in *The Birth of the Clinic* (1963), Foucault writes, "In the alleviation of physical misery, it [the clinic] would be close to the old spiritual vocation of the Church, of which it would be a sort of lay carbon copy." He continues, "Are not doctors the priests of the body?" (32). Berger tightly sums up the secularization thesis of the 1950s and 1960s as "more modernity, less religion" (Interview [Tippett]). By the 1990s, however, Berger and Cox, along with writers like Charles Taylor, began to question the validity of that thesis. Berger stated in 2006, "The belief is still quite prevalent among intellectuals — secular intellectuals — that religion is a kind of backwoods phenomenon that with rising education will increasingly disappear. That's not happening. It's not going to happen" ("Interview" [Mathewes] 157). Indeed, sociologists today divide into those who want to discard the secularization thesis and those who still accept it with some well-defined parameters. This moment that I call the third wave, others call the postsecular.

In the first fifteen years of his work, Foucault examines what he sees as the last epistemic shift from around 1775 to 1825, in which the Christian pastoral became the modern pastoral and the care of the self passed from the church to the sciences. In the first two weeks of the course, in a unit called "The Christian Pastoral Becomes the Modern Pastoral," I have the students read some of the poetry of Anne Bradstreet, Jonathan Edwards's "Sinners in the Hands of an Angry God," and Ben Franklin's letter to Ezra Stiles and Thomas Jefferson's to his nephew Peter Carr. These letters better explain deism than most textbooks I have found, so in this unit the students can examine American literature moving from a position very much within a religious worldview to a position with one foot out the door. In one iteration of the course, I begin with a unit exploring Darwin's influence on Kate Chopin's fiction; in another, which this essay describes, I begin at the height of secularization theory in the 1950s, with O'Connor and her battle with Freud.

One can position O'Connor as writing during a time when the secularization thesis was ascendant in the circles she encountered at Georgia State College for Women, the Iowa Writers' Workshop, and the artists' colony Yaddo. The disbelief in God that she discovered at Yaddo "disgusted" and "shocked" her (Cash, *Flannery O'Connor: A Life* 69; Gooch 176). Freud stands as one of the chief proponents of the idea that a belief in God represents an illusion, and, indeed, Freud, psychoanalysis, and psychotherapy haunt O'Connor's letters. In October 1955, she wrote to Betty Hester, "As to Sigmund, I am against him tooth and toenail" (*Habit* 110). That she would oppose Freud comes as no surprise: she lived as a devout, outspoken believer, whereas Freud once described himself as "a completely godless Jew" (Freud and Pfister 63). For him, religion was the enemy and Roman Catholicism its most threatening manifestation. Nathan Hale describes the analyst during his time in Austria as "a Jew in an anti-Semitic Roman Catholic Empire" (*Freud* 333). Freud worried that the conflation of church and state in 1920s Austria would conspire to squelch his nascent psychoanalysis.

Freud's criticism of religion worried O'Connor less than how America approached psychoanalysis and psychotherapy. In June 1962, she wrote to Alfred Corn, "One of the effects of modern liberal Protestantism has been gradually to turn religion into poetry and therapy" (*Habit* 479). The writer worries here about religion turning into therapy, but she also worried about its opposite: therapy turning into religion. Hale tells us that even before World War I a stereotype existed of the uncanny analyst "who combined the qualities of secular priest, uncondemning listener, and scientific soul surgeon" (*Rise* 95). Does psychoanalysis represent a science, as Freud claimed? Dietrich Bonhoeffer describes it as "the secularized offshoots of Christian theology" (179), Betty Friedan as "a new religion" (115), and Karen Armstrong as a "secularist spirituality" (*Battle* 199). O'Connor did not use these writers' language to describe psychoanalysis, but her letters show that she intuited a slippage between religion and how Americans practiced psychotherapy, a slippage she fought "tooth and toenail."

This slippage also explains her greater concern with Carl Jung. In September 1962, she wrote to Cecil Dawkins, "You probably hear a lot about Freud at Yaddo. To religion I think he is much less dangerous than Jung" (*Habit* 491). Why she would see Jung as more dangerous becomes apparent by examining the Terry Lectures that Jung gave at Yale in 1937. These talks make clear that he saw psychotherapy as confronting phenomena empirical science did not recognize and taking up issues that religion no longer effectively addressed. He describes "the fact that an idea of God, utterly absent from the conscious mind of modern man, returns in a form known consciously three hundred or four hundred years ago" (69). That is, since the Reformation, God has withdrawn into the unconscious, so modernity can access God better on a therapist's couch than in a church pew. Jung describes a case he believes exemplifies the modern condition when he tells of a lapsed Catholic who comes into therapy convinced he has cancer, though tests prove otherwise. His problem resolves one night when he has a dream of a mandala—what Jung calls an archetype of the deity—that fills the analysand with "the most sublime harmony." Jung concludes, "It was what one would call—in the language of religion—a conversion" (80). In October 1958, O'Connor wrote, "The religious sense seems to be bred out of them [modern people] in the kind of society we've lived in since the eighteenth century. And it's bred out of them double quick now by the religious substitutes for religion" (*Habit* 299–300). She saw Freud as religion's adversary, Jung as religion's substitute.

Freud and Jung, however, embodied a much larger zeitgeist in the 1950s. Eva Moskowitz claims that in this decade "popular culture became saturated with therapeutic messages" (217), and the facts bear this out: from 1948 to 1976, the number of psychiatrists in America grew from 4,700 to 27,000, and in 1956, on the hundred-year anniversary of Freud's birth, America witnessed university lectures, public addresses, congratulations from President Eisenhower, and the publication of Ernest Jones's three-volume biography that positioned Freud as Copernicus's and Galileo's equal (Hale, *Rise* 286–87). O'Connor's letters and lectures show that she clearly sensed the spirit of her time; in 1955 she wrote, "My audience are people who think God is dead" and "The man of our time is certainly not a believer" (*Habit* 92; *Conversations* 104). One realizes the extent of this problem for her from a recurring metaphor in her letters. In August 1955 she wrote, "If you live today you breathe in nihilism," and four years later she remarked on "the disbelief in it [the Holy] that we breathe in with the air of the times" (*Habit* 97, 349).

One of O'Connor's most anthologized stories, "Good Country People," can be taught using her concern around Freud and Jung as background. If Freud was "a militant atheist" (Gay 37), the story's protagonist, Hulga Hopewell, follows his lead. When Manley Pointer says to her, "I guess God takes care of you," she responds, "I don't even believe in God" (*Flannery . . . Works* 277). Earlier, when Manley notices that the Hopewells' living room does not contain a bible, Mrs. Hopewell cannot tell him the truth: "My daughter is an atheist and won't let me keep the Bible in the parlor" (270). In his famous criticism of religion, *The Future of an Illusion* (1927), Freud, true to the book's title, argues that all religion is one of civilization's great illusions. Hulga, in fine Freudian fashion, insists, when she and Manley reach the barn, "I don't have illusions. I'm one of those people who see *through* to nothing" (*Flannery . . . Works* 280). In another O'Connor story, "The Enduring Chill," Asbury's Buddhist friend, Goetz, like Hulga, sees "it all as illusion" (549).

My father used to say no such thing as an atheist exists: everyone has his or her god. At the end of *Future of an Illusion*, once Freud has dismissed religion, he names the new god, "our God, Λόγος," which James Strachey translates as *Logos* or reason (54). In "Good Country People," Hulga, too, demonstrates her complete faith in her intellect. When Manley first kisses her,

> the power went at once to the brain. Even before he released her, her mind, clear and detached and ironic anyway, was regarding him from a great distance, with amusement but with pity. She had never been kissed before and she was pleased to discover that it was an unexceptional experience and all a matter of the mind's control.
>
> (*Flannery . . . Works* 278)

Richard Giannone describes how she substitutes her mind for God, but the story points to another god, of which she remains unaware, her leg (*Flannery O'Connor, Hermit Novelist* 76). When Manley asks her to show him where her leg joins on, the narrator tells us, "[S]he was as sensitive about the artificial leg as a peacock about his tail. No one ever touched it but her. She took care of it as someone else would his soul, in private and almost with her own eyes turned away" (281). The association of Hulga's leg with a peacock's tail must give us pause, in that O'Connor kept a steady flock of the birds at Andalusia. Her 1961 essay "The King of the Birds" describes how the bird's opened tail silences viewers (836), and "The Displaced Person" associates the peacock's tail with the transfiguration of Christ (317). That is, O'Connor's work associates the peacock's tail with the mystery of religion, but this passage associates it with Hulga's leg. Like a pilgrim at a shrine, Hulga must avert her eyes from her leg, and like a monk safeguarding a holy relic, only she handles it.

The moment in the barn loft when Hulga agrees to let Manley remove her leg, therefore, reads as her substituting one god for another. She gives up her leg because she believes she has found the true god, Manley Pointer:

> She decided that for the first time in her life she was face to face with real innocence. This boy, with an instinct that came from beyond wisdom, had touched the truth about her. When after a minute, she said in a hoarse high voice, "All right," it was like surrendering to him completely. It was like losing her own life and finding it again, miraculously, in his.   (281)

She thought she had wisdom, but this boy has something beyond wisdom; she thought she knew the truth, but only this boy can touch the truth. Robert Coles and Louise Westling believe this scene parodies a Christian conversion, but one could also read it as parodying a secular conversion like the one we see in Jung's Terry Lectures (Coles 140; Westling, *Sacred Groves* 152).

Manley mirrors Hulga in that he, too, loudly declares his atheism—"[Y]ou ain't so smart. I have been believing in nothing ever since I was born"—and he, like Hulga, has his religious substitutes (*Flannery . . . Works* 283). Once he has acquired her leg, the traveling bible salesman opens one of his bibles to reveal that he has hollowed it out to make room for whiskey, condoms, and pornography, literally hollowing out one religion to make room for another. The narrator says, "He laid these out in front of her one at a time in an evenly-spaced row, like one presenting offerings at the shrine of a goddess" (282). The adjective "evenly-spaced" suggests that he views this action as a carefully executed religious ritual; for a moment, Hulga becomes his pagan goddess, he the pilgrim making offerings before her. In "The Church and the Fiction Writer" (1957), O'Connor writes that she sees the modern world as divided about mystery, "part of it trying to eliminate mystery while another part tries to rediscover it in disciplines less personally demanding than religion" (*Mystery* 145). This quotation describes Hulga: she begins "Good Country People" trying to eliminate mystery and ends the story trying to find it in disciplines less demanding than religion. The quotation also sums up O'Connor's concerns with Freud and Jung: the former tries to eliminate mystery, while the latter finds it in substitute disciplines.

I begin the unit on O'Connor by having the students read Freud's *Future of an Illusion*, a short work that can be covered in two classes, if one teaches three times a week. I then go through O'Connor's work chronologically, starting with *Wise Blood* and moving to "Parker's Back," but at two points I break from the fiction to have the students read some of her letters and lectures (my selections are given above). The second iteration of this class opens up the syllabus a bit so that one can also have the students read Jung's *Psychology and Religion*, which contains the Terry Lectures. Like *Future of an Illusion*, the book can be covered in two classes.

Students have an easier time understanding O'Connor's battle with Freud and the secularization thesis of the 1950s than they do understanding Morrison's stance on religion, the idea of the postsecular, and how her fiction embodies this nuanced concept. I begin the section on Morrison by outlining her somewhat guarded attitude toward religion and using it as an entrée into talking about postsecularism. O'Connor is a staunch monotheist: one God exists, one man, one book, one church, and one truth. She fought entities that denied this monotheism and those she believed diluted it. The dilution of faith does not concern Morrison; in fact, her fiction and interviews both distrust claims to a single truth because they can be used to validate one group and marginalize another. Most scholars know that O'Connor was Catholic; few know that Morrison is.

Morrison first mentioned her Catholicism in a 1993 *Paris Review* interview. Speaking about the space out of which she writes, she stated, "It just so happens that that space for me is African American; it could be Catholic, it could be Midwestern. I'm those things too" ("Toni Morrison" 119). Ten years later, Hilton Als wrote, "When she was twelve years old, Morrison converted to Catholicism, taking Anthony as her baptismal name, after St. Anthony. Her friends shortened it to Toni" ("Ghosts" 67–68). Morrison gave her most definitive statement in 2005: "I am a Catholic; some of my family is Catholic, some of them are Protestant, some of them are all sorts of things. And what saved me was, I think—what helped me at any rate—was knowing that I was going to take religion seriously" ("Pam Houston" 254). One year later, however, Antonio Monda asked her to talk about her "religious journey." She answered, "I had a Catholic education, even though my mother, who was very religious, was Protestant. As a child I was fascinated by the rituals of Catholicism, and I was strongly influenced by a cousin who was a fervent Catholic." Monda followed up, "When did your relationship with Catholicism end?" She answered by talking about Vatican II, but she did not correct him in saying that she was still Catholic, as she said the year before. He asked, "Do you think that those who believe are deluded?" She answered, "No, on the contrary: I feel the greatest respect for them" (qtd. in Monda 117–19). Morrison positions herself here as outside Catholicism and outside "those who believe." One might see this contradiction as indicating hypocrisy or uncertainty in her beliefs, but it could also reflect postmodernism. John Duvall writes that Morrison's later work "suggests a more postmodern articulation of identity as a process plural and fluid" (*Identifying Fictions* 8). It could also reflect postsecularism, in that John McClure states that postsecular fiction rarely treats any "single discourse . . . as a complete and authoritative representation of the real" (5). Morrison appears cagey when it comes to naming her religious identification; her statements resist fixity.

After this prelude, the students dive in to Morrison's most decorated novel, *Beloved*. In "Memory, Creation, and Writing," Morrison writes, "If my work is to confront a reality unlike that received reality of the West, it must centralize and animate information discredited by the West" (388). Christianity and Morrison's Catholicism constitute part of that Western "received reality." When critics do address the question of religion in Morrison, they write about how she "refigures," "retells," "revises," and "rewrites" biblical texts and Christian stories (C. Mitchell 28; Taylor-Guthrie, "Who Are" 119; Ochoa 114; C. Lee 44).

We see such a moment at the end of *Beloved*, when Ella and the group of women go out to 124 Bluestone Road to confront Beloved, the ghost of Sethe's murdered child. When the women arrive, half of them drop to their knees, but the moment changes when "Ella hollered," and "[i]nstantly the kneelers and the standers joined her. They stopped praying and took a step back to the beginning. In the beginning there were no words. In the beginning was the sound, and they all knew what that sound sounded like" (259). When Sethe sees and hears the women singing, she thinks of the Clearing, where Baby Suggs clandestinely preached to Cincinnati's African American community and "where the voices of women searched for the right combination, the key, the code, the sound that broke the back of words. Building voice upon voice until they found it, and when they did it was a wave of sound wide enough to sound deep water and knock the pods off chestnut trees. It broke over Sethe and she trembled like the baptized in its wash" (261).

This passage clearly references the Gospel of John, so when I teach this scene, I bring a bible into the classroom and read John 1.1–4: "In the beginning was the Word, and the Word was with God, and the Word was God. He was in the beginning with God. All things came to be through Him, and without Him nothing came to be. What came to be through him was life, and this life was the light of the human race" (New American Bible). The passage from *Beloved* also echoes Genesis 1.1–3: "In the beginning when God created the heavens and the earth, the earth was a formless wasteland, and darkness covered the abyss, while a mighty wind swept over the waters. Then God said, 'Let there be light,' and there was light." I ask the students what the passage from *Beloved* appears to be doing with these biblical passages. With luck, we end up discussing how, according to the Bible, which makes up part of Morrison's "received reality," everything—the Word, life, all things made, the heavens, earth, light—begins with God the Father and his son. Western iconography figures God as a white man with a white beard, as in the ceiling of the Sistine Chapel, and Western film figures Christ as a white man with brown hair and blue eyes, as in Ted Neeley in Norman Jewison's *Jesus Christ Superstar*, Robert Powell in Franco

Zeffirelli's *Jesus of Nazareth*, Willem Dafoe in Martin Scorsese's *Last Temptation of Christ*, and Jim Caviezel in Mel Gibson's *Passion of the Christ*. Morrison pushes back against this "received reality" with her first novel, *The Bluest Eye*, where blue eyes come to symbolize white beauty idealized.

Beloved, too, rewrites this tradition by ending with thirty poor black women — what Taylor-Guthrie calls an "amplified trinity" (128) — going back to a time before the word when only sound existed and only they knew what "that sound sounded like." When the women sing, their voices search for the right combination that will break "the back of words." In *Playing in the Dark*, Morrison writes, "I am a black writer struggling with and through a language that can powerfully evoke and enforce hidden signs of racial superiority, cultural hegemony, and dismissive 'othering' of people" (x). The very language in which she writes represents part of her received tradition, so her fiction must find a way to break "the back" of that racialized language. Part of her strategy remains to create stories that imagine a time before language.

In this unit, I have only enough time to cover *Beloved*, but I bring in passages from Morrison's other work to add to the discussion. For example, the students examine a scene from *Song of Solomon*, which contains a similar prelingual moment. Late in the novel, its protagonist, Milkman Dead, sits in a North Carolina forest in the middle of the night listening to the sounds surrounding him. "It was all language," he thinks, but then he corrects himself. "No, it was not language; it was what there was before language. Before things were written down. Language in a time . . . when man ran *with* wolves, not from or after them" (278). This moment represents his "spiritual rebirth," when he turns from his father's values, which unquestioningly replicate Western capitalistic values, and toward those more grounded in his black, southern ancestry (C. Lee 56). Milkman's rebirth and Sethe's baptism come not from encountering the Word but from entering a time and sound predating words.

I bring a passage into class from Morrison's *Love* in which, again, she rewrites her biblical received tradition. The novel revolves around Bill Cosey, a powerful, wealthy black man who owned and operated Cosey's Hotel and Resort. When the story begins, his granddaughter, Christine Cosey, and his second wife, Heed Cosey, are bitter enemies. They have been fighting over his will since his death, but at the novel's end, as they reconcile, they think back to a time in 1940 when, as ten-year-olds, they played at the beach. One day, Heed went back to the hotel to get jacks for their games and ran into Bill Cosey, who, after talking to her briefly, fingered her nipple, though she was a child and he a grown man. Heed ran to find Christine to tell her what her grandfather did. Christine, coming up from the beach to look for Heed, saw her grandfather masturbating. At first she laughed but then vomited. When the girls reunited at the beach, Heed said she could not find the jacks: "That first lie, of many to follow, is born because Heed thinks Christine knows what happened and it made her vomit. So there is something wrong with Heed" (191). Christine, for her part, cannot look Heed in the eye because "[s]he is ashamed of her grandfather and of herself." Now, at the novel's conclusion, toward the end of one of their lives, "they don't speak of the birth of sin" (192).

In Christian theology, sin begins when Eve eats the fruit in the Garden and then gives it to Adam. Once they eat of the tree of knowledge, they become aware of their nakedness and hide when God calls. God punishes Eve by making childbirth painful and Adam by making him till the soil for his sustenance: "Thorns and thistles shall it bring forth to you" (*New American Bible,* Gen. 3.18). God then drives them from Eden. The Fall, the pain of childbirth, shame, deceit, having to till the ground, thorns and thistles—in Christian theology these emanate from a woman, but in Morrison's *Love*, the first lie, shame, self-loathing, and the birth of sin emanate from a man. In Christianity, the world and the Word begin with a man, but sin begins with a woman. Morrison once said, "One must critique [history], test it, confront it, and understand it in order to achieve a freedom that is more than license, to achieve true, adult agency" ("Toni Morrison" 114). In these passages, we see Morrison critiquing her own history, her received sacred stories, in order to achieve a freedom and agency within them.

I have had students argue that these moments in *Beloved* and *Love* represent Morrison's dismissal of Christianity. Gay Wilentz believes *Song of Solomon* subverts "dominant white Christian values" and replaces them with Afrocentric ones (158; see also Peach 163). In 1985, however, Morrison stated:

> I have a family of people who were highly religious—that was part of their language. Their sources were biblical. They expressed themselves in that fashion. They took it all very, very seriously, so it would be very difficult for me not to. But they combined it with another kind of relationship, to something I think which was outside the Bible. They did not limit themselves to understanding the world only through Christian theology.
> ("Interview" 177–78)

One could respond, following D. H. Lawrence, Trust the tale, not the teller. Insight into this tension between these passages and her interviews comes from examining a three-part lecture series she gave at the University of Toronto entitled The Foreigner's Home. In the first of these talks, "Grendel and His Mother," she referenced Seamus Heaney's then-recent translation of *Beowulf*, but as the title of her lecture suggests, she did not focus on the titular character but rather on those whom the text figures as monstrous, Grendel and his mother. In the talk, she noted that Grendel's mother has no name, and "in true mythic fashion, evil is female."[1] She ended her address meditating on foreignness, home, and belonging—and asking who or what gets defined as a foreigner.

She began her keynote address, however, with a simple statement: "I'm just going to tell a story." Her entire oeuvre tells stories that question and interrogate the narratives passed down in Western literature, including those passed down in her own religious tradition. She questions the tales not to eradicate them or the tradition but to rethink, rework, and rewrite them. Emily Griesinger writes of Morrison and "the syncretism of her method, the way she blends Christianity with black folklore, African tribal religion, and magical realism" (700). The word *syncretic*, which shows up often in Morrison criticism, better encapsulates the author's work, especially in a postmodern and postsecular context, than does a position arguing that she replaces one tradition with another. In "Grendel and His Mother," she spoke of the poet's word and "its power to transform" and of the poet as "the shaper." As a poet, she wants to transform and reshape the stories passed down to African Americans, particularly African American women, in order to create a home, a space of belonging for those who are foreign, those excluded from and demonized in the dominant culture's narratives.[2]

Students struggle most with this section, so I end the unit having them read the introduction to McClure's *Partial Faiths: Postsecular Fiction in the Age of Pynchon and Morrison*. Drawing on the work of Harold Bloom, William Connolly, Charles Taylor, Jacques Derrida, Pierre Hadot, and Jürgen Habermas, McClure defines postsecularism as "a mode of being and seeing that is at once critical of secular constructions of reality and of dogmatic religiosity" (ix). Characters in postsecular fiction "are not conducted from the barren confinements of a secular universe into a temple of ultimate truths or a great hall of light"; instead, these texts "conduct us into a vividly reenchanted, but dauntingly open, world" (129). Ultimately, McClure sees postsecularism as a "sort of reconciliation of secular and sacred modes of being" (103).

One can teach O'Connor and Morrison by introducing the question of religion into the classroom—a space that tends to be highly secularized in today's academy—and examining them with the history of secularization as a backdrop. O'Connor once wrote to Betty Hester, "You have to push as hard as the age that pushes against you" (*Habit* 229), and from *Wise Blood* to "Parker's Back" she pushes against the secularism of her day. An encroaching secularism does not concern Morrison; nonetheless, she spoke of her writing ritual as "my preparation to enter a space that I can only call non-secular" ("Toni Morrison" 65). Like *postsecular*, the word *nonsecular*, and O'Connor's and Morrison's bodies of work, asks us to pause and rethink our unexamined secular assumptions. Such an examination then opens up a space for approaching these two authors in the classroom.

NOTES

[1] The quotations from "Grendel and His Mother" come from my notes at the lecture. I use quotation marks to record Morrison's words verbatim; the material not in quotation marks is paraphrased.

[2] One sees Morrison's interest in interrogating the stories passed down to her also in a commencement address called "Cinderella's Stepsisters" and in her Nobel acceptance speech, which critiques the story of the Tower of Babel ("Pam Houston" 239; "Nobel Lecture" 270).

O'Connor in Popular Music

Irwin Streight

Flannery O'Connor had very little interest in or appreciation for music of any kind. In her letters she jokingly suggests that she possesses "the First and Prime Tin Ear" and confesses, "I am a complete musical ignoramus. . . . I never hear any music and don't seek it out" (*Flannery . . . Works* 1200, 1092). Although conscious of her deficiency in appreciating music, she was not completely oblivious to the popular music of her day. She likely saw Elvis Presley's first appearance on *The Ed Sullivan Show* in 1957, a performance that may well inform Rufus Johnson's hip-swiveling Elvis imitation (606) to an altered version of his first million-selling hit "Shake, Rattle and Roll" in "The Lame Shall Enter First." And she accurately quotes the lyrics for the Albert Brumley song "When I Looked Up and He Looked Down" that Ruby Turpin inwardly sings along to as she sits in the doctor's waiting room in "Revelation" (635). Released in 1957 and 1958 by the popular gospel group the Chuck Wagon Gang, this song would have had extensive airplay in the South in the late 1950s and early 1960s. O'Connor's "A Good Man Is Hard to Find" takes its title from a popular blues song famously recorded in 1927 by Bessie Smith, though O'Connor may have been familiar only with the title and not the song, as her editor and friend Sally Fitzgerald suggests (*Flannery . . . Works* 1266, note for page 137, line 1). Regardless, O'Connor was not as culturally deficient as she let on. Gifted with a cast-off record player and box of LPs in the last months of her life, she does appear to have been singularly unsuccessful in a final attempt to appreciate either classical or popular music. She confides comically to a correspondent, "All I can say about it is that all classical music sounds alike to me and all the rest of it sounds like the Beatles" (*Habit* 566). There is considerable irony therefore in the extent to which her art and vision have had a profound and extensive influence on the works and songcraft of a number of accomplished contemporary singer-songwriters and pop musicians.

Cultural critics have noted and suggested references to O'Connor's fictions in songs by an A-list of artists that includes Bob Dylan, Bruce Springsteen, U2, Lucinda Williams, Tom Waits, Nick Cave, PJ Harvey, R.E.M., and Sufjan Stevens, along with many other less commercially successful pop groups and singer-songwriters. There are a considerable number of contemporary songs that make glancing reference to O'Connor's works and person, but there is a sizable subset of songs that draw considerable lyrical substance from her fictions or that bear acknowledged evidence of her influence. These songs can be used in the classroom both to complement approaches to teaching and to enrich students' understandings of a number of her fictional works. This essay discusses songs and artists that are substantially influenced by O'Connor's art and vision. It is organized in part around her works and in part around individual songwriters.

"A Good Man Is Hard to Find"

Foremost among pop artists influenced by O'Connor is the American rock star Bruce Springsteen. In a 1997 interview, Springsteen acknowledged that reading O'Connor's fiction transformed both his sensibilities as an artist and his craft as a songwriter. Students may be interested to discover the formative depth and arc of her influence:

> The really important reading that I did began in my late twenties, with authors like Flannery O'Connor. There was something in those stories of hers that I felt captured a certain part of the American character that I was interested in writing about. They were a big, big revelation. She got to the heart of some part of meanness that she never spelled out, because if she spelled it out you wouldn't be getting it. It was always at the core of every one of her stories—the way that she'd left that hole there, that hole that's inside of everybody. There was some dark thing—a component of spirituality—that I sensed in her stories, and that set me off exploring characters of my own.   ("Rock" 37)

In this interview, Springsteen further reflected that "Songwriting . . . has a little in common with short-story writing in that it's character-driven." He observed that his songwriting underwent a transformation to "a more scaled-down, more personal, more restrained" form of lyrical expression, which he credited to the fact that he was "deep into O'Connor" as he wrote for *Nebraska* his narrative-style songs (38). As late as a 2014 interview published in the *New York Times Sunday Book Review*, he singled out O'Connor's collected stories as the "one book" that had most profoundly informed his artistic sensibilities ("By the Book" 8). In his autobiography, *Born to Run*, he cited O'Connor as a "model" of an individualistic artist, like himself, "who worked on the edges of society" and whose art had been "assimilated and become a part of the culture at large" (430–31).

The lyrics for "Nebraska" are included in the eleventh edition of the *Norton Introduction to Literature*—the only work in this popular anthology that is a song—with a footnote giving Springsteen's allusion to O'Connor's "A Good Man Is Hard to Find" in the closing words of the song's narrator: "I guess there's just a meanness in this world" (464n1). His appropriation of the term *meanness* in his song narrative invites an examination of what it means in the story and how that might extend to his song. The narrator of "Nebraska" is based on real-life serial killer Charles Starkweather, who, along with his fifteen-year-old girlfriend Caril Fugate, in 1958 went on a killing spree from Lincoln, Nebraska, to eastern Wyoming, senselessly murdering ten people in eight days. Springsteen's unrepentant Starkweather character remarks, "I can't say that I'm sorry for the things that we done / At least for a little while, sir, me and her we had us some fun." Students might recognize here the concluding words of the Misfit's accomplice, Bobby Lee, who after shooting Bailey and his family remarks, "Some fun!," to which the Misfit, in the last line of the story, replies tellingly, "It's no real pleasure in life" (*Flannery . . . Works* 153). O'Connor's story of a cold-blooded killer ultimately touched by grace hinges on the "pleasure" he previously derived from acts of violence. The testimonial of Springsteen's narrator underscores, by contrast, the transformational nature of the Misfit's encounter with the grandmother: an antidote to the "meanness" that hitherto defined his existence.

As Springsteen did on his album of outtakes, *Tracks*, indie pop artist Sufjan Stevens borrowed a song title from O'Connor's "A Good Man Is Hard to Find" and in a form of postmodern appropriation borrowed as well her character the Misfit as his narrator. Stevens's first aspiration was to be a fiction writer like O'Connor, "his idol," according to an interview in *The Village Voice* (Sylvester). His artistic vision and work, like O'Connor's, are deeply informed by the Christian faith. Further, his song cycles explore themes similar to those found in her stories: the effects of original sin, the subtle ways in which we are moved by the motions of grace, and the redemptive possibilities in physical suffering. Stevens's "A Good Man Is Hard to Find," from his twelve-song low-fi recording *Seven Swans*, is a simple, brief folk song in a minor key played on an acoustic guitar, strummed in the off-balance time signature 5/4, which is unusual for a folk song.

Stevens's "A Good Man Is Hard to Find" comments on the meaning of O'Connor's story from the Misfit's point of view. Stevens imagines the character's inner response to the moment of revelation in the story when the prattling Grandmother recognizes her kinship with the spiritually distraught killer, reaches out to touch him, and is shot point-blank. Stevens's narrator begins by observing "she was once like me" and repeats this phrase three times in the first part of the song to underscore its truthfulness, a rhetorical strategy that O'Connor frequently employs in her fiction. The song suggests that the Misfit experiences a moment of insight similar to that of the Grandmother. Thus it engages in an act of literary appropriation while also offering to the classroom a distinctive interpretation of O'Connor's complex short story. The lyrics conclude with reference to the Misfit's epiphanic encounter at the touch of the Grandmother: "So I go to hell. I wait for it, / but someone's left me creased. / Someone's left me creased." Bullets from the Misfit's gun claim the Grandmother the moment she acts on the Gospel truth that she has denied. But the mystery manifest in her gesture ricochets and creases the Misfit in Stevens's interpretation of the story. Both are shot through with the revelation of their common condition—that each is in need of grace.

Stevens's lyrics suggest that the Misfit too would have been a good man had there been someone in his life to act in a Christlike way in response to his spiritual anguish. Yet Stevens's Misfit narrator has "put off" all hope of finding "peace" and considers himself damned, whereas O'Connor, as she remarks in one of her published talks, would "prefer to think, however unlikely this may seem" that "the old lady's gesture . . . will be enough of a pain" to the Misfit that he will "turn . . . into the prophet he was meant to become." She adds, "But that's another story" (*Mystery* 113). Stevens's lyrics both expound on the effect of the Grandmother's gesture and offer another angle on the story through the eyes of the Misfit.

Playing Springsteen's "Nebraska" and Stevens's "A Good Man Is Hard to Find" when teaching O'Connor's story helps students engage with this widely anthologized yet difficult work and enables a deeper exploration of O'Connor's moral and religious vision. Springsteen's song expands on the meaning of the Misfit's reference to meanness, and Stevens's lyrical exploration of the Misfit's consciousness adds both a supportive interpretation and a conflicting point of view to the violent two-way revelation that concludes O'Connor's story.

"Everything That Rises Must Converge"

A song titled "Everything That Rises," by the Canadian husband-and-wife duo Wild Strawberries, draws on and interprets O'Connor's story "Everything That Rises Must Converge." Originally recorded in 1991, the song was rereleased as a synth-pop dance mix on *Heroine*, the duo's best-selling recording, earning a gold record in the Canadian marketplace.

The first verse of "Everything That Rises" offers a condensed description of the characters in O'Connor's story and refers to the symbolic penny that Julian's mother offers the African American boy, followed by a chorus composed solely of the translated phrase O'Connor borrows from Pierre Teilhard de Chardin for her story's title: "Everything that rises must converge." This song belongs to a subset of O'Connor-influenced pop tunes that might be labeled *song as criticism*. Its second verse begins with an observation in the form of social criticism: "This is my country—this is your sign— / We are painting fences, drawing lines." Played alongside a reading of O'Connor's story, the song expands the issue of racism in the American South that O'Connor addresses in her one "topical" story (*Flannery . . . Works* 1147) into Canadian social history. In recent decades, Canada has had to account for its own legacy of racist government policies toward its indigenous peoples, Ukrainian and Japanese immigrants, and African Canadian community. This pop song speaks to the cultural translatability of O'Connor's art and vision and to issues of racism that continue to create social fences in North America and increasingly in the global community. The image of a "whitewashed fence" in the song lyrics provides students with a metaphor through which to view both the inherited racist attitudes of Julian and his mother in the story and to address racism in contemporary society, where a systemic culture of white privilege and a whitewashing of implicitly racist government and social policies are similar, and damning, on both sides of the United States–Canada border.

"The Comforts of Home" and "Revelation"

Mary Gauthier, a Nashville-based, Louisiana-born country blues artist, remarked in a personal interview that as a woman and a writer she owes a debt to O'Connor for her willingness to be "an unladylike writer," echoing an early reviewer in *Time* magazine ("Such Nice People"). O'Connor gave women "permission to explore their own darkness," said Gauthier, and to talk about it in often violent terms. She readily connects O'Connor's violent and shocking stories with her own songs about desperate and destitute characters (Interview). Allusions in Gauthier's songs to characters and events in O'Connor's stories help illuminate O'Connor's themes. Gauthier's "most Flannery O'Connor-inspired song" is titled "Snakebit," the first track on her fifth collection of songs, *Between Daylight and Dark*. Like the desperate characters in Springsteen's *Nebraska* songs, whose sense of meaninglessness drives them to commit acts of violence, Gauthier's snakebit character has impulsively "pulled [a] pistol from [a] dresser drawer" and is poised to commit some deadly act—or perhaps has already done so. The chorus cries, "Oh Lord, oh Lord / Oh Lord, what have I done? / Everything worth holding slips through my fingers / Now my hand's wrapped around the handle of a gun."

O'Connor's influence on the song might be observed in the description of the distraught and regretful first-person narrator, whose voice takes over the lyrics after the first chorus. The narrator is forty years old, feels put upon, "forsaken, forgotten, without love," and is subject to the dark shadow cast by the narrator's deceased father, whose repeated foretellings of misfortune now replay in the narrator's consciousness: "Kid, I knew when you was born you'd end up snake bit like me." Thomas in O'Connor's story "The Comforts of Home" comes to mind in that stupefying moment after the gun he is holding goes off at the story's conclusion. He fatally fires as though his hand were "guided by" the "hissed" imprecations of his lying father / the Father of Lies (*Flannery . . . Works* 593, 592). The Misfit, recoiling from the proffered grace of the Grandmother's touch on his shoulder "as if a snake had bitten him" also comes to mind (152). Gauthier acknowledges that she drew on O'Connor's the Misfit in shaping the sensibilities of her "Snakebit" character (qtd. in Hight 110). Students will find that her haunting blues song helps reveal the anguished inner states of O'Connor's two gun-toting characters; it also intimates a cosmic evil that can animate human actions.

Gauthier's song "Wheel inside the Wheel," from *Mercy Now*, invokes a vision similar to that which the chastened Ruby Turpin sees in her moment of revelation at the end of O'Connor's "Revelation." In Ruby's vision of that "vast horde of souls . . . rumbling toward heaven," the social order that she so hypocritically applies to those she meets is inverted. The "white trash" she despises, the blacks, and a whole company of "freaks and lunatics" who, "leaping like frogs," appear even farther off the bubble than the seemingly temporarily mad Mary Grace, are all headed up that "vast swinging bridge" toward heaven ahead of respectable good Christian folk like Ruby and Claud (*Flannery . . . Works* 654).

More important than the inverted social hierarchy here is the revelation that the vastness of divine grace includes them all. This is the shock that we are led to understand has ultimately altered Ruby's pharisaic outlook.

The parade of souls in Gauthier's "Wheel inside the Wheel" is a motley and unexpected collection of folk, metaphorically winding their way heavenward. The song invokes the familiar Mardi Gras parades in New Orleans that precede the season of Lent: flambeau dancers, French Quarter queens, Native Americans in "colored feathers and beads," and African Americans led by the New Orleans native Satchmo (Louis Armstrong) are envisioned parading and chanting behind a brass band playing "When the Saints Go Marching In." In Gauthier's heavenly procession, Marie Laveau, the famous nineteenth-century voodoo queen who was eventually given a Catholic burial, "promenades with Oscar Wilde," who, despite his sins against the morals of his age, died a baptized Catholic. All are joined in a "soul parade" that "winds its way down Eternity Street." Gauthier's song presents her listener with a vision of an eclectic procession of souls who have been marginalized on account of race, religion, and sexual orientation, all marching toward Zion and with the same shocking message implicit in Ruby's vision. Gauthier updates O'Connor's story of a bigoted, hypocritical good Christian woman and her social targets by adding transgender people, gays, and Native Americans to the litany of others who might have been included in Ruby's judgmental vision and thoughts. Studying Gauthier's song alongside "Revelation" may assist student listeners in finding further insight into the "abysmal life-giving knowledge" that is revealed to Ruby at the end of O'Connor's story (*Flannery . . . Works* 653).

"Good Country People," "The River," and "The Life You Save May Be Your Own"

By her own confession, British alt-rocker PJ Harvey likes to make things from found objects—pictures, photographs, things she has collected in walks along the beach (Blandford 117). In a trio of songs on *Is This Desire?*, she has done the same with characters, phrases, and bits of dialogue from three of O'Connor's stories collected in *"A Good Man Is Hard to Find" and Other Stories*. Students may be interested to examine the pervasive intertextuality between Harvey's lyrics and O'Connor's stories and to explore the ways in which the song lyrics lend critical focus to and add to a critical understanding of the stories.

Harvey's hard-driven rock song "Joy" presents a lyric summary of O'Connor's story "Good Country People" with elements of critical commentary as well. Its opening line draws attention to a crucial detail about the protagonist: "Joy *was* her name" (emphasis added). Joy's choice at age twenty-one to change her name legally to the ugly-sounding Hulga signals her disdain for her upbringing and community as well as her self-loathing at her maimed condition. Her mother laments the hopeless state of her daughter, describing her as a "poor stout girl in her thirties who had never danced a step or had any *normal* good times" (*Flannery . . . Works* 266)—a line with details and a phrase that Harvey incorporates into the first verse of her song. Indeed, a close comparative reading of the "Joy" lyrics reveals that it is a pastiche of quoted phrases and dramatic details drawn from the story. But Harvey does more than mine the story for its pitiful portrait of Joy/Hulga and a few poetic phrases. "Joy" is also an example of song as criticism, offering a reading of Hulga's moment of revelation in the hayloft, where she has gone to seduce the seemingly guileless bible salesman Manley Pointer. Hulga believes that in her tryst with the young Pointer "she [is] face to face with real innocence" (281). But in the aborted sexual encounter with Pointer, she is the one who is parted from innocence. As Joy/Hulga sits immobilized and abandoned in the hayloft, bereft of her false leg and, symbolically, of her false philosophy, she is brought, as Harvey sings, "face to face" with "her own innocence," which in Harvey's reading is an "innocence so suffocating / now she cannot move, no question." Students may find a satisfying conclusion to O'Connor's open-ended story by considering the insight Harvey suggests in Hulga's immobilizing and "suffocating" state of innocence at the end.

The tenth track on the *Is This Desire?* CD, "The River," shares more than a title and a dramatic event with O'Connor's story. Like found poetry, Harvey's text is in part a found lyric. Words and phrases and plot details from "The River" have been extracted and reformed into a lyrical pastiche. Most significant is that Harvey's chorus borrows, with a variant word, the young preacher's exhortation to the people who have come to the river: "Throw your pain in the river / To be washed away slow" (cf. *Flannery . . . Works* 161–62). Harvey's song supports the emphasis in O'Connor's story on the mysterious agency of the river as a sacramental symbol. The revelatory "white light" that "scatters" over the surface of O'Connor's river is emphasized in the closing refrain of Harvey's lyrics, drawing attention to the salvific act of baptism that is the story's central concern. Similarly, the second half of Harvey's song "No Girl So Sweet," track 11 on *Is This Desire?*, substantially borrows description and dialogue from "The Life You Save May Be Your Own," but unlike "Joy" and "The River," this song does not directly engage in a lyric retelling of O'Connor's story. The raucous refrain at the end of the song quotes Mr. Shiftlet's voiced revelation at the story's end: "He took her from heaven and giver to me . . ." (183). Harvey's impassioned, almost shouted repetition of this key phrase emphasizes its importance to O'Connor's intended anagogical meaning.

Harvey places quotation marks around several bits of dialogue taken from O'Connor, but whole phrases and key words and images from the stories are extracted and melded to form her lyrics without acknowledgment. Careful sifting through these O'Connor stories with Harvey's song lyrics at hand will reveal her artistic bricolage and raise interesting—and perhaps contentious—issues regarding artistic inspiration and influence.

Wise Blood *and* The Violent Bear It Away

Lucinda Williams's brief biography in the *Rolling Stone Encyclopedia of Rock and Roll* notes that she regards Flannery O'Connor as "a major influence on her songwriting" (George-Warren and Romanowski 1068). Now a multiple Grammy Award–winning country blues artist, Williams as a four- and five-year-old would chase O'Connor's peacocks around the family farm at Andalusia as her father, the poet Miller Williams, sat in a rocking chair on the farmhouse porch for one of his monthly visits while the Williams family was residing in nearby Macon (M. Williams 2).

Reflecting on her formative years, her southern family background, and the reading that has lent itself to the rich literary quality of her lyrics, Lucinda Williams remarked in a *Rolling Stone* interview:

> I have a certain Southern Gothic sensibility. I related to Flannery O'Connor at a young age. My mother's father was a fire-and-brimstone Methodist preacher. I saw a lot of that kind of thing growing up, and I read about it in O'Connor. Her writing was really dark but also ironic and humorous. It informs a lot of my songs.   ("Last Word" 66)

Like O'Connor, Williams is interested in exploring human experience at its sometimes terrible extremes, including the practices and perspectives of southern religious extremists: people who, like O'Connor's Hazel Motes, would torture and blind themselves, even risk death, in penance for their sinfulness or in a manic pursuit of righteousness. The Christ-hauntedness that informs several of her song lyrics is cast without irony in the garb and language of the Bible Belt, and her artistic representations of religious extremism may well come from her reading of O'Connor. She has named *Wise Blood* as her favorite novel and its film adaptation by John Huston as her favorite movie (House 86).

Williams's pursuit of the agonizing grace that O'Connor writes about is evident in her Grammy Award–winning song "Get Right with God," from *Essence*. The lyrics list some of the potentially harmful practices that southern religious extremists engage in, particularly snake handling. The singer then offers a litany of self-mortifying acts she would perform if by doing so she could "walk righteously again": burn the soles of her feet and the palms of her hands and sleep on a bed of nails "[t]ill my back was torn and bleeding"—all this resolving in a plea to God to "take me as one of your daughters." Like O'Connor's Hazel Motes after he has killed his false prophet double, the female narrator of "Get Right with God" appears willing to pay for righteousness by torturing her flesh and risking death. One thinks of Haze's acts of mortification at the end of *Wise Blood*: overpowered by the sense that he is "not clean," Haze blinds himself with caustic lime, walks in shoes filled with gravel and bits of broken glass, and wraps his chest in three strands of barbed wire (*Flannery . . . Works* 127). The distant religious grotesque in O'Connor's story that students may resist is brought forward into the twenty-first century in Williams's song.

Like O'Connor's hillbilly prophet Mason Tarwater in *The Violent Bear It Away*, who at times "couldn't stand the Lord one instant longer" (358), Williams too has surfeited on southern religion. Her grating rock song "Atonement," from *World Without Tears*, was written as a backlash to the presumptuous religion of southern Baptists she encountered while living in Nashville ("Fruits"). "Atonement" crowds all of southern Pentecostalism into a single song that "[locks] you in a room / With a holy roller and a one-man band" listening to "[s]houting with twisted tongues" from "Hell fire scorched lungs." It describes the fire-and-brimstone religion of the Carmodys, O'Connor's southern evangelist family from *The Violent Bear It Away*. Williams voices this song as though she were both repelled and enraptured by the scene. Despite its abrasive, pulsating assault on the listener, "Atonement" takes an O'Connoresque twist at the end and becomes more an invocation to than a condemnation of the gospel of the grotesque. In introducing the song from the stage, Williams frequently remarks to her audience that it was influenced by her reading of O'Connor's fiction.[1]

Williams's "Get Right with God" and "Atonement" are particularly useful in the classroom when either of O'Connor's novels are taught for the way in which they evoke the rhetoric and extreme practices of the southern Pentecostalism that defines the religious ethos in these novels. Students unfamiliar with the culture of the Bible Belt are offered a kind of aural introduction to that world through the musical styles and religious content of Williams's songs.

Wise Blood *and Alternative Music*

O'Connor reports in her letters that she received some rather quirky and occasionally disturbing correspondence from readers of her first novel, *Wise Blood*, and remarks, "I seem to attract the lunatic fringe" (*Flannery . . . Works* 935). The same might be said about most of the contemporary musicians who are attracted to her characters and vision in this flawed novel—largely of the punk and alternative rock genre in what some still refer to as the underground music scene. *Wise Blood* is uncannily the most widely referenced of O'Connor's works in commercial music. Instructors may wish to assign students the untypical task of listening critically to the lyrics and music of songs in the heavy metal and death metal genres. "Death has always been brother to my imagination," O'Connor once remarked as an explanation for her concerns as a writer with a Catholic worldview (*Conversations* 107). Her works of imagination have in turn informed the works of artists on the darker, gothic extremes of contemporary music.

A recording titled *Wiseblood*, by the heavy metal band Corrosion of Conformity from Raleigh, North Carolina, contains a number of songs that allude to

themes and key phrases in *Wise Blood* and to O'Connor's false preacher protagonist Hazel Motes. Students should pay particular attention to the title song
and to "Good Bye Windows" and "Born Again for the Last Time"—a song of
spiritual anguish that contains the telling refrain "My life is hazy hazy hazy / So
I'm born again for the last time," a possible allusion to the condition and fate
of Hazel Motes. Under the band name Wiseblood, a collective of industrial
and noise metal artists from Australia and the United Kingdom released several recordings in the mid-1980s through early 1990s that venture both morally
and spiritually into "territory held largely by the devil," as O'Connor phrases it
(*Mystery* 118). Bits of dialogue by Hazel Motes's character from the 1979 film
version of *Wise Blood*—including the memorable line "Nobody with a good
car needs to be justified"—are sampled throughout the opening section of the
extended mix of "Jesus Built My Hotrod (Redline/Whiteline Version)," a maxi
single recorded by the Chicago-based industrial metal band Ministry. The post-
punk band King Swamp alludes to O'Connor's Enoch Emory character in the
title song from their album *Wiseblood*. But students will find references to the
themes, content, and title of O'Connor's *Wise Blood* in works by a sizable number of experimental, alternative rock, punk, and heavy metal bands. The question of why her work is particularly attractive to songwriters in these marginal,
less accessible, and often excessive musical genres may give students insight into
her pervasive and abiding influence on the darker products of popular culture.

Flannery at the Grammys

To top the irony of O'Connor's lack of appreciation for music and her nonetheless significant influence on current pop musicians is the fact that she has been
named at the Grammy Awards. In accepting the second award for U2 at the
1988 Grammys for *The Joshua Tree*, their guitarist, the Edge, read out names
from a list of people whom the band wished to thank, which included Desmond
Tutu, the South African Anglican bishop, followed by Martin Luther King, Jr.,
and Bob Dylan. Fourth from the top, before Jimi Hendrix, John the Baptist, and
a comic roster of lesser worthies, was O'Connor (see www.youtube.com/watch
?v=NgRErUkTdFM&index=2&list=RDr_31c15CMqM). Her influence on the
lyrical content of U2's celebrated recording is at least evident in an allusion
to one of her story titles found in the first line of the elegiac "One Tree Hill,"
which refers to mourners who "turn away to face the cold, enduring chill" of
lives doubtless filled with some form of guilt and sorrow. Bono, the front man
and lyricist for U2, was introduced to O'Connor's writings by Springsteen when
they met backstage at the Hammersmith in London in 1981. In a communiqué
distributed in the U2 organization, Bono remarked of O'Connor, "I've never felt
such sympathy with a writer in America before."

A good number of contemporary songwriters and pop performers have been
influenced and inspired by O'Connor's art and vision. Their songs both comple-

ment and critique her remarkable stories and add depth to our understanding of them.

NOTE

[1] On the limited edition live recording of *World without Tears*, track 11, *The West East North Tour* (Lost Highway), Williams tells her audience that "Atonement" is "influenced by the books I read by Flannery O'Connor."

SPECIALIZED PERSPECTIVES

Feminism and Identity Politics in a Critical Close Reading of "Good Country People"

Julie Goodspeed-Chadwick

In virtually every short story anthology, American literature anthology, or introduction to literature anthology, Flannery O'Connor's work is spotlighted. Her work is included in women-and-literature collections, too, and yet it is not yet treated as standard content in a women's studies course, because O'Connor is not positioned (currently) as a feminist writer or a writer who participates in discursive formations related to identity politics or content relevant to women's studies. However, her canonical work does speak to the very conversations we have in women's studies and feminist theory, and I teach her annually in a 200-level and 300-level concurrent women-and-literature and feminist theory course that is coded as a women's studies course. Approaches to her from women's studies perspectives will open up further her texts to students and engage them in conversations on an important author and her work in the context of real-world concerns about identity and power, concerns that are already embedded in critical theory in English studies. In this essay, I focus on one story, "Good Country People," as a case study to show how O'Connor might be approached in a women's studies course.

Although I teach O'Connor in a semester-long course that focuses on feminist theory and literature by women, it would be easy to create a unit in other courses—for example, an introduction to literature, a course on literary interpretation, a course on contemporary American literature, or a course on literary theory—that features O'Connor and women's studies. Additionally, an intro-

duction to women's studies course could include a unit that incorporates feminist interpretations of literature, as I do when I teach Introduction to Women's
Studies, so that students are exposed to the intersection of the humanities and
women's studies in a course that is informed by social sciences primarily and by
the humanities and the hard sciences to a lesser extent.

Because O'Connor's work strikes students as challenging on several levels, it
is useful to teach it in an explicit theoretical framework that will help ground
their reading. In my classes we read "Good Country People" through feminist theories—specifically, through the ideas of gender performativity, binary
opposition, identity politics in relation to power and subjectivity, and *écriture
féminine*. Close reading and the interpretation of literature or other highly stylized texts require students to think critically. Stephen D. Brookfield defines
critical thinking as a process that involves "(1) identifying the assumptions that
frame our thinking and determine our actions, (2) checking out the degree to
which these assumptions are accurate and valid, (3) looking at our ideas and
decisions (intellectual, organizational, and personal) from several different perspectives, and (4) on the basis of all this, taking informed actions" (1). As professors we can lead our students through this process by explaining what we are
doing and why we are doing it, with both lectures and assignments (61). Elaine
Showalter asserts that "students will learn better if we not only explain what
skills or techniques we expect them to master, but also show them models and
examples" (55).

In approaching "Good Country People," I identify along with my students
the assumptions that frame our thinking when we articulate what our expectations are of "good country people," and we draw the binary oppositions on the
board: good versus bad and country versus urban. We mine the story for examples of whether our assumptions are accurate and valid, especially in regard to
Joy/Hulga and her perspectives on her mother, Mrs. Hopewell; their neighbor
Mrs. Freeman; and the "Chrustian" bible salesman (270). We also consider the
perspectives of her mother and the salesman on Hulga. By bringing feminist
theorists to bear on our text, we can try on and try out the range of different
positions. Our informed action as a class is to interpret the story, reflect on its
significance, and consider how it can be factored into our final paper.

I recommend that students study each page of the short story. If time does
not allow such study, it is easy to select passages, have different students read
them aloud, and then discuss how we can interpret them and how the passages
fit our feminist theme. We examine the degree to which power undergirds subject positions and how identity types are overturned or reaffirmed and who
benefits through privilege by the end of the story.

The teacher should adopt an ideological and political approach to a text and
entertain positions or ideas that are in opposition to that approach, as Gerald
Graff advocates in *Beyond the Culture Wars*. Graff suggests that classics, like
O'Connor's work, have "less to fear from newfangled ideological hostility than
from old-fashioned indifference" (47). His "young female professor (YFP)" who

teaches "Dover Beach" from a women's studies perspective does a better job of allowing the poem to be a *"live issue* in the culture again than does the respect-ful treatment of traditionalist teachers . . . [like the one who] fails to arouse his students" (49).

Gender performativity is an important term in any gendered approach to O'Connor's work. Judith Butler argues that gender is a script (409). She al-ludes to "binary genders" (i.e., femininity and masculinity), because "gender is in no way a stable identity or locus of agency from which various acts [pro-ceed]; rather, it is an identity tenuously constituted in time—an identity cre-ated through a *stylized repetition of acts*" (402). She clarifies, "[T]o be a woman is to have *become* a woman, to compel the body to conform to an historical idea of 'woman,' to induce the body to become a cultural sign" (405). She observes that the body is bound up in a performance: "One is not simply a body, but, in some very key sense, one does one's body. . . . [The] body is always an embody-ing *of* possibilities both conditioned and circumscribed by historical conven-tion" (404). In "Good Country People," students can locate examples in which they think Joy/Hulga tries to subvert gender constraints, but they will discover that she responds to the expectations of her gendered script (i.e., femininity) reluctantly but steadfastly. There is never a time when she stops performing her gender. She dresses in a feminine, albeit dowdy fashion, in her skirt and faded sweatshirt. Enamored of the traditional seduction plot, she assumes the role of seducer with the bible salesman, then winds up becoming the passive and feminine victim of a seduction and a crime, which further feminizes her. Moreover, she is socialized into cultural notions of what a disabled woman is: a freak. With her amputated leg and heart condition, she is treated as a child by her ableist mother, who tolerates Hulga's bratty and sulky behavior because of Hulga's physical disability.

We are told that "Joy was [Mrs. Hopewell's] daughter, a large blonde girl who had an artificial leg," then immediately that "Mrs. Hopewell thought of her as a child though she was thirty-two years old and highly educated" (*Flan-nery . . . Works* 263). It tears the mother's heart "to think of the poor stout girl in her thirties who had never danced a step or had any *normal* good times" (266). Tellingly, from Mrs. Hopewell's perspective, "every year [Joy/Hulga] grew less like other people and more like herself—bloated, rude, and squint-eyed" (268). A feminist analysis, problematizing the binary constructions, suggests that people would be thought about and treated differently—that is, fairly—if power were redistributed. Hulga would be viewed as differently abled instead of disabled.

Stomping around her home, making much more noise with her wooden leg than necessary, Hulga performs her disability by calling attention to it in unat-tractive ways (267). Joy chooses the name Hulga because she finds it ugly and therefore fitting for her ugly body, which becomes the basis of her identity as a woman. She selects the name "first purely on the basis of its ugly sound and then the full genius of its fitness had struck her" (266).

We learn about her disability: "As a child she had sometimes been subject to feelings of shame. . . . No one ever touched [her artificial leg] but her. She took care of it as someone else would his soul, in private and almost with her own eyes turned away." When the bible salesman tells her that her artificial leg makes her "different" and she "ain't like anybody else," she feels that for the first time in her life she is "face to face with real innocence" and the bible salesman has "touched the truth about her" (281).

Students can be asked to find passages in which Hulga's disabled female body defines her life by setting a cultural script for her. Other characters support that script. Her mother encourages her to act like a child; Mrs. Freeman's subtle though perverse attention suggests that Hulga is grotesque; and the bible salesman teaches her that she and others like her are vulnerable to victimization.[1] Students can also offer close readings of the bible salesman (see 269–73, 275–84). How does he perform (and misperform) what it means to be a "good country" person? Is he performing masculinity or femininity? Students can work in small groups to cull examples from the story; analyze and discuss what these examples mean in terms of gender, identity, and power; then present their interpretations to the class, with the teacher moderating.

Audre Lorde summarizes what we need to know about binary oppositions or binary constructions: "Much of western European history conditions us to see human differences in simplistic opposition to each other: dominant/subordinate, good/bad, up/down, superior/inferior" (630). With the Western Cartesian mindset, in order to know what the positive term or position is, we must have a negative term or position to put it into relief and define it. Hulga learns what Lorde makes clear: the "master's tools will never dismantle the master's house" and "the future of our earth may depend upon the ability of all women to identify and develop new definitions of power and new patterns of relating across difference" (636). In shunning her mother and her neighbor as able-bodied women who cannot understand her and in dismissing the bible salesman—along with her mother and female neighbor—as good country people (hence the title), Hulga emerges as the most naive character, because she accepts and trusts stereotypes, leaving the people themselves unexamined. Mrs. Freeman is introduced as one who cannot admit she is wrong, who insinuates herself where she is unwanted (e.g., at dinner, when she stands and watches the seated Hopewells eat), and who enjoys gossip. Yet she and her daughters are good country people. They may live in the country, but there is nothing in the story that indicates they are good (263–65). The bible salesman takes the characterization of "good country people" to be an insult when Hulga asks if it applies to him: "'Yeah,' he said, curling his lip slightly, 'but it ain't held me back none. I'm as good as you any day in the week'" (282).

Hulga's binary mind-set—people are all one way or another—puts her in danger.[2] I open the discussion of binary oppositions by having the students help me list some that might be pertinent to our discussion: good versus bad, able-bodied versus disabled, male versus female, and mind versus body. We see that Hulga seems to occupy the disempowered side of every binary.

In her overview of the aims of feminist criticism, Toril Moi charts how one school argues that literature by women needs to be empirical and ultrarealist so it "can and should reflect life accurately and inclusively and in every detail." She wryly comments that "toe-nail clipping and the disposal of sanitary towels . . . seem neglected as fictional themes" (45). O'Connor would not disappoint the literary empiricists or the ultrarealist feminists: although Hulga is not depicted in the act of shaving her legs, she removes her leg. Her faded schoolgirl sweatshirt (with a cowboy on a horse) and her lack of social grace signal her inability to fit in. Although she reads nihilistic philosophy, she does not rebel against patriarchy.

Lillian Robinson identifies an important aim for feminist criticism: "It can emphasize alternative readings of the tradition, readings that reinterpret women's character, motivations, and actions and that identify and challenge sexist ideology" (155). What we do when we read "Good Country People" from a feminist perspective is consider women's studies issues in the text in relation to power and identity constructions. The term *identity politics* refers to the categories that shape (as a taxonomy) our understanding of differences along the intersectional axis lines of sex/gender, race and ethnicity, socioeconomic class, sexual orientation, nationality, religion, and other facets of identity. *Politics* also suggests the power (i.e., empowerment or disempowerment, enfranchisement or disenfranchisement) involved in our construction and perception of binaries and subjectivity. To this end, Hélène Cixous argues that *écriture féminine* or marked writing, what O'Connor produces in her literary texts, "is *the very possibility of change*, the space that can serve as a springboard for subversive thought, the precursory movement of a transformation of social and cultural structures" (1456). I would argue that O'Connor writes in white ink (1458) in this story, with its ties to the female body and female experience and desires (and metaphorical invisibility) that Cixous sees as integral to feminist literature and aesthetics. In our study of the textual world of "Good Country People" and in our real-world reflection of binary oppositions, stereotypes, and identity politics, we are investigating power and subjectivity, especially in connection with gender, that affect our students and ourselves. In the process we are honing our critical thinking and close reading skills.

I monitor students' understanding by calling on every student (a feminist teaching practice) and by asking open-ended questions and allowing each student to weigh in on, reiterate, or comment on any aspect of the story or the interpretation at hand.[3] More formal, written assessment occurs in my class a few weeks after we finish our unit on O'Connor. The students produce a paper for which they select a woman writer we have not studied together in our course and argue that her work should be included in the course syllabus. They describe the work and link it in detailed and developed fashion to the issues of feminist theory. The assignment requires that they connect their recovered author to the canonical authors we have already read. They are expected to situate the text they chose in the genealogy we have constructed of women writers in class. In this paper, students tend to treat the southern grotesque and the post-structuralist notions of the world as textual, identity as socially constructed and deconstructed, and identity politics as something that requires them to grapple with uncomfortable discussions about subject positions in relation to O'Connor. In their constellation of literary stars, they often connect O'Connor with Carson McCullers and Eudora Welty. My students have not had trouble referencing a textbook or theory when they are scaffolding their analysis, because we have studied the textbook or theory together. I make it a point to block out passages and tell students to mark them, so they can reference them appropriately in their written work and in class discussions.

Reading O'Connor's work in tandem with feminist theoretical concerns allows for a nuanced study of her representations of women (and men) and of the sexual and identity politics embedded in her work. The ability to read closely, persuasively, and ethically is a skill we prize in literary studies and in academia at large. This ability can be developed by studying an author like O'Connor and exploring a text like her "Good Country People" in a feminist framework and contextualized by women's studies. Students' education can and should have "a sustained, substantial, and positive influence on the way they think, act, and feel" (Bain 24). Students can change the way they think if they read critically, which professors can facilitate by offering different perspectives and posing problems and feminist concerns that are profoundly important in literature and the real world.

NOTES

[1] For the mother's permissiveness with regard to Hulga's rudeness and disability, see *Flannery . . . Works* 266; for the neighbor's keen interest in Hulga, see 267; for the bible salesman's manipulation and assault of her and stealing from her, see 278–83.

[2] The irony of the ending of the story ("I guess the world would be better off if we were all that simple") underscores the danger of subscribing to stereotypes (283).

[3] In her classroom, bell hooks requires students, even those "who are afraid to speak," to "assert themselves as critical thinkers" (53). She enacts this praxis by calling on students and expecting participation in the classroom; students cannot "refuse to read paragraphs" when asked to do so in class (54).

Teaching the Body in O'Connor

Ben Saxton

Because of her accessible style and wicked humor, Flannery O'Connor appeals to students with a wide range of literary competence. I teach her fiction in courses on the modern short story (advanced undergraduates), illness narratives (freshman undergraduates), and medical humanities (medical students). Whatever their level of expertise, students are captivated and confused by the strange bodies in O'Connor's stories. Her extraordinary characters are there on the page, demanding to be seen and understood.

This essay presents three complementary methods for teaching the body in O'Connor: an aesthetic approach that sees her grotesque characters as symbols, a disability studies approach that sees the deformed body as a conspicuous sign of social exclusion and oppression, and a medical humanities approach that foregrounds the personal dimension of her stories. Attention to the body allows students to confront the central issues of O'Connor's fiction: the grotesque, the strange confluence of violence and grace, the special significance of the material world, the suffering of her characters, and her own experience with illness and disability.

The Grotesque Body as Symbol

In order to give students a picture of the grotesque body in O'Connor, I often begin with a scene from "The Life You Save May Be Your Own":

> [Shiftlet] turned his back and faced the sunset. He swung both his whole and his short arm up slowly so that they indicated an expanse of sky and his figure formed a crooked cross. The old woman watched him with her arms folded across her chest as if she were the owner of the sun, and the daughter watched, her head thrust forward and her fat helpless hands hanging at the wrists. She had long pink-gold hair and eyes as blue as a peacock's neck. (*Flannery . . . Works* 172–73)

Vivid imagery accompanies unmistakable deformity. Shiftlet is missing half an arm; the daughter, mute and passive, watches with dangling hands. The passage raises many questions. What is the relationship among these three characters? How does the natural world work in this scene? Shiftlet's arms form a "crooked cross"; is he some kind of crooked Christ? What do Lucynell's deep-blue peacock eyes suggest about her? How might her deafness function as a symbol (see Ciuba, "'To the Hard of Hearing,'" esp. 5–9)?

O'Connor tended to see her characters' physical deformities as an index of their spiritual deformities. Shiftlet, for instance, dupes old Mrs. Crater into giving him Lucynell for a wife, and then he steals the family car in order to continue his shiftless life. He's a bad man. The symbolic function of his deformed arm is negative: it measures, by degrees of distortion and monstrosity, his separation from spiritual well-being. Negative images of grotesquerie are everywhere in O'Connor's stories. Hulga's prosthetic limb, Claud Turpin's ulcerous leg, Rayber's deafness, General Sash's senility, Mrs. McIntyre's failing health, Julian's mother's obesity, Asbury Fox's undulant fever, Rufus Johnson's clubfoot—all these infirmities indicate failures of pride, intellect, greed, and hypocrisy.[1]

Although O'Connor often focused on the negative side of the grotesque, she also believed that, when looking at the good, "its face too is grotesque" (*Mystery* 226).[2] We return to the passage above and discuss Lucynell Crater, the young girl whom Shiftlet marries and promptly abandons on his joyride out of town. In addition to her deep-blue peacock eyes—a color that relates Lucynell to a bird that O'Connor loved and associated with spiritual purity—Lucynell is called "an angel of Gawd" (*Flannery . . . Works* 181). O'Connor thus suggests that the prospect of renewal is present even—and sometimes especially—in the ugliest, most deformed human bodies. What seems repulsive or worthless may in fact be redemptive. Students respond in various ways. Some see cruelty in the images of shiftless wanderers, mute misfits, tormented intellectuals, and deformed children. Others see love in these images. The grotesque body prompts conversation about whether O'Connor's fiction is incarnational or Manichaean, hopeful or hurtful.[3]

Teaching the Disabled Body

"The Life You Save May Be Your Own" is useful because it presents two images of deformity in one scene, the first representing sinfulness (Shiftlet) and the other purity (Lucynell). In both cases, though, the body points somewhere—it works as a symbol. Disability studies scholars often oppose aesthetic readings of the body, arguing that these readings turn the deformed or disabled person into an abstraction.[4] For Rosemarie Garland-Thomson, who repeatedly singles out O'Connor and her interpreters, too many critics see the disabled body "as a sign for a degenerate soul or a bankrupt universe" (112). These negative representations, she argues, conflate disability with ugliness and marginalize the already marginalized. "If Flannery O'Connor's Hulga Hopewell were pretty, cheerful, and one-legged instead of ugly and bitter," she writes, " 'Good Country People' would fail" (136).

A disability studies approach assumes, in Paul Longmore's words, that "[f]or most people with most kinds of disabilities most of the time the greatest limitations are not somatic but social: prejudice and discrimination, inaccessibility and lack of accommodation" (2). One of the discipline's central commitments is to show that disability is at the center, not the periphery, of art, literature, and culture. O'Connor's fiction, with its profusion of distorted and deformed bodies, offers a useful context for exploring disability in the literature of the American South (see Yaeger, *Dirt*; Watson).

When we read "Good Country People," an excellent story for teaching disability in O'Connor,[5] I ask my students to imagine what prejudice and discrimination would be like for Hulga Hopewell. Her bellow "If you want me, here I am—LIKE I AM" (*Flannery . . . Works* 266) is perhaps a cry for acceptance. Much of her suffering has to do with her inability to be involved in masculine pursuits. Her feminine and fragile body rule out living a manly lifestyle. Her father accidentally shot off her leg on a hunting trip, preventing more trips in the future. Her "weak heart" excludes her from the male-dominated world of academic philosophy (268). She changes her name from Joy to the not-so-ladylike Hulga. Nearly an old maid by the standards of the 1940s South, she is unmarried at thirty-two.

As an unmarried female atheist philosopher living in the American South, Hulga sticks out like a—well, like a wooden leg. Her disability is a "narrative prosthesis," a visual supplement that, according to David Mitchell and Sharon Snyder, encourages readers to link outward "flaws" with a character's inner qualities (45). But Hulga's leg is also a material need that, when removed, impairs her free movement. "If you want to say that the wooden leg is a symbol," wrote O'Connor, "you can say that. But it is a wooden leg first, and as a wooden leg it is absolutely necessary to the story" (*Habit* 99). We focus on a moment when she follows and then playfully departs from the romance plot. "Show me where your wooden leg joins on" (*Flannery . . . Works* 288), Manley whispers, urging Hulga to provide proof of her love. Manley points to her spiritual prosthesis—her pride—and renders her vulnerable. No longer Joy/Hulga, she is simply a "girl" who can finally move past the hunting accident and start a new life (280).

Pathography: A Medical Humanities Approach

Some scholars think that disability studies is antithetical to medical humanities. Diane Price Herndl explains the difference this way: "The definition of disability used in disability studies focuses not on the body but on the social. . . . Disease, on the other hand, is almost always understood as located in the body itself" (593). Medical humanities does see disability and disease as material things rather than social constructions, as Herndl points out. But the field is also committed to treating illness. Disease—what happens to the body—is understood through science. Illness—what the person experiences—is understood though an attention to stories (Eisenberg 11). In classes on illness narratives and medical humanities, we read O'Connor's fiction as a kind of pathography: a narrative with illness as its centerpiece (see Hawkins). We assume, in other words, that O'Connor's fictive presentation of illness and disability was transformed by the news, when she was twenty-five, that she was dying of lupus (Gooch 185). For fourteen years, until her death at thirty-nine, she suffered from systemic lupus erythematosus, the worst form of the disease, which caused hair loss, malaise, nausea, rashes, joint pain, insomnia, and weight loss.

"I have never been anywhere but sick," O'Connor confessed in 1960. "In a sense sickness is a place more instructive than a long trip to Europe, and it's always a place where there's no company, where nobody can follow" (*Habit* 163). Sickness and its neighbor, loneliness, housed her for most of her life. They were part of the daily routine that she followed with monastic rigor. Every morning around six, when she woke in bed on the first floor at Andalusia, she read from her Benedictine prayer book. Then she rose and, with the aid of metal crutches, carried herself to the bathroom. After selecting a covering outfit so that her lupus would not be inflamed by the sun, she met her mother, Regina, in the kitchen and listened to the local weather report on the radio. Perhaps the weather would be mild. Pulling a black wool tam-o'-shanter over her head, she stepped into the Georgia sunlight and drove with Regina to mass at Sacred Heart Church. She sat in the fifth pew on the right side and worshiped. When she returned home around nine, she was already tired. But there was work to do. She entered her bedroom, tucked her shriveled body beside a small wooden desk, and began to write (Gooch 223–25).

How can I understand my illness? How can I tell its story? Although she rarely spoke about her lupus, O'Connor surely confronted these questions. After considering how writing fiction might have helped her, we discuss a passage from Susan Sontag's *Illness as Metaphor*: "Illness is the night-side of life, a more onerous citizenship. Everyone who is born holds dual citizenship, in the kingdom of the well and in the kingdom of the sick. Although we all prefer to use only the good passport, sooner or later each of us is obliged, at least for a spell, to identify ourselves as citizens of that other place" (1). Keeping O'Connor and Sontag in mind, students write about their own experience with illness or that of someone close to them. A medical humanities perspective considers how, for both authors and readers, for both the sick and the well, the act of writing might facilitate recovery: the healing of the whole person.

Seeing the Body, Others, Oneself

The aesthetic approach, disability studies approach, and medical humanities approach are linked, in class, through consistent conversation and written reflection. The Sontag passage above may prompt broad reflection about health or illness. Rita Charon's parallel chart, which offers an alternative to the impersonal hospital chart, is a writing exercise that can contribute to professional formation:

> Every day you write in the hospital chart about each of your patients. You know exactly what to write there and the form in which to write it. You write about your patient's current complaints, the results of the physical exam, laboratory findings, opinions of consultants, and the plan. If your patient dying of prostate cancer reminds you of your grandfather, who

died of that disease last summer, and each time you go into the patient's room, you weep for your grandfather, you cannot write that in the hospital chart. We will not let you. And yet it has to be written somewhere. You write it in the Parallel Chart.   (155–56)

The parallel chart is especially useful in classes of advanced undergraduates or medical students, who, as future health professionals, will be forming powerful emotional connections with patients.

"Good Country People" taught Nicholas Phillips, a fourth-year medical student, about the challenges of empathy and professional boundaries. After a joyless week on psychiatry rotations, his clinical team visited a fifty-year-old man with symptoms of substance abuse. The man's attitude rescued Phillips from the gloom. "Sure, his hair was a little messed up and he was wearing a KISS t-shirt," he recalled, "but he might have been the friendliest patient ever. When we finished I thought to myself, 'I wish that guy was my neighbor.'"[6] After the meeting, Phillips was certain that the patient should be discharged. The case had been solved. The patient had been cured. The man would enjoy a healthy life free of addiction and full of KISS concerts. But the next morning, to Phillips's dismay, the patient was still on the list. Even worse, the lab results indicated that he needed a level of care greater than his team could provide. The patient's charisma prevented Phillips from seeing clearly: the man, it turned out, was an addict who desperately needed help. Phillips had been fooled.

"I am most dangerous to my favorite patients." Phillips's blunt admission prompted discussion about the powerful and problematic bonds that doctors form with favorite patients—especially those who, like Manley Pointer, are intentionally deceptive. Hulga first supposes that she will enlighten this bumbling bible salesman ("True genius can get an idea across even to an inferior mind," she thinks [*Flannery . . . Works* 276]). But Manley is the one who enlightens her. Skimming Christlike over a green speckled lake, a newly acquired prosthetic leg in hand, he teaches Hulga that she "ain't so smart" after all (283). "Good Country People" draws attention to the ethics of reading, to the fragile bonds among authors, characters, and readers.[7] Just as Hulga misreads Pointer, readers risk misreading Pointer and the narrative. Will we, like Mrs. Hopewell and Mrs. Freeman, be perpetually fooled by him? Or will we, like Phillips, learn from our mistakes and see more clearly the next time?

There are many ways of seeing and teaching the body in O'Connor. I have tried to show that aesthetic, disabilities studies, and medical humanities approaches are complementary, not contradictory. Aesthetic readings should acknowledge the social and material conditions of disability. Disability studies scholars should remember that, in Michael Bérubé's words, "there's a *there* there," that social relations always involve a material reality (43). Medical humanities should attend to both disease and illness, paying special attention to the ways in which suffering is shaped into a story.

NOTES

[1] Hulga appears in "Good Country People" (*Flannery . . . Works* 263–84), Claud Turpin in "Revelation" (633–54), Rayber in *The Violent Bear It Away* (329–480), General Sash in "A Late Encounter with the Enemy" (252–62), Asbury Fox in "The Enduring Chill" (547–72), Mrs. McIntyre in "The Displaced Person" (285–327), Rufus Johnson in "The Lame Shall Enter First" (595–632), Julian's mother in "Everything That Rises Must Converge" (485–500).

[2] Christina Lake's *Incarnational Art* is an excellent resource for teaching O'Connor's negative and positive images of grotesquerie. For her discussion of "The Life You Save May Be Your Own," see 93–100.

[3] Tim Caron provides an excellent summary of the principle division in O'Connor scholarship between (his categories) "True Believers" and "Apostates" ("'Bottom Rail'" 138–39).

[4] For a survey of disability studies, which is far from a monolithic field, see Pfeiffer.

[5] For a full treatment of disability in O'Connor, including a reading of "Good Country People," see Basselin.

[6] The quotation is taken from Phillips's reflective writing exercise.

[7] See Newton. For a discussion of narrative ethics in O'Connor, see Gordon, *Flannery O'Connor: The Obedient Imagination*, esp. 32–82.

Teaching O'Connor's Narrative Style through "The River"

Donald E. Hardy

The word *style* brings to mind authors like William Faulkner, Henry James, and Cormac McCarthy, but style in much but not all of their writing is highlighted in part through obliquity rather than clearness. O'Connor's style, on the other hand, is deceptively simple. Seeming to lie easily within our reach, what O'Connor called her "one-cylander syntax" (*Flannery . . . Works* 1075) is far more complex than she would have us think, and for most students that style demands an introduction. Otherwise some will skim the surface, coming to easy conclusions that paradoxically make her fiction unsatisfying. A stylistic approach in the classroom can guide students' interpretations of complex O'Connor stories like "The River." In teaching "The River," I explore in passing two common interpretations: how the drowning of a small child is either suicide or a result of Christian fundamentalism gone awry (arguments against the latter interpretation are in Wood, "'Scandalous Baptism'"). But I concentrate on some of the linguistic devices that help create the grotesque world that Harry Ashfield lives in, one in which the deadly choice to literalize a metaphor might indeed be motivated.

I demonstrate how to bring students to a realization of such literalization through a modification of Robert F. Bergstrom's pedagogy of first using Piagetian "[c]oncrete operations" of reading, which are largely based on "the physical world and the thinker's own direct experience" (746). These operations can be explored though a series of discussion questions that for the students mostly come from language used in the text:

> Are body parts used in unusual ways in "The River"?
> Does Harry live in a threatening environment?
> How much of identity can reliably be conveyed through dialect?
> How much of identity can be conveyed through the representation of knowledge, false knowledge, and lack of knowledge?
> Which of the metaphors in "The River" might a child of four or five interpret literally?

Students' responses to these questions can be gently guided through an introduction to the narrative devices described in this essay. Each device, which is non-self-explanatory, is accompanied by a discussion to guide students. These discussions will lead, ideally, to what Bergstrom refers to as "[f]ormal operations," which are at one abstraction from concrete reasoning patterns (746–47). It is at this level that students may decide whether or not Harry's drowning is an act resulting from the literalization of Bevel Summers's metaphors. Bergstrom's article "Discovery of Meaning: Development of Formal Thought in the Teaching of Literature" is well worth an independent reading, because in it he illustrates how his method may be used to develop a "formal," advanced cognitive understanding of O'Connor's *Wise Blood* (754–55).

Stuart L. Burns argues that there is a kind of paradox in O'Connor's appeal to "an audience largely skeptical and secular" (495). I believe there is a way to read "The River" that retains the narrative depth needed without appealing to the Christian notion of grace or even baptism received by a child four or five years old. (For both an introduction to the mystery of baptism and a pedagogical approach to that mystery in "The River," see Maloney.) My approach is not only realistic, given O'Connor's skeptical audience, but also likely to make O'Connor accessible to some younger readers, those in high school or even undergraduates, who might otherwise reject her art upon a superficial reading and then reject her faith. Topics in narrative stylistics that this essay offers in an analysis of "The River" include literalization, simile, negation, presupposition, body-part imagery, represented thought and speech (e.g., free indirect discourse), dialect representation, and embedded narration.

"The River" is in part a study of the contrast between innocence and fashionable cynicism (Behrendt 144). The narration provides consistent contrasts between Harry Ashfield's innocence and the more developed knowledge, if sometimes flawed, of other characters, such as Mrs. Connin, and of the reader. In this story in particular there is a device that is analogous to the "comic literalization" that Josephine Hendin has recognized in O'Connor's fiction (28). Harry suffers as a very young child from what we might call literal-mindedness or literalization. Thus he drowns himself not suicidally but in an effort to reach the Kingdom of God that he believes is under the river. There is a radical mismatch between his childishly literal understanding of the world and that of his elders—his neglectful parents; his sitter, Mrs. Connin; her abusive sons; and especially the sometime healer and itinerant preacher Bevel Summers.

The first paragraph of the story presents readers with a completely passive Harry Ashfield (who has yet to rename himself Bevel). The word choice and syntax are noteworthy because they not only characterize Harry as a sacrificial animal but also communicate that passivity with remarkable clarity: "The child stood glum and limp in the middle of the dark living room while his father pulled him into a plaid coat. His right arm was hung in the sleeve but the father buttoned the coat anyway and pushed him forward toward a pale spotted hand that stuck through the half-open door" (*Flannery . . . Works* 154). Because Harry is not named here but referred to only as "the child," we see him as a representative of childhood. O'Connor points out that because he is only four or five years old, he "hasn't reached the age of reason; therefore he can't commit suicide." She argues further that he "goes to his Maker [and] this is a good end" (*Conversations* 58). One can agree or disagree with this statement, depending on one's acceptance or rejection of her rather rigid approach to the meaning of her stories. After the first clause, where "stood" is reinforced in its nonactive sense by the words "glum" and "limp," Harry is not the subject of any of the sentences. He is acted on physically by his father, who pulls him into his coat, not pulling his coat on him, and who pushes him. Only the boy's right arm, a body part, "hung in the sleeve," appears as a subject. Mrs. Connin is also represented first metonymically as a body part, "a pale spotted hand." The metonymic use of body parts is a common device in O'Connor, as it is in many other writers (e.g., Charles Dickens, Nathanael West, Edgar Allan Poe), to create the grotesque, the dehumanization or reduction of the human to either the animal or the partially human (see Hardy, *Body*). When Mrs. Connin first appears to Harry's father in the doorway, she is "a speckled skeleton in a long pea-green coat and felt helmet" (*Flannery . . . Works* 154). The artifacts of civilization are also reduced to grotesque body imagery. For instance, once everyone is at the river for the preaching, the narrator observes, "the city rose like a cluster of warts on the side of the mountain" (162).

In keeping with her focus on the grotesque, O'Connor does not show an ounce of sentimentality in her fiction, including her fiction about children. Harry steals Mrs. Connin's handkerchief and the children's book that she tells him she "wouldn't part with . . . for nothing on earth" (160). He then lies to his mother, telling her that Mrs. Connin gave them to him. O'Connor's children can be menacing. In "The River," an embedded narrative signals the looming threat of the Connin boys: "The three boys watched him while he unbuttoned the coat and took it off. Then they watched him hang it on the bed post and then they stood, watching the coat. They turned abruptly and went out the door and had a conference on the porch" (157). The mindlessness of these lower-class children is hinted at by the nine relatively bare clauses.

O'Connor is known for her skillful use of dialect to distinguish class. In "The River," Harry, his parents, their friends, and Mr. Paradise all speak what seems to be Standard English, while Mrs. Connin, her children, Bevel Summers, and some of the congregants at the river all speak what can be recognized as a general southern dialect, marked mostly by accent, word choice, and some syntactic patterns. The use of dialect is important to demonstrate to students because it frequently tells where readers' sympathies are supposed to lie. But in O'Connor's world, nothing is simple.The characters who speak Standard English, except for Harry, are all corrupt in one way or another, through neglect of him (his parents), through theft from him (on the morning after the party George seems to have made off with the book that Harry himself stole from Mrs. Connin), or perhaps through (but this is ambiguous) intended sexual assault on him (Mr. Paradise follows Harry to the river carrying candy bait [see Behrendt]). College students commonly have a negative response to O'Connor's characters who speak in southern dialect: the dialect is sometimes taken to be a marker for rural, relatively uneducated, Bible-believing people.

Mrs. Connin and Bevel Summers have the most to say in the story, and much of their speech is marked by southern dialect: in accent (*twict* for *twice*, *pervide* for *provide*, *borry* for *borrow*, *swang* for *swing*), word choice (*ain't*, *favor* for *resemble*, *drew* for *drawn*), and syntax ("Friday me and my wife drove to

Lulawillow to see a sick man there," "I wouldn't part with it for nothing on earth"). Because Harry, his family, and their friends are southerners as well, their speech too would have features, but few writers attempt to record accent accurately, using it instead to indicate class, race, or a combination of the two. Many students do connect nonstandard speech with morality of the sort with which Stephen Behrendt associates Mrs. Connin. I do not agree with Behrendt that Mrs. Connin holds "the complacent and self-congratulatory moral stance of the superficially spiritual individual for whom religious experience consists in simplistic stories like those in her old book and in visible signs and shows like those attributed to Bevel Summers" (149). Theological interpretation of this sort can lead to exactly the opposite conclusion about Mrs. Connin, as we see in Ralph Wood's comment: Mrs. Connin "discerns . . . that the child hungers for spiritual satisfaction, that he yearns in some inchoate way for the love of God, that he needs not generic love or vague philanthropy, therefore, but the quite particular and incarnate love of God" ("Scandalous Baptism" 193).

If students were to read Behrendt and Wood back to back, they might conclude that anything is possible in the world of interpretation of O'Connor, as long as one talks about Christian salvation. I suggest rather that one of the appeals of O'Connor is the language itself and that there is a depth to the manipulation of that language that deserves close attention. That scrutiny could prevent the disengagement students unconcerned with theological matters might feel. Wood argues explicitly, "The story's dire outcome cannot be justified by insisting that the child unfortunately literalized the preacher's message and thus mistakenly ended his own life. The story would thus become a trite exercise in the sentimentality that O'Connor despised" ("Scandalous Baptism" 190). But I argue that literalization is not trite, that it is in fact a common, although complex and context-dependent, pattern in child language development (Pouscoulous) and that every story that O'Connor wrote need not be interpreted as an exercise in grace.

Harry's interpretation of Bevel Summers's metaphors reveals not only his literalization but also his reinterpretation of them. An important stylistic device in O'Connor's fiction is speech and thought representation through free indirect discourse, for which a good introduction can be found in Geoffrey Leech and Mick Short (255–81): it conveys the thoughts of a character mixed with those of the narrator, allowing for either empathy or irony, which is always context-dependent. O'Connor used this device most commonly with older children and with adults, not with a character as young as Bevel. The device is on display frequently in "A Good Man Is Hard to Find," for example, where the narrator reports on what the Grandmother is wearing and what the Grandmother thinks of what she is wearing: "In case of an accident, anyone seeing her dead on the highway would know at once that she was a lady" (*Flannery . . . Works* 138). The Grandmother's thoughts are given free of a reporting verb such as *thought*, *believed*, or *knew*. In "The River," Bevel Summers says to Harry, "You'll be washed in the river of suffering, son, and you'll go by the deep river of life. Do you want that?" The narrator reports, "'Yes,' the child said, and thought, I won't go back to the apartment then, I'll go under the river" (165). Harry somehow thinks of the Kingdom of Christ as under the river, although Bevel Summers never describes it that way. O'Connor's use of direct thought free of quotation marks distances the narrator from the thought while still showing Harry's naïveté.

Literalization, of course, presumes metaphorical expression, which is woven throughout Bevel Summers's preaching at the river: "This old red suffering stream goes on, you people, slow to the Kingdom of Christ." Bevel himself recognizes that he is speaking in metaphor when he says, "[I]t ain't this muddy water here that saves you" (163). This is the statement that Harry both misinterprets and takes literally. It is the disjunction between the literal and the nonliteral that is at the core of the story. The narrator comments when Harry realizes that Bevel is serious and is not joking, "Where [Harry] lived everything was a joke" (165). The reader too is caught between the real and the metaphorical and therefore prepared for Harry to be sacrificed. Just after the startling simile that compares a four- or five-year-old child to a sheep, a second simile shocks in the depth and nature of its revelation of his home life. When Harry's father says good-bye to Bevel, Bevel returns the farewell "and jumped as if he had been shot" (155). O'Connor's use of the as-if construction in this passage implies neglect and perhaps even violence at home, a violence that may motivate the boy's self-drowning later. Edward Kessler and others have considered O'Connor's famous use of the quasi-simile ("as if") and have recognized that part of its powerful effect is that sometimes it is true and sometimes it is clearly metaphorical (15, 52). (See Pillière for an extended discussion of O'Connor's "as if" as well as other stylistic features in her fiction.) When Harry changes his name to Bevel, Mrs. Connin "stood looking down at him as if he had become a marvel to her" (156).

I always like to point out to students that one of the most subtle linguistic constructions that O'Connor uses throughout her fiction is problematic presupposition. She uses it to communicate questionable knowledge. A presupposition is assumed to be true whether the sentence containing it is true or false. The combinations of positive and negative statements and problematic presuppositions allow her to fine-tune the disjunction between what a character knows and what the reader knows. In "The River," "Bevel had never seen a real pig but he had seen a pig in a book and knew they were small fat pink animals with curly tails and round grinning faces and bow ties" (158). Note that even if one changes the main verb to "didn't know," it is still presupposed that pigs are cute, friendly, and dressed to entertain. In the last sentence of the story narrated from Harry's perspective, O'Connor returns to presupposition and the verb *know*, this time with a much more ambiguous and problematic reading: "[T]hen since he was moving quickly and knew that he was getting somewhere, all his fury and his fear left him" (171; see Pillière 98 for further discussion). Whether Harry is indeed getting somewhere depends on what one understands *somewhere* to mean. If one accepts O'Connor's preferred reading of the story, Harry has been baptized and is now literally going to God. If one does not, *somewhere* is a cruel joke.

Another syntactic device, negation, is intimately related to knowledge in O'Connor, both false and true knowledge. (See Hardy, *Narrating*, on presupposition and supposition in "The River" [57, 66, 109] and other stories.) Negation is normally used when there is a positive lurking in the background. Take, for example, the narrator's comment about what there is to do in the Ashfield apartment: "There was very little to do at any time but eat; however, he was not a fat boy" (*Flannery . . . Works* 169). If the assumption is that one would become fat if practically all one did was eat, then one has to question why Harry isn't a fat boy. The answer might be that Harry's parents not only neglect him emotionally but also don't feed him well, and he ends up not eating or eating nonnutritious food. Recall the description of the Ashfield refrigerator: "some shriveled vegetables," "a lot of brown oranges," "three or four kinds of cheese," "something fishy," and "the rest was a pork bone" (168–69). One of Bevel Summers's obsessions is correcting suppositions of others about both what the river can and cannot do and what he as a preacher can and cannot do: "'You can't leave your pain in the river,' he said. 'I never told nobody that'" (162).

O'Connor returns to these narrative strategies—all of which help communicate her vision of a grotesque world largely lacking in human compassion—again and again throughout the novels and throughout both story collections and even in some of her MFA thesis stories. Concentration on these devices can help instructors bring students to the fiction with an eye for textual detail and with less inclination to remain stuck in an outright rejection or uncritical acceptance of O'Connor's preferred anagogical Christian reading of her fiction.

Convergence: The Duped Shall Enter Last: But They Shall Enter

Alice Walker

"Really, Mama," Adrianne practically snorted, feeling desperately close to tears, but angry too, and as if she were about to throw up. It was all so useless! "Won't you ever understand that the white man doesn't give a damn about you!"

"Heah chile, you cut out that cussin' round me. Respect these gray hairs." And her mother kept rocking back and forth in the beat-up old rocker, her silvery head like a burst of white rose petals over a burnt cork jug. Back and forth, back and forth she rocked, busy at her sewing.

"And I wish you wouldn't bring home that filthy white man's drawers to sew up!" cried Adrianne, her voice getting away from her, out of control. She wanted to scream at her mother, to claw the hideous yellowed flannel under-suit out of her hands. But her mother sat there, placidly sewing, like a squat little black toad in glasses, like a cow, like any idiot who would sew up the drawers of someone who hated them.

"They ain't done nothing to me. Ain't done nothing to you neither. I don't know what the matter is with you. Your daddy and me scraped and saved to send you to school," biting the thread and smoothing out the worn long-johns over her knee, "and whut do we git for it? Nothing but disrespect and abuse from you who ain't even dry behind the ears yet. And you shore God don't seem to be gitting no smarter." She sighed. "I wonder if I ought to take in this here seam. Mr. Kelly's got so thin here recently."

"Well, come on if you want me to go with you to work today." Adrianne wondered how she would be able to stand being in the white house where her mother worked. But in order to have any time with her at all during vacations she had to go to the house and talk to her while she scrubbed and waxed and polished and cooked apple pie and fried chicken for the Kelly brats. She never let Adrianne help her with the work and had lectured her severely when Adrianne had suggested it. Heaving a deep sigh that shook her thick chest and small breasts, her mother dragged herself out of her hunched over position, groping around the bottom of her chair for the fan that had fallen as she moved to get up.

Adrianne followed her as she treaded heavily across the rickety porch to the sagging screen door. Her mother ran her fingers tenderly and proudly around some flower petals near the door with an awed curiosity in her small weak eyes that never failed to make Adrianne sorry for whatever she had done. Today, however, her mother's soft vulnerability had less effect on her than ever, as it always was on Adrianne's first days home from college.

"I wonder if I ought to take miz Kelly a sprig of this here callidendrum," her mother mused as she fingered a plant on the front steps that pushed out aggressive thick green and white leaves from a rusty old coffee can painted thinly and sadly in "cheerful" yellow paint.

"For God's sake, Mama, don't give that old buzzard a thing!"

She could never get used to her mother's saying "yes ma'am" and "no ma'am" to a lot of pissy little creeps who were no older than she was. And it burned her up that Mrs. Kelly, the woman her mother had started working for soon after Adrianne started college, called her mother "Katie" instead of "Mrs. Taylor," and although her mother knew how much she hated it she made a point, even when talking to Adrianne, to call Mrs. Kelly "Mrs.," although they had played together as children.

"Ain't I told you to be more respectful, young'un?" said her mother, remorsefully rather than forcefully, for she loved this angry daughter of hers. Her reproaches were always soft-spoken, as if her disagreement with her daughter's philosophy was too settled to be stirred by words, no matter how vehemently spoken. "Why cain't you never understand nothing," she murmured on, busily attacking the root of the calodendrum with a hoary and calloused finger. "You is just lak your uncle Ulus, all the time griping about the white man—and lord look at whut happened to him." She straightened up, a hand pressed hard to her right side. "Been dead these many years."

"Oh, Mama, be quiet and just come on!" Adrianne said, stamping her foot childishly with frustration, then holding her mother tight around her protruding middle and kissing her leathery cheeks. She felt near tears and knew her mother felt even worse, for her brother, Ulus, had been roasted alive, then lay around the town for nearly a week before anybody got up nerve enough to get him and bury what was left of him.

"Let's go."

Getting the battered old Packard out of the yard was always a feat. It choked and gurgled, and snorted and farted and finally quit altogether. "May be it need some air in the tires," was the curiously naïve remark her mother always made when the car wouldn't start, or choked down, or ran over something.

"No, Ma, it *ain't* the tires," and, pulling up the emergency brake Adrianne went and peeked under the hood, blew her breath over the motor a couple of times, and got back in. The ancient blue and white beauty, freshly washed and polished, but rotten to the core, started with a lurch, only to stop again as it came against fat raised oak roots that crawled about the yard like so many twisted snakes. "Damn it all!" Adrianne muttered. Then, "oh hell, I'm sorry," for her mother had thrown her a look of such mild reproach that she could do nothing else. The mother, for her part, watched her girl out of the corner of her little overstrained eyes and could not seem to understand the actuality of what sat beside her. "I shore don't see a-tall how you got to be my daughter. Ain't none of my people been big cussers. I reckon you takes after your pa's side. You take his sistuh, your Aunt Rye, not that I believes in talking bout peoples, but that sistuh of your pa's — say, Andy, I just thought of something, maybe whut the car needs is some wa-tuh. You never can tell when thangs is thirsty. Now firanexample, you take my flowers, they cain be just as pritty as they cain be and just bout ready to die from lak of wa-tuh. Or lak some peoples — " but by then the car had started and Adrianne had given her mother another quick kiss, this time between chin and collarbone, a very "winning" spot as she knew from long practice aimed at stopping charming but inane monologues, and they were off, the farty old car dispelling gallons of bilious smoke in its extravagant wake.

What angered Adrianne more than anything or as much as anything or as little as anything was that her mother refused to leave the house without her apron on. So that when they came abreast of the post office her mother suddenly remembered that she expected a package from "the House of God," located somewhere in Chicago, and, bouncing out of her side of the car with more speed than gracefulness, she hurriedly waddled up the steps of the post office while Adrianne was torn between running after her and ripping off the stupid apron, which streamed out in snowy butterfly wings behind, and finding a place to park close by the post office building so that when her mother came bobbing out she would not have to walk through the entire congregation of the town.

"SHIT!" Adrianne cried in her rage as she narrowly missed a pursed-mouth, dried up old white lady in a crepy black suit that nearly touched the ground. The old lady shook her umbrella at her, and Adrianne heard her screech "nigger!" and it was all she could do to keep from swirling the car around and sweeping down upon the little black and white insect, crushing it like a wrinkled moth into the dusty concrete.

Oh fuck it all, Adrianne frowned, who had her mother stopped to chat with!? On the steps of the post office her mother was talking to a pallid, round milk jug dressed in gray. Grinning, they both turned and looked in her direction. "Cum here, Andy baby," her mother called. "Here's mis Thomson wants to see you!" Her mother knew she hated these confrontations. And Mrs. Thomson (the milk jug) was especially unbearable to her; for she had provided her with baby clothes as a child, that her own daughter had out-grown, and seemed to feel that Adrianne owed her a special debt. And although Adrianne had never felt and still did not feel gratitude for her magnanimous gift she knew that her mother did. "Deah God, please hep me to be more respectful," she thought, and she slowly prodded herself across the street where her be-aproned mom, "Katie" to them, stood beaming at her, her eyes glowing, as if she were about to present the queen of the May.

"How do you do," Adrianne said formally, throwing her mother a look that said "YOU *KNOW* BETTER, and whatever happens is your fault, although I'll try to do my best FOR *YOUR* SAKE!" Her mother smiled nervously and pushed her fat little arm through Adrianne's skinny one.

"We-ll, we-ll, if it ain't 'our' lil Andy-girl!" the old southern charmer gushed. "My, my, my, how you *have* grown. Bet you thank you're a lil lady now—don' she Katie," she beamed, turning to her mother, good will and condescension written all over her face, obvious and superficial, like her make-up. "You're here on va-cation?" the bloated belle thrust onward.

"Yes." Adrianne heard her mother's pitiably audible intake of breath when the "yes" came out, but she ignored it.

"How do you like being up yonder in Atlanta at school and away from us down here?" The red painted mouth, smiling widely, kept twitching at the corners.

"Love it." Adrianne replied shortly and with emphasis.

"You mean to say you don' miss us a-tall?" asked the scarlet mouth, letting the smile go.

Adrianne's look said plainly enough "are you nuts?" before she condescended to answer in her own southern dialect and drawl, "Thet's jest zackly whut ah mean to say, miz Thomson," she refused an impulse to scratch the back of her head, "as the lord iz mah widnis, although ah sometimes misses mah Ma, ah jest didn't miss de rest of yall a-tall." Adrianne was aware that her mother was pulling at her arm. Mrs. Thomson, that old weatherer of grudges, storms, and wars, overlooked the pointed mimicry, but Adrianne felt her draw away from her. "All of my *good* lil ba-be close," the cold blue eyes seemed to say. "All my *good* lil ba-be close, gone to wa-ste on that gal who don' even preshate it enough to say 'yes ma'am' to me, who am old enough to be her mother! Lordy, lord, what *is* this world coming to." After a few bland pleasantries during which Adrianne gave in to her mother's pressure on her arm and spoke in her normal voice, the threesome broke up. Adrianne tried to joke about Mrs. Thomson, calling her "Mrs. Tumson" because of her jutting hillock of stomach, but Mrs. Taylor hugged the corner of the seat and would not speak to her.

"By the way, what ya got in that package from God's house?" She asked in the light "homey" manner she used when she wanted to bring her mother out of a pout. Her mother was holding a thin package wrapped in brown paper, a picture of a thin fellow with a beard and his arms raised like he was about to fly, pasted on the outside. The picture was in color and the Christ, for that's who the man was supposed to be, was a waxen, sick-looking pink, like a plastic doll. She knew that if she asked about the picture and the package her mother would feel prompted to give her a lecture on religion, but to get back into her good graces she was willing to talk about anything, the church, and baptisms, and preachers, and revivals, and even Jesus Christ, of whose very sacred person her mother was holding an exact color drawing, done from life.

Her mother wasn't stupid, just full of faith. Once she had tried to convince her that Christ couldn't possibly look like that. All rouged and painted. But her mother had smiled at her naiveté and said that *she knew that,* but that they had to make him look wasted away for he was newly risen and hadn't eaten probably for "snever so long," and at the same time they had to paint him brilliant so as to show the glory was on him . . . etc., etc. She wondered if she would ever recover from her mother's faith? She thought not. She had tried, in many a brightly lit study room at school, in many a book-laden library in college, in many a bar and in many a strange and motley company (of which her mother would die if she knew, feeling that any discussion that expressed doubt about the existence of God—and especially with white folks and particularly with white young men—would put Adrianne "way out of her 'place'"). But the fact that God was dead and Jesus ailing along as only a prophet and incapable of bringing about miracles could never be brought home to her mother. And whereas a few God-deniers she knew had thrown themselves from fifteen-story apartment windows and others had "flipped out," her mother stayed sane as an ant.

"Say, Lovie, what's in the package?" she asked pleadingly. She wanted to make a quip about the picture on the outside of the package, but thought she'd better not. Nothing riled her mother as quickly as having somebody make fun of "her Jesus." "With all my education, I'm a goddamn bum," Adrianne thought. "And she's a bloody saint capable of miracles much more essential than that creep on the outside of that package!" How else could she have sent Adrianne to college on twelve dollars a week? There was something miraculous about that, one had to admit. Even "her Jesus" couldn't have done it, if he had had the guts to father and try to raise a nigger child in the first place.

In a small pathetic and distracting way "Lovie" began a hymn. The thumping revival always in session in her breast, came pulsing out, and mourn after mourn of "Je-sus ke-ee-p me ny-aer the cross!" rolled out of her chest and her lumpy short fingers pulled in time at the crisp cotton of her bright print house-dress. Why did this chile of hers plague her so? "I reckon I got a right to try to keep in contact wid my Je-sus," her eyes said, making a scathingly wounded sweep of Adrianne's body behind the wheel. She pulled the wrapped package, which Adrianne guessed contained new Sunday school books—her mother was a teacher—closer to her humming body. "Je-sus ke-ee-p me ny-aer the cross!" she intoned, looking meaningfully at Adrianne, as if to drive away an evil spirit that lurked within her daughter's flesh.

"The trouble wid you all young'uns is that you don't know your place." Her mother started in just where Adrianne had hoped most she would not. She groaned to hear her start on the subject of how all "new generation" people were "mix-placed" and "mis-placed" persons.

"Good grief! Sweetie-pie," said Adrianne, masking her annoyance with a strained profile grin, "what I been trying to tell you for god knows how many years, is that I don't *have* a place, that I've got to *make* myself a place, and if some old white bitch is in the place I want to be then she'd better move over and make some room, or else vacate the spot altogether! Now I ask you, what could be wrong with that? Ain't there at least some right in my wanting in the first place to share? It ain't exactly as if I wanted to eat the whole damn cake by myself!" Ah crap, what was the use? When if ever was her mother going to wake up and begin to fight for the "place" she deserved?

"Well, all I know is that I is satisfied wid where I is, wid what I is, and as I is," and she smoothed out the apron over her lap, a gesture aimed at making Adrianne ashamed that she had been ashamed of it. "At least my generation knows its place—leastways most of us do. Though here recently I seen a whole lot of peoples who ain't got no respect for themselves and nobodies else out marching and gallivantin' around like they think they know more'en anybody else whut's been going on in the world. Like they been saved and the rest of us ain't. But I been in this here world just as long as they and I know whut's been going on, and a whole lot of marching and sanging ain't going to change nothing. They got to git right wid they maker fore anything going to change. They seem to be forgitting about him; but let me tell you young'un, widout him, the sun don't shine and the moon don't wane!"

There was a pause. Her mother always ended lectures like these by saying that she knew all this for a fact. And since the sun had always shone and the moon had always waned, Adrianne figured she had the proof, though how her mother figured the shining and waning were anybody's doing was beyond her.

"And I know all this here I'm telling you for a fact," her mother said, vigorously nodding her head.

The old car battered down the dirt roads of the Negro "quarter" in greasy whorls of smoke and dust. A little Negro girl was on her way, late, to school, and wore a bright blue dress with white around the tail and a pair of brand-new red sneakers. She was practically in a trot.

"That there's one of the ones going to the white school," Mrs. Taylor offered with the cool speculation in her tone of someone calmly expecting an argument. "That's annuther thang—I don't see why you all (meaning everybody under twenty-five) wants to go to the white folks school. You all claim you hates them so much. Yit and still you wants to go to they school. Why you all cain't be satisfied wid your own thangs is whut I cain't understand. I'm telling you chile, the secret of success is that you makes do wid whut you got!"

"Yes Ma," Adrianne sighed, "all that you say is very logical. Not the point at all, but logical. How many times have I got to tell you that 'going to the white folks school' just because it's got white folks in it is not the point. The point is that our schools are inferior to their schools, and as long as there is a choice between attending a school that is first rate and a school that is second rate a person would be a fool to choose the one that is second rate. Now that's got some logic too, hasn't it? Don't you see yet that although it may be true that the key to success is 'making do wid whut you got,' we ain't got nothing to make do wid!"

"Well, it ain't they fault if you all ain't as bright as they," Mrs. Taylor said, glancing back at the hurrying girl climbing the hill to the white folks school. Adrianne felt like strangling her for being so brainwashed and dense. She pushed in on the accelerator but quickly slowed the car lest careening around one of the bumpy twisted "streets" she ran over some unheeding, late young rebel on her way to school "wid the white folks."

"Mama, don't you think that little girl is as bright as they are?"

"We-ull—"

"Alright then, don't you think I'm as bright as any of them? And if you say no you can just get out and walk to work!"

"But Andy, you's different—"

"No I'm not Ma. I'm black too. By the way," dropping the subject of intelligence because it always ended with her mother saying that it looked like to her the blacker the child the dumber he was, and Adrianne always had to fight the temptation to suggest that maybe that was why she wasn't any genius, "how did the white folks act the first day that little girl went? Did they give her a hard time, or did they act civilized for once?"

"Nearly blinded her," her mother said laconically, as someone agreeing with a judgement.

"But Mama," Adrianne kept wanting to run the side of the car her mother was on against a tree, "where were all of *you* all? Where was the goddamn 'Negro leadership'?" ("I wish you would quit that cussin' it don't make whut you trying to say come out no stronger") "I mean what did she have to do, walk down a line of clubs to get to that da—place!"

"Her ma was wid her. The two of them got stoned pretty bad—But I had done tol'em and tol'em, 'you all ain't got no bidnis gitting out your place!' 'That's the *all white* school' I tol'em, but they got sassy wid me. 'Well, it won't be the all white school once *my* daughter gets in it!' is whut the ma said to me." Mrs. Taylor mimicked the woman's language. She was a school teacher and talked "proper." "So I just tol'em to go on ahead, but just remember when the bricks started flying that they was out of they place!"

"Oh screw y—," Adrianne began, then quickly bit her lip and counted to five.

"But Mama," she began again, "what if it had been you and me? What if we had gone up that walk and all those little babies you had nursed on your knee suddenly started throwing rocks at you—what would you have done, and what would you have felt? Don't tell me you would have stood there thinking about 'place'!"

"Wouldn't have been me in the first place. I knows where I belongs and I stays there, and longs' I stays there ain't nobody going to bother me, be they white, green or colored."

"Green is colored, Lovie."

Her mother always worried about getting to work on time but since they had to drive from one small townlet to another—both in the same county and obnoxious—Adrianne could not understand how Mrs. Kelly could scold her mother for being late. After all, she wasn't building her mother a fortune with those twelve dollars a week.

"Whut time is it Andy?"

"Nearly nine, we'll be there before long." And the car swung onto the smooth black asphalt, which coiled and twisted like a lean black cat slowly falling through the green countryside. To the right and left were tiny cattle farms, dairy barns, chewing cows bunched together under flat-leaved oaks and silvered poplars. The spring sun was very warm and the blossom of the honeysuckle glistened like pale yellow flames and the heady wine of the scent pervaded the whole air, leaving not one space, even inside the car, empty of its presence.

There did not seem to be grounds this morning for an argument. An argument of any kind, and Adrianne felt with relief how far the pastoral scene all around was from all the recent demonstrations, the publicity surrounding the President's latest gall-bladder operation, the war in Asia. In her town of Briersville, Georgia, life went on its way, always the same as before, and even she, at nine o'clock on such a peaceful June morning was lulled into thinking that nothing should disturb the rest of the quaint and drowsy little village.

They swung around the corner of the street that led to the courthouse on the square, and the first thing she noticed was a picket line spread out around the drugstore on the other side. Her fingers tightened on the wheel and she would have said nothing to her mother, whose eyes were bouncing indignantly about the sidewalk, had not Mrs. Taylor said disgustedly: "Well, I see there's some more poor peoples out pounding the sidewalk this morning instead of working—I wonder whut *they* wants?"

About forty Negro girls and boys, almost none of them out of their teens, were marching, two abreast, twelve feet apart, up and down the quickly awakening street. The drug store under attack had pulled down its shades and the man who operated it was scuttling across the street to collaborate with the sheriff, who stood outside his tiny house of glass that was in one corner of the courthouse lawn. He looked both helpless and dismayed. All he could do was scowl at the young pickets, since they were obeying all the laws of picketing.

The signs the picketers carried were bold and imaginative, but some completely off the subject, which was that in future Negroes demanded the right as customers to sit down while they drank the cokes they bought in the drugstores. One left-wing slogan said, "Support the Black Panthers, Support Black Power," picked up no doubt from a passing SNCC group. Another very colorful sign, carried by an old Negro granny of about ninety, urged "MAKE LOVE NOT WAR!" Adrianne could have kissed her. Apparently the old woman couldn't read and had no idea what the sign said, for when a young boy walked up and whispered something in her ear she tore it off her chest, not bothering to unfasten the safety pins. Adrianne laughed gleefully as the spry old woman immediately took up another sign that read "Burn, Whitey, burn. Soon, Whitey, soon." Grinning widely and showing that she had not a tooth in her head she marched away, chin up and stepping high, the last white baby she had dawdled on her ancient knee the steadily reddening sheriff who gave her wine and hard candy at Christmas and called her "his" Aunt Lou-ise.

"Ought to be shamed of herself, the silly old fool. Ought to be down on her knees right this minute thanking the lord she done made it for as long as she has. Whut she need to be setting anywhere dranking a co-cola anyhow!" Mrs. Taylor said as Adrianne slowly passed by, waving and yelling and throwing kisses to the old lady—who *was* a bit out of her head if the truth were known.

"Times are changing!" Adrianne said.

"Bob Dylan's right you know Mama," she said happily, even though her mother claimed she never could understand what the boy was "sanging" about, he "slurged" his words together so bad, "I tell you the truth," her mother said to her one day as she sat listening to Dylan, "I have always said that white folks cain't sang, but that poor chile—he cain't even talk!"

"The times they sure are a changin' and brother, am I glad to see the day!" Adrianne said.

"Might be changin' for the wust," her mother said, and gave a nervous look of impending doom which Adrianne knew meant all was not right in her little country world.

"Slow down Andy."

"Why, what's the matter?" She wanted to drop her mother quickly and get back to the picket line. Strings of whites were beginning to fill the streets and she felt her blood tingle. The only way she wanted to confront the whites in this town was from a picket line telling them just where the hell to get off.

"Heah, just a minute. Looks to me lak I see the Kelly boy over yonder in the crowd. He ain't got no bidnis gallivantin' round heah. He ought to be in school. I wish you could have seen his grades last year—they almost put his ma and pa both in the horspital. Stop the car."

"Mama," Adrianne hollered. "I certainly will not stop the car! Have you lost your *mind*! It is not your business and not your duty to see that that snotty brat gets to school." Brainwashed she knew her mother to be, as much as she loved her, but was she crazy as well? She couldn't be serious, she just couldn't! That was all!

"You heah me, Andy. I say stop this car and lemme out," said her mother, beginning to look at her with a look that promised she would jump out while the car was still running. "Ah," her mother looked pained, "he's just lak the rest of his generation. He don't know his place. It shore ain't here watching a bunch of misguided cullid chillen who ought to be in school this morning trying to start trouble. You going to stop this car or not?"

"Oh hell." Adrianne grimaced. She pulled over to the curb as far away from the pickets and the obscenity-throwing whites as she could without having her mother bash something over her head for not obeying her sooner. Then Mrs. Taylor, "Katie" to them, was bustling down the sunny street, bumping into everybody, seeing nobody, saying a brisk "scuse me" to everyone she hit, going on toward the Kelly boy lost somewhere in the jeering white crowd. "Oh lord," sighed Adrianne, as she followed as closely as she could her mother's flying streamers, "why has thou forsaken us!" And I tell you right now Jesus—she felt the hatred welling up inside her as she conducted the mental angry monologue—I don't want nothing to do with you if you desert little fools like Mama who never did nobody no harm and send then flying through a goddamn white mob trying to make some goddamn stupid white boy go to school and make good marks so his "poor ma and pa" won't end up in the "horspital." One of the few decent things her father had told her before he ran out on them was that although it might be true, as her mother often said, that God was on their side, they were not to be running through no damn mobs to find out. But Mama hadn't listened and hadn't learned. Was she just dumb, or what?

"Mama wait!" Adrianne whispered as she caught up with her. "Don't you realize you can't do this. Don't you realize you don't know these people, have never known these people, and if you keep going on this way, *will* never know these people? And you needn't think they know you either. You're just another 'nigger' to them. Won't you see that Mama. Please stop and come home with me. To hell with the Kelly boy. Let him stay where he is, the most that can happen to him is that he'll pick up some new names to call you. What do you care about *his* education. You think the Kellys give a damn about *my* education? Do you?" She was almost in tears. "They don't give a shit whether I get good marks or not, whether you get put in the hospital or not, whether you die or not. How many times have I got to tell you that!" Her mother was about to tell her to quit her cussin' but changed her mind because they were approaching the thick crowd of whites who presented a fiercely solid wall in front of the pickets across the street. Her eyes scanned the crowd, the obscene remarks they threw at the children in front of the drugstore lost on her as she tried to catch sight of the Kelly boy.

"Mama, darling, please—won't you come back with me. Your place isn't here trying to make these white folks behave. They haven't ever behaved and the only way you can make them is to beat it into them that you ain't gonna take no shit from 'em. Mama, that across the street is not a social gathering—that in front of us is a mob. And the sooner you realize that the happier you will be—" but they had already reached the edge of the crowd. "Niggers!," "Coons," and "Go back to the jungle" were shouts yelled into their very ears. They plunged into the crowd where feeling was most intense, the fire hottest, the breathing of the men making a menacing rustle of hatred that splayed over them like cascading slime. Her mother, sensing some danger for Adrianne, had grabbed her by the hand and held her tight as she worked her way, with more determination than ever, through the red-necked crowd. At first the whites, especially the women, were too dazed to notice that they were being pushed aside by a colored woman and a girl. But as they passed heads turned, for no other black person had dared turn his face in their direction, except for the "misled children" picketing the drugstore. So it was, with the entire crowd's attention, that Mrs. Taylor, "Katie," bustled up to Tommy Kelly, a thirteen year old with a confederate flag in his lapel, and grabbing him under the elbow began to tow him away, all the while saying, "Ain't you shamed of your self. Whut would your ma and pa say if they knowed you was here and not in school. Stop that hanging back and cum on here!" and holding Tommy with one hand and Adrianne with the other she began to drag them both away from the scene so "degeneratin' to their morals."

It was easy to see Tommy had no idea what to do. On the one hand she had always been his friend. On the other she was a nigger. He seemed almost on the point of letting himself be carried off, his little flag dangling loosely by its wood handle from his pocket. His narrow blue eyes blinked a couple of times as he looked down at the ground between his sneakers. Then his scrawny, none-too-clean neck began to redden. He had seen Adrianne and recognized her as a "colored *girl*," according to his mother one of the most hateful kinds of uppity niggers. "Take your hands off of me, you crazy old nigger woman!" and Adrianne saw her mother's back sway as if she had been hit. The next minute she had been, for the non-repentant Tommy drew back a bony fist and hit her as hard as he could right under the arm she was holding him by. "You cain't tell me what to do, you ugly old monkey!" And he ran back to his friends, who had watched his capture and escape with approval and loud yells and hand-clapping. Adrianne started to go after him, she wanted to get his skinny neck between her hands, but her mother pulled her back. She was holding her side with the hand that had been holding Tommy, and her eyes rested on the crowd of whites milling and muttering around her as if she'd never seen them before. Yet she knew them all, knew them by name, knew their fathers and mothers and birthdays, knew their children, had cooked and cared for them when they were ill—as some of them had done for her when she had been sick. Now she just looked at them, and a few of them dropped their heads and slinked away to the back of the group, a few of them walked away altogether, sobered by what they had seen. They did not even glance at the singing, clapping Negroes who had gained entry to the drugstore and swayed and bounced up and down on the shiny red stools, their hard-earned cokes downed in one exuberant gulp.

"Dear God, what has this mess done to her?" Adrianne wondered, as they made their way slowly back to the car. Some laughter directed at the pitiful spectacle they made coming from whites behind them. Her mother had never looked so gray. She was breathing hard and her eyes were brimful of tears. Her crumpled butterfly apron strings dangled limply behind her as she walked.

"Why the hell doesn't she say something!" Adrianne's own heart had contracted into a tight ball of pity for her. She had wanted her to learn her lesson, but not this way. This was too hard for an ailing old black woman whose brother had been roasted alive.

"Mama, you want to go back to the house now?"

Her mother seemed not to hear, but as they neared the car she began pulling off her apron and brushing at the stray wisps of white hair that had come out from under her hairnet. "You got a comb, Andy?" she asked as she leaned over to look into the side-view mirror, and tossed her apron into the car. She took the comb and ran it around the band of the hairnet, pushing the hair back into it. Then she brushed down her bosom with a heavy hand but firm, thorough strokes. Adrianne was surprised to see another look beginning to take the place of the hurt. What she saw growing in her mother's formerly meek eyes was a veritable blaze of anger. But at whom was it directed? At herself? At Adrianne?

"Mama, aren't you going to get in the car?" she asked over the top of the hot automobile. Her mother had begun to walk back down the street. "It's too hot for you to be walking in this sun."

"—Mama, where on earth are you going. Don't you know you can't go back there fooling with that ass-hole of a boy?" Her mother walked on, her eyes straight ahead. Adrianne followed her, feeling like the world's second biggest fool. And down the street they went again. Bumping into the same people, saying "scuse me" to the same people, hurrying on down the street, a fat black tugboat and its charge.

"Mama, don't *do* this—" Adrianne had begun to plead, when she noticed her mother had slowed down as she came abreast the pickets, and looking still a bit suspicious of them, crossed their lines and stalked into the drugstore, pulling Adrianne behind her. And now they stood in the middle of the white-vacated drugstore, with the exception of the soda jerk, who was not white but red as he served dozens of laughing Negroes who took turns replacing each other on stools under which was written "White Seats Only."

Going up to the only vacant stool Mrs. Taylor plopped her body on it, and the dark-skinned, grinning boy who occupied the one next to it quickly hopped up and offered it to Adrianne, who accepted it with a smile. "What are we having?" she asked her mother, still a little afraid that what her mother had really come into the store to do was preach a sermon on "place" to the Negroes who were gathered there. But when the soda jerk got to them and asked in a contemptuous drawl "whut ya'll *want*?" her mother casually remarked to him, looking him straight in the eye with a blue-ringed look, "We wants two of them cokes that's causing so many peoples here today to forgit they place—and make it snappy young'un, we ain't got all day!"

"Hallelujah!" Adrianne shouted, as she looked with bright eyes at her mother's militant profile.

"Out of the mouths of babes," her mother retorted, drily, slurping her coke complacently, as if this wasn't the first time she'd been able to sit down with it.

28 June 1966

Dedicated to the memory of Flannery O'Connor

NOTE

This story can be accessed through the library Web sites of either Georgia College or Emory University.

NOTES ON CONTRIBUTORS

Jon Lance Bacon is an independent scholar and filmmaker from Raleigh, North Carolina. He is the author of *Flannery O'Connor and Cold War Culture* (1993) and the cofounder of Dagtype Films, where he serves as writer-director. His most recent film is a romantic comedy short called *Oh Crappy Day*.

Mark Bosco, vice president for mission and ministry and professor of English at Georgetown University, focuses on the intersection of religion and art, especially in twentieth-century Catholic literature. He is the author of *Graham Greene's Catholic Imagination* (2005) and coeditor of *Revelation and Convergence: Flannery O'Connor and the Catholic Intellectual Tradition* (2017). He is a producer and director of the documentary feature film *Flannery*.

Will Brantley is professor of English at Middle Tennessee State University, where he teaches modern American literature, southern literature, and film studies. He is the author of *Feminine Sense in Southern Memoir* (1993), the editor of *Conversations with Pauline Kael* (1996), and coeditor of *Conversations with Edmund White* (2017).

Miriam Marty Clark is associate professor of English and affiliated faculty of the Office of University Writing at Auburn University, where she specializes in twentieth-century American literature. She is finishing a book on meaning in contemporary American poetry and is at work on another book focused on assignment design for literature courses.

Doug Davis is professor of English at Gordon State College in Barnesville, Georgia, where he teaches literature and writing. He is the author of essays on topics ranging from the extinction of the dinosaurs to the technological sublime in the literature of the American South and the technoscientific foundations of O'Connor's storytelling.

Robert Donahoo is professor of English at Sam Houston State University, where his teaching focuses on twentieth-century American literature and American drama. He codirected with Marshall Bruce Gentry the 2014 NEH Summer Institute "Reconsidering Flannery O'Connor" and coedited with Avis Hewitt *Flannery O'Connor in the Age of Terrorism: Essays on Violence and Grace* (2010).

John N. Duvall is Margaret Church Distinguished Professor at Purdue University and editor of the English department's journal *MFS Modern Fiction Studies*. He is the author of *Faulkner's Marginal Couple: Invisible, Outlaw, and Unspeakable Communities* (1990) and *Race and White Identity in Southern Fiction* (2008) and coeditor, with Tim Engles, of the MLA volume *Approaches to Teaching Don DeLillo's* White Noise (2006).

Christine Flanagan is associate professor of English at University of the Sciences in Philadelphia, where she teaches creative writing and environmental humanities. She is the author of *The Letters of Flannery O'Connor and Caroline Gordon* (2018) and received the 2017 Lindback Foundation Award for Distinguished Teaching.

Doreen Fowler is professor of English at the University of Kansas. She is the author of *Drawing the Line: The Father Reimagined in Faulkner, Wright, O'Connor, and Morrison* (2013) and *Faulkner: The Return of the Repressed* (1997) and coeditor of eleven collections of essays on Faulkner. She is currently writing a book that approaches issues of race in Flannery O'Connor's fiction through psychoanalytic frames.

Marshall Bruce Gentry is the editor of the *Flannery O'Connor Review* and professor of English at Georgia College. He is the author of *Flannery O'Connor's Religion of the Grotesque* (1986), the editor of *The Cartoons of Flannery O'Connor at Georgia College* (2010), and coeditor of *At Home with Flannery O'Connor: An Oral History* (2012).

Julie Goodspeed-Chadwick is professor of English, director of the Office of Student Research, and an affiliated faculty member in Women's Studies at Indiana University–Purdue University, Columbus. She is the author of *Modernist Women Writers and War: Trauma and the Female Body in Djuna Barnes, H.D., and Gertrude Stein* (2011) and a recipient of the Indiana University Trustees' Teaching Award and the Chancellor's Award for Excellence in Teaching.

Virginia Grant teaches college English in and near Philadelphia. She works on American literature, particularly the work of Flannery O'Connor at mid-century. In 2013, she won the Sarah Gordon Award for the best submission by a graduate student to the *Flannery O'Connor Review*.

Donald E. Hardy, professor emeritus at the University of Nevada, Reno, is the author of *Narrating Knowledge in Flannery O'Connor's Fiction* (2003), *The Body in Flannery O'Connor's Fiction: Computational Technique and Linguistic Voice* (2007), and *Because I'd Hate to Just Disappear: My Cancer, My Self, Our Story* (2018).

Carole K. Harris teaches writing and literature at New York City College of Technology. She is the author of essays about the ritualized nature of clichés and small talk in Flannery O'Connor's stories.

Christina Bieber Lake is Clyde S. Kilby Professor of English at Wheaton College, where she teaches classes in contemporary American literature and literary theory. She is the author of *The Incarnational Art of Flannery O'Connor* (2005) and *Prophets of the Posthuman: American Fiction, Biotechnology, and the Ethics of Personhood* (2013).

Ben Saxton is a clinical instructor at Tulane Medical School and an adjunct professor at the McGovern Medical School. His essays and nonfiction have appeared in *The Big Roundtable*, *Academic Medicine*, *Cambridge Quarterly of Healthcare Ethics*, *The Health Humanities Reader*, *Tolkien Studies*, and the *Flannery O'Connor Review*, which gave him the Sarah Gordon Award in 2011. He lives in New Orleans.

Irwin Streight is associate professor of English at the Royal Military College of Canada in Kingston, Ontario. He is coeditor, with R. Neil Scott, of *Flannery O'Connor: The Contemporary Reviews* (2009) and coeditor, with Roxanne Harde, of *Reading the Boss: Interdisciplinary Approaches to the Works of Bruce Springsteen* (2010).

John D. Sykes, Jr., is Mary and Harry Brown Professor of English and Religion at Wingate University. He is the author of *The Romance of Innocence and the Myth of History: Faulkner's Religious Critique of Southern Culture* (1989) and *Flannery O'Connor, Walker Percy, and the Aesthetic of Revelation* (2007).

Alice Walker, a feminist, human rights activist, fiction writer, poet, and essayist, won the Pulitzer Prize and the National Book Award for her novel *The Color Purple*. Her most famous comments on O'Connor are found in the essay "Beyond the Peacock," in her essay collection *In Search of Our Mothers' Gardens: Womanist Prose*. She has published short stories in such collections as *In Love and Trouble* and *You Can't Keep a Good Woman Down*, and her *Complete Stories* appeared in 1994.

Nagueyalti Warren is professor of pedagogy in African American Studies at Emory University. She is the author of *Grandfather of Black Studies: W. E. B. Du Bois* (2011); *Margaret* (2008), winner of the Naomi Long Madgett Poetry Award; and *Alice Walker's Metaphysics: Literature of Spirit* (2019). She is the editor of *Tembe Tupu! (Walking Naked): The Africana Women's Poetic Self-Portrait* (2008) and *Critical Insights: Alice Walker* (2013).

David Z. Wehner is associate professor of American literature at Mount St. Mary's University, the alma mater of Flannery O'Connor's father, Edward Francis O'Connor. He is the author of articles and book reviews on Kate Chopin, Flannery O'Connor, and Toni Morrison in journals such as *American Literary Realism*, *Flannery O'Connor Review*, *Mississippi Quarterly*, and *Women's Studies*.

Margaret Earley Whitt is professor emerita of English at the University of Denver. She is the author of *Understanding Flannery O'Connor* (1995) and *Understanding Gloria Naylor* (1999) and the editor of *Short Stories of the Civil Rights Movement* (2006). She is a frequent group tour leader through historical civil rights places in the South.

Jessica Hooten Wilson is associate professor of English at John Brown University in Siloam Springs, Arkansas. She is the author of *Giving the Devil His Due: Demonic Authority in the Fiction of Flannery O'Connor and Fyodor Dostoevsky* (2017), *Walker Percy, Fyodor Dostoevsky, and the Search for Influence* (2017), and *Reading Walker Percy's Novels* (2018).

SURVEY PARTICIPANTS

The editors thank the many scholars and teachers whose answers to survey questions guided our work throughout the composition of this volume.

Richmond B. Adams, *Andrew College*
Lynn M. Alexander, *University of Tennessee, Martin*
L. Troy Appling, *Florida Gateway College*
Karla Armbruster, *Webster University*
Rhonda Armstrong, *Augusta State University*
Grant Bain, *University of Arkansas*
Michele Balze, *Glen Burnie, MD*
Stephanie Batcos, *Savannah College of Art and Design, Atlanta*
Stephen C. Behrendt, *University of Nebraska, Lincoln*
Mary M. Bendel-Simso, *McDaniel College*
Nikola Benin, *University of Ruse*
Linda C. Nicole Blair, *University of Washington, Tacoma*
Victoria Madden Bonillas, *Baldwin-Wallace College, Cuyahoga Community College, and Bryant and Stratton College*
N. S. Boone, *Harding University*
Mark Bosco, *Loyola University, Chicago*
Beau Boudreaux, *Tulane University*
Will Brantley, *Middle Tennessee State University*
Jamie Brummer, *Christian Brothers High School, TN*
Michael J. Burke, *Art Institute of Atlanta*
Lauren S. Cardon, *Tulane University*
Jean W. Cash, *James Madison University*
Ricia Anne Chansky, *University of Puerto Rico, Mayaguez*
John Claborn, *University of Illinois*
Miriam Marty Clark, *Auburn University*
Mary S. Comfort, *Moravian College*
Thom Conroy, *Massey University*
Paul J. Contino, *Pepperdine University*
Eurie Dahn, *College of Saint Rose*
Patsy J. Daniels, *Jackson State University*
Doug Davis, *Gordon College*
Jeremy Delamarter, *Northwest University*
Nancy Dixon, *University of New Orleans*
Jordan Dominy, *Berry College*
James J. Donahue, *State University of New York, Potsdam*
William Donnelly, *University of Houston*
Stacey Donohue, *Central Oregon Community College*
David C. Dougherty, *Loyola University, Maryland*
Mark Eaton, *Azusa Pacific University*

Jennifer Elmers, *Missouri Valley College*
Ellen Feig, *Bergen Community College, NJ*
Theresa Fine-Pawsey, *Durham Technical Community College*
Doreen Fowler, *University of Kansas*
Margaret Vallone Gardineer, *Felician College*
Allen Gee, *Georgia College*
Mimi R. Gladstein, *University of Texas, El Paso*
Sarah Gleeson-White, *University of Sydney*
Julie Goodspeed-Chadwick, *Indiana University–Purdue University, Columbus*
James Patrick Gorham, *University of Rhode Island*
Bruce Gospin, *Northampton Community College*
Jeffrey Gray, *Seton Hall University*
Amanda Hagood, *Hendrix College*
Melissa Hardie, *University of Sydney*
Donald E. Hardy, *University of Nevada, Reno*
Carole K. Harris, *New York City College of Technology*
Hayley Haugen, *Ohio University Southern*
Alison Heney, *State University of New York, Empire State College, and Binghamton University*
Avis Hewitt, *Grand Valley State University*
Linda Houck, *Nashville State Community College, TN*
Tony J. Howard, *Collin College*
Jolene Hubbs, *University of Alabama*
Chris Hudson, *St. Mary-of-the-Woods College*
Patricia Ireland, *University of Tennessee, Knoxville*
Tommie L. Jackson, *St. Cloud State University*
Monica F. Jacobe, *College of New Jersey*
Danielle Jones, *University of Montana Western*
Steven G. Kellman, *University of Texas, San Antonio*
Mabel Khawaja, *Hampton University*
Kevin Kiely, *University College Dublin*
Albert LaFarge, *Boston University*
Christina Bieber Lake, *Wheaton College*
Demetri Lallas, *Wagner College*
Michael LeMahieu, *Clemson University*
Marie Lienard-Yeterian, *Universite de Nice-Sophia Antipolis*
John Lihani, *University of Kentucky*
Judith Lockyer, *Albion College*
Matthew Luter, *Davidson College*
Denise MacNeil, *University of Redlands*
Patricia Maida, *University of the District of Columbia*
Lauren Rule Maxwell, *The Citadel*
Kathryn E. McFarland-Wilson, *Wheaton College*
Fiona McWilliam, *Florida State University*
Rae Ann Meriwether, *Le Moyne College*
Joseph Millichap, *Western Kentucky University*
Shamika Ann Mitchell, *Rockland Community College, State University of New York*
Michelle Monte, *Bryant and Stratton College*

Marita Nadal, *University of Zaragoza*
Donna Nalley, *South University*
L. Lamar Nisly, *Bluffton University*
Laurah Norton, *Georgia State University*
Heather Ostman, *Westchester Community College, State University of New York*
Steven Ostrowski, *Central Connecticut State University*
William Pannapacker, *Hope College*
Ann M. Pelelo, *Clarke University*
Susan K. Petrole, *Northampton Community College, PA*
George Piggford, *Stonehill College*
Bruce Plourde, *Rowan University*
Joseph Quinn Raab, *Siena Heights University*
Moshe Rachmuth, *University of Oregon*
Lisa Rado, *Harvard-Westlake (Upper) School, CA*
Brian Abel Ragen, *Southern Illinois University, Edwardsville*
Guy Reynolds, *University of Nebraska, Lincoln*
R. Clay Reynolds, *University of Texas, Dallas*
Andrew Robles, *Citrus College, CA*
Lisa Ruddick, *University of Chicago*
Patrick Samway, *St. Joseph's University, Philadelphia*
Benjamin Saxton, *Rice University*
Amy Schmidt, *Lyon College*
Matthew Sewell, *Minnesota State University, Mankato*
Jolly Kay Sharp, *University of the Cumberlands*
Susan Srigley, *Nipissing University*
Sunny Stalter, *Auburn University*
Jeffrey Stayton, *University of Mississippi*
Jacob Stratman, *John Brown University*
Melissa J. Strong, *Northeastern State University*
Peter Swirski, *University of Missouri, St. Louis*
Lynda Szabo, *Geneva College*
Claudia Tienart, *Concordia University Texas*
Joanne Valin, *Nipissing University*
Lara Vetter, *University of North Carolina, Charlotte*
Richard Vogel, *Wilton High School, CT*
Bethany White, *Carson-Newman College*
Lorna Wiedmann, *Wisconsin Lutheran College*
Jessica Hooten Wilson, *University of Mary Hardin-Baylor*
Harbour Winn, *Oklahoma City University*
Virginia Wray, *Lyon College*
Jacqueline A. Zubeck, *College of Mount Saint Vincent*

WORKS CITED

Achebe, Chinua. "An Image of Africa: Racism in Conrad's 'Heart of Darkness.'" *Heart of Darkness: An Authoritative Text: Backgrounds and Sources: Criticism*, 3rd ed., edited by Robert Kimbrough, Norton, 1988, pp. 251–61.

Adam, Karl. *The Spirit of Catholicism*. Translated by Justin McCann, Martino Fine Books, 2016.

Allison, Dorothy. *Bastard out of Carolina*. 1992. Plume, 1993.

Allitt, Patrick. *Religion in America since 1945: A History*. Columbia UP, 2003.

Als, Hilton. "Ghosts in the House: How Toni Morrison Fostered a Generation of Black Writers." *New Yorker*, 27 Oct. 2003, pp. 64–75.

———. *White Girls*. McSweeney's, 2013.

"Ann Petry." *FemBio*, www.fembio.org/english/biography.php/woman/ann-petry.

Anzaldúa, Gloria. *Borderlands / La Frontera: The New Mestiza*. 3rd ed., Aunt Lute, 1999.

Armstrong, Karen. *The Battle for God: A History of Fundamentalism*. Ballantine, 2000.

———. *A History of God: The Four-Thousand-Year Quest of Judaism, Christianity, and Islam*. Ballantine, 1993.

Asals, Frederick, editor. *Flannery O'Connor: "A Good Man Is Hard to Find."* Rutgers UP, 1993. Women Writers: Texts and Contexts.

———. *Flannery O'Connor: The Imagination of Extremity*. U of Georgia P, 1982.

———. "The Mythic Dimensions of Flannery O'Connor's 'Greenleaf.'" *Studies in Short Fiction*, vol. 4, 1968, pp. 317–30.

Bacon, Jon Lance. *Flannery O'Connor and Cold War Culture*. Cambridge UP, 1993.

Bain, Ken. *What the Best College Teachers Do*. Harvard UP, 2004.

Bakhtin, M. M. *Art and Answerability: Early Philosophical Essays*. Edited by Michael Holquist and Vadim Liapunov, supplement translated by Kenneth Brostrom, U of Texas P, 1990.

Baldwin, James. "Sonny's Blues." *Going to Meet the Man*, Vintage, 1995, pp. 101–41.

Balée, Susan. *Flannery O'Connor: Literary Prophet of the South*. Chelsea House, 1995.

Barrett, William. *Time of Need: Forms of Imagination in the Twentieth Century*. Wesleyan UP, 1972.

Bartley, Numan V. "Society and Culture in an Urban Age." *A History of Georgia*, edited by Kenneth Coleman et al., 2nd ed., U of Georgia P, 1991, pp. 375–89.

Basselin, Timothy J. *Flannery O'Connor: Writing a Theology of Disabled Humanity*. Baylor UP, 2013.

Baym, Nina, editor. *The Norton Anthology of American Literature*. Shorter Eighth ed., vol. 2, Norton, 2013.

Beerbohm, Max. *Zuleika Dobson*. Heinemann, 1911.

Behrendt, Stephen. "Knowledge and Innocence in Flannery O'Connor's 'The River.'" *Studies in American Fiction*, vol. 17, no. 2, 1989, pp. 143–55.

Ben-Hur. Directed by William Wyler, MGM, 1959. Warner Home Video, 2012. Blu-Ray Disc.

Berger, Peter. Interview by Krista Tippett. *Speaking of Faith*, National Public Radio, KNOW, St. Paul, MN, 22 May 2005.

———. "An Interview with Peter Berger." By Charles T. Mathewes. *The Hedgehog Review*, vol. 8, nos. 1–2, 2006, pp. 152–61.

Bergstrom, Robert F. "Discovery of Meaning: Development of Formal Thought in the Teaching of Literature." *College English*, vol. 45, no. 8, Dec. 1983, pp. 745–55.

Bérubé, Michael. "Afterword: If I Should Live So Long." *Disability Studies: Enabling the Humanities*, edited by Sharon L. Snyder et al., MLA, 2002, pp. 337–43.

The Best Years of Our Lives. 1946. Screenplay by Robert E. Sherwood, directed by William Wyler, Warner Home Video, 2013. DVD.

Blandford, James R. *PJ Harvey: Siren Rising*. Omnibus, 2004.

Bloom, Harold, editor. *Flannery O'Connor*. Bloom's Literary Criticism, 2009.

———, editor. *Flannery O'Connor*. Chelsea House, 1999. Bloom's Major Short Story Writers.

———. *Genius: A Mosaic of One Hundred Exemplary Creative Minds*. Warner, 2002.

Blotner, Joseph. *Faulkner: A Biography*. Quality Paperback Book Club, 1994.

Bonhoeffer, Dietrich. *Letters and Papers from Prison*. Translated by Reginald Fuller, edited by Eberhard Bethge, 3rd ed., Macmillan, 1953.

Bono. "Bono and the Two Americas." Interview. @U2, www.atu2.com/news/the-enduring-chill.html.

Booth, Wayne C. *The Rhetoric of Fiction*. 2nd ed., U of Chicago P, 1963.

Bosco, Mark, and Brent Little, editors. *Revelation and Convergence: Flannery O'Connor and the Catholic Intellectual Tradition*. Catholic U of America P, 2017.

Boyle, Anne M. *Strange and Lurid Bloom: A Study of the Fiction of Caroline Gordon*. Fairleigh Dickinson UP, 2002.

Bradbury, Malcolm, and James McFarlane. "The Name and Nature of Modernism." *Modernism: 1890–1930*, edited by Malcolm Bradbury and James McFarlane, Humanities, 1978, pp. 19–56.

Branch, Taylor. *Parting the Waters: America in the King Years, 1954–63*. Simon, 1988.

Brinkmeyer, Robert H., Jr. *The Art and Vision of Flannery O'Connor*. Louisiana State UP, 1989.

Brodhead, Richard H. "A Life of Letters." *Yale Review*, vol. 69, no. 3, 1980, pp. 451–56.

Brookfield, Stephen D. *Teaching for Critical Thinking: Tools and Techniques to Help Students Question Their Assumptions*. Jossey-Bass, 2012.

Buell, Lawrence. *The Environmental Imagination. Thoreau, Nature Writing, and the Formation of American Culture*. Harvard UP, 1995.

———. *The Future of Environmental Criticism: Environmental Crisis and Literary Imagination*. Blackwell, 2005.

Buffington, Daniel Taylor. "A South in the North: Emplacing the South in American National Myth." *National Identities*, vol. 13, no. 3, 2011, pp. 235–51.

Burns, Stuart L. "O'Connor and the Critics: An Overview." *Mississippi Quarterly*, vol. 27, no. 4, 1974, pp. 483–95.

Burroway, Janet. *Writing Fiction: A Guide to Narrative Craft*. 8th ed., Longman, 2003.

Butler, Judith. "Performative Acts and Gender Constitution: An Essay in Phenomenology and Feminist Theory." *Writing on the Body: Female Embodiment and Feminist Theory*, edited by Katie Conboy et al., Columbia UP, 1997, pp. 401–17.

Camus, Albert. *The Rebel: An Essay on Man in Revolt*. Vintage, 1991.

"Carl Linnaeus." *Carl Linnaeus*, Regents of the U of California, 7 July 2000, www.ucmp.berkeley.edu/history/linnaeus.html.

Caron, Timothy P. " 'The Bottom Rail Is on the Top': Race and 'Theological Whiteness' in Flannery O'Connor's Short Fiction." McMullen and Peede, pp. 138–64.

———. *Struggles over the Word: Race and Religion in O'Connor, Faulkner, Hurston, and Wright*. Mercer UP, 2000.

Carson, Clayborne, et al., editors. *The Eyes on the Prize Civil Rights Reader: Documents, Speeches, and Firsthand Accents from the Black Freedom Struggle*. Penguin, 1991.

Caruso, Teresa, editor. *"On the Subject of the Feminist Business": Re-reading Flannery O'Connor*. Peter Lang, 2004.

Cash, Jean W. *Flannery O'Connor: A Life*. U of Tennessee P, 2002.

———. "Flannery O'Connor as Lecturer: '. . . a Secret Desire to Rival Charles Dickens.' " *The Flannery O'Connor Bulletin*, vol. 16, 1987, pp. 1–15.

Cather, Willa. "Paul's Case." *McClure's Magazine*, vol. 25, May 1905, pp. 74–83. *Willa Cather Archive*, cather.unl.edu/ss006.html.

———. Prefatory Note. *Willa Cather: Stories, Poems, and Other Writings*, Library of America, 1992, p. 812.

———. *The Selected Letters of Willa Cather*. Edited by Andrew Jewell and Janis Stout, Knopf, 2013.

Cenatus, Lordia. "The Displaced Person: The Beginning to an End." Paper for English 2001, Introduction to Fiction, New York City College of Technology, Fall 2013.

Charon, Rita. *Narrative Medicine: Honoring the Stories of Illness*. Oxford UP, 2006.

Chatman, Seymour. *Story and Discourse: Narrative Structure in Fiction and Film*. Cornell UP, 1980.

Chow, Sung Gay. " 'Strange and Alien Country': An Analysis of Landscape in Flannery O'Connor's *Wise Blood* and *The Violent Bear It Away*." *The Flannery O'Connor Bulletin*, vol. 8, 1979, pp. 35–44.

Ciuba, Gary M. *Desire, Violence, and Divinity in Modern Southern Fiction: Katherine Anne Porter, Flannery O'Connor, Cormac McCarthy, Walker Percy*. Louisiana State UP, 2007.

———. " 'To the Hard of Hearing You Shout': Flannery O'Connor and the Imagination of Deafness." *Flannery O'Connor Review*, vol. 12, 2013, pp. 1–18.

Cixous, Hélène. "The Laugh of the Medusa." Translated by Keith Cohen and Paula Cohen. *The Critical Tradition: Classic Texts and Contemporary Trends*, edited by David H. Richter, 2nd ed., Bedford, 1998, pp. 1453–66.

Clark, Keith. *The Radical Fiction of Ann Petry*. Louisiana State UP, 2013.

Cleary, Michael. "Environmental Influences in Flannery O'Connor's Fiction." *The Flannery O'Connor Bulletin*, vol. 8, 1979, pp. 20–34.

Cobb, James C. *Away Down South: A History of Southern Identity*. Oxford UP, 2005.

Cobb, James C., and William Stueck. *Globalization and the American South*. U of Georgia P, 2005.

Cofer, Jordan. *The Gospel according to Flannery O'Connor: Examining the Role of the Bible in Flannery O'Connor's Fiction*. Bloomsbury, 2014.

Coles, Robert. *Flannery O'Connor's South*. Louisiana State UP, 1980.

Corrosion of Conformity. *Wiseblood*. Columbia, 1996. CD.

Crews, Frederick. *The Critics Bear It Away: American Fiction and the Academy*. Random, 1992.

"The Curse of Ham." *New World Encyclopedia*, www.newworldencyclopedia.org/entry/Curse_of_Ham.

Danticat, Edwidge. *Krik? Krak!* Soho Press, 2015.

Davis, F. James. "Who Is Black? One Nation's Definition." *Frontline*, www.pbs.org/wgbh/pages/frontline/shows/jefferson/mixed/onedrop.html.

Davis, Joe Lee. "Outraged or Embarrassed." Robillard, pp. 23–24.

Day, Matthew. "Flannery O'Connor and the Southern Code of Manners." *Southern Crossroads: Perspectives on Religion and Culture*, edited by Walter H. Conser, Jr., and Rodger M. Payne, UP of Kentucky, 2008, pp. 133–44.

Desmond, John F. *Risen Sons: Flannery O'Connor's Vision of History*. U of Georgia P, 1987.

Díaz, Junot. *Drown*. Riverhead, 1996.

———. "Fiction Is the Poor Man's Cinema: An Interview with Junot Díaz." By Diogenes Céspedes and Silvio Torres-Saillant. *Callaloo*, vol. 23, no. 3, 2000, pp. 892–907.

———. "Junot Díaz." Interview by Edwidge Danticat. *BOMB*, no. 101, 2007, pp. 89–95.

———. "Junot Díaz." Interview by Lourdes Torres and Carina Vásquez, *Diálogo*, vol. 15, no. 1, 2012, pp. 29–35.

———. "Junot Díaz, Diaspora, and Redemption: Creating Progressive Imaginaries." Interview by Katherine Miranda. *Sargasso*, vol. 2, 2008–09, pp. 23–39.

Di Renzo, Anthony. *American Gargoyles: Flannery O'Connor and the Medieval Grotesque*. Southern Illinois UP, 1993.

Dirlik, Arif. "The Global South: Predicament and Promise." *The Global South*, vol. 1, no. 1, 2007, pp. 12–23.

The Displaced Person. 1976. Directed by Glenn Jordan, performances by John Houseman, Irene Worth, Shirley Stoler, Lane Smith, Robert Earl Jones, and Samuel L. Jackson, Monterey Media, 2007.

Donahoo, Robert. "Beholding the Handmaids: Catholic Womanhood and 'The Comforts of Home.'" McMullen and Peede, pp. 79–101.

———. "O'Connor and *The Feminine Mystique*: A Southern Slant on Post-war American Women." Caruso, pp. 9–28.

————. "On Flannery O'Connor: Recovering the Histories in Flannery O'Connor's Short Fiction." *Short Fiction of Flannery O'Connor: Critical Insights*, edited by Robert C. Evans, Salem, 2016, pp. 3–24.

————. "Recasting the Monuments: O'Connor and Histories of the South." *Flannery O'Connor Review*, vol. 11, 2013, pp. 1–21.

————. "Subject to Limitations: O'Connor's Fiction and the South's Shifting Populations." *Flannery O'Connor Review*, vol. 2, 2004, pp. 16–30.

Donaldson, Susan V. "Southern Roots and Routes: Mobility, Migration, and the Literary Imagination." *Mississippi Quarterly*, vol. 65, no. 1, 2012, pp. 5–15.

Driggers, Stephen G., and Robert J. Dunn. *The Manuscripts of Flannery O'Connor at Georgia College*. With Sarah Gordon, U of Georgia P, 1989.

Du Bois, W. E. B. *The Souls of Black Folk*. 1903. Dover, 1994.

Duvall, John N. *The Identifying Fictions of Toni Morrison: Modernist Authenticity and Postmodern Blackness*. Palgrave, 2009.

————. *Race and White Identity in Southern Fiction: From Faulkner to Morrison*. Palgrave, 2008.

Dziakiewicz, Olga. E-mail in response to Fall 2013 Introduction to Fiction class at New York City College of Technology. 15 Apr. 2014.

Edmondson, Henry T., III, editor. *A Political Companion to Flannery O'Connor*. UP of Kentucky, 2017.

Eisenberg, Leon. "Disease and Illness: Distinctions between Professional and Popular Ideas of Sickness." *Culture, Medicine, and Psychiatry*, vol. 1, 1977, pp. 9–23.

Elie, Paul. *The Life You Save May Be Your Own: An American Pilgrimage*. Farrar, 2003.

Engel-Ledeboer, M. S. J., and H. Engel. "Carolus Linnaeus and the Systema Naturae (1735)." *KTH Royal Institute of Technology*, www.kth.se/polopoly_fs/1.199546!/Menu/general/column-content/attachment/Linnaeus—extracts.pdf.

Engle, Paul, and Hansford Martin. Introduction. *Prize Stories 1955: The O. Henry Awards*, edited by Engle and Martin, Doubleday, 1955, pp. 9–12.

Erkkila, Betsy. "Ethnicity, Literary Theory, and the Grounds of Resistance." *American Quarterly*, vol. 47, 1995, pp. 563–94.

Evans, Robert C. *The Critical Reception of Flannery O'Connor, 1952–2017: "Searchers and Discoverers."* Camden House, 2017.

Evans, Robert C., et al., editors. *Short Fiction: A Critical Companion*. Locust Hill, 1997.

Farmer, David. *Flannery O'Connor: A Descriptive Bibliography*. Garland, 1981.

Faulkner, William. *Faulkner in the University: Class Conferences at the University of Virginia, 1957–1958*. Edited by Frederick L. Gwynn and Joseph Blotner, Vintage, 1951.

————. *Go Down, Moses*. 1942. Vintage International, 1990.

————. *Light in August*. 1932. Vintage International, 1990.

————. *Novels, 1936–1940*. Edited by Joseph Blotner and Noel Polk, Library of America, 1990.

————. *The Sound and the Fury*. 1929. Vintage International, 1990.

Fickett, Harold, and Douglas R. Gilbert. *Flannery O'Connor: Images of Grace*. Eerdmans, 1986.

Fitzgerald, Sally. "Chronology." O'Connor, *Flannery O'Connor: Collected Works*, pp. 1237–56.

————. Letter to the editor. *The Flannery O'Connor Bulletin*, vol. 24, 1994–95, pp. 175–82.

————. "A Master Class: From the Correspondence of Caroline Gordon and Flannery O'Connor." *The Georgia Review*, vol. 33, no. 4, 1979, pp. 827–46.

"Flannery O'Connor." *Catholicism: The Pivotal Players*, vol. 2, pivotalplayers.com/.

"Flannery O'Connor." *Religion and Ethics Newsweekly*, reported by Rafael Pi Roman, WNET, 20 Nov. 2009, *PBS*, www.pbs.org/wnet/religionandethics/2009/11/20/november-20-2009-flannery-oconnor/5043/.

Foucault, Michel. *The Birth of the Clinic: An Archaeology of Medical Perception*. Translated by A. M. Sheridan Smith, Vintage, 1994.

Fowler, Doreen. *Drawing the Line: The Father Reimagined in Faulkner, Wright, O'Connor, and Morrison*. U of Virginia P, 2013.

Francis. "Encyclical Letter *Laudato Si'* of the Holy Father Francis on Care for Our Common Home." *The Holy See*, 18 June 2015, w2.vatican.va/content/francesco/en/encyclicals/documents/papa-francesco_20150524_enciclica-laudato-si.html.

Frank, Frederick S. *Guide to the Gothic III: An Annotated Bibliography of Criticism, 1994–2003*. Scarecrow Press, 2005.

Freire, Paulo. *The Pedagogy of the Oppressed*. 1970. Bloomsbury, 2014.

Freud, Sigmund. *The Future of an Illusion*. Edited and translated by James Strachey, Norton, 1961.

————. *The Standard Edition of the Complete Psychological Works of Freud*. 24 vols., edited and translated by James Strachey, Hogarth, 1961.

Freud, Sigmund, and Oskar Pfister. *Briefe, 1909–1939*. Edited by Ernst L. Freud and Heinrich Meng, S. Fischer Verlag, 1963.

Friedan, Betty. *The Feminine Mystique*. Dell, 1963.

Friedman, Melvin J. Introduction. *Critical Essays on Flannery O'Connor*, edited by Friedman and Beverly Lyon Clark, Hall, 1985, pp. 1–15.

Friedman, Melvin J., and Beverly Lyon Clark, editors. *Critical Essays on Flannery O'Connor*. Hall, 1985.

Friedman, Melvin J., and Lewis A. Lawson, editors. *The Added Dimension: The Art and Mind of Flannery O'Connor*. 1966. Fordham UP, 2nd rev. ed., 1977.

Frydman, Jason. "Violence, Masculinity, and Upward Mobility in the Dominican Diaspora: Junot Díaz, the Media, and *Drown*." *Columbia Journal of American Studies*, vol. 8, Spring 2007, pp. 99–118.

Furman, Jan, editor. *Toni Morrison's Song of Solomon: A Casebook*. Oxford UP, 2003.

Garland-Thomson, Rosemarie. *Extraordinary Bodies: Figuring Physical Disability in American Culture and Literature*. Columbia UP, 1997.

Gates, Henry Louis, Jr. *The Signifying Monkey*. Oxford UP, 1988.

Gauthier, Mary. Interview. By Irwin Streight, 25 Apr. 2009.

———. "Snakebit." *Between Daylight and Dark*, Universal Music Group, 2007.

———. "Wheel inside the Wheel." *Mercy Now*, Lost Highway, 2005.

Gay, Peter. *A Godless Jew: Freud, Atheism, and the Making of Psychoanalysis*. Yale UP, 1987.

Gentry, Marshall Bruce. *Flannery O'Connor's Religion of the Grotesque*. UP of Mississippi, 1986.

———. "O'Connor as Miscegenationist." Hewitt and Donahoo, pp. 189–200.

Gentry, [Marshall] Bruce, and Craig Amason, editors. *At Home with Flannery O'Connor: An Oral History*. Flannery O'Connor–Andalusia Foundation, 2012.

George-Warren, Holly, and Patricia Romanowski, editors. *Rolling Stone Encyclopedia of Rock and Roll*. 3rd ed., Fireside, 2001.

Gerber, David A. "Heroes and Misfits: The Troubled Social Reintegration of Disabled Veterans in *The Best Years of Our Lives*." *Disabled Veterans in History*, edited by David A. Gerber, U of Michigan P, 2000, pp. 70–95.

Giannone, Richard. *Flannery O'Connor and the Mystery of Love*. 1989. Fordham UP, 1999.

———. *Flannery O'Connor, Hermit Novelist*. U of Illinois P, 2000.

Giles, Paul. *American Catholic Arts and Fictions: Culture, Ideology, Aesthetics*. Cambridge UP, 1992.

Girard, René. *Violence and the Sacred*. Translated by Patrick Gregory, Johns Hopkins UP, 1979.

Glotfelty, Cheryll. "Literary Studies in an Age of Environmental Crisis." Introduction. Glotfelty and Fromm, pp. xv–xxxvii.

Glotfelty, Cheryll, and Harold Fromm, editors. *The Ecocriticism Reader: Landmarks in Literary Ecology*. U of Georgia P, 1996.

Golden, Robert E., and Mary C. Sullivan. *Flannery O'Connor and Caroline Gordon: A Reference Guide*. Hall, 1977.

Golsan, Richard. *René Girard and Myth: An Introduction*. Routledge, 2002.

Gooch, Brad. *Flannery: A Life of Flannery O'Connor*. Little, 2009.

Gordon, Sarah, editor. *Flannery O'Connor: In Celebration of Genius*. 2000. U of South Carolina P, 2010.

———. *Flannery O'Connor: The Obedient Imagination*. U of Georgia P, 2000.

———. *A Literary Guide to Flannery O'Connor's Georgia*. With Craig Amason and Marcelina Martin, U of Georgia P, 2008.

Graff, Gerald. *Beyond the Culture Wars: How Teaching the Conflicts Can Revitalize American Education*. Norton, 1992.

Gray, Richard, and Owen Robinson, editors. *A Companion to the Literature and Culture of the American South*. Blackwell, 2004.

Graybill, Mark S. "O'Connor's Deep Ecological Vision." *Flannery O'Connor Review*, vol. 9, 2011, pp. 1–18.

Greif, Mark. *The Age of the Crisis of Man: Thought and Fiction in America, 1933–1973*. Princeton UP, 2015.

Gretlund, Jan Nordby, and Karl-Heinz Westarp, editors. *Flannery O'Connor's Radical Reality*. U of South Carolina P, 2006.

Griesinger, Emily. "Why Baby Suggs, Holy, Quit Preaching the Word: Redemption and Holiness in Toni Morrison's *Beloved*." *Christianity and Literature*, vol. 50, no. 4, 2001, pp. 689–702.

Gubar, Susan. *Racechanges: White Skin, Black Faces in American Culture*. Oxford UP, 1997.

Haddox, Thomas F. *Hard Sayings: The Rhetoric of Christian Orthodoxy in Late Modern Fiction*. Ohio State UP, 2013.

Hale, Nathan G. *Freud and the Americans: The Beginnings of Psychoanalysis in the United States, 1876–1917*. Oxford UP, 1995.

———. *The Rise and Crisis of Psychoanalysis in the United States: Freud and the Americans, 1917–1985*. Oxford UP, 1995.

Halliday, Josh. "Savile Told Hospital Staff He Performed Sex Acts on Corpses in Leeds Mortuary." *The Guardian*, 26 June 2014, www.theguardian.com/media/2014/jun/26/savile-bodies-sex-acts-corpses-glass-eyes-mortuary.

Han, John J., editor. Wise Blood: *A Re-consideration*. Rodopi, 2011.

Hanson, Ellis. *Decadence and Catholicism*. Harvard UP, 1998.

Haraway, Donna. "A Cyborg Manifesto: Science, Technology, and Socialist-Feminism in the Late Twentieth Century." *Simians, Cyborgs and Women: The Reinvention of Nature*, Routledge, 1991, pp. 149–82.

Hardy, Donald E. *The Body in Flannery O'Connor's Fiction: Computational Technique and Linguistic Voice*. U of South Carolina P, 2007.

———. *Narrating Knowledge in Flannery O'Connor's Fiction*. U of South Carolina P, 2003.

Harpham, Geoffrey Galt. *On the Grotesque: Strategies of Contradiction in Art and Literature*. Princeton UP, 1982.

Harris, Carole K. "James Baldwin, Flannery O'Connor, and the Ethics of Anguish." *Hunger Mountain: VCFA [Vermont College of Fine Arts] Journal of the Arts*, www.hungermtn.org/james-baldwin-flannery-oconnor-and-the-ethics-of-anguish/.

———. "On Flying Mules and the Southern Cabala: Flannery O'Connor and James Baldwin in Georgia." *Renascence*, vol. 65, no. 5, 2013, pp. 328–50.

———. "The Politics of the Cliché: Flannery O'Connor's 'Revelation' and 'The Displaced Person.'" *Partial Answers*, vol. 9, no. 1, 2011, pp. 111–29.

Harvey, David. *The Condition of Postmodernity: An Enquiry into the Origins of Cultural Change*. Blackwell, 1989.

Harvey, PJ. *Is This Desire?* Island Records, 1998.

Hawkes, John. "Flannery O'Connor's Devil." *Sewanee Review*, vol. 70, no. 3, 1962, pp. 395–407.

Hawkins, Anne. *Reconstructing Illness: Studies in Pathography*. Purdue UP, 1999.

Hendin, Josephine. *The World of Flannery O'Connor*. 1970. Wipf and Stock, 2009.

Herberg, Will. *Protestant, Catholic, Jew: An Essay in American Religious Sociology*. Anchor Books, 1960.

———. "Religion and Culture in Present-Day America." *Roman Catholicism and the American Way of Life*, edited by Thomas T. McAvoy, U of Notre Dame P, 1960, pp. 4–19.

Herndl, Diane Price. "Disease versus Disability: Medical Humanities and Disability Studies." *PMLA*, vol. 120, no. 2, 2005, pp. 593–98.

Hewitt, Avis, and Robert Donahoo, editors. *Flannery O'Connor in the Age of Terrorism: Essays on Violence and Grace*. U of Tennessee P, 2010.

Hicks, Granville, editor. *The Living Novel: A Symposium*. 1957. Collier, 1962.

Hight, Jewly. *Right by Her Roots: Americana Women and Their Songs*. Baylor UP, 2011.

The Holy Bible: Douay-Rheims Version. Saint Benedict Press, 2009.

The Holy Bible: English Standard Version. Crossway, 2016.

The Holy Bible: New International Version. Zondervan, 1984.

hooks, bell. *Talking Back: Thinking Feminist, Thinking Black*. South End, 1989.

House, Silas. "Happy Woman Blues." *No Depression*, May-June, 2001, pp. 86–93.

Hughes, Richard. *A High Wind in Jamaica*. Chatto and Windus, 1929.

Hughes, Thomas P. *American Genesis: A Century of Invention and Technological Enthusiasm*. Penguin, 1989.

Jabbur, Adam. "Tradition and Individual Talent in Willa Cather's *Death Comes for the Archbishop*." *Studies in the Novel*, vol. 42, 2010, pp. 395–420.

Jansson, David. "Racialization and 'Southern' Identities of Resistance: A Psychogeography of Internal Orientalism in the United States." *Annals of the Association of American Geographers*, vol. 100, no. 1, 2010, pp. 202–21.

Jesus Christ Superstar. Directed by Norman Jewison, Universal Pictures, 1973. Universal Pictures Home Entertainment, 2004. DVD.

Jesus of Nazareth. Directed by Franco Zeffirelli, ITC Films, 1977. Shout Factory, 2016. DVD.

Johnson, E. Patrick. *Appropriating Blackness: Performance and the Politics of Authenticity*. Duke UP, 2003.

Johnson, Loretta. "Greening the Library: The Fundamentals and Future of Ecocriticism." *Choice*, Dec. 2009, pp. 7–13.

Jones, Bill T. "Dance: The Sincerest Form of Flannery." Interview by Fletcher Roberts. *The New York Times*, 1 Feb. 2014, www.nytimes.com/2004/02/01/arts/dance-the-sincerest-form-of-flannery.html.

Joyce, James. Dubliners: *Text, Criticism, and Notes*. Edited by Robert Scholes and A. Walton Litz. Penguin, 1996.

———. *Letters of James Joyce*. Edited by Stuart Gilbert, vol. 1, Viking, 1966. 3 vols.

Jung, Carl. *Psychology and Religion*. Yale UP, 1938.

Kahane, Claire. "The Artificial Niggers." *The Massachusetts Review*, vol. 19, no. 1, 1978, pp. 183–98.

Kang, Seng Yeal. "Life of Immigrants." Paper for English 2001, Introduction to Fiction, New York City College of Technology, Spring 2012.

Katz [Kahane], Claire. "Flannery O'Connor's Rage of Vision." *American Literature*, vol. 46, 1974, pp. 54–67.

Kessler, Edward. *Flannery O'Connor and the Language of Apocalypse*. Princeton UP, 1986.

Kilcourse, George A., Jr. *Flannery O'Connor's Religious Imagination: A World with Everything Off Balance*. Paulist, 2001.

King Swamp. *Wiseblood*. Virgin/WEA, 1990.

Kinney, Arthur F. *Flannery O'Connor's Library: Resources of Being*. U of Georgia P, 1985.

Kirk, Connie Ann. *Critical Companion to Flannery O'Connor: A Literary Reference to Her Life and Work*. Facts on File, 2008.

Kowalewski, Michael. *Deadly Musings: Violence and Verbal Form in American Fiction*. Princeton UP, 1993.

Kreyling, Michael. Introduction. Kreyling, *New Essays*, pp. 1–24.

———, editor. *New Essays on* Wise Blood. Cambridge UP, 1995.

Lacan, Jacques. *Écrits: A Selection*. Translated by Alan Sheridan, Norton, 1977.

Lake, Christina Bieber. *The Incarnational Art of Flannery O'Connor*. Mercer UP, 2005.

The Last Temptation of Christ. Directed by Martin Scorsese, Universal Pictures, 1988. Universal Pictures Home Entertainment, 2012. DVD.

Latour, Bruno. "Give Me a Laboratory and I Will Raise the World." *Science Observed: Perspectives on the Social Study of Science*, edited by Karin D. Knorr-Cetina and Michael Mulkay, SAGE, 1983, pp. 141–69.

———. *We Have Never Been Modern*. Harvard UP, 1993.

Lebeck, Sherry Lynn. *Paradox Lost and Paradox Regained: An Object Relations Analysis of Two Flannery O'Connor Mother-Child Dyads*. PhD dissertation. Dissertation.com, 2000.

Lee, Catherine Carr. "The South in Toni Morrison's *Song of Solomon*: Initiation, Healing, Home." Furman, pp. 42–65.

Lee, Harper. *To Kill a Mockingbird*. 1960. Grand Central Publishing, 1982.

Leech, Geoffrey, and Mick Short. *Style in Fiction: A Linguistic Introduction to English Fictional Prose*. 2nd ed, Routledge, 2007.

"The Life You Save." *Schlitz Playhouse*. Directed by Herschel Dougherty, performances by Gene Kelly, Agnes Moorehead, and Janice Rule, CBS, 1 Mar. 1957.

Longenbach, James. *Modern Poetry after Modernism*. Oxford UP, 1997.

Longmore, Paul. *"Why I Burned My Book" and Other Essays on Disability*. Temple UP, 2003.

Lorde, Audre. "Age, Race, Class, and Sex: Women Redefining Difference." *Literary Theory: An Anthology*, edited by Julie Rivkin and Michael Ryan, Blackwell, 1998, pp. 630–36.

Lubin, Alex, editor. *Revising the Blueprint: Ann Petry and the Literary Left*. UP of Mississippi, 2007.

Lynch, William. *Christ and Apollo: The Dimensions of the Literary Imagination*. 1960. Intercollegiate Studies Institute, 2004.

———. "Theology and the Imagination." *Thought*, vol. 29, 1954–55, pp. 61–80.

MacKethan, Lucinda. "Redeeming Blackness: Urban Allegories of O'Connor, Percy, and Toole." *Studies in the Literary Imagination*, vol. 27, no. 2, 1994, pp. 29–39.

Maloney, Anne. "Flannery O'Connor: Apostle to the Blind." *Crisis: A Journal of Lay Catholic Opinion*, 1 Nov. 1994, www.crisismagazine.com/1994/flannery-oconnor-apostle-to-the-blind. Accessed 4 Jan. 2016.

Maritain, Jacques. *Art and Scholasticism*. Translated by J. F. Scanlan and Joseph W. Evans, Cluny Media, 2016.

Marrs, Suzanne. *Eudora Welty: A Biography*. Harcourt, 2005.

Marx, Leo. "The Machine in the Garden." *New England Quarterly*, vol. 29, no. 1, Mar. 1956, pp. 27–42.

———. *The Machine in the Garden: Technology and the Pastoral Ideal in America*. Oxford UP, 1964.

May, Charles E., editor. *Critical Insights: Flannery O'Connor*. Salem, 2011.

May, John R. *The Pruning Word: The Parables of Flannery O'Connor*. U of Notre Dame P, 1976.

McClure, John A. *Partial Faiths: Postsecular Fiction in the Age of Pynchon and Morrison*. U of Georgia P, 2007.

McCullers, Carson. *The Member of the Wedding*. 1946. Bantam, 1962.

McGann, Jerome. "Interpretation." *Introduction to Scholarship in Modern Languages and Literatures*, edited by David G. Nicholls, 3rd ed., MLA, 2007, pp. 160–70.

McGurl, Mark. "Understanding Iowa: Flannery O'Connor, B.A., M.F.A." *American Literary History*, vol. 19, no. 2, 2007, pp. 527–45.

McKee, Kathryn, and Annette Trefzer. "Preface: Global Contexts, Local Literatures: The New Southern Studies." *American Literature*, special issue edited by McKee and Trefzer, vol. 78, no. 4, 2006, pp. 677–90.

McKenzie, Barbara. *Flannery O'Connor's Georgia*. U of Georgia P, 1980.

McMullen, Joanne Halleran. *Writing against God: Language as Message in the Literature of Flannery O'Connor*. Mercer UP, 1996.

McMullen, Joanne Halleran, and Jon Parrish Peede, editors. *Inside the Church of Flannery O'Connor: Sacrament, Sacramental, and the Sacred in Her Fiction*. Mercer UP, 2007.

The Men. 1950. Screenplay by Carl Foreman, directed by Fred Zinnemann, Olive Films, 2013.

Michaels, J. Ramsey. *Passing by the Dragon: The Biblical Tales of Flannery O'Connor*. Cascade, 2013.

Miller, J. Hillis. *The Disappearance of God: Five Nineteenth-Century Writers*. Harvard UP, 1963.

Miller, Matthew L. "Trauma in Junot Díaz's *Drown*." *Notes on Contemporary Literature*, vol. 41, no. 1, 2011, pp. 2–4.

Ministry. "Jesus Built My Hotrod" (Redline/Whiteline Version). Single. Sire / Warner Bros, 1991.

Minter, David. *A Cultural History of the American Novel: Henry James to William Faulkner*. Cambridge UP, 1994.

Mitchell, Carolyn A. "'I Love to Tell the Story': Biblical Revisions in *Beloved*." *Religion and Literature*, vol. 23, no. 3, 1991, pp. 27–42.

Mitchell, David T., and Sharon L. Snyder. *Narrative Prosthesis: Disability and the Dependencies of Discourse*. U of Michigan P, 2000.

Moi, Toril. "'Images of Women' Criticism." *Sexual/Textual Politics: Feminist Literary Theory*. Routledge, 1985, pp. 42–49.

Monda, Antonio. *Do You Believe? Conversations on God and Religion*. Vintage, 2006.

Montgomery, Marion. *Hillbilly Thomist: Flannery O'Connor, St. Thomas, and the Limits of Art*. 2 vols., McFarland, 2006.

Morales, Alejandro. "Dynamic Identities in Heterotopia." *Alejandro Morales: Fiction Past, Present, Future Perfect*, edited by José Antonio Gurpegui, Bilingual, 1996, pp. 14–27.

Moran, Daniel. *Creating Flannery O'Connor: Her Critics, Her Publishers, Her Readers.* U of Georgia P, 2016.

Moreno, Marisel. "Debunking Myths, Destabilizing Identities: A Reading of Junot Díaz's 'How to Date a Browngirl, Blackgirl, Whitegirl, or Halfie.'" *Afro-Hispanic Review*, vol. 26, no. 2, 2007, pp. 103–17. JSTOR, www.jstor.org/stable/pdf/23054623.pdf.

Morrison, Toni. *Beloved*. Penguin, 1987.

———. *The Bluest Eye*. Penguin, 1994.

———. "Grendel and His Mother." The Congress of the Social Sciences and the Humanities, U of Toronto, 27 May 2002. Address. The Foreigner's Home: Meditations on Belonging.

———. "An Interview with Toni Morrison." Interview by Bessie W. Jones and Audrey Vinson. Taylor-Guthrie, *Conversations*, pp. 171–87.

———. *Love*. Knopf, 2003.

———. "Memory, Creation, and Writing." *Thought*, vol. 59, 1984, pp. 385–90.

———. "Nobel Lecture 1993." *Toni Morrison: Critical and Theoretical Approaches*, edited by Nancy J. Peterson, Johns Hopkins UP, 1997, pp. 267–73.

———. "Pam Houston Talks with Toni Morrison." Interview by Pam Houston. *Toni Morrison: Conversations*, edited by Carolyn C. Denard, UP of Mississippi, 2008, pp. 228–59.

———. *Playing in the Dark: Whiteness and the Literary Imagination*. Vintage, 1992.

———. *Song of Solomon*. Penguin, 1977.

———. "Toni Morrison: The Art of Fiction CXXXIV." Interview by Elissa Schappell. *The Paris Review*, no. 128, 1993, pp. 82–125.

Moskowitz, Eva. *In Therapy We Trust: America's Obsession with Self-Fulfillment*. Johns Hopkins UP, 2001.

Muller, Gilbert H. *Nightmares and Visions: Flannery O'Connor and the Catholic Grotesque*. U of Georgia P, 1972.

Murfin, Ross C., and Supryia M. Ray. *The Bedford Glossary of Critical and Literary Terms*. Bedford, 1997.

Murphy, Patrick D. "'The Women Are Speaking': Contemporary Literature as Theoretical Critique." *Ecofeminist Literary Criticism: Theory, Interpretation, Pedagogy*. Edited by Greta Gaard and Patrick D. Murphy, U of Illinois P, 1998, pp. 23–39.

Murray, Lorraine V. *The Abbess of Andalusia: Flannery O'Connor's Spiritual Journey*. Saint Benedict, 2009.

Nesbitt, Laurel. "Reading Place in and around Flannery O'Connor's Texts." *Post Identity*, vol. 1, no. 1, 1997, pp. 145–97.

The New American Bible. United States Council of Catholic Bishops, 2015.

Newstrom, Scott L. "Saying 'Goonight' To 'Lost' Ladies: An Inter-textual Interpretation of Allusions to *Hamlet*'s Ophelia in Cather's *A Lost Lady* and Eliot's 'The Waste Land.'" *Willa Cather Pioneer Memorial Newsletter*, vol. 39, nos. 2–3, 1995, pp. 33–37.

Newton, Adam Zachary. *Narrative Ethics*. Harvard UP, 1997.

Ngũgĩ wa Thiong'o. *Writers in Politics*. Heinemann, 1997.

Nisly, L. Lamar. *Impossible to Say: Representing Mystery in Fiction by Malamud, Percy, Ozick and O'Connor*. Greenwood, 2002.

North, Michael. *Reading 1922: A Return to the Scene of the Modern*. Oxford UP, 1999.

Oates, Joyce Carol. *The Profane Art: Essays and Reviews*. Dutton, 1983.

Obama, Barack. *Dreams from My Father: A Story of Race and Inheritance*. Three Rivers Press, 2004.

Ochoa, Peggy. "Morrison's *Beloved*: Allegorically Othering 'White' Christianity." *MELUS*, vol. 24, no. 2, 1999, pp. 107–23.

O'Connor, Flannery. *The Cartoons of Flannery O'Connor at Georgia College*. Edited by Marshall Bruce Gentry, Georgia College and State University, 2010.

———. "The Coat." *DoubleTake*, vol. 2, no. 3, 1996, pp. 38–41.

———. *The Complete Stories*. Farrar, 1971.

———. *Conversations with Flannery O'Connor*. Edited by Rosemary M. Magee. UP of Mississippi, 1987.

———. *The Correspondence of Flannery O'Connor and the Brainard Cheneys*. Edited by C. Ralph Stephens, UP of Mississippi, 1986.

———. *Everything That Rises Must Converge*. Farrar, 1965.

———. *Flannery O'Connor: Collected Works*. Edited by Sally Fitzgerald, Library of America, 1988.

———. *Flannery O'Connor: The Cartoons*. Edited by Kelly Gerald, Fantagraphics, 2012.

———. *"A Good Man Is Hard to Find" and Other Stories*. Harcourt, 1955. *Boyd County Public Schools*, www.boyd.k12.ky.us/userfiles/447/Classes/28660/A%20Good%20Man%20Is%20Hard%20To%20Find.pdf.

———. *The Habit of Being: Letters*. Edited by Sally Fitzgerald, Farrar, 1979.

———. "Home of the Brave." Albondocani, 1981.

———. Letter to LaTrelle Blackburn. 1 Nov. 1962. O'Connor Collection, Emory University MARBL folder 13.

———. Manuscripts of Flannery O'Connor. Flannery O'Connor Collection, Ina Dillard Russell Library, Georgia College and State University, Milledgeville.

———. *Mystery and Manners: Occasional Prose*. Edited by Sally Fitzgerald and Robert Fitzgerald, Farrar, 1969.

———. *A Prayer Journal*. Edited by W. A. Sessions, Farrar, 2013.

———. The Presence of Grace *and Other Book Reviews*. Compiled by Leo Zuber, edited by Carter W. Martin, U of Georgia P, 1983.

———. *The Violent Bear It Away*. Farrar, 1960.

———. *Wise Blood*. 1952. 2nd ed., Farrar, 1962.

O'Connor, Flannery, and Caroline Gordon. *The Letters of Flannery O'Connor and Caroline Gordon*. Edited by Christine Flanagan, U of Georgia P, 2018.

O'Donnell, Angela Alaimo. *Flannery O'Connor: Fiction Fired by Faith*. Liturgical, 2015.

O'Gorman, Farrell. *Peculiar Crossroads: Flannery O'Connor, Walker Percy, and Catholic Vision in Postwar Southern Fiction*. Louisiana State UP, 2004.

Omi, Michael, and Howard Winant. *Racial Formation in the United States: From the 1960s to the 1980s.* Routledge, 1986.

Oteng, Sandra. "A Hole in the Floor is a Blemish and Can Even Be Dangerous but It Won't Make the Entire House Fall Down." Paper for English 2001, Introduction to Fiction, New York City College of Technology, Spring 2012.

Park, Clara Claiborne. "Crippled Laughter: Toward Understanding Flannery O'Connor." *The American Scholar*, vol. 51, 1982, pp. 249–57.

The Passion of the Christ. Directed by Mel Gibson, Icon Productions, 2004. Zondervan, 2004. DVD.

"Paul's Childhood and Education." *Paul, the Man and the Teacher in the Light of Jewish Sources*, by Risto Santala, translated by Michael G. Cox, www.ristosantala .com/rsla/Paul/paul05.html.

Paulson, Suzanne Morrow. *Flannery O'Connor: A Study of the Short Fiction.* Twayne, 1988.

Peach, Linden. "Competing Discourses in *Song of Solomon*." *Modern Critical Interpretations: Toni Morrison's* Song of Solomon, edited by Harold Bloom, Chelsea, 1999, pp. 159–76.

Peacock, J. L., et al., editors. *The American South in a Global World.* U of North Carolina P, 2005.

Peebles, Stacey. "He's Huntin' Something: Hazel Motes as Ex-Soldier." Han, pp. 371–88.

Percy, Walker. *Conversations with Walker Percy.* Edited by Lewis A. Lawson and Victor A. Kramer, UP of Mississippi, 1985.

Perreault, Jeanne. "The Body, the Critics, and 'The Artificial Nigger.'" *The Mississippi Quarterly*, vol. 56, no. 3, 2003, pp. 389–410.

Pessar, Patricia R. *A Visa for a Dream: Dominicans in the United States.* Pearson, 1996.

Petrides, Sarah I. "Landscape and Community in Flannery O'Connor's *The Violent Bear It Away* and Walker Percy's *Love in the Ruins.*" *Flannery O'Connor Review*, vol. 1, 2001–02, pp. 9–25.

Petry, Ann. "The Witness." *Children of the Night: The Best Short Stories by Black Writers, 1967 to the Present*, edited by Gloria Naylor, Little, Brown, 1995, pp. 240–51.

———. "The Witness." *"Miss Muriel" and Other Stories.* 1971. Beacon Press, 1989, pp. 211–34.

———. "The Witness." *Redbook Magazine*, Feb. 1971, pp. 80–81, 126–34.

Pfeiffer, David. "The Philosophical Foundations of Disability Studies." *Disability Studies*, vol. 2, no. 22, 2002, pp. 3–23.

Pilgrim, David. "Lawn Jockeys—July 2008." *Jim Crow Museum of Racist Memorabilia*, ferris.edu/HTMLS/news/jimcrow/question/2008/july.htm.

Pillière, Linda. "Revealing the Mystery—an Approach to Flannery O'Connor's Use of Language." *The Complete Stories: Flannery O'Connor*, edited by Annick Duperray, Ellipses, 2004, pp. 93–103.

Poe, Edgar Allan. *Edgar Allan Poe: Poetry and Tales.* Library of America, 1984.

Pollock, Donald Ray. *Knockemstiff*. Anchor Books, 2009.

Pouscoulous, Nausicaa. "Metaphor: For Adults Only?" *Belgian Journal of Linguistics*, vol. 25, 2011, pp. 51–79.

Prince, Gerald. "Point of View." *Routledge Encyclopedia of Narrative Theory*, edited by David Herman et al., Routledge, 2005.

Prown, Katherine Hemple. *Revising Flannery O'Connor: Southern Literary Culture and the Problem of Female Authorship*. U of Virginia P, 2001.

Quinlan, Kieran. *Strange Kin: Ireland and the American South*. Louisiana State UP, 2005.

Quo Vadis. 1951. Directed by Mervyn LeRoy, Warner Home Video, 2008. DVD.

Ragen, Brian Abel. *A Wreck on the Road to Damascus: Innocence, Guilt, and Conversion in Flannery O'Connor*. Loyola UP, 1989.

Rath, Sura P., and Mary Neff Shaw, editors. *Flannery O'Connor: New Perspectives*. U of Georgia P, 1995.

Reese, Rita Mae. *The Book of Hulga*. Illustrations by Julie Franki, U of Wisconsin P, 2016.

Reichardt, Mary R., editor. *Encyclopedia of Catholic Literature*. Greenwood Press, 2004.

Reiter, Robert E., editor. *Flannery O'Connor*. Herder, [1968].

Ring, Natalie J. "Linking Regional and Global Spaces in Pursuit of Southern Distinctiveness." *American Literature*, special issue edited by Kathryn McKee and Annette Trefzer, vol. 78, no. 4, 2006, pp. 712–14.

Riofrio, John. "Situating Latin American Masculinity: Immigration, Empathy and Emasculation in Junot Díaz's *Drown*." *Atenea*, vol. 28, no. 1, 2008, pp. 23–36.

The Robe. Dir. Henry Koster. 1953. Twentieth Century Fox, 2014. DVD.

Robillard, Douglas, Jr., editor. *The Critical Response to Flannery O'Connor*. Praeger, 2004.

Robinson, Gabriele Scott. "Irish Joyce and Southern O'Connor." *The Flannery O'Connor Bulletin*, vol. 5, 1976, pp. 82–97.

Robinson, Lillian. "Treason Our Text: Feminist Challenges to the Literary Canon." *Falling into Theory: Conflicting Views of Reading Literature*, edited by David Richter, 2nd ed., Bedford, 2000, pp. 152–66.

Rodriguez, Richard. "A Twenty-First Century Writer: Richard Rodriguez on Flannery O'Connor." Interview by Farrell O'Gorman. *Flannery O'Connor Review*, vol. 4, 2006, pp. 27–31.

Rogers, Jonathan. *The Terrible Speed of Mercy: A Spiritual Biography of Flannery O'Connor*. Thomas Nelson, 2012.

Rosenfeld, Isaac. "To Win by Default." Robillard, pp. 21–23.

Samway, Patrick. *Flannery O'Connor and Robert Giroux: A Publishing Partnership*. U of Notre Dame P, 2018.

Schaub, Thomas Hill. *American Fiction in the Cold War*. U of Wisconsin P, 1991.

Schloesser, Stephen. *Jazz Age Catholicism: Mystic Modernism in Postwar Paris, 1919–1933*. U of Toronto P, 2005.

Scott, R. Neil. *Flannery O'Connor: An Annotated Reference Guide to Criticism*. Timberlane, 2002.

Scott, R. Neil, and Valerie Nye, compilers. *Postmarked Milledgeville: A Guide to Flannery O'Connor's Correspondence in Libraries and Archives*. Edited by Sarah Gordon and Irwin Streight, Georgia College and State University, 2002.

Scott, R. Neil, and Irwin H. Streight, editors. *Flannery O'Connor: The Contemporary Reviews*. Cambridge UP, 2009.

"Secular." *Oxford English Dictionary*, www.oed.com.

Seel, Cynthia L. *Ritual Performance in the Fiction of Flannery O'Connor*. Camden House, 2001.

Sharp, Jolly Kay. *Between the House and the Chicken Yard: The Masks of Flannery O'Connor*. Mercer UP, 2011.

Shenandoah: The Washington and Lee University Review. 60th anniversary issue, vol. 60, nos. 1–2, 2010. Special issue on O'Connor, edited by R. T. Smith.

Shloss, Carol. *Flannery O'Connor's Dark Comedies: The Limits of Inference*. Louisiana State UP, 1980.

———. "S/kin: Writing across Relatives." *Flannery O'Connor Review*, vol. 12, 2014, pp. 70–80.

Showalter, Elaine. *Teaching Literature*. Blackwell, 2003.

Shurr, William H. *Rappaccini's Children*. UP of Kentucky, 1981.

Siegel, Ben. "The Visionary Exuberance of Saul Bellow's *The Adventures of Augie March*." *A Companion to the American Novel*, edited by Alfred Bendixen, Wiley-Blackwell, 2012, pp. 625–40.

Simpson, Lewis P. *The Brazen Face of History: Studies in the Literary Consciousness in America*. Louisiana State UP, 1980.

Simpson, Melissa. *Flannery O'Connor: A Biography*. Greenwood, 2005.

Singal, Daniel J[oseph]. "Towards a Definition of American Modernism." *American Quarterly*, vol. 39, no. 1, 1987, pp. 7–26.

———. *William Faulkner: The Making of a Modernist*. U of North Carolina P, 1997.

Smith, Jon, and Deborah Cohn, editors. *Look Away! The US South in New World Studies*. Duke UP, 2004.

Smith, Lawanda. "Confronting Ghosts of the Christ-Haunted South: Teaching Theology through Story." *Teaching Theology and Religion*, vol. 7, no. 2, 2004, pp. 95–100.

Smith, Lillian. *Killers of the Dream*. Norton, 1994.

Smith, R. T. *The Red Wolf: A Dream of Flannery O'Connor*. Louisiana Literature, 2013.

Sokol, Jason. *There Goes My Everything: White Southerners in the Age of Civil Rights, 1945–1975*. Knopf, 2006.

Sontag, Susan. *Illness as Metaphor*. Farrar, 1978.

"Southern Dissonance." Robillard, pp. 19–20.

Spivey, Ted R. *Flannery O'Connor: The Woman, the Thinker, the Visionary*. Mercer UP, 1995.

Springsteen, Bruce. *Born to Run*. Simon, 2016.

———. "By the Book." Interview. *The New York Times Book Review*, 2 Nov. 2014, p. 8.

———. "A Good Man Is Hard to Find (Pittsburgh)." *Tracks*, Columbia, 1998.

———. "Nebraska." *Nebraska*, Columbia, 1980.

———. "Nebraska." *Norton Introduction to Literature*, edited by Kelly J. Mays, portable 11th ed., Norton, 2013, pp. 463–64n1.

———. "Rock and Read: Will Percy Interviews Bruce Springsteen." *DoubleTake*, vol. 4, no. 2, 1998, pp. 36–43.

Srigley, Susan, editor. *Dark Faith: New Essays on Flannery O'Connor's* The Violent Bear It Away. U of Notre Dame P, 2012.

———. *Flannery O'Connor's Sacramental Art*. U of Notre Dame P, 2004.

———. "The Violence of Love: Reflections on Self-Sacrifice through Flannery O'Connor and René Girard." *Religion and Literature*, vol. 39, no. 3, 2007, pp. 31–45.

Stephens, Martha. *The Question of Flannery O'Connor*. Louisiana State UP, 1973.

Stevens, Jason W. *God-Fearing and Free: A Spiritual History of America's Cold War*. Harvard UP, 2010.

Stevens, Sufjan. "A Good Man Is Hard to Find." *Seven Swans*, Asthmatic Kitty Records, 2004.

"Such Nice People." Review of *"A Good Man Is Hard to Find" and Other Stories*. *Flannery O'Connor: The Contemporary Reviews*, edited by Neil R. Scott and Irwin H. Streight, Cambridge UP, 2009, p. 36. Originally published in *Time*, 6 June 1955, p. 114.

Sullivan, Walter. *A Requiem for the Renascence: The State of Fiction in the Modern South*. U of Georgia P, 1976.

Sykes, John D., Jr. *Flannery O'Connor, Walker Percy, and the Aesthetic of Revelation*. U of Missouri P, 2007.

———. "How the Symbol Means: Deferral vs. Confrontation in 'The Artificial Nigger' and *The Sound and the Fury*." Hewitt and Donahoo, pp. 125–41.

———. "Portraits of the Artist: O'Connor's 'The Enduring Chill' and Faulkner's 'Elmer.'" *Flannery O'Connor Review*, vol. 8, 2010, pp. 22–30.

Sylvester, Nick. "Without a Prayer." *The Village Voice*, 2 Aug. 2005, www.villagevoice.com/2005-08-02/music/without-a-prayer/2.

Tate, Mary Barbara. "Flannery O'Connor at Home in Milledgeville." *Studies in the Literary Imagination*, vol. 20, no. 2, 1987, pp. 31–35.

Taylor, Alan C. "Redrawing the Color Line in Flannery O'Connor's 'The Displaced Person.'" *Mississippi Quarterly*, vol. 65, no. 1, 2012, pp. 69–80.

Taylor-Guthrie, Danille. "Who Are the Beloved? Old and New Testaments, Old and New Communities of Faith." *Religion and Literature*, vol. 27, no. 1, 1995, pp. 119–29.

Thomas Aquinas. *Summa Theologica*. New Advent, www.newadvent.org/summa/index.html.

Till the End of Time. 1946. Screenplay by Allen Rivken, directed by Edward Dmytryk, Warner Archive Collection, 2014.

Torres, Lourdes, and Carina Vásquez. "Junot Díaz." *Diálogo*, vol. 15, no. 1, 2012, pp. 29–35.

Torres-Saillant, Silvio, and Ramona Hernández. "Dominicans: Community, Culture, and Collective Identity." *One out of Three: Immigrant New York in the Twenty-First Century*, edited by Nancy Foner, Columbia UP, 2013, pp. 223–45.

Tracy, David. *The Analogical Imagination: Christian Theology and the Culture of Pluralism*. Crossroads, 1986.

Turner, Victor. *The Forest of Symbols: Aspects of Ndembu Ritual*. Cornell UP, 1967.

Twain, Mark. *Pudd'nhead Wilson*. 1894. Signet, 1964.

Twice Blessed. Screenplay by Ethel Hill et al., directed by Harry Beaumont, MGM, 1945.

Uncommon Grace: The Life of Flannery O'Connor. Directed by Bridget Kurt, Beata Productions, 2015.

U2. "One Tree Hill." *The Joshua Tree*. Island Records, 1997.

Végsö, Roland. "Flannery O'Connor and the Politics of Realism: Reading 'The Artificial Nigger.'" *Hungarian Journal of English and American Studies*, vol. 6, no. 2, 2000, pp. 59–75.

Viramontes, Helena María. "Viramontes on O'Connor." Interview by Bridget Kevane. *Flannery O'Connor Review*, vol. 4, 2006, pp. 5–11.

Wachlin, Marie. *The Bible Literacy Report: What Do American Teens Need to Know and What Do They Know?* Bible Literacy Project, Inc., 2005.

———. "Why and What Professors of English Say Students Need to Know about the Bible: A Research Report Summary." *Society of Biblical Literature Forum*, Feb. 2008, www.sbl-site.org/publications/article.aspx?ArticleId=757.

Walker, Alice. "Beyond the Peacock: The Reconstruction of Flannery O'Connor." Walker, *In Search*, pp. 42–59.

———. "Convergence: The Duped Shall Enter Last: But They Shall Enter." *Flannery O'Connor Review*, vol. 12, 2014, pp. 3–12.

———. *In Search of Our Mothers' Gardens: Womanist Prose*. Harcourt, 1983.

———. *Possessing the Secret of Joy*. New Press, 1992.

———. *We Are the Ones We Have Been Waiting For*. New Press, 2006.

Wallace, Jeff. *Beginning Modernism*. Manchester UP, 2011.

Waller, Willard. *The Veteran Comes Back*. Dryden, 1944.

Walsh, John Evangelist. *Into My Own: The English Years of Robert Frost, 1912–1915*. Grove, 1988.

Warne, Kennedy. "Organization Man." *Smithsonian.com*, May 2007, www.smithsonian mag.com/science-nature/organization-man-151908042/?no-ist.

Watson, Jay. *The Recalcitrant Materiality of Southern Fiction, 1893–1985*. U of Georgia P, 2012.

Weber, Donald. "From Limen to Border: A Meditation on the Legacy of Victor Turner for American Cultural Studies." *American Quarterly*, vol. 47, no. 3, 1995, pp. 525–36.

Welty, Eudora and William Maxwell. *What There Is to Say We Have Said: The Correspondence of Eudora Welty and William Maxwell*. Edited by Suzanne Marrs, Houghton Mifflin Harcourt, 2011.

West, Nathanael. *Miss Lonelyhearts*. Liveright, 1933.

Westarp, Karl-Heinz, compiler. *Flannery O'Connor: The Growing Craft: A Synoptic Variorum Edition of "The Geranium," "An Exile in the East," "Getting Home," "Judgement Day."* Summa, 1993.

———. "'Judgement Day': The Published Text versus Flannery O'Connor's Final Version." *The Flannery O'Connor Bulletin*, vol. 11, 1982, pp. 108–22.

Westling, Louise. "Flannery O'Connor's Revelations to 'A.'" *Southern Humanities Review*, vol. 20, no. 1, 1986, pp. 15–22.

———. *Sacred Groves and Ravaged Gardens: The Fiction of Eudora Welty, Carson McCullers, and Flannery O'Connor.* U of Georgia P, 1985.

"The Westminster Shorter Catechism." *The Westminster Presbyterian*, www.westminster confession.org/confessional-standards/the-westminster-shorter-catechism.php.

Whitfield, Stephen J. *The Culture of the Cold War.* Johns Hopkins UP, 1991.

Wild Strawberries. "Everything That Rises." *Heroine*, Nettwerk, 1995.

Wilentz, Gay. "Civilizations Underneath: African Heritage as Cultural Discourse in Toni Morrison's *Song of Solomon.*" Furman, pp. 137–63.

Williams, George. "Learning to Hate." *City Tech Writer: Outstanding Student Writing from all Disciplines*, vol. 5, 2010, pp. 71–75.

Williams, Jeffrey. Introduction. *The Institution of Literature*, edited by Williams, State U of New York P, 2002, pp. 1–15.

Williams, Juan. *Eyes on the Prize: America's Civil Rights Years, 1954–1965.* Penguin, 1987.

Williams, Lucinda. "Atonement." *World without Tears*, Lost Highway, 2003.

———. "Fruits of Her Labor." Interview by Dan Ouellette. *Archive.today*, 17 July 2012. archive.li/BEfn. *Acoustic Guitar*, Aug. 2003.

———. "Get Right with God." *Essence*, Lost Highway, 2001.

———. "The Last Word: Lucinda Williams." Interview by David Browne. *Rolling Stone*, 11 Feb. 2016, p. 66.

Williams, Miller. "Remembering Flannery O'Connor." Gordon, *Flannery O'Connor: In Celebration*, pp. 1–4.

Wilson, Charles Reagan, editor. *The New Encyclopedia of Southern Culture.* U of North Carolina P, 2006–13. 24 vols.

Wilson, Charles Reagan, and William Ferris, editors. *Encyclopedia of Southern Culture.* U of North Carolina P, 1989.

Wilson, Jessica Hooten. *Giving the Devil His Due: Demonic Authority in the Fiction of Flannery O'Connor and Fyodor Dostoevsky.* Cascade Books, 2017.

Wimsatt, Mary Ann, and Karen L. Rood, editors. *Southern Women Writers: Flannery O'Connor, Katherine Anne Porter, Eudora Welty.* Gale, 1995.

Wise Blood. 1979. Directed by John Huston, performances by Brad Dourif, Harry Dean Stanton, Amy Wright, Ned Beatty, William Dickey, Dan Shor, and Mary Nell Santacroce, Criterion Collection, 2009.

Wolfe, Tom. *A Man in Full.* Farrar, 1998.

Wood, Ralph C. *Flannery O'Connor and the Christ-Haunted South.* Eerdmans, 2004.

———. "The Scandalous Baptism of Harry Ashfield: Flannery O'Connor's 'The River.'" McMullen and Peede, pp. 189–204.

———. "Where Is the Voice Coming From? Flannery O'Connor on Race." *The Flannery O'Connor Bulletin*, vol. 22, 1993–94, pp. 90–118.

Woodress, James L. *Willa Cather: A Literary Life*. U of Nebraska P, 1987.

Woolf, Virginia. *Collected Essays*, edited by Leonard Woolf, 4 vols., Harcourt, 1967.

———. "Modern Fiction." Woolf, *Collected Essays*, vol. 2, pp. 103–10.

———. "Mr. Bennett and Mrs. Brown." Woolf, *Collected Essays*, vol. 1, pp. 319–37.

Wright, Richard. "Blueprint for Negro Writing." *New Challenge*, vol. 2, no. 1, 1937, pp. 53–65.

Yaeger, Patricia. *Dirt and Desire: Reconstructing Southern Women's Writing, 1930–1990*. U of Chicago P, 2000.

———. "Southern Orientalism: Flannery O'Connor's Cosmopolis." *Mississippi Quarterly*, vol. 56, 2003, pp. 491–510.

Zaidman, Laura Mandell, editor. *"A Good Man Is Hard to Find": Flannery O'Connor*. Harcourt College Publishers, 1999. Harcourt Brace Casebook Series in Literature.

Zaidman, Laura M[andell], et al. "A Teachers' Forum: O'Connor and the Issue of Race." *Flannery O'Connor Review*, vol. 1, 2001, pp. 99–102.

INDEX OF O'CONNOR'S WORKS

INDEX OF NAMES